Comedian of the Frontier

Comedian of the Frontier

*The Life of Actor/Manager
Jack Langrishe, 1825–1895*

MARGARET MCCUTCHEON LAUTERBACH
and CHARLES E. LAUTERBACH

McFarland & Company, Inc., Publishers
Jefferson, North Carolina

ISBN (print) 978-1-4766-6409-5
ISBN (ebook) 978-1-4766-2495-2

LIBRARY OF CONGRESS CATALOGUING DATA ARE AVAILABLE

BRITISH LIBRARY CATALOGUING DATA ARE AVAILABLE

© 2016 Margaret McCutcheon Lauterbach and
Charles E. Lauterbach. All rights reserved

*No part of this book may be reproduced or transmitted in any form
or by any means, electronic or mechanical, including photocopying
or recording, or by any information storage and retrieval system,
without permission in writing from the publisher.*

Front cover portrait of John (Jack) S. Langrishe
(ca. 1861–1870), Denver Public Library

Printed in the United States of America

*McFarland & Company, Inc., Publishers
Box 611, Jefferson, North Carolina 28640
www.mcfarlandpub.com*

I dedicate my work on this project to the memory
of my late father, Richard K. McCutcheon,
who ignited in me an interest in western American history
—Margaret McCutcheon Lauterbach

I dedicate my work on this project to the memory
of my late mentor and colleague,
Dr. Willis Lloyd "Jerry" Turner,
former artistic director of the Oregon Shakespeare Festival,
who first introduced me to the wonder that is theatre.
—Charles E. Lauterbach

Table of Contents

Acknowledgments ix
Preface 1
Introduction 5

1. New Land, New Life — 9
2. Moving West: The Old Northwest Territory — 19
3. A New Theatre Home — 22
4. Riding High — 31
5. Profits Shrink — 46
6. Rootless — 53
7. Colorado — 61
8. Gold Circuit — 75
9. Into Unknown Perils — 91
10. Return to Montana — 109
11. Chicago — 115
12. The *Black Crook* Venture — 124
13. Battered but Not Beaten — 131
14. Deadwood — 137
15. High in the Rockies — 153
16. Mining, Managing and Acting — 164
17. On the Last Tour — 174
18. End of the Last Tour — 182
19. Another Gold Rush — 189

20. A New Career and Reflections	196
21. Shattered Peace	202
22. The Last Act	209
Epilogue	219
Chapter Notes	225
Bibliography	249
Index	255

Acknowledgments

The biography of Jack Langrishe could not have been written without the cooperation and contribution of scores of individuals and institutions across the continent. The authors wrote hundreds of query letters to libraries and historical societies which were answered swiftly and professionally. Space will not allow mentioning every correspondent who deserves recognition. Apologies and a blanket "thank you."

Major contributions came from Boise State University's and the Idaho Historical Society's inter-library loan departments that provided numerous reels of microfilmed nineteenth century newspapers to us. The Boise State University Library also aided our research by purchasing microfilm of the entire runs of the theatrical trade papers *The New York Clipper* and *The New York Dramatic Mirror*, as well as almost all available theses and dissertations dealing with American theatre history.

The authors are indebted to a pair of institutions who awarded grants to finance travel for research. They are the Idaho Humanities Council and Boise State University.

While on her 40-day research tour of the East and Midwest, Margaret received assistance from the staffs of numerous universities, libraries and historical societies. These include institutions in Cincinnati, Columbus and Cleveland, Ohio; Philadelphia, Pittsburgh, Harrisburg and York, Pennsylvania; Providence, Rhode Island; New Haven, Connecticut; Detroit, Michigan; and Chicago, Illinois. Other aid came from institutions in the New York cities of Albany, Troy, Syracuse, Ithaca, Rochester, Buffalo and New York. Still more help came from the Massachusetts cities of Cambridge, Worcester and Boston and two New Jersey universities: Princeton and Rutgers. Lastly, she made use of the Library of Congress. In a shorter tour of California, Margaret availed herself of services offered by the Huntington Library, the Bancroft Library, the public library of Grass Valley and the library at the University of California, Davis.

Institutions deserving special mention for their contributions are the

University of Chicago library, the Newberry Library (Chicago), the Denver Public Library, the Colorado Historical Society (History Colorado), the Wisconsin Historical Society, the Idaho Historical Society, the Minnesota Historical Society, the Walter Hampden-Edwin Booth Theatre Collection at the Players' Club of New York City and the Utah Historical Society.

Photographs were obtained with the cooperation of the Denver Public Library, the Colorado Historical Society, the Wisconsin Historical Society, Harvard University, the Idaho Historical Society, University of Utah, the Utah Historical Society, Brigham Young University, Boston Public Library, University of Washington, Yale University, the New York Public Library and the New Bedford Free Public Library.

William Folds of the Isle of Wight conducted research in Dublin to find the birth record of Jack Langrishe (born John Sewell Folds, Jr.). He was employed at the suggestion of Charles Folds of Illinois, Jack Langrishe's distant cousin. Dr. Allan S. Jackson was consulted about the use of gas lighting in nineteenth century theatres. Helen June Hamlin donated portions of Charles B. Well's memoir of his days with the Langrishe Black Crook Company. Frank Parker and Catherine Barth, the only grandchildren of comedian John Dillon, contributed pictures, programs and a diary. Jeanette Young of Idaho's *Kellogg Evening News* was most helpful in research done in northern Idaho. Edith Jackson contributed information on Jeanette Langrishe's daughter Rosalthe. Judy Austin provided her expertise in the nuances of the *Chicago Manual of Style*.

Staff members of the Colorado's Clear Creek County Recorder's office and Idaho's Shoshone Recorder's Office went out of their way to dig up legal papers, mining claim records and real estate information.

During her eastern research trip, Margaret enjoyed the hospitality of Dr. Sally Hayden Mitchell of Philadelphia, Dr. and Mrs. David Ewbank of Kent, Ohio, and Mr. and Mrs. Carl Brookins of St. Paul. She also visited the home of Charles Weston Folds of Winnetka, Illinois. There she was served tea in a cup of antique china brought to America from Ireland in the nineteenth century by Langrishe's uncle and aunt, Mr. and Mrs. George Folds. Charles Folds also shared genealogical information about his ancestors in Dublin.

Preface

John Sewell Folds Langrishe was a major figure in the theatre history of the American frontier from 1850 to 1895. Most commonly known as Jack Langrishe, he brought theatrical entertainment to a floating world of prospectors, miners, gamblers, adventurers and opportunists who followed successive gold rushes in Colorado, Montana, South Dakota and the Coeur d'Alene region of Idaho.

Langrishe is an all but forgotten name in the annals of nineteenth century American theater. He himself observed that an actor's life is "writ on water." His name does appear in publications from time to time, notably Melvin Schoberlin's *From Candles to Footlights: A Biography of the Pike's Peak Theatre—1859–1876* and Annie D. Tallent's *The Black Hills*, as well as numerous graduate theses. Some websites, mainly those dealing with the history of South Dakota, feature his photograph and a brief biographic sketch. He is the subject of a Wikipedia article with content mainly limited to his years in South Dakota and some inaccurate information about his origins. His name was used for a character in the Home Box Office series *Deadwood*. However, to date no one has presented a comprehensive treatment of the life and career of Jack Langrishe.

We have been involved in a collaborative pursuit of the story of Jack Langrishe for over a half-century, which began with Charles reading Melvin Schoberlin's *From Candles to Footlights* while an undergraduate at the University of Colorado in the 1950s. While that book is not specifically about Jack Langrishe, he is so frequently referenced that a partial outline of his life is apparent. His participation in the Colorado gold rush of the 1860s is covered rather thoroughly by Schoberlin, but there is little about him before he arrived in the Colorado gold fields and only infrequent notes about his activities in the decades after leaving Colorado.

In 1961, when Charles was a doctoral candidate in theatre arts at Michigan State University, he considered a Langrishe biography as his dissertation, but he dropped the idea.

Over two decades passed, during which time we married and became immersed in life and work, but finally it was time to begin our work on Langrishe's biography in earnest. Margaret, also a native of Colorado and sharing knowledge of Langrishe's history, suggested we work on the frontier actor's biography. In our household, the work, which came to be known as "The Langrishe Project," went on for nearly three decades.

We started a chronology of Langrishe's career beginning with the information in Schoberlin's book. From this base we began research backward and forward to expand the chronology. Intensive use of the interlibrary loan service at Boise State University's library and the Idaho Historical Society brought us numerous rolls of microfilmed nineteenth century newspapers. More information came in from our inquiries to various Western and Midwestern historical societies, libraries and theatre collections. Grants from Boise State University and the Idaho Humanities Council financed travel to conduct on-site research. The university grant allowed Charles to carry out research at the Wisconsin Historical Society in Madison and three sites in Chicago.

Margaret traveled extensively, making research trips from coast to coast, conducting a 40-day tour of libraries, historical societies and theatre collections in New York, New England, other eastern locales and the Midwest. This was preceded by research in California at the Huntington Library in San Moreno, the University of California, Berkeley's Bancroft Library, collections at the University of California, Davis, and San Francisco Museum and Historical Society Library. This research odyssey concluded with a visit to Northern Idaho, the last home of Jack Langrishe, where Margaret interviewed locals about Langrishe, obtained copies of the newspaper he edited, and located Langrishe's grave in the Kellogg, Idaho, cemetery, the lower part of the tombstone partially buried.

By the late 1980s we had expanded the Langrishe chronology to over 70 pages and had accumulated enough notes and photocopies of newspaper items to fill two four-drawer filing cabinets. After gathering this material, work on the Langrishe project was again postponed. Charles turned his research efforts to creating a history of theatre in Idaho for the state's celebration of its centennial in 1990. Margaret also began a new career, writing a weekly column on gardening for the local Boise newspaper. As a result all work on the Langrishe project ceased until retirement in 2001.

Recreating John Langrishe's life with primary and secondary sources has been challenging. Langrishe often declared he was working on his memoir, but if he did, it has never come to light. His Denver home burned, he lost all his possessions in the great Chicago fire in 1871 and probably lost everything again when Deadwood burned in 1879. Fortunately, Langrishe was at home in newspaper offices, having been raised in his father's printing plant in Ireland, so contemporary newspapers often published items about him. He also included materials about himself when he was editor of newspapers in South Dakota and Idaho. Some of his fellow actors and admirers wrote about him in their memoirs. Lamentably, too many of his friends had the attitude of "Everybody knows Jack Langrishe, so it is useless to write about him."

Finding items about his life and organizing them into a coherent narrative has been an arduous but rewarding task. Here at last is the story of Jack Langrishe, a fabulous figure who played an important role in the history of nineteenth century theatre on the American frontier.

Introduction

John S.F. Langrishe is a central figure in the largely neglected history of theatre in the nineteenth century American West. Noted theatre historian William Carson considered Langrishe and John Potter VIPs in frontier theatre. While Langrishe's name shows up from time to time in various historical society publications and a few dissertations, there has been no coherent nor complete coverage of his life and accomplishments. This is regrettable since his story is significant in its contribution to the cultural life of mining camps and early settlements in frontier days.

Looking back at the American frontier from the twenty-first century, many of us are aware of the violence—holdups, shootouts, rustling and hangings—thanks to motion pictures and television. Yes, these incidents did happen occasionally, but only to a minority of people settling new towns and cities. The majority, as now, were merchants, wage earners, ranchers, farmers, bankers, millers and milliners, bakers and other good people who lived quiet lives, attending church or visiting other's homes for tea or dinner.

When Jack Langrishe brought his troupe to town, he brought a cultured type of amusement: plays by Bulwer-Lytton, Coleman, Richard Brinsley Sheridan, Dion Boucicault, Alexander Dumas *fils*, William Shakespeare and others, dramas to show patrons a way to improve their lives in the eyes of their mothers and their God. He presented many exciting melodramas and hilarious farces and comedies. Usually he offered a full-length play and a brief "afterpiece," a comedy in which he starred. He insisted on presenting only dramas that were uplifting and at times he presented plays even before they were staged in the East. One of the hazards he and his troupe faced when presenting Shakespearean dramas was that the audience often knew the dialogue better than the actors; woe to a performer who skipped a line. Many settlers moving West owned only two books: the Bible and the works of William Shakespeare.

In many towns Langrishe's shows were the only legitimate theatre available. His competition was variety theatres that catered to a rowdier crowd with songs, dances, risqué comedy, acrobats and, for a price, behind-the-curtains rendezvous with waitresses or performers. Variety theatres were frequently connected with brothels. Langrishe's theatres did their best to exclude prostitutes from their audiences.

Variety theatre performers were regarded as a lower class, especially by actors and actresses in legitimate theatre. Only on rare occasions, *in extremis*, did a legitimate actor perform in a variety theatre.

The choice of amusements ran thus: one dollar to Langrishe's theatre to spend an evening thrilling to a melodrama or laughing uproariously at a comedy and observing the behavior of well-mannered citizens (and being able to see nicely dressed, decent women without offensive staring) or going to a variety theatre to gamble (often to be cheated), drink alcohol, get into fights or engage a woman for illicit purposes. One could survive the former, perhaps not the latter at higher cost.

In the early West, there were also conflicts with Native Americans, commemorated in countless films and television programs. Contrary to the stereotype, Langrishe camped out with some, entertained some in his theatres and calmly journeyed through areas rife with angry, hostile tribes. Some members of his party of seven later said they had fought off Indian attacks a time or two, but that may have been *braggadocio*; Langrishe never publicly mentioned those battles.

Langrishe has been recognized as the father of legitimate theatre in Colorado, Montana and South Dakota. One could legitimately call him the father of theatre in the west were it not for the fact that he was also the founder of theatre in Madison, Wisconsin, Minnesota and the Old Northwest. It is said he "built" more theatres than any man but John S. Potter, a legendary showman in the South and East. Langrishe had some theatres built and bought some, but many of his "theatres" were creative uses of space in restaurants, hotels, military forts and even a butcher shop.

Langrishe, the opportunist, toured his companies all over the northern states, Canadian provinces and into Mexico. During his youth in Dublin his father's home had been lighted by gaslights and tended by servants. In America, he did not enjoy such civilized niceties on the rugged American frontier until he neared retirement.

In addition to pursuing a virtual odyssey across the American continent, Langrishe participated in a substantial number of varied theatrical enterprises. While most of his time was spent as an actor-manager of various resident and touring stock companies, he also functioned as a magician in his early career, as an actor on London and New York stages, as a manager of an equestrian circus and drama combination, as a co-owner of a "floating palace" theatre, as a leader of a spectacular *Black Crook* company of 143 members and as a western tour manager for noted eastern producer M.B. Leavitt. His skill in theatre management was all the more remarkable in that he performed shows on the frontier without the luxuries of theatre equipment found in eastern United States, often making do in spaces such as tents, restaurants or hotels.

Besides his many theatre contributions as an actor-manager, Langrishe had several other notable career accomplishments. He co-authored an imitation of *The Black Crook*, served as a newspaper editor in Deadwood, South Dakota and Wardner, Idaho, owned a Colorado silver mine, prospected for gold, functioned as a justice of the peace, served as an elected member of the first Idaho state senate and aided Episcopal clergy in lay readings.

It was said that in his time Langrishe was as well-known in the West as Ulysses Grant was in the East. A major figure in a population of prospectors and miners, he moved from gold strike to gold strike and was well received on all levels of society. He numbered among his acquaintances generals, politicians, newspapermen and members of the clergy. He could claim that he knew railroad magnate George Pullman, inventor of the Pullman railroad car, when that millionaire was a hard rock miner earning three dollars a day. Langrishe was also well-regarded by fellow theatre producers and actors. When he died his obituary appeared in newspapers from New York to San Diego.

While his personal accomplishments certainly mark him as a man of interest, many occurred in periods of historical importance. According to the often quoted Irish adage, he lived in interesting times.

- He and his theatre companies performed in most of the major gold and silver mine camps in the West where fortunes were made and lost overnight. Langrishe filed several mining claims himself in those heady times.
- Although his theatre at Wood's Museum in Chicago was destroyed, he escaped that city's Great Fire of 1871 and managed to take over the only theatre building to escape the conflagration, thus gaining a virtual monopoly on theatre presentations in the devastated city.
- The inquiry into the assassination of Wild Bill Hickok was held in Langrishe's theatre in untamed Deadwood, Dakota Territory.
- Before arriving in South Dakota, Langrishe and his troupe, traveling by horse and wagon, passed through hostile Indian territory while General George Armstrong Custer and his troops were being slaughtered some 150 miles away.
- An ill-advised 1875 tour of Mexico landed him and his *Black Crook* company in that nation in the days of social unrest. There, he and his troupe trav-

eled down roads lined with the hanging bodies of dozens of captured bandits.

- In 1883 his was the first troupe to travel over the newly completed Great Northern Railroad.
- In 1890 he was elected a Senator in the first state legislature of Idaho, serving on a committee that selected that state's flag and official seal.

John Langrishe died over a century ago in Wardner, Idaho, just a few years after the closing of the American frontier he had been so much a part of. His funeral had the largest attendance of any ever held in northern Idaho, but now he lies obscurely in the cemetery of adjacent Kellogg, Idaho. Though the man and the West he reveled in are long past, his story deserves to be preserved and the pages that follow are a tribute to his remarkable life and eventful times.

> Because Langrishe spent most of his career in western territories, for clarity, the towns and camps that he appeared in are identified by their state names, although most of them were admitted to the union much later. Denver, for example, was part of the Jefferson Territory when Langrishe arrived there in the 1860s but Colorado did not attain statehood until 1876.

1

New Land, New Life

A 40-year journey traversing the North American continent began with a crossing of the Atlantic Ocean. The man who was to be known as Jack Langrishe left Dublin, Ireland, in 1845 to seek a new life in a new land.

Two days overdue, the steamship *Britannia* arrived in Boston the morning of Friday, September 19, 1845, after a lurching 15-day voyage from Liverpool. Among the passengers were "I.P. Langrishe and lady" and "Standish and lady." I.P. Langrishe was John Sewell Folds, Jr., the "lady" his sister Isabella. Standish was his brother-in-law George, recently married to Folds' younger sister Eliza.[1] They debarked at New York City, Langrishe remaining in the city while his sisters and brother-in-law went on to Wisconsin to join the elder Folds.

John S. Folds, the father of John S. Folds, Jr., Isabella and Eliza Standish, had sailed to America earlier in the year on the same steamship.[2] Langrishe, born September 24, 1825,[3] was a tall, lanky young man with a very large straight nose like that of his grandfather, William Folds. John S. Folds aka Langrishe loved theatre and aspired to be an actor, his comedic portrayals facilitated by his mobile nose.

John S. Folds, Jr., aka Langrishe was just 19, so even though he was titular partner of his father's printing plant in Ireland, he was not legally responsible for the company's crushing debts. John S. Folds, Sr., had owned one of Dublin's most extensive printing plants and printed popular journals, magazines and government publications. His business had made him sufficiently affluent to have a home in Dublin and a summer home in Black Rock on the coast, where he entertained distinguished literary men and government officials.[4] The elder Folds' affluence vanished due to a costly printing plant fire and the loss of his government printing contract. Newly widowed, facing bankruptcy, and believing that the sale of his properties would reimburse his creditors, Folds quietly left for America, his grown children following.

Young Langrishe's role models while growing up were men whom he had met in his father's print shop and at home gatherings, men renowned for wit, intelligence and courtly manners. He arrived in America with those nascent attributes and some skills: He could set type, and evidently had studied acting and magic. He may have been taught magic by the "Great Wizard of the North," who had given lessons in Dublin a year before the Folds family emigrated.[5] Folds-Langrishe did put on "natural magic" shows twice in New York, and theatrical illusion was a lifelong interest.

John S. Folds, Jr. (Langrishe) had some acting experience before arriving in New York, but neither surname appeared in Dublin playbills. "Folds" was an inappropriate name for an actor, because shows that close or fail are said to "fold," probably dating from the days of traveling tent shows. Why did he choose the stage name "Langrishe"? It was not a family name, but a name known to him: One Langrishe was a policeman, one a judge, another a Church of Ireland official in Dublin. Sir Hercules Langrishe in Kilkenny was renowned for hosting private theatricals which sometimes included a Folds family friend,[6] poet Sir Thomas Moore.[7] John Folds, Jr., may have just thought it a grand name.

Langrishe probably made his stage debut the same way other actors did: He bought enough tickets to entitle him to act the role he wanted in a benefit, then gave the tickets to his friends who would provide enthusiastic encouragement.[8] With that experience, getting other acting jobs would be easier.

A May 1844 benefit at the Theatre Royal, Dublin, was to feature a "gentleman amateur, his first appearance on any stage" in the character of Pat Rooney in *The Omnibus*.[9] A benefit for another actor at the same theatre in August of that year was to feature a scene from *The Gamester* with Beverley played by a gentleman amateur.[10] A "gentleman amateur" played Gratiano to Mr. Dawson's Shylock in *The Merchant of Venice* at the Theatre-Royal Abbey-street on December 10, 1844. Some or all of these could easily have been John Folds, Jr.-Langrishe who acted these roles for the rest of his life. And he could have gained further experience as a minor player not identified in ads or reviews.

After landing in America in 1845, Langrishe worked in New York City as a reporter and perhaps typesetter for Horace Greeley's *New York Tribune*.[11] All of the Folds males (his own father, uncle and cousins) had learned the placement of type in cases as children, replacing pied or used type in their proper niches for spending money.[12] Langrishe was undoubtedly working for the *Tribune* under his real name, Folds, but it wasn't long before "John S. Langrishe" performed in a New York theatre. Greeley's dislike of theatre would have been another reason for Folds to have used a stage name, retaining his day job.[13]

A playbill for the Chatham Theatre, New York City, announced that "Mr.

Langrishe! The Irish Comedian" would play Pierce O'Hara in *The Irish Attorney* on Monday, December 8, 1845, his "first appearance in this city."[14] Topping the bill was *The Lady of Lyons*, *The Irish Attorney* second. Six months later he tried magic, appearing at the Apollo Room as "Langrishe, the Great Wizard of the East."

> Mr. Langrishe, having just arrived from Europe, where he has appeared in all the principal cities to crowded and overwhelming audiences, and ... before the royal families of France and England, will appear for the first time in America at the [Apollo Room], Thursday, June 18 and following evenings, with a splendid apparatus, illustrating the wonders of Natural Magic and Experimental Philosophy.[15]

His previous experience was greatly exaggerated. Having performed for "all the principal cities" and "royal families" was also the claim of "The Great Wizard of the North," under whom Langrishe probably had studied. On August 17, 1846, an unnamed "Wizard of the East" astonished the audience at the New Greenwich Theatre.[16] This may have been Langrishe or it could have been another who used that pseudonym.[17]

Langrishe needed more experience and a theatrical wardrobe to make theatre a career. Actors had to supply their own costumes, and an actor aspiring to his line of acting roles had to supply ruffs, collars, frills, boots, shoes and pantaloons, as well as a "countryman's coat and inexpressibles [trousers] ... stockings of different colors in silk and worsted ... hats, sword belts" and various wigs including a skullcap.[18] Irish comedians such as Langrishe portrayed commonly wore a red vest, red wig, green Balbriggan hose and corduroy pants and, of course, carried a shillelagh.[19]

Langrishe learned of the taint associated with legitimate theatre in America at that time, a stigma absent in Ireland. In America, actors were regarded as less than respectable (partly because of actor-actress divorces), and theatres were avoided by respectable people because liquor was often sold in the theatre building and "improper people" allowed in the audience.[20] This Puritanical attitude prevailed throughout settled America in the 1840s, inspiring Langrishe to often proclaim that "Nothing to offend the most fastidious" would occur in his theatres.

He was an energetic and ambitious young man, who may have joined like young men in amateur theatrical endeavors. There were several theatre groups in New York City such as the amateur dramatic company that performed *Hamlet* and *Bombastes Furioso* with proceeds going to the city's poor. The review in *Spirit of the Times* recommended that the unnamed players "throw aside tragedy entirely" and only perform comedy.[21]

While Langrishe was working in New York City, a few stock companies toured towns in upstate New York, one under the management of Allen and

Bridges. During the summer of 1846, they played in Utica, Syracuse, Onondaga, Albany and Buffalo,[22] probably traveling on the Erie Canal. Manager John H. Allen[23] may have been related to the actress Jeannette Allen who later married Langrishe, but was probably not a sibling. The *Syracuse Daily Star* remarked that the women of the company were more talented than the men, but none of the cast was named. Jeannette Allen was performing at this time in western New York, but with what company remains a mystery.

Performance conditions at the time were far from ideal. Outside of New York City, Boston, Philadelphia and Washington, D.C., few buildings at that time were used only for theatrical performances. Most communities in western New York did not have theatres, so actors performed in any large room that could hold an audience, in courthouses, in churches and hotel dining halls. Some traveling companies had playbills printed, leaving blank the name of the hall, date and admission price.[24] That information was added just before the bills were posted.

These room-theatres were poorly ventilated and even more poorly heated. Chairs (or, more often, benches) were uncomfortable, but actors were usually in even more deplorable surroundings than the audience, for dressing rooms were usually not heated at all,[25] many having a flimsy piece of cloth for privacy. Actors boarded in private residences with often cramped accommodations (two or three to a bed was common), ate indifferent food, then traveled to the next engagement in a wagon or gut-wrenching stagecoach, either conveyance liable to tip over and distribute passengers at any moment. The company usually performed six nights per week, rehearsing every afternoon. Mornings were devoted to memorizing lines. For those talented women who sewed their own costumes by hand, true leisure time was rare. It was a strenuous life, but one of few fairly respectable occupations for a woman.

Newspapers for western New York, Pennsylvania and Ohio for the 1840s exist only in broken files, so Langrishe's daily activities are not apparent as in later years. Many theatrical companies were only mentioned by the particular newspaper that had printed their bills, programs or tickets, and few mentioned members of the casts other than the stars or managers of the troupes.

Langrishe apparently left New York City in 1847 to perform full time. In Utica, New York, on September 14 and 15, 1847, "Mr. Langrishe, the Great Irish Comedian," drew large crowds, so was re-engaged for more dates.[26] The post office in Rochester, New York, held a letter for Langrishe on October 15, 1847, and Syracuse held one on November 1, 1847.[27] (Newspapers regularly published lists of letters that had not been picked up from the local post offices, the only way travelers could receive mail.) On November 3, the

Rochester newspaper announced: "Museum: Mr. Languishire [sic], famous for extempore singing, &c. holds forth at the Museum this week."[28]

The J.S. Potter Co. played in Utica for most of November and December, some of the cast leaving and others arriving. Complete casts were never given, but on December 23, 1847, a Mrs. Sullivan was listed in the cast.[29] Mrs. Sullivan was the name used at that time by Jeannette Allen, the future Mrs. Langrishe.

In Rochester in November 1847, a "variety of comic singing and the laughable farce of *State Secrets*—the principal parts by Mr. Collins[30] and Mr. Langrishe" amused audiences, who were also treated to the "truly amusing pantomime" of *Don Juan* performed by the members of the Olympic Vaudeville Company.[31] Langrishe and the Olympic Vaudeville Company continued to perform in Rochester for a month.[32]

A letter waited in the post office in Lockport, New York, on February 9, 1848, for John S. Langrishe. In his obituary nearly 50 years later, the *New York Clipper* noted that he had met Jeannette Allen in Lockport, later marrying her.[33] Lockport was on the Erie Canal, a major route of summer transportation from the Hudson River to Lake Erie, often used by theatre troupes weary of the jolting, jarring and danger of wagon or stagecoach travel.[34]

On August 16, 1848, the Adelphi Theatre in Rochester opened with the tragedy of *The Gamester* with Langrishe and Mrs. R.J. Miller appearing as Mr. and Mrs. Beverley, concluding with the farce *The Irish Lion*.[35] (*The Gamester* is the play in which a "gentleman amateur" performed at the Theatre Royal, Dublin, in August 1844.) They drew full and "highly respectable" audiences, presenting different plays each evening.[36]

A letter awaited "J.T. Langrishe" [sic] in Geneva, New York, on October 6, 1848, indicating he had told others he would be in that area. A "New York Temperance Vaudeville Company" performed in Fredonia, New York, in early December,[37] Jamestown the following week, then to Erie, Pennsylvania.[38] The name changed to Mr. Burgette's Vaudeville Company, in which "Mr. Langrishe, who plays the principal part is [said to be] rarely excelled in comedies ... [and the company] intends to travel south to Waterford, Meadville, &c." American vaudeville, synonymous with the English "music hall," is generally regarded to have started in 1881; this earlier use of the term was used probably because actors sang between the acts.[39]

An advertisement ran on December 30 for that night's performance of *Maid of Croissey* or *Theresa's Vow* at the Meadville, Pennsylvania, Court House. Langrishe was to play "Walter Berrier," Mrs. Burgette "Theresa," and Mrs. Sullivan "Manette." Langrishe was to sing a "comic song," and then the company would perform a comedy and a farce.[40] "Considering the difficulties under which they necessarily labor ... having to travel with their scenery, wardrobe, &c., the performances are very creditable. Mr. Langrishe, especially, possesses a fund of good humor, which cannot fail to keep the audience in a roar...."[41]

A hazard common to all actors is a bad notice or review. In late March 1849, Langrishe received the worst review of his entire career, from someone who hadn't even seen the show.

> Vi [sic] la Humbug! Olympic Olio Company.—This *grand* [sic] humbug company is in town (Youngstown, Ohio), and performed on Monday evening. We was [sic] not present, but learned that it was a low contemptable [sic] affair. We saw the actors, and from their appearance, they are not of the first water [sic]. Mr. Langrishe and Mrs. Sullivan, we understand, wish to get up a school in magic. From their appearance we judge them to be natural [sic] magic actors behind the curtains.[42]

The *Pittsburgh Daily Gazette* reported a letter waiting May 1, 1849, at the Pittsburgh post office for "Mrs. Jennette Sullivan."[43] A letter had been waiting for "John S. Languish" at the Pittsburgh post office in March, too.[44] It may have been about this time that Langrishe and Jeannette Allen Riddell Sullivan were married, for a source reports they did marry in Pittsburgh in 1849,[45] and this was the only time they were known to have been in Pittsburgh that year.

Mrs. Langrishe was born Jeannette Allen in Thetford, Vermont; her age varied wildly in censuses. She claimed to be a granddaughter of Ethan Allen of Ticonderoga fame, but her sister Augusta, wrote that Ethan Allen was a cousin of their father Bela Allen.[46] Folds family members report that Jeannette was older than Langrishe, who was born in Dublin in 1825. Her obituary reported she was 84 at her death, making her birth year 1816.

Prior to her 1849 marriage to Langrishe, she had been married to a Mr. Riddle or Riddell and, about 1840, had borne a daughter, Rosalthe.[47] At age seven or eight, Rosalthe contracted a disease such as scarlet fever or meningitis that left her deaf. Thereafter she attended boarding schools for the deaf, and never lived with or visited her mother and Langrishe in the West.[48] Jeannette's prior marriages and the existence of her daughter were kept secret from all but family in her effort to appear a "respectable lady." Divorce and/or multiple marriages were the principal reasons that actresses were not acceptable in polite society.

J.H. Powell's Theatre Company closed in Erie, Pennsylvania, on May 12, 1849,[49] then went to Sandusky, Ohio, probably by ship across Lake Erie. Langrishe was a member of the company, although not mentioned until July 7.[50] A cholera epidemic was raging in the summer of 1849, but by July 28 the epidemic was rapidly waning in Cincinnati.[51] In Sandusky, "it is estimated that there are less than 1000 people remaining in town [three or four thousand inhabitants had left]. Even the sexton left town, so those city authorities who remain have given permission to all to dig graves for friends when and where they please...."[52]

Apparently the troupe played Tiffin, Springfield, probably Columbus, and Cincinnati.[53] Travel in Ohio at that time was arduous, many of the roads "corduroy" roads (round logs laid on swampy land to sink, some more than others). Stagecoaches and wagons bounced and lurched over the bumpy road southward,[54] through swamps, tall grass, fens and bogs.

The Langrishes turned up in Oswego, New York, on September 20, 1849. Mrs. Langrishe was also with the "New York Vaudeville Company,"[55] and a "report speaks very favorably of their performances.... Langrishe, the great comedian of the Western Theatre is with them...." "Western Theatre" referred to Ohio, western Pennsylvania and New York.

Most beginning actors exaggerate gestures, and Langrishe probably was no exception. Jeannette Allen was an exceptionally talented actress, more experienced than he, proficient with subtle expression and gesture to convey meaning, and throughout subsequent years she demonstrated an ability to coach others. After Langrishe met her, he began getting better notices for his performances. They often referred to the naturalness of his acting, perhaps displaying her influence.

Their September 1849 engagement in Oswego had a choppy beginning: Mrs. Langrishe was ill one day, so the performance was cancelled, and two nights later, the weather turned foul enough to prevent the performance.[56] The local press commented: "Those who have not seen Langrishe, the truly droll and eccentric comedian, lately of the Pittsburgh and Cincinnati theatres, should bear in mind that he plays three of his best parts to-night ... assisted by.... Miss Laurette Allen (Jeannette Langrishe's sister) and Mr. Sefton, forming one of the best vaudeville companies ever here...."[57]

In February 1850 the Langrishes were in Corning, New York, having come from Addison. By then it was Langrishe's Vaudeville Company, and citizens of Addison wrote that this company would warrant a "full return in mirth and fun for your trouble and money."[58] March 20, a new theatre company was managed by W.H. Scoville and Langrishe.[59] In Ithaca they performed Shakespeare's tragedy *Macbeth*, among other plays.

From Ithaca they went to Auburn, New York, where they performed until at least April 1. That partnership dissolved, and the Langrishes then linked up with Mr. and Mrs. R.J. Miller in Utica. Langrishe was to sing between the plays and perform in comic farces.[60] Mrs. Langrishe was not mentioned as part of the cast until May 25. Two days later, the *Utica Daily*

Gazette reported, "The managers, with Mr. Vance and Mrs. Miller take the lead and evince discrimination and taste in their representations.... They are very well sustained in the female parts by Mrs. Miller, Miss Allen and Mrs. Langrishe. In the latter will be recognized an old favorite of the Utica theatre goers...."[61]

The newspaper reporter may not have remembered what name or names Jeanette Langrishe had previously used in Utica. She could have played there as "Miss Allen," "Mrs. Riddle (or Riddell)," "Mrs. Sullivan" or all three prior to her appearance as "Mrs. Langrishe."

The company was to open in Oswego a few days later.[62] Over the next several nights in Oswego they performed *The Gamester* (with R.J. Miller, not Langrishe, portraying Beverley)[63] and a nightly change of bill, including Shakespeare's *Hamlet* and *Richard III*.

June 14, they added an orchestra, and on June 17, they displayed their new scenery and drop curtain, painted by E. Bowers.[64] John McKibbin, a portrayer of old women's roles, joined the troupe June 28.[65] Thirty-five plays in about three weeks was quite a flex of histrionic effort for Langrishe. Most nights they performed a full-length play plus a comic farce.

After Oswego, they opened in Syracuse on July 8. The company now included Mr. and Mrs. R.J. Miller, Mr. and Mrs. Langrishe, Laurette Allen, T.M. Vance, J.C. McKibbin, D.T. Cooper and Mr. French. A sign of their success was traveling with their own scenery painter, E. Bowers, and an "orchestra" led by Mr. Martin. In reality, theatre "orchestras" often consisted of just two or three musicians.[66]

Over the next 54 days they performed a new bill each night except Sundays, a full-length play plus a farce, introducing guest stars W.J. Whitney, W. Plato, Mr. and Mrs. Sloan from the Broadway and London theatres, and W.H. Scoville.[67] The company enjoyed very good houses during its two-month run, partly because of the cast's talent and partly because guest artists provided a change of "scenery" at times. The press observed: "Mrs. Langrishe and Mrs. Miller are both very ladylike women, and.... Miss Allen has a very pleasant way with her, is extremely comely, and has already become a great favorite...."[68]

Newspapers had expressed admiration for Langrishe's comic portrayals using playwrights' works. For his benefit in Syracuse on August 10, he distributed blank cards to audience members, inviting them to select a subject on which he would "poetize without previous preparation."[69] He drew a very crowded house.

At the end of engagements, Langrishe offered benefit performances. Benefits, a common practice at this time, were held to give a specific per-

John McKibbin, character actor with Langrishe companies for decades, in Indian costume (Wisconsin Historical Society, image number WHi 121072).

former (or manager) the profits for the evening, increasing his or her remuneration and giving his or her admirers a chance to show their esteem by buying tickets, augmenting the attendance. The practical effect of such benefits was to encourage actors and actresses to make friends among audience members rather than to be aloof.

The company was still in Syracuse on September 6, but not performing, when the census taker arrived. Langrishe was identified as 28 (he was 25), as were R.J. Miller and his wife. Thomas M. Vance was 23, William Plato 30, D.J. Cooper 22, Laurette (spelled Lorette) Allen 22 and John McKibbin (spelled McCibbon) 63. Mrs. Langrishe was absent. Neither of the Langrishes were included in the census index.[70]

In January 1851, they reappeared in Corning, New York. "Mr. Langrishe and Company, whose Theatrical performances here last winter gave such unusual satisfaction, will again perform in this village commencing on Wednesday [January 15]."[71] The *Corning Journal* reported that the company was going on to Addison, New York. "As a general rule, we have a very poor opinion of traveling Theatrical Companies, but we must do them justice to say that Langrishe's Company are far superior to any other itinerant Co., we ever saw ... [T]he members ... are in every respect Ladies and Gentlemen of acknowledged talent and worth."[72]

With this appraisal, they were ready for lifetime careers.

2

Moving West: The Old Northwest Territory

Langrishe and his actors probably took a steamboat to Milwaukee. A Lake Michigan Line ship, the *St. Lewis*, regularly traveled between New Buffalo, Chicago and Milwaukee.[1] In 1851, settlement of Wisconsin was in its infancy, new towns emerging like spring mushrooms. The government was selling land for $1.25 an acre in Wisconsin, and men and their families, especially those from blight-stricken Ireland, converged on Wisconsin.[2]

By June 30, "Messrs. Atwater and Co." announced a series of "chaste and elegant dramatic entertainments at Gardiner's Hall, commencing this evening with 'Naval Engagements,' 'The Old Guard' and 'The Yankee Duellist.'" The "Messrs." included Langrishe and Manager G.A. Hough, although Langrishe's name was not published for a number of days. Laurette Allen and Jeannette Langrishe were in the cast.[3]

Three managers made this an expensive company. J.B. Atwater had recently returned to the East from the California gold rush, having survived an arduous overland journey, arriving in California "barefoot and destitute."[4] When he did not find gold plentiful, he was happy to return to acting in Sacramento so he could buy ship passage back home. C.B. Mulholland and John McKibbin were in the new Wisconsin company, along with Mrs. Langrishe and Mrs. Hough. Mr. Hess, of Milwaukee, led the orchestra.

McKibbin, who had joined Langrishe and Miller's company in 1850, was much older than the others, portraying old men and old women on stage and performing a comic dance between the acts. In spite of the age difference, he was a close friend and actor for Langrishe for nearly 16 years, until he retired from the stage about 1866, then almost 80 years old.[5]

The Atwater-Hough-Langrishe theatre company in Milwaukee put on three performances on July 4. Over the next several days they performed a variety of inspiring melodramas, spectacles and side-splitting (but moral) farces. They changed the bill every night, one night putting on *Jenny Lind in*

Milwaukee. [The real Jenny Lind was to give a concert in Syracuse, New York, with tickets priced at $4, $3, and $2; tickets to the pretend *Jenny Lind in Milwaukee* performances were 50 cents.[6]] Then they performed a benefit to raise money for widows and orphans of the IOOF (International Order of Odd Fellows) on July 12. A Grand Lodge meeting of the IOOF in Milwaukee was to commence a few days later. Holding a benefit for widows and orphans would introduce the company to the members of that organization, and encourage members to support their theatre.[7]

The company, comprising "15 to 20" people, traveled to Racine to open a short season July 29. Admission was 25 cents.[8] A week later, that newspaper reported that the company "has been quite successful … plays have been both well selected and well performed, and the audiences have been improving in respectability … Messrs. Mulholland, Hough and Langrishe were the favorites among the men, and Mr. McKibbin as an old man was very much liked."[9]

The Kenosha newspaper announced that the company would start a season in that city starting Monday, August 11, at the Sons' Hall.[10] The hall was small for a theatrical production, according to the *Kenosha* Telegraph.[11] They were to play in Kenosha a "short season," then go on to Sheboygan. "Mr. Atwater, who is the proprietor of the Theatre, was formerly a resident of [Kenosha], and is well known to most of our citizens…."[12] Instead, the company returned to Racine, where in the early part of the week the houses were not full, because the company was not expected back so soon.[13]

The actors left Kenosha editors with a new hunger for theatre: One reporter wrote,

> Men can no more fulfill the object of their whole being, without indulging and being indulged with amusements; than they can become religious without exercising that faculty of the mind, which points to their Creator as an object of reverence.
> We are led to this train of remark, from the impression left on our mind after looking over the crowd that nightly visited the theatre…. On whatsoever side of the room the eye rested, might be seen a representation of some one of the churches of the city. And such a harmony of feeling we don't believe was ever manifested by those different sectarians before….[14]

The *Sheboygan Journal* wrote they were pleased to learn that J.B. Atwater's theatre company would come to the village and "remain during the balance of the week."[15] Once the company had arrived, however, there was no further mention of Atwater. The paper named the rest of the company, both Atwater and Laurette Allen missing.[16]

Apparently the large company then split, Langrishe taking some actors to Fond du Lac for the week of September 7–13, then on to Oshkosh. There were only seven in the company at this time. The Langrishe company opened in Watertown on September 25.[17] Members of the company were Mr. and Mrs. Langrishe, Mr. and Mrs. Wilkes, John McKibbin, Plato and Cooper. Tickets were 25 cents.[18]

The Wisconsin State Agricultural Fair opened on October 1, in Janesville, to run for two days.[19] There was a ready-made audience, and Langrishe was eager to take advantage of it. He opened at Apollo Hall *on* October 3;[20] next they traveled to Beloit, then Waukegan, Illinois, the first week in November.[21] By November 21, the company was named Langrishe & Atwater and back in Kenosha, where audiences laughed and cheered the "feast of fun." They closed their Kenosha engagement on November 22.[22]

The company had been augmented by three people: Mr. and Mrs. Atwater (Laurette Allen's first mention as Mrs. Atwater) and Miss Helen Allen. Mrs. Atwater and Helen Allen were Jeannette's younger sisters.[23] The *Kenosha Telegraph* viewed their second visit happily: "[W]e are glad to see that the performers so far respect themselves as not to indulge in any of those *double entendres*, which would properly offend a refined taste."[24] The company opened December 1 in Racine. The newspaper encouraged all to attend the theatre, to induce the company to "prolong its stay here, as we are satisfied it is far better for our city that so orderly a place of amusement be kept opened...."[25] A little more encouragement and we shall have a company here making regular circuits throughout the state."[26]

In Janesville on December 16, the crowded audience proved too much for the theatre and a "part of the boxes gave way and let about fifty gentlemen and ladies into the pit.—Fortunately no one was seriously injured."[27] Langrishe and Atwater continued to draw sufficiently good houses through the holidays to remain in Janesville. "From this place they go to Madison, where they will entertain the citizens of that village, and the visitors who will be attracted by the sitting of the legislature."[28]

3

A New Theatre Home

In Madison, Wisconsin, Langrishe and Atwater ordered the remodeling of a theatre on the second floor of Lewis's Hall, on the southwest corner of Wisconsin Avenue and Johnson Street. Patrons would buy tickets in the general store on the main floor, then go to an outdoor back stairway to ascend to the theatre.[1] Seats there "wouldn't do credit to a cattle show."[2] Nevertheless, this was Langrishe's new theatre home and Madison's principal theatre.

Langrishe and Atwater promised to open the first theatrical season in Madison in January 1852. The "Corps Dramatique" was comprised of "Mr. J.L. [*sic*] Langrishe, J.B. Atwater, T.W. Plato, D.T. Cooper, H. Wilks, Mrs. Langrishe, Mrs. Wilks and Miss Helen Allen." Mrs. Atwater was not listed,[3] but she was a member of the company. While the theatre was being fitted up, Langrishe and Atwater took their company to Beloit.[4]

They opened in Madison on January 15 with Kotzebue's *The Stranger* or *Misanthropy and Repentance.* Langrishe was to sing a song, then star with Mrs. Atwater in a farce, *Two Gregories* or *Where Did the Money Come From?* Box seats were 50 cents, sloping raised seats 25 cents.[5] The *Wisconsin Daily Argus* reported that Langrishe and Atwater were performing to crowded houses in Madison. "We are glad of their great success, as we never knew a company more worthy."[6] It's a very good thing they were drawing crowded houses because Wisconsin was dangerously cold in winter; the larger the audience, the more body heat generated, the more comfortable the theatre. That same issue of the newspaper reported that the temperature was 24° below zero at daybreak.

The following week they continued to perform a nightly change of bill, each night a melodrama plus an amusing farce.[7] Usually during these evenings, Langrishe entertained with songs between the main play and the afterpiece. This company performed *Othello*, the first Shakespeare presentation in Madison, drawing their usual crowded house.[8] Langrishe and Atwater continued to present serious dramas with comic farces until February 20, then took a few days off to spruce up the theatre. They were to re-open on February 27 with new scenery, new plays and improved seats. Monday, March

15, was the last night of the Madison season, a benefit for the three sisters: Mrs. Langrishe, Mrs. Atwater and Miss Allen.[9]

Well, not quite the last night. They resumed March 19 and 20, and the paper reported they were to leave for Galena, Illinois, the first of "next week." "During their brief sojourn among us, they have acquired many warm friends, and have won the respect and esteem of all."[10]

En route to Galena, they performed in Mineral Point, Wisconsin, at the Court House. The *Wisconsin Tribune* praised midsummer efforts at beautification and building sidewalks about town, but added that the Mineral Point Court House could use a good coat of paint and proper seats installed.[11]

"The first entertainment of the Theatrical company under the management of Messrs. Langrishe and Atwater was given at the [Galena] Court House last evening. The whole performance was excellent—to our judgment, better than anything we have seen in Galena—and that is praise enough."[12]

A few days later, the *Galena Jeffersonian* praised the "spirit with which Mrs. Langrishe enters into her parts, and the fidelity with which she brings them out. Her laugh in comedy is contagious, and her reading and action leave little room for criticism...."[13] They played through at least April 30, 1852, in Galena, then went to St. Paul, Minnesota. The river was free of ice that far north, and steamboats were plying between Galena and St. Paul in 33 hours, 30 minutes.

The company had a great deal of baggage, including painted scenic drops for the plays in their large repertoire. They took the new steamship, *The Nominee*, to St. Paul to open Saturday, May 22.[14] The press praised them: "The Company ... is the best provincial company we have ever seen; and will afford the people here a great deal of pleasure.... They appear to be people who highly respect themselves; and were treated with much consideration in Galena."[15] Reviews were favorable, plays changed every night following the serious drama-*entr'acte*-farce schedule, and apparently at least some residents attended every night. "While the whole public mind is tortured with suspense about the ratification of the [Indian] treaties, it is as refreshing as ice in dog-days, to be amused and entertained every night, with the excellent dramatic performances at Mazourka Hall...."[16]

They performed through June 5 and then went on to La Crosse, Fort Winnebago, Oshkosh and Fond du Lac, Wisconsin.[17] In February, a *Fort Winnebago River Times* correspondent who had attended a theatre performance in Madison wrote, "We believe both the [theatrical] company and our citizens would be gainers if Messrs. Langrishe and Atwater should pay us a short visit. The theatre here [Fort Winnebago] is more extensively patronized than is that now at Madison."[18]

Langrishe and Atwater opened in Fort Winnebago on June 22.[19] A reporter wrote: "We wish the 'pious families' could have been present on Friday evening to witness *The Serious Family* ... promotive of a high tone of morality and honorable feeling, and [combining] the instructive, the amusing and the refining lessons of the drama to an extent which must secure crowded houses and reputation wherever they make a stay."[20]

In Fond du Lac, they performed for a week, then on to Green Bay.[21] The *Green Bay Advocate* wrote warmly of the actors' talents: "[I]f for no other thing, they deserve the esteem of the public for demonstrating that a provincial company can be free from a vulgar and tainting character...."[22] They took Lake Michigan transport to Waukegan, Illinois.[23]

Langrishe and Atwater opened at the Court House in Waukegan August 7. "An Auditor" wrote the newspaper: "Nothing could have bourn [sic] greater proofs of the peculiar powers of this company, than the large and intelligent audiences which they drew each night, and the immense cheering with which every piece was received.... [I]n this place they have not only proved themselves gentlemen in *every* respect, but worthy the worldwide celebrity they have already established."[24] More than a week before the troupe actually showed up, the *Kenosha Tribune* noted, "Although we should at any time greet their coming with uncommon pleasure, yet this summer we hail them as budgets of sweet delight."[25]

They played in Son's Hall, Kenosha, from August 16 to 28, to overflowing houses.[26] A letter from "Thespis" appeared in the *Kenosha Tribune*, offering a "trifling tribute to those who are doing so much ... to divert us from the ghost of hard times. I mean the Theatre. [Members of the company are] very quiet, citizen-like, and even [exhibit] courteous behavior.... There is not one *uproarious* character among them....[reflecting] great credit upon the proprietors.—Much worse playing than that of this company, in Boston and New York, costs us from two to ten dollars, while it is now brought to our doors for a nominal price...."[27] From Kenosha they crossed Lake Michigan and traveled to Grand Rapids, where they opened on September 1.[28]

Their playing was well-received in Grand Rapids, whose newspaper praised them for avoiding "the vulgar jest, and *double entendre* ... [that] pander to a corrupt taste [that] have driven respectability from the boxes of the Theatre.... *The Serious Family* was capital. Mr. Langrishe's Aminidab, we venture to say, can't be beat. Mr. McKibbin's old lady was perfect; we could scarcely realize that the character before us was not a veritable sainted old woman."[29]

September was harvest time in agricultural areas, with audiences hard to attract, so it was an appropriate time for theatre people to rest. Langrishe usually went to New York City to obtain new plays and/or new actors; Mrs. Langrishe may have gone to visit her daughter at a boarding school for the deaf (in Ohio, then New York in later years).

Langrishe took the company to Janesville October 18, without the Atwaters. For leading man, he had R.J. Miller, with whom he had partnered in New York in earlier years. Mrs. Miller was also a member of the company as were Mrs. Langrishe and T.W. Plato.[30] They played in Janesville through November 6.[31] They played in Freeport, Illinois, from November 16 to about the 19th, and then the weather turned disagreeably colder.[32]

Langrishe and Miller's company arrived in Galena, Illinois, on November 25 and the press remarked: "It will be remembered that Mr. Langrishe was the soul of the Company when here last spring...."[33] As of December 4, the newspaper reported the "horrid walking has hitherto prevented as large an attendance as could be justified. With the first frost, the ladies will turn out to make the Hall glad with their presence. Without their smiles, places of amusement become dull indeed."[34]

The *Madison Daily Argus and Democrat* reported Langrishe's theatrical company was performing in Galena, but intended to be back in Madison at the start of the legislative session.[35] The company remained in Galena until about January 1, 1853. They opened at the Court House in Mineral Point, Wisconsin, on January 3, 1853, performing through January 11.[36]

Langrishe and Atwater, back together, opened in Badger Hall, Madison, on January 15, with the *Orphan of Geneva* and *The Artful Dodger*. Madisonians welcomed the company warmly with a crowded house.[37] The company was the same as the previous season.[38]

They started this season with some new plays and some old favorites.[39] Newspaper reporters seldom reviewed shows, but occasionally an audience member wrote a review such as:

> Mr. Editor: ... [*The Stranger's*] chief attraction was Mrs. Langrishe, in the character of Mrs. Haller—her countenance, her air, her gestures, were all in keeping with that tender melancholy, that deep remorse, that unutterable anguish of a breaking heart, laboring under the scorching consciousness that her own misdeeds had wrought the heavy curse upon her. I have seen the most distinguished actresses in the same character, and yet I never saw it better illustrated. The Farce brought down the house in perpetual peals of laughter. Plato and Langrishe, in the characters of Captain Tribet and Wigler, kept the audience in convulsions of laughter—Yours, &c., B.[40]

Under "state matters," the *Kenosha Telegraph* noted that the Madison Theatre "is said to be in hallelujah blast, and to excel in grandeur the Olympic games.—Here, any and all are enabled to gratify their taste for mental degradation at the extreme low price of two or four bits."[41] "The company have recently made large additions to their scenery...."[42]

A Madison paper noted:

> What we should do here without the amusement afforded by Messrs. Langrishe and Atwater, it would be difficult to tell.—One visit to the Tiger [i.e., Faro game] is enough to satisfy any gentleman not over eager to make a fortune, and the consumption of Rock River Whiskey, flavored with kreosote [sic], may be an exhilarating diversion, but is rather destructive to the human constitution, yet for a homeless bachelor, or for a married man exiled to the Legislature or Lobby, these would be the only resources for amusement in the long winter evenings, had not the above-named gentlemen kindly stepped in to provide another means of escape from weariness of one's self and neighbors....[43]

The company began introducing new plays, interspersing them with old favorites, and changing the bill each night. On March 7, 1853, they performed *Uncle Tom's Cabin*, based on Harriet Beecher Stowe's then-newish novel. Their production was not the popular version by George Aiken, and it ran only a single night.

For Langrishe's benefit, we copy the following from the bill: "To wake the soul with humorous strokes,/To crack the sides of honest folks,/To banish care, dispel ennui,/With special merriment and glee/To make you smile— aye, laugh outright/ With Langrische [sic] Thursday night."[44]

The legislature adjourned April 4, until June 6. John S. Folds Langrishe had cemented friendships with Madison men by joining Lodge No. 5 of the Free and Accepted Masons of Wisconsin.[45] Many of these Masonic gentlemen would be his friends for the rest of his life, and being a member gave him instant access to brother Masons wherever he went.

Langrishe and Atwater left Madison and traveled to Galena for a short season,[46] then opened in Mineral Point on May 10, drawing very good crowds. The paper commented: "The performance on Monday evening [May 16] was one of the best we have ever witnessed. Mrs. Langrishe, in the character of Lucretia Borgia, performed her part most admirably, and called forth peals of approbation from the audience; but where all act their several parts as well as do this company, distinction is unnecessary...."[47] They went on to Shullsberg for a very brief season.[48]

The Wisconsin legislature re-convened on June 6, and an item in the *Madison Daily Argus and Democrat* asked, "Have we a Jack Langrishe among us? *Well*, we have; and Atwater, Plato and all of 'em that make up the theatrical company that contributed so much to the entertainment of our citizens and those who were sojourning with us during the past winter season."[49]

They reverted to their repertoire of sentimental and historical comedies, melodramas, serious and historical dramas and farces.[50] They slipped a number of new plays and afterpieces into their repertoire, conducting rehearsals of new pieces on the days familiar pieces were scheduled to be put on those evenings. Only once this month did they repeat a play a second night; that was the spectacle *The Carpenter of Rouen*,[51] an expensive production requiring new scenery.

They went on to play Oshkosh, Fond du Lac and Green Bay, then on to Waukegan, Illinois.[52] They had good houses each night. As the paper observed: "It does a man good in these dog-days to have his sluggish blood sent through his veins at railroad speed under high pressure, by witnessing and *realizing* these life-like representations upon the stage."[53] The plan was to play Waukegan through September 3, then move to Kenosha for a two-week run, arriving in Racine the week after that.[54]

A Kenosha playgoer wrote: "[I]f there's anything *bizarre* and comical to the death, Langrishe will elicit it, from the gall of Hypochondria the bitterness of grief and from the very skull cap of holy horror. …The most serious word he ever said is sufficient to stagger the sobriety of Loyola, and bewitch dark melancholy to a smile…. CIEL"[55] The *Kenosha Tribune* reported that "the inimitable Langrishe convulses an audience with a look or a word…."[56]

With this reputation it must have required extraordinary effort to portray serious characters as Langrishe did once in a while. A Kenosha audience member warmly reviewed the company's work, and praised Mrs. Langrishe as a very fine actress: "[H]er actions are impressive and appropriate. At the point where Ingomar approaches her and she fears from his indelicacy, and exclaims, while her dagger is raised above her bosom,—'Back! one more step and I die at your feet!'—her position was beautifully statuesque and imposing. In general, her positions are uncommonly fine, and would do honor to the best actresses in the country…."[57]

Her husband was likewise lauded:

> But Langrishe in *Poor Pillicoddy,* and *The Omnibus*, is unsurpassed. Dan Marble is dead, and Yankee Hill is dead, and Winchell has retired, but Langrishe is left, and he is enough to kill all, with laughter. If any body can look at him without hearing a word he says and not be convulsed they have more gravity than the most of mankind. His fun is not gross or vulgar, but is of the kind, which you cannot define, which you would not define if you could—which you would despise a man for endeavoring to define. It is delicate, keen, original, diversified. As "Aminidab Sleek," you cannot think him himself. As "Pillicoddy," he kills you downright. He is as far above Mossop in his comicalities as Mossop was above Hypochondria itself. He makes things funny that were never dreamed to be so before. He sends the audience home with the side-ache and they return the next night with swollen cheeks and bloated with the pure sting of fun. If any body is more creative than he is, that somebody is a criminal, that's all, and he should be kept fasting for the health of the people…. CID.[58]

The first week of September, Langrishe traveled alone to Watertown, Wisconsin, to arrange for erection of a 30x40-foot building close to the Wisconsin State Fair grounds, the Fair to be held there in October.[59] They opened in Racine on September 19, promising to present "all the new Tragedies,

Comedies, Dramas, Farces, Burlesques, &c., &c." Langrishe and Atwater's company played in Racine through September 30.[60]

They performed every afternoon and evening during the run of the Fair in Watertown, and may have out-drawn the Fair. As the press observed: "The Fair is not so well attended as I expected, the price of admission being fixed by the officers at twenty-five cents, and membership at three dollars, has kept thousands away that would have attended, had it been conducted in the usual way.... The best part of the 'show' I have neglected to mention, and that was ... our old friends 'Langrishe and Atwater' with their admirable company.... DANE"[61] A reporter from the *Green Bay Advocate* dropped in on the Langrishe-Atwater show one afternoon "and calculated there were five hundred people present, besides about two hundred babies, full seventy-five percent of which were taking an active part in the oratoria...."[62] The Fair concluded October 8, after which the theatre company traveled to Waukesha and performed from October 10 through 15, 1853, and then to Janesville, October 20, playing in that city for the rest of 1853 and a few days into 1854.[63]

By Monday, January 9, Langrishe and Atwater and their theatre company were back in Madison, to open at Badger Hall January 11, the day the legislature was to convene in that city.[64] Their ad claimed they had new scenery painted by "the celebrated Artist, R.H. Smith, now attached to the Chicago Theatre. Their stage has been greatly enlarged—New and Splendid Wardrobe added.... All the new pieces of the day are received by Express ... and will be produced here immediately after their appearance in New York...."

The company's plays were mainly those they had previously performed in Madison, although a few were new.[65] On February 8 they premiered *The Corsican Brothers*.[66] "For three nights in succession the thrilling tragedy of *The Corsican Brothers* has been performed ... to full houses. This piece was gotten up at great pains and expense ... the parts were all extremely well sustained.... The Tableaux were strikingly beautiful...."[67]

March came in like a lamb and streets were full of mud which kept many from attending Mrs. Langrishe's March 2 benefit, when she starred as Lady Gay Spanker in Dion Boucicault's *London Assurance*.[68] This item appeared before Langrishe's benefit on March 29: "Theatre—Langrishe, the comic, the fun-inspiring the side-splitting Langrishe, who has kept his audiences 'on a roar' all winter, has his benefit to-night. Those who have held both their sides as his inimitable phiz [face] in the mock heroic attitude cannot but feel warmly towards the man who has made them so merry for an hour.... Langrishe will appear in all his glory, and if he don't get a thundering benefit, then merit will not receive its reward."[69]

The troupe traveled to Janesville, opening about April 8, 1854.[70] They

3. A New Theatre Home 29

probably performed in Janesville several more days, while Langrishe went to Chicago to obtain new actors and perhaps new plays. The company opened in Milwaukee at the Market Hall Monday, April 24, with *The Corsican Brothers*,[71] one of the minor characters played by John Dillon, in his theatrical debut. Apparently audiences were smaller than expected.[72] They finished the week at Market Hall, then moved to Young's Hall, "a much better locality for their business than Market Hall...."[73] It proved to be a smart move, and the company was rewarded with better-sized audiences from the beginning. Milwaukee gentlemen (S.B. Grant and 62 others) signed a petition to create a benefit for the former Allen sisters, and the ladies chose the bill. The Milwaukee gentlemen, by tendering the benefit, paid all production expenses so the ladies could keep all box office receipts.[74]

Kenosha residents expected Langrishe and Atwater's company would play in Kenosha[75] but they were not enamored of just any theatre. They wanted good actors and good pieces, well presented. A correspondent lambasted a troupe called the Calladine Company, the editor concurring, condemning it as a burlesque and "a very poor one at that."[76]

Langrishe and Atwater's company traveled 30 miles south of Milwaukee and began playing at Racine. A reporter or editor of the *Kenosha Tribune* described traveling to Racine and attending their performance of *Damon and Pythias*.

> Mr. Atwater, as Damon, and Mrs. Langrishe as Calanthe, were excellent.... Calanthe's address to the sun on the execution block of Pythias, before the arrival of Damon, was fine beyond our capacity to express. We felt something like a *furor* of excitement, while her love and Minerva-like dignity kept the officers at bay, after the moment of the execution of her lover was even past.... A little lady by our side, said she 'would not cry, any how!' while the little perfumed 'kerchief was drinking the nectar of her pearly tears to intoxication....[77]

In Kenosha it was observed:

> The Military Hall resounds every evening to the thunders of applause and the ring of merry laughter from delighted and respectable audiences. Messrs. Langrishe & Atwater have earned their well-established reputation, by persevering and honorable effort to cultivate and maintain the dramatic taste of the western States.... We have never yet known them to act to thin houses.... The afterpiece *The Omnibus* was one in which Mr. Langrishe appears to immense advantage and in a manner which Mossup never equalled. We say this reverently of the favorite comedian Mossup who is now dead but the preference must be given to Langrishe on account of the greater naturalness and less restraint.... [*Serious Family*] is a favorite comedy, and we always greet Mr. L. in the character of Aminidab Sleek with great pleasure, for it proves the Irish character is not the only one within the range of his powers, as was evidently the case with Mossup....[78]

Langrishe also received extravagant praise for his portrayal of Nichol Jarvie in *Rob Roy*:

> In this, Langrishe is the *Star,* and if one would see Langrishe in his glory let him perform the part of Nichol Jarvie *in Rob Roy*. In it the natural comicality of the man has a full and free scope and it does take a free scope overturning the sobriety of his audience and carrying with it his extraordinary power where he will. One quite forgets that the same Langrishe has been the scrupulous Mr. Sleek or the Irish servant or the drunken B'hoy or, as in the *Deserter,* making love to king Frederick, winning his fractious sovereign to his favor by a series of the most ludicrous and even killing counterfeits of the drunken grenadier we have ever seen....[79]

The company opened at the Court House in Waukegan, Illinois, on June 12, 1854.[80] They remained there through at least June 17, and perhaps longer,[81] then to Fond du Lac, Oshkosh and Green Bay where the press reported that their company "are general favorites in Wisconsin, and in no place have they *more* or warmer friends, among the pleasure-loving people, than in Green Bay. Since their recent arrival here, we have seen people who have come 30 miles to enjoy an evening or two in their theatre, which speaks well for their power to please and *attract* the crowd...."[82]

Settlers were still moving into Wisconsin, swelling the population of small towns and creating new communities. This year, 1854, Langrishe and Atwater played Menasha, Neenah and Berlin for the first time.[83] Jack Langrishe was not with the company and had not been with it for three weeks. A Madison paper explained: "Langrishe, who has been ... in the Eastern cities, has been fortunate in securing the services of Mrs. Frary, late of Burton's Theatre, New York. They passed through here [Madison] en route for Janesville, and will probably open here about the last of December."[84] The Langrishe and Atwater company probably played in Janesville from about October 2, 1854, to the end of the year. The press apologized: "We have somehow ... omitted to notice the theatrical company of Messrs. Langrishe and Atwater ... [but] everyone knows they are among us, and they are deservedly popular. Our friends from the country staying in town over night will find a pleasant entertainment any evening at Apollo Hall."[85]

Three months was a lengthy season to play in Janesville, population 6000, yet the newspapers indicated they were enjoying sufficient attendance to support this large company of actors.[86] In New York, theatres were complaining of hard times.[87]

4

Riding High

Near the close of 1854, editors of some Wisconsin newspapers joked about Langrishe and Atwater's plans to open at Madison with the play *The Forty Thieves*. A *Milwaukee Sentinel* editor wrote, "A judicious selection. What the Company lack in strength, to give full effect to the piece, they can find plenty of 'supernumeraries' about the Capitol to fill up with."[1]

Fairchild Hall was fitted up for the new Langrishe and Atwater season,[2] with a larger seating capacity than the old theatre, but the proscenium opening the same size, for they used the same drop curtain, the scene of Columbus' arrival in the New World that drew this comment: "Columbus ... attempting to land so long that we have quite despaired of his success."[3] This theatre may have been an acoustic improvement, due to a thin wooden sounding board installed under a skylight, and probably was more comfortable for the audience, with "good" ventilation.[4]

A news item in the Saturday, January 6, 1855, *Madison Daily Argus and Democrat* indicated that Langrishe and Atwater would open their season Tuesday, January 9. At this time the company was composed of Mr. and Mrs. Langrishe, J.B. Atwater, Miss Allen and "Mrs. Frary, a pleasing comic actress and exquisite singer" from the New York theatres. Her husband, J. Frary, was prompter.[5] Mrs. Atwater was not listed because she had given birth or was about to give birth to a child this month.[6]

The *Chicago Tribune* noted, "The gentlemanly troupe of Messrs. Langrish [sic] and Atwater are at present in Madison, Wis. Some of Shakespeare's heaviest characters, Macbeth, Hamlet, and etc. have been produced to overflowing houses. Mrs. Frary, formerly of this place, a good actress and beautiful singer, adds greatly to the strength of the company."[7]

The company suffered a setback when Mrs. Langrishe slipped on an icy sidewalk on March 1 and severely sprained her wrist.[8] The company didn't have anyone to take her place. Then Atwater fell ill.[9] They struggled to finish the Madison season. Interruption of their theatre season struck a hard financial blow to Langrishe and Atwater, and the community realized it. Forty prominent Wisconsin citizens tendered a benefit to Langrishe, stating "they [the undersigned] deem that this testimonial is due both to yourself and Mr. Atwater, as a token of their esteem for your personal and professional characters, as well as their regrets for the temporary but still serious misfortunes...."[10]

In mid–April, the *Mineral Point Tribune* wrote that the company still had the Langrishes, Atwaters, Miss Allen and McKibbin, and if those performers "fail to please the Theatre-going portion of our citizens, no others need make the attempt."[11] The company enjoyed a few days off in Portage City, then started their season there May 5, running through May 19.[12]

One man in Portage disparaged the theatre. The *Portage Independent* printed his attack and defended the theatre:

> We have lived long enough in this world to become convinced that men must and will have amusement of some kind—and if it is not presented to them in one form, they will seek for it in another.... So as far as Messrs. Langrishe and Atwater's Theatre is concerned, we can only say that we have attended on several occasions; and have never yet witnessed anything to which the most fastidious could object.... Their plays are well selected, and for the most part convey an excellent *moral*. We wish that every man, woman and child in the community could have heard *The Serious Family* as performed by them last week.... There are too many "Aminidab Sleeks" in the world; and the canting, sniveling, hypocritical crews which are brought together under their influence, do more to retard the progress of true religion and morality than all the Theatres in Christendom....[13]

The Langrishe and Atwater company opened in Oshkosh on May 22, then went to Fond du Lac June 18.[14] On July 2 they put on *The Corsican Brothers* and during the performance, an audience member threw a bouquet on stage at the feet of Mrs. Langrishe, playing "Emilie De Lesparre." The attached poem, from "Nelly Wildwood," began:

> To Mrs. Langrishe. 'Oh Lady! Would this harp of mine, /Could breath [sic] strains worthy thee, /Its every string/ should be attuned,/To holiest melody/ ...

And on, in maudlin fashion, for nine similar stanzas.[15]

They opened in Green Bay about September 2 with new scenery, new plays plus new actors and actresses "from the [U.S.] Eastern Theatres."[16] The company performed several new plays in Green Bay, delighting audiences. Some thought the acting of the "old favorites" was better than ever.[17] In 1855 Green Bay had a population of 1644, but repeat attendance made a 25-day theatrical season profitable for Langrishe and Atwater.[18] The managers planned to go on to Neenah, Oshkosh, Fond du Lac and Janesville before proceeding to Madison for the winter season.[19] The new faces in the company were Charles Wilson and John Dunn.[20] Wilson performed various types of roles for Langrishe, both in Wisconsin, a decade later in Colorado, and in Chicago in 1871.[21]

4. Riding High

The troupe left Fond du Lac about October 21, went to Waupun, Ripon and Watertown. A Ripon critic appraised the troupe: "Among them are a number of first rate actors, and the whole of them are much above mediocrity ... [praises the Langrishes and Atwater] Mrs. Atwater makes the finest woman we ever saw in br– ah well—[probably breeches] any way—and as 'King Charles' and in many other characters, both in the agreeable and comical, fitted our ideas exactly...."[22] Then to Janesville on November 28[23] where a Madison paper reported, "Mrs. Langrishe, an accomplished actress..., is seriously ill at Janesville. We trust she may recover, at least, in time, for the winter's season in Madison."[24]

Langrishe and Atwater's company opened the National Theatre in Madison with *Richelieu*, never previously performed in Madison, and Mrs. Langrishe was fully recovered from her illness.[25] A critic wrote: "In comedy Langrishe keeps the audience in a laugh the whole time and even those who come to cavil or to show what they have seen by grumbling, often break up their growling by a laugh at some unexpected comicality. In the pathetic comedy he astonishes the audience almost as much by his exhibition of true feeling...."[26]

An audience member wrote "Mrs. Langrishe ... possesses a versability [*sic*] of talent that is amazing. Langrishe the 'unimitated, unimitable Langrishe,' what can we say of him in the way of commendation which has not been said and which he does not deserve. In everything that pertains to the comic, Langrishe is perfect. In the 'rich brogue' of the Irish, the broad Scotch, and the still broader Yorkshire, he is equally at home, and when Langrishe would make the audience laugh, they must laugh...."[27] Even Langrishe's advertisements were humorous. One carried a note, "No charge, except a small collection taken up at the door to pay expenses."[28]

When Langrishe appeared in *The School for Scandal*, a critic wrote that he "was superbly dressed in the costume of the day, glittering in silver and satin. He performed his part admirably, and his quiet effective acting in the character excited a great deal of admiration, though it was too efficient to draw much applause. People forgot the actor and looked at Sir Peter...."[29]

On March 25 a Madison paper revealed: "*Black Hawk* is the title of a new play by a lady of this State known by the *nom de plume* of Nelly Wildwood.—It will be brought out in the course of the season by Langrishe and Atwater, at the National Theatre."[30] Nelly Wildwood was the author of the saccharine poem accompanying the bouquet thrown to Mrs. Langrishe about a year previous in Fond du Lac.[31]

In March 1856, the Wisconsin legislature passed a private bill, changing

Picture of Jeannette Langrishe as an Indian in the production of *Blackhawk* in Madison, Wisconsin (Wisconsin Historical Society, image number WHi 7066).

Langrishe's name from John S. Folds to "John S.F. Langrishe." Langrishe was the surname he'd been using professionally for over ten years.[32]

A reader submitted his estimation of "Our Theatre" on March 31:

> The audience (and the whole state is more or less that very audience) that can listen to the choicest productions of Shakespeare, Bulwer, Sheridan, Knowles, Colman, &c., &c., is an audience that ... does honor to the author and the actor. The very selection of such a highly intellectual class of drama is at once a mark of the clear discriminating and discerning character of the managers and a reflex compliment to the people.... The Wisconsin state dramatic

company is a company of which Wisconsin may justly be proud, nor has the dramatic company less reason to be proud of its audience, the people of Wisconsin.

Langrishe and Atwater have not only earned for themselves an enviable reputation as theatrical managers, but (perhaps separately) they have added to this the no less enviable reputation of actors, actors whose standing though it may fall short of a Charles Kemble, a Macready or a Power, in the absence of these illuminates, entitles them to tread the boards of these their masters as representatives of high artistic mental and moral worth.

There is not a stage in London where Langrishe would find his superior. Since the loss of the *President* in which poor Power went down [the SS *President*, bearing the comedian Tyrone Power, sank in 1842].[33] neither the English nor the Irish stage has a home representative of Irish character.... No other stage at the present day has any honest, Irish, inimitable Jack Langrishe.... Aubyn.[34]

John Dillon's reappearance in Madison was cause for an "uproarious cheer."[35] There was more than one reason for Dillon's rejoining the Langrishe and Atwater company: He had married Helen Allen on April 20.[36]

Langrishe and Atwater picked up another partner, Edgerton, for an ambitious tour of the region with a brass band, an acting company, scenery and costumes, plus a very large tent seating up to 5000 people. They opened that tour in Madison on April 19, near the Congregational Church.[37] The *Sheboygan Journal* observed that the company's taking their own tent would get "to the windward of owners of halls, who charge high prices."[38] This touring was a costly undertaking, but if their audiences were indeed large, revenues would be large too. Admission was 50 cents.

They opened in Monroe on April 24,[39] Beloit April 29,[40] Waukegan, Illinois, May 8,[41] Kenosha May 9,[42] Geneva, May 14 and Janesville, May 17. They had an excellent run of business when weather permitted,[43] but rains were frequent and heavy, producing mire that bogged down their heavy wagons.[44]

The company performed both a matinee and an evening performance in Janesville on May 17, Whitewater May 19[45] and Jefferson May 21, after they entered grandly with their brass band. The *Whitewater Gazette* said the Langrishe and Atwater company drew a respectably large crowd, the afternoon performance better than the evening show because in the latter "the principal player seemed to have mistaken indecency for wit, and to consider profanity his principal accomplishment, judging from the great display he made of it."[46]

Thus rebuked, they went on to Beaver Dam May 29,[47] Portage June 2,[48] Oshkosh June 11,[49] Fond du Lac June 17 and 18[50] and back to Beaver Dam.[51] From there they traveled to Galena, Illinois, a considerable distance by horse. They would have left Beaver Dam June 21 and arrived in Galena by July 2, having traveled about 125 miles. They might have sent the heavy scenery, trained horses and huge pavilion on ahead of the company. Or they could have taken a steamer on the Fox River, connecting to the Mississippi.[52]

The *Galena Daily Courier* began running ads for the "Langrishe and Atwater & Co." on June 24:

> This magnificent establishment combining all that is Beautiful in Painting, novel in Horsemanship, Talent in the distribution of characters, Dazzling and picturesque in Costumes,

Earliest image found of Jack Langrishe. From an ambrotype (Wisconsin Historical Society, WHi (X3) 121071).

4. Riding High

Decorations, Appointments, Processions, Battle Tableaux, Music and Orchestra Aid, &c., &c., with the Full Stud of Horses, and an Entire Star Company! Consisting of 40 Ladies and Gentlemen, aided by two superb Bands of Music. The Renowned New York Brass Band! Led by the celebrated Cornet Player, Mr. Shriner. An unequaled string band, under the direction of the great violinist, Mr. R.S. Bensel, formerly leader of the Park Theatre, New York. Afternoon performance will commence with the great Scottish drama of *Lochinvar*, in which the entire Company will appear and Mr. Atwater's Highly Trained Horse, Waverly. Mademoiselle Therese, the beautiful danseuse will appear in a great variety of Fancy Dances. Yankee Bowman[53] in a side-splitting story. Dan Scott, the great clown and grotesque dancer. Mr. J. Dillon, the great comic singer of the age in a budget of comicalities. Jack Langrishe, in the great farce of *Catherine Hayes*. Evening performance will commence with the Great Drama of *The Forty Thieves*, with the entire company and full stud of Horses. To be followed by an endless variety of Dancing and singing. To conclude with the laughable farce of *The Limerick Boy*.[54]

Wednesday, July 9, they paraded into Prairie du Chien with their prancing horses and "splendid band music."[55] The local paper commented: "Sucks.– Among the greatest sucks that make their appearance in this neighborhood are C-i-r-c-u-s-e-s, which never fail to suck in the curious; but it must be allowed that Langrishe, Atwater and Co.'s Great Western Amphitheatre has proved an agreeable exception."[56]

Harvesting of crops began in late July in Iowa and Wisconsin, so Langrishe and Atwater took a hiatus.[57] They resumed traveling with the amphitheater in late September, appearing in Mineral Point, Wisconsin, September 29,[58] Sauk City, October 3, Baraboo October 4[59] and Portage from October 7 to 18.[60] The *Baraboo Republic* noted, "If any of our readers are troubled with the blue-devils, they had better go and hear Langrishe—just once, that's enough to scatter them."[61] Langrishe left the company in Portage and went to Madison.[62] In Portage they played in a rented hall; there was no mention of the fate of the large tent. As of October 23, the company was still playing at Vandercook's Hall in Portage.[63]

On November 15 they were in Janesville, performing in Lappin's newly completed hall, complete with gas lights. The hall was 100 feet long, a 51x70 foot area devoted to audience, plus a gallery along the sides of the hall, the total seating from 1200 to 1500 people.[64]

The *Madison Daily Argus and Democrat* looked forward to the season. "Amusements for the Season.—Messrs. Langrishe and Atwater, now playing in Janesville, are to be here next Monday. Their company consists of Mr. Langrishe, who, as a comedian, has no superior in the West; Mr. Atwater, a justly celebrated tragedian; Mrs. Langrishe, a general favorite in all characters of the Drama; Mrs. Atwater, a charming actress—as is also Mrs. Dillon—formerly Miss Allen; Mr. Dillon the comic singer and punster; Mr. Davis, distinguished in genteel comedy; Messrs. Cline, Shaffer and O'Neil, all old favorites...."[65]

Langrishe played the role of Sir Harcourt Courtly in *London Assurance*, not a comedy role. A spectator commented:

> He displayed an artistic skill almost surprising. There is no opportunity in that character for bold or startling outlines, but the consistency and finish which he gave to the picture set his shallow-brained man of fashion down as a *bona fide* individual in the upper walks of society, making mercantile calculations about matrimony, and considering his toilet the great ultimatum of duty.... Mr. Langrishe excels in finished pictures, and his genius as an artist is always visible more in the polish of the ludicrous than in any strong points that are, clearly enough, wholly dependent on the imagination. He never takes anybody else's conception of character, but possesses a nice discrimination of his own....[66]

Mrs. Langrishe played Alice Darvil in *Ernest Maltravers*, and the paper's reviewer pronounced this role her masterpiece. "We defy the histrionic world to produce her superior in it ... her picture of the madwoman forcibly reminded us of Mr. Conway's 'Mad Tom' in *King Lear*. It was no foolish creation, but one so true to nature of madness that it could make the blood creep coldly back in the artist's veins...."[67]

Another item said: "We do not imagine that Mrs. Langrishe possesses great versatility of genius, but in this character she has the power of an inspired *artiste*; her voice is susceptible of a tender, liquid sweetness, and the most intense modulation; her attitudes are all graceful and natural; and the interpretations of her eyes are irresistibly eloquent...."[68]

The company had been presenting plays new to them and to Madison, one after another.[69] A report from Madison to readers in Kenosha said Langrishe and Atwater's theatre was the main reliance for relaxation from the cares of State. "It is thronged night after night with the dignitaries of the land...."[70] "Mr. Langrishe is well known to the laughter-loving.... Everybody pronounces him inimitably droll, transcendently comical, irresistibly humorous—provokingly ludicrous—and capable of giving expression to any joke in the whole range from simply quizzical to profoundly sardonic. He is a gentleman, notwithstanding his wit...."[71]

Mrs. Langrishe may have been at the height of her acting prowess. The *Madison Daily Argus and Democrat* was effusive with praise for her acting in *Lady of the Lake*: "[She] was possessed of her usual quiet and winning grace. She is essentially quiet, always at home, and never 'tears a passion to tatters' in attempting to express what she has the power to do more perfectly with a glance, or a silvery tone, both of which she can command with an ease that is surprising to the audience...."[72]

On tap were more plays new to Madison and the members of this company[73]; at the end of the first act of *The Last Man*, a newly painted drop curtain fell and was "greeted with thundering applause." The advent of a new scenic drop curtain was always hailed as the beginning of a new era in theatricals. The unique and well-designed scene—representing summer ruins by the side of a beautiful stream that mirrors them—was bordered with green trees and shrubbery.⁷⁴ On Friday the 13th they performed *White Horse of the Peppers* (with Langrishe as Gerald Pepper) and *Naval Engagements*. That bill

Laurette Allen Atwater, sister of Jeannette Langrishe, ambrotype of a scene from *Blackhawk*, original drama by Wisconsin native, Nellie Wildwood (Wisconsin Historical Society, image number WHi 7068).

drew a full house. A reviewer said: "Langrishe distinguished himself by his sudden changes between genteel and low Irish comedy. He is natural and easy in either, and capable of making anything laugh that is possessed of 'facial muscles or nervous qualities....'"[75] They were in rehearsal of an original play written by "Nellie Wildwood," presenting old favorites in the evenings.[76]

On February 26 the paper announced: "The company of Messrs. Langrishe and Atwater is at present composed of more members than ever before since commencing their successful career in this place. There is no larger dramatic company west of Chicago and north of St. Louis—They ... are now about to embark on the rendition of a thrilling original and *aboriginal* drama written expressly for them...."[77] Mr. Walters and his tamed elk were on the bill as prominent characters in *Black Hawk* or *The Lily of the Prairie*, a play abounding in native incident and based on western history.[78] There was no description of how they enticed the trained elk to walk up the stairs to the floor where the theatre was located, or how they were lowered or led down the stairs.

For whatever reason—tact, taste, business or cowardice—Langrishe was not in that cast when *Black Hawk* opened. He conveniently left for New York.[79] The theatre was filled "to suffocation," and many turned away with the promise that the play would be repeated. The play's reviewer wrote: "As for the play itself, a criticism of it, as a work of art, would hardly do it justice.—It must be judged leniently to be judged fairly...."[80] They repeated *Black Hawk* Saturday night, and again Monday, for the benefit of authoress Elizabeth Farnsworth Mears (Nelly Wildwood),[81] when Langrishe may have acted in the cast. Apparently he did pose for an ambrotype in a *Black Hawk* costume.

Langrishe returned from New York City, and the paper reported that the "first sound of his voice on Monday evening

From an ambrotype of John Bowman Atwater as an army officer in *Blackhawk* (Wisconsin Historical Society, image number WHi 7065).

[March 16] 'brought down the house'—amphitheater, dress circle, boxes and all. He cannot fail to be gratified with such ample testimonials of appreciation among critics and the *ton*. There is a peculiar suavity about him that makes him the life of comedy and farce, and renders all his productions finished and easy."[82] The company left for Watertown, and after playing standard dramas there a few weeks they were to commence traveling again, "giving dramatic entertainments under canvas."[83]

The 1855 state census showed that Watertown had a population of 8526 and Madison a population of 8664. Not that many more, but the convening of the legislature enlarged the population of Madison during its session and the delegates and suppliants were eager for respectable entertainment in evenings, sustaining the theatre company through the winter months.[84] The Langrishe and Atwater company began performing in Watertown on April 7, at Cole's Hall.[85] The company remained in Watertown the rest of April, enjoying large enthusiastic audiences.[86] From Watertown they traveled to Beaver Dam, opening May 6, 1857.[87]

One of the first of many "I knew him when" remarks was printed in the *Horicon Argus:* "Langrishe and Atwater are performing to crowded houses at Beaver Dam. Come this way gents, and give us Horiconians a taste of the beautiful. We remember when the good folks of Elmira, Corning &c. were compelled to sew their buttons on nightly at Langrishe's inimitable comicalities."[88] In Beaver Dam, Langrishe and Atwater "succeeded beyond their expectations in drawing good houses...."[89]

The company next appeared with their Great Western Amphitheatre in Watertown, May 22. The local paper described the event:

> They traveled with a full stud of horses, a star company consisting of 40 ladies and gentlemen, all that is beautiful in the Dramatic Art, Novel in Painting, talent in the distribution of Characters, Dazzling and Picturesque in Costume, Decorations, Appointment, Processions, Battle Tableaux, Music and Orchestral Aid, &c., &c.... The company includes artists of known celebrity from the principal Theatres of Europe and America; among whom will be found Mr. J.B. Atwater, Mr. J.S.F. Langrishe, Mr. W. Davis, Mr. Dillon, Mr. Bensel, Mr. McKibbin, Mr. O'Neill, Mr. Deering, Mr. Shafer, Mr. Turner, Mr. Sefton, Messrs. Willis, Jones, Lewis and Croft; Mrs. Langrishe, Mrs. Atwater, Mrs. Deering, Miss Fanny Turner, Miss Emily Dulang, &c., &c., and an immense Corps de Ballet.

The afternoon performance was to be *The Castle of Lausanne* and the farce *Prize in the Lottery*. Evening performances were to be the "grand dramatic spectacle" of *The Carpenter of Rouen* and *The Siamese Twins*. Tickets were 50 cents, children half price.[90] They were in Kenosha May 29, Albany June 8, Monroe June 9, and Shullsberg June 11. In Shullsberg, a balloon ascension outside the tent (free admission, obviously) attracted attention to the Langrishe and Atwater exhibition.[91]

Comedian John Dillon, Jack Langrishe's brother-in-law. Photo taken early in his career (authors' collection, donated by Mrs. Catherine Barth, granddaughter of John Dillon).

4. Riding High

Langrishe and Atwater's advance man ran an ad in the La Crosse paper that was much reduced in size, primarily featuring "two of the best Clowns in the world, Jack Langrishe and John Dillon." They were to play at Hokah on July 2, La Crescent, Minnesota, July 3, and La Crosse, Wisconsin, July 4.[92] "It is estimated that from 1200 to 1500 were present to witness the theatrical performance of Langrishe and Atwater's company on the evening of the Fourth."[93] The company crossed back into Minnesota again, and planned to show in St. Paul on July 1. The day they were giving three performances in St. Paul, a warm wind blew so much dust it was quite unpleasant.[94] It must have been a strain for the actors to be heard in such a large facility even without wind; best permanent theatres have seating capacity of 500 or fewer.

Back in Madison, Langrishe's loyal friends at the *Madison Daily Argus and Democrat* noted that William E. Burton, considered one of the greatest comedians of the day, had appeared in Chicago as "Aminidab Sleek" in *The Serious Family*, and the audience was disappointed in his performance. "We think Jack Langrishe, in the above character, would give as good satisfaction, if not more, than Burton, and feel assured that such could be the unanimous decision of the theatre-going public of Chicago...."[95]

Editors of the *Mantorville Express* were not impressed with the Langrishe and Atwater troupe. "This Company exhibited at this place yesterday [July 29] to a large gathering of people. Their plays are chiefly of the comic order, and the audience seemed highly amused. We cannot but think however that in regard to refinement and intellectuality their pieces are below the standard best suited to a [sic] intelligent Minnesota audience."[96]

Their ad in the McGregor, Iowa, *North Iowa Times* advised people to "Come and see two of the best Clowns in America, JACK LANGRISHE and JOHN DILLON." They were calling it "The Big Show of 1857" and planned to perform in McGregor on September 11, afternoon and evening, and Prairie du Chien, Wisconsin, on September 17.[97] The press greeted them: "Langrishe and Atwater passed through this country a year ago, and it is not a bad sign to see them travel over the same ground.... Children all like shows and you know the good book says, 'Be ye like little children!' Measured by this rule our Christianity is unquestionable."[98]

The Madison paper reported: "Langrishe and Atwater's Company entered town to-day [September 25, 1857] in fine style, looking and feeling in high glee. They have done an excellent business this season, which they well deserve. They perform this evening in their pavilion ... this evening only."[99] The next day there was an item that read: "The pavilion of Messrs. Langrishe and Atwater was filled last night, to the extent of all extra seats the company could muster...."[100]

Langrishe and Atwater returned to Madison from Janesville by October 5.[101] The press revealed that the [Fairchild] theatre "had undergone an entire revision, being enlarged, fitted up with new seats, and re-ornamented throughout ... until the first of December there will be but two performances a week—these on Wednesday and Saturday evenings."[102]

A week later the paper revealed: "The crowded house of last evening, and the cordial reception given to all the members of the [Langrishe and Atwater] corps, as they made their appearance was evidence most conclusive of the esteem in which they are held by those who patronize the drama...."[103]

At the season opening, special praise was reserved for Mrs. Langrishe: "Indeed we have seldom witnessed an impersonation that proved so irresistible a key to the 'softer emotions' of the audience.... As a portrait we look upon the representation as one which cannot be over-estimated; its outlines are bold, yet it is chaste, and symmetrical beyond exception; there is something about it that bespeaks at once extraordinary dramatic power, and a correct, analytical judgment."[104]

Then it was Jack Langrishe's turn for an extended review of his performance in *Langrishe's Adventure with a Polish Princess*. With tongue firmly in cheek, a reporter wrote:

> Langrishe as *Mr. Langrishe* was passable in his impersonation, though open to criticism in some of the more prominent points of what we know to have been the author's ideal! In fact we were somewhat puzzled to know which he was delineating, *Langrishe* the comedian, or Langrishe the gentleman. If the former, he succeeded in doing his portrait only partial justice; if the latter, he indulged in too much caricature—not only as to dress, but in point of manner and general suavity. The house was full of critics, and we must admit that most of them indulged the performance with applause; yet it did not come up to our standard,—as the Langrishe of Society—one of the most courteous and gentlemanly of our acquaintance; neither was there pliability, vivacity and irresistible drollery enough about it for 'Langrishe in his element.'[105]

After a few weeks of old favorites, the company was augmented by a tragedian of note, H. Gossin, who debuted in *Damon and Pythias* on December 8.[106] The afterpiece was *Phenomenon in a Smock Frock*, in which Mrs. Atwater played "Betsey Chirrup." That was probably her last stage appearance as a "show actor" (her term).[107]

On December 18 a Madison paper revealed: "Retired.—Mr. and Mrs. J.B. Atwater ... have retired to private life ... with the intention of resuming no more the histrionic profession. This announcement is a very abrupt one...."[108] The same day, an ad began running in the *Madison Daily Argus and Democrat*, introducing Langrishe's new partner, Charles George Mayers, both partners promising to keep the Theatre respectable, comfortable and "in every way worthy of support."[109] Mayers had played a few roles with Langrishe and Atwater's company as a volunteer, and was also an Alderman, Street Commissioner and Superintendent of the Poor in Madison.[110]

The fact that Gossin, a tragedian, had moved to Madison and Mayers was ready to take on the partnership indicates at least Langrishe and perhaps others in the company knew of Atwater's impending departure sometime in advance of the public announcement.[111]

5

Profits Shrink

The dawn of 1858 saw the Langrishe troupe in Madison before the legislature convened, one of the partners managing the company a politician rather than a professional actor. The Atwaters were still in Madison, although they no longer were involved with the theatre.

The financial panic spreading in the East had extended to the Midwest. Banks were going broke, the notes they had issued worthless, and businesses and individuals holding those notes struggling to stay solvent.

The Madison newspaper sounded as if all was well on the dramatic front, but a letter to the *Prairie du Chien Leader* expressed a contrary opinion: "From Madison Correspondent, Feb. 4.—Our theatre is in full blast. Mr. Atwater and his estimable lady have retired from the boards, and a Mr. W.H. Gossin does up the tragic, and nightly foams, and rants, and mouths, and murders the drama, in the most tragical manner in the presence of empty seats. [Signed] X."[1] A contrary opinion of the theatre company was expressed by "E.A.C.," perhaps E.A. Calkins, who attended a Harrisburg, Pennsylvania, performance: "I visited a theatre last evening and saw *Camille* executed. That last word has a double signification: 'There double murder fills the greedy eye, Shakespeare and Duncan, stabbed, together lie.' While comedy was played like high tragedy, tragedy looked a perfect farce. It was little as the charming Mrs. Langrishe, the gifted Gossin, and the inimitable Langrishe would have rendered *The Fate of a Coquette*...."[2]

In Madison, the company was said to have had a full house for *Hamlet* that was expected to draw even better when repeated. After several other old favorites, the company staged a significant new piece, *The Poor of New York*.[3] A critic observed:

> [We] were not prepared for the happy hit made last evening in the presentation [of *The Poor of New York*]. The scenery took us by surprise to begin with, and then the characters en suite were rendered with such well tuned discrimination, that we gave the entertainment the palm of the season before it was half concluded.... The fire scene and the view of the park given in the play 'brought down the house.' The piece is on the bill again for this evening, and will, no doubt, draw a bigger crowd than ever.[4]

The Poor of New York was a new play by Dion Boucicault, introduced in New York City about two months previous to the Madison showing. The show took Madison by storm, and ran for five nights in succession.[5]

Of this event, the *Prairie du Chien Leader's* correspondent wrote (February 7): "The people of Madison seem to lack all appreciation for the intellectual, and prefer rather to witness the wretched representation of the 'legitimate drama,' at a one-horse theatre, than to listen to the most intellectual discourse, upon the most interesting subject.... X"[6]

That "X" was in the minority was evidenced by the fact that *The Poor of New York* ran for three nights the following week as well. On February 23 they introduced another new play, *The Last Days of Pompeii,*[7] one reviewer commenting: "The refined taste of the managers is shown in their selection from that class of plays which combine instruction with amusement.... [Regarding Mrs. Langrishe:] One could hardly imagine that the same person who presented to our view the noble traits of a virtuous, high-souled, confiding and most-loveable woman in the *Town and Country* could become so suddenly metamorphosed into the simple, bawling, jam-loving 'Tommy Dobbs,' of the afterpiece, but her versatility as an artist is without limit."[8]

Then, for Langrishe's benefit night, they put on another new play, Mrs. Sidney F. Bateman's *Self,* or *The Rich of New York.* When it was mounted at Burton's Theatre in New York, it ran for 100 consecutive nights to crowded houses.[9] The theatre in Madison was "crowded" for the production, and Langrishe was "called out after the fall of the curtain and loudly applauded. In return he made a very handsome little speech and retired gracefully amid hearty cheers...." It was repeated the next evening and the next.[10] "Mr. Langrishe's 'John Unit' is certainly a very happy 'hit.' His elimination of the crusty old bachelor, who 'can't make the institution of matrimony pay,' but who loves virtue and truth, and really has a heart overflowing with kindness, was so perfect as to add new honors to those he has already won by his masterly powers of impersonation...."[11]

Winter snows persisted in the Midwest, but (as the paper reported): "for several days the weather has been spring-like—the south and southwest wind prevailed—vegetation begins to show itself—if no sudden change occurs, we may look for grass by the first of April...."[12] Then the theatre was to close until the following Thursday, to make preparations for *Uncle Tom's Cabin.*[13] The press greeted this event:

> This wonderful play, this impressive moral lesson, since its advent upon the stage has everywhere been supported by a liberal and generous public, and not a single instance has been known where the firm and steadfast supporters of religion have not likewise given this inimitable drama their sanction and encouragement.

> It is to be hoped that our citizens will appreciate the efforts of the management in presenting this piece at a heavy expense, and go and see those wonderful characters which heretofore have existed in ideality alone. The first representation in Madison of this renowned Moral Drama....[14]

A curious claim, in view of the fact that Langrishe and Atwater had performed *Uncle Tom's Cabin* on March 7, 1853. They had probably put on C.W. Taylor's version that had a happy ending, a version that was soundly criticized in other parts of the country.[15]

In Langrishe and Atwater's 1853 *Uncle Tom's Cabin*, the cast included characters named George, Uncle Tom and Cassy. There was no Little Eva.[16] The hugely popular version of the play (with Little Eva) was written by George Aiken in one week for $40 and a gold watch.[17]

In Madison the theatre was crowded for the first presentation of *Uncle Tom's Cabin*, and it was promised to be presented just two more nights, April 23 and 24.[18] Some members of the legislature didn't believe the run was at an end, so a resolution was introduced, asking the managers of the National Theatre (Langrishe and Mayers) "to remove from the boards the popular play of *Uncle Tom's Cabin*, believing as we do, it is impossible to run the Legislature during its continuance before the public."[19]

Then Mayor George B. Smith and other prominent men in Madison tendered a complimentary benefit to Mr. and Mrs. Langrishe. The published letter read: "To Mr. and Mrs. Langrishe: The undersigned who have witnessed your representations of 'many colored life' upon the stage, during the season about closing, and who entertain a high respect for you personally, desire to manifest their appreciation of your efforts to amuse and instruct the public, by the tender of a farewell complimentary benefit...."[20] The weather took a turn for the terrible, and the benefit was postponed until the following evening.[21]

The company then traveled to Portage City. The only report from that community was on May 12: "Langrishe's Theatrical company was attended last evening by a very respectable number of the citizens of Portage, who seemed to be highly pleased with the play entitled *The French Spy*, or *The Fall of Algiers*." The Langrishe and Mayer company opened in La Crosse with *The Poor of New York*, playing in Barron's Hall.[22]

During the next week the citizens of La Crosse enjoyed an antidote for the "blues." The press reported: "Langrishe, (who is equal to Burton, and in 'Toodles' better) ... Mrs. Langrishe, whose versatility of genius finds no bounds ... are worthy of liberal patronage.... Their plays are well selected, and nothing is witnessed of an objectionable character. We regret that 'hard times' have prevented the liberal patronage, which, under ordinary circumstances, would fill Barron's Hall nightly for months."[23]

5. Profits Shrink 49

Mayers and Langrishe bought a barge in Red Wing, Minnesota, for $1200 (paid $620, actually and four horses worth that amount on account).[24] Mayers also spent $90 repairing and "fitting up" the barge for theatrical performances on the river, the barge to be towed to different communities.[25] They closed their season in La Crosse about June 10.[26] The other La Crosse paper reported that the Langrishe company had had "thin houses, owing to the tightness of the times."[27] They apparently played in Pepin, Wisconsin, on June 19 on their barge.[28]

The company arrived in Prairie du Chien with their "Floating Dramatic Temple" about July 3 and played *The Poor of New York*, *The Toodles*, and *His Last Legs* to enthusiastic audiences.[29] They crossed the river to perform at McGregor, Iowa, meeting with favor there, although probably not the attendance they wished.[30] They re-crossed to Prairie du Chien and performed *The Toodles* and *His Last Legs*, Saturday, July 10.[31]

Langrishe tied up the barge and abandoned it at Prairie du Chien by mid–July 1858.[32] It was probably a disastrous time to be performing on the river. Throughout the summer, heavy rains in the Mississippi Valley raised the river, causing a lot of flooding.[33] By July 1, the water level was falling, exposing sand bars and grounding a number of rafts.[34]

Meanwhile, the Langrishe and Mayer Theatrical Company "came to grief." The local paper reported:

> We regret to chronicle the last appearance of this truly meritorious dramatic company. During the past six months [should have been six weeks] they had been playing, up the river and elsewhere throughout the State, to losing houses, and after a series of but partially successful performances here and at McGregor, the "Floating Temple" gave up the ghost, and the proprietor, on "His Last Legs," retired from the stage of action. It was worthy of a better fate. By this occurrence, the company have been somewhat scattered....[35]

As a sidelight, John Langrishe's father may have been with them, performing as a minor actor.[36]

Langrishe was not the only manager of a traveling theatre company to take a beating that summer. The *New York Clipper* reported: "The season has not been as profitable for our traveling friends as we could have wished, the panic, the inclement weather during the early period of their peregrinations, and various other causes combined, interfering sadly with the calculations of managers."[37]

In Madison, workmen were busy erecting staging around Van Bergen's Hall so they could raise the roof and extend the walls ten feet higher, so it could be used as a theatre. Rumor was that Langrishe had leased it for a long term.[38] The paper responded: "Mr. and Mrs. Langrishe have for years been favorites with the theatre-going public of Wisconsin.... We believe that they have been the means of doing much good to the City, by the agreeable opportunity which they have afforded strangers visiting the city, of improvingly passing a winter's evening...."[39]

That September 1858, an item was circulating among the nation's newspapers that gold had been discovered at Pike's Peak: "Two men with inferior implements washed out $900 in one week, in a small stream 50 miles from Pike's Peak."[40] Towns bordering the great plains were agog with excitement over the find, anticipating a new "rush" of emigrants and prospectors to buy supplies. Gold was worth $18 an ounce. This news would later impact the life and career of the Langrishes.

The remodeled theatre had been christened "The Madison Lyceum." As described in the press: "The access to this fine room is through broad and convenient halls, ladies can approach without being crowded and jostled by everybody, and without wading through a sea of mud and dirt. The entrance is wide and capacious, and in case of fire or any other accident, the entire audience can get out without difficulty or accident. The fears on this subject kept many away from their former place...."[41]

When Langrishe did open, October 4, they had a brilliant audience, proving that "Langrishe's friends are legion."[42] Then they mounted *The Poor of New York* and drew "at least 500 persons" to the audience. It was augmented with "singing and dancing and a side-splitting farce."[43] On October 6 the press reported:

> The extensive gallery in the new Lyceum was packed to such a degree that the manager had to refuse the sale of any more tickets to that part of the house, not fearing its stability, but properly regarding the comfort of those favoring them with their presence. It held its own until the boys commenced stamping for the music, when the angle next to the street slid down, causing a disarrangement which can be better imagined than described. The utmost confusion prevailed for a time, and a number of timid ones left, but on being assured no danger need to be apprehended, the excitement subsided and the play commenced.
>
> *The cause of the accident*—In the great hurry to get the Lyceum completed for the Fair, the beam extending under the section which gave way was only fastened by a nail at each end, just sufficient to keep it in its place, and the omission to complete that portion of the gallery did not become known until an examination was had as to the cause of the break. The error will be rectified this morning.... The large crowd that remained through the performance will readily bear testimony as to the entire safety of the gallery.[44]

On Monday, October 16, the "great American tragedian, Mr. J.B. Roberts," opened a limited engagement with Langrishe's company. His first night he was to play the lead in *Cardinal Richelieu*. Roberts had just returned from Europe where he "achieved the most brilliant triumphs and has been pronounced by the London press the best American artist that has yet visited the great Metropolis."[45] Langrishe continued to use his company as a stock company supporting stars such as Mrs. Charles Howard and H. Watkins for a six-night run.[46]

5. Profits Shrink

The *Wisconsin Daily Patriot* hinted that Mrs. Langrishe was more involved in running the theatre than most realized. "We think that Mrs. Langrishe is entitled to the hearty support of our citizens for her exertions in bringing forward the best talent in the Union, regardless of self-profit, for the gratification of our citizens...."[47]

Langrishe escaped the bad weather following the day of the election (November 2) when Madison had "nothing but rain, mud and slush with umbrellas and rubber overshoes in good demand."[48] He had apparently been out of town for several days, but was back with the company by November 8. The company, minus stars, performed several nights,[49] then November 15 saw a complete change of pace at the Lyceum. The Hutchinson Brothers, extraordinary gymnasts, were the featured stars, the theatre company contributing only the afterpieces.[50]

On November 26 the paper disclosed that Langrishe "started this morning for Beaver Dam in company with the celebrated Hutchinson Brothers, whose performances have created such excitement in New York and all the principal cities of the Union.... Miss Emily Dow, a charming vocalist, and Mr. Dow, an actor of good parts, make up the troupe. They will visit Oshkosh, Fond du Lac, Berlin, Ripon and other northern cities...."[51] The next day a letter appeared, signed by the mayor and prominent officials and businessmen of Madison, tendering a complimentary benefit to Mrs. Langrishe in appreciation of her efforts to entertain and amuse them.[52] On December 2, they opened "the new French drama, *The Sea of Ice*." The paper pleaded: "The management have devoted much time and been to considerable expense in preparing for this great drama, and we hope our citizens will now do their part and remunerate them for their trouble."[53]

The company left for Janesville. It was snowing and the temperature 26° below, making travel life-threatening.[54] Ten days later, the temperature rose. On New Year's Eve a Madison paper read: "Rain, Mud, Slush! Yesterday it seemed as though the floodgates of heaven were opened.... O, what abominable walking it is!!—worse, by far than the streets of 'Muddy-cum-slushes,' so pathetically mentioned by the pious Aminidab Sleek [a favorite character portrayed by Langrishe]."[55]

The weather must have been cold again, for the *Madison Wisconsin Daily Patriot* found it necessary to report the "Theatre is now well warmed and very comfortable."[56] Langrishe had new scenery painted for this production and had "spared no expense" in sets and costumes, but all was not well in the theatre. According to the press:

> The theatre in this city, under the management of Mrs. Langrishe, has been indefatigable in its endeavors to produce novelty for the amusement and instruction of the public. Their

endeavors should meet with better appreciation than is at present bestowed.... Last evening *Uncle Tom's Cabin* was performed in a very effective manner. It will be repeated this evening ... [A]s the sentiments of the play are in accordance with the majority of our Legislative *savants*, they should appreciate the same by attending *en masse* this evening.[57]

On Monday, R.E.J. Miles took his benefit. He enlisted the assistance of several Madison gentlemen to appear in *The Mormons*.[58] There was an "immense crowd" at the theatre for *The Mormons*, so the Langrishe company repeated it the following night.[59] Then in a departure from tradition, Emily Dow's benefit was held on Saturday, January 29. This permission for benefits on Saturday, a night which should draw an audience generally, may have been in lieu of salary.[60]

On February 1, J.B. Roberts rejoined the company, starring in a season of heavy tragedies.[61] Then Langrishe engaged "the unrivaled comedian Yankee Locke, the only acknowledged successor of Dan Marble and Yankee Hill."[62] "Yankee" actors were those who specialized in the costume, speech mannerisms, gait and gestures of stereotypical New England characters, generally to comic effect.

A member of the press wrote:

> Mr. and Mrs. Langrishe—These able and indefatigable caterers to the theatrical taste of the public, deserve some substantial mark of appreciation for the efforts they have made, to keep the Theatre open and supply an innocent and intellectual entertainment for the amusement of the citizens and strangers living in Madison, under the discouragement of having night after night but thin audiences. We think they deserve a ROUSING benefit, and as we know that many of the legislators would be anxious to attend upon such an occasion, we should like one to be given before all of the members leave the City.

This was followed with an announcement:

> Farewell Benefit of Mr. and Mrs. Langrishe To-Night.—A performance for the benefit of these well-known and respectable caterers to the theatrical amusement of the public, will be presented at the Theatre this evening.... The knowledge that they have played throughout the season, which will close with this evening's performance, without being benefitted one cent, has occasioned a desire on the part of the theatre goers to give them an evidence that their exertions have been appreciated, if not rewarded—We trust this intention will be substantially seconded and manifested by an overflowing audience attending their farewell and benefit performance. Those residing in Madison may never have the pleasure of witnessing the talented impersonations of Mr. and Mrs. Langrishe again, except in some other distant city, as we understand that they intend seeking for better luck elsewhere.[63]

The *Madison Weekly Argus and Democrat* sadly looked back:

> Closed Out.—The Theatre has closed after a period of rather poor success. The hard times are the worst on places of amusement, and they suffer most greatly. Langrishe has made every effort possible, and has deserved remunerative houses. He has kept an excellent company, has had some first rate Stars, and has produced all the novelties, but with few exceptions, has had small houses, and poor pay, for which all our friends are sorry. So clever a fellow should be successful in his undertakings.[64]

6

Rootless

It was either the end of a brief theatrical career or a new beginning for Jack Langrishe and his wife. The world that had welcomed them with open arms and purses had changed and could no longer support them. To survive, they would have to relocate or change professions.

America was reeling from economic failures, coins were scarce and paper money was worthless. It had started with bank failures in New York, then spread westward like giant falling dominoes, one bank after another succumbing. Prior to 1861, all paper money was issued by private or state banks.[1] When a note-issuing bank failed, their bank notes were worthless. Even though theatre box offices took in many notes, they might as well have taken in air.

Langrishe, manager of the company, could no longer pay his actors or technicians. They struggled through their winter theatrical season in Madison, Wisconsin, until spring, 1859, money reserves dwindling rapidly. They had hired stars, but their salaries consumed the larger box office receipts.

Serendipitously, at the same time that America slumped into deep financial straits, there was a new gold discovery, this one on the eastern slope of the Rocky Mountains. Although prospectors didn't find much at first, as in every such excitement rumors circulated and exaggerated.[2] "Gold lay in the streets." "A man with ample pockets could get rich just from picking up nuggets." "Get a sled mounted on a rasp, and as you slid down Pike's Peak it would shave off enough gold to make a man rich for life."[3] Langrishe doubtless had heard stories of freely circulating gold dust from Atwater's experience in the California Gold Rush.

Farmers weary of bad weather's nullifying a season's hard work, disease and insects destroying crops and banks foreclosing on their farms scrounged every last bit to assemble equipment for the trek west. A throng of people traveled to St. Joseph, Missouri, and so did Jack and Jeannette Langrishe, along with R.E.J. Miles and the "old man" of their acting company, John C. McKibbin.[4]

They bade adieu to their many friends and admirers, Langrishe to his father, John S. Folds, Sr.,[5] sisters and cousins,[6] and Jeannette Langrishe said goodbye to her daughter Rosalthe, sisters, brother, nieces and nephews, all of whom lived at a fairly reasonable visiting distance. Now Jack and Jeannette were to move west over 1000 miles, not an easy distance to cross and visit. The Langrishes left Madison for the Mississippi, and probably took a steamship from Prairie du Chien, Wisconsin, to St. Joseph, Missouri.[7]

As in the California Gold Rush ten years earlier, St. Joseph, Missouri, was a principal jumping-off point for emigration. Horse and mule traders, sellers of ponderous oxen, wheelwrights, wagon builders, farriers, blacksmiths, grocers, butchers, gunsmiths and hardware store owners smiled as crowds flowed into that riverside city, buying necessities for the overland journey. The din and clang, bawling oxen and children, braying mules and donkeys, hammering and shouting was a thunderous cacophony.

Card sharps, men with shells and peas, patent medicine salesmen, pickpockets and highway robbers rubbed shoulders with poor farmers, pastors in wide black hats, half-breed Indians, lawyers, mountain men clad in greasy skins, and banished or impoverished gentlemen from England, Ireland, Germany, France, Sweden, Norway, Italy, Wales, Scotland and Russia.

Where people gather, there's an audience, so actors joined the emigrants in St. Joseph. Many of the emigrants couldn't afford to attend the theatre, but merchants could. Too, there were those among the emigrants, especially remittance men, who had been accustomed to attending theatre in their homelands, and they could pay for amusements. An evening in the theatre was cheaper and safer than an evening in a saloon or variety hall, and could be instructive and amusing. Few women attended, but many men chose this means of diversion.

In May, Langrishe joined the acting company of John R. Allen[8] in St. Joseph.[9] The company was large, and there was evidently no place in it for Mrs. Langrishe or McKibbin. Langrishe himself was hired to play "old men roles" since the company already had three comedians.[10] Seating was inadequate, so many audience members sat on window sills. In late June, benefits for the actors began, a sign that the season was drawing to a close.

By that time, disappointed gold seekers already were returning to St. Joseph, inflamed by rumors that merchants of that city had spread tales of gold in order to increase their business. Angry men threatened to torch the town, the militia was called out and nightlife abruptly shut down.[11] Letters from disappointed gold-seekers began to appear in newspapers around the country, reporting there wasn't any gold to be found, no food could be purchased, and some prospectors starved.[12]

Horace Greeley, the famous *New York Tribune* publisher, arrived in Denver to see the diggings for himself, accompanied on the stagecoach from Leavenworth by Albert D. Richardson, then a correspondent of the *Boston Journal*. Objective reports from these renowned writers were widely printed, and they, in concert with new gold discoveries, kept gold fever hot.

In St. Joseph, the Langrishes linked up with Harry Richmond, a member of John Allen's troupe. Richmond was handsome, young, ambitious to make acting a career, and temperate.[13] They traveled to Kansas City, Missouri, to open July 6, 1859. The theatre was tiny, the audience practically in the actors' laps.[14] The editor of the *Kansas City Western Journal of Commerce* claimed to have been acquainted with Langrishe's "comedy from old time experience."[15] They played through July 16. Occasional performances kept their pockets jingling, plays confined to old favorites.[16]

Langrishe's dry wit was evident in "The admission fee has been changed from fifty cents to half-a-dollar, which it is confidently hoped will cause an increase in the nightly attendance."[17] McKibbin made his first appearance in Kansas City on August 8, as Mrs. Sowerby Creamly in *The Serious Family*.[18] The Langrishes took a farewell benefit August 12, at which they performed a "local comedy written by a gentleman of this city ... filled with local hits," and Langrishe sang a "new and original song, replete with hits at everything in town and funny remarks about people in the room."[19] They concluded their Kansas City performances August 12, but performed in Kansas towns for the next several days. The next extant newspaper that mentions their performing

Harry Richmond, leading man in several Langrishe companies on and off for over twenty years. Infamously involved in Colorado's Sand Creek Massacre (Chamberlin Collection, Scan# 10036835, History Colorado).

is the *Lecompton* (Kansas) *National Democrat,* on September 10, 1859, promoting their performance in Lecompton September 15.

They re-opened in St. Joseph on September 19, 1859. That city was more subdued and thinly populated than in early summer, and attendance must have been disappointing, for the Langrishe people closed their "season" six days later.[20] Langrishe, Allen and their combined troupe traveled to Leavenworth, Kansas, and played there for three weeks.[21] In Leavenworth, the "critic" said that Langrishe's performance as Aminidab Sleek in *The Serious Family* was of a sort "whose exhortations might move stones to repent, and hogs to contrition, but the only effect upon those who heard, was to keep them in roars of laughter...." The rest of that Leavenworth run, they performed dramas and comedies that the Langrishes and McKibbin were familiar with, but the Allens (John R. and Mary) may have had to learn.[22] On Saturday, October 29, the theatre was so cold it was "very disagreeable."[23] Langrishe and Allen apparently split their troupes about November 1.[24]

Langrishe took his troupe, the "Langrishe Vaudeville Company,"[25] to the interior cities of Kansas including Lecompton, Atchison, Topeka, Junction City, Lawrence and, for the first time, military posts. They found soldiers readily parted with their coins for an evening's entertainment, relishing a break from monotony. The legislature was due to convene in Lecompton, and Langrishe said he'd play there for the session of the legislature.[26]

Years later, Langrishe said he had played for "over seven months at Fort Riley."[27] This was an exaggeration. In spite of newspapers' broken files, his location is known each month of that winter. From November 18-20, 1859, he was in Lecompton, KS[28]; December 12-20, Topeka; and in late December, Atchison.[29] In January 1860, he was in Weston, MO, and then back in Lecompton; and February 1860, back to Topeka. He may then have taken his company to Ft. Riley, playing until May, perhaps seven weeks, not months.

One of the main routes to the Colorado gold diggings followed the route of the Oregon and California trail along the Platte River valley. That trail was a virtual train of humans in 1860, many traveling west, others returning. The *Elwood* (Kansas) *Express* reported that "the numbers now leaving the Missouri river from this point are larger than at any time in our history...."[30] The furor the rushes caused is amazing; gold priced at only $18 per ounce. Since the Langrishes were performing in Atchison at the time the report was published, they undoubtedly read his account. On April 3, 1860, the first horse and rider of the famous Pony Express left St. Joseph amid cheers and shouts, with souvenir hunters plucking hairs from the horse's tail.[31] The destination of the relays of horses and riders carrying mail was Sacramento.[32]

"A Different Class of Emigration" was noticed by the *Nebraska City News* on April 14, 1860. "The scurvy horde of pauper immigrants who started for the mines last season, but whose courage for the most part oozed out about fifty miles west of this city, will not soon be forgotten in this city...."[33] Some returning gold seekers had threatened to burn the towns along the Missouri, undoubtedly coloring the attitude of the editors.

In Missouri or Kansas, Langrishe must have acquired at least one, probably two wagons to haul his company, costumes and cloth sets. Such hauling capability was essential to touring companies. In that day, costumes were often stored and hauled in zinc-lined trunks. In view of the fact that many deodorants contain zinc, it's reasonable to assume that zinc-lined trunks "sweetened" odoriferous costumes. Colors were not fast either, so for most costumes, washing in water was not a good solution. Many traveling actors preferred to use wicker champagne baskets to haul (and air) their costumes to the theatre from residences, but usually stored them in trunks.[34]

This area between Leavenworth and Denver had been called the "Great American Desert" by Stephen Long (for whom Long's Peak was named) in 1823, but it was not quite that arid. If an ocean were transformed to soil and sand, it would look much like those high plains between the Missouri River and the Rocky Mountains. Waves, swells and troughs dapple the landscape which, after all, was an ancient sea bed. Occasional large rocks are conglomerates of ancient seashells, hundreds of miles from the nearest present-day ocean. The silty sand drains quickly, leaving only drought-tolerant buffalo bunch grass, flat-padded Opuntia cacti, sagebrush and Spanish dagger, plus occasional encrusted lakes of alkali. Dust rising behind a ridge could be dust devils, Indians on the prowl, pronghorns or even lumbering herds of buffalo.

The Langrishes paused to perform at the tiny settlement of Marysville, Kansas, that spring, leaving an indelible impression on at least one of the small audience. Thirty years later, a woman who had witnessed that performance wrote *Field and Farm* that she saw the Langrishes' Marysville performance when she was 15 years old, and had since visited theatres and seen "some of the best plays, yet nothing in that line has ever given me more pleasure than those simple plays by old Jack and his estimable wife, who notwithstanding the hastily constructed stage and primitive surroundings, tried to please and do their best."[35]

The Langrishe company next appeared at Fort Kearny, Nebraska, about 130 miles distant, where they performed for about eight weeks.[36] The company enjoyed good houses at Fort Kearny,[37] where they added George McArthur to their company.

The route between Marysville and Fort Kearny was peppered with numerous "ranches" [inns]. Not known for elegance or fastidiousness, the

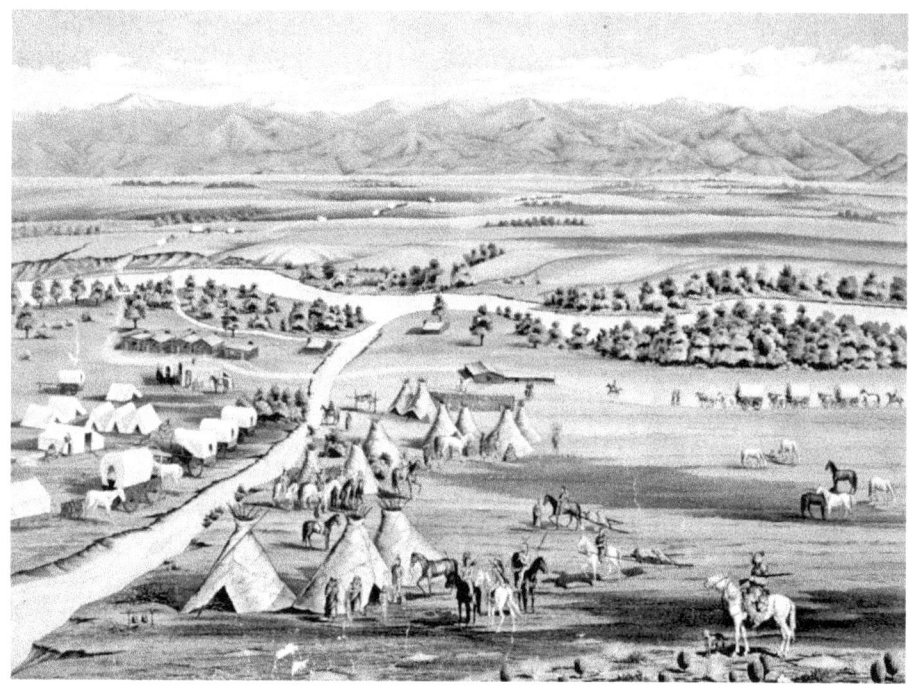

Early Denver, Colorado, as Langrishe would have seen it when he entered the territory in 1860 (Library of Congress, Prints and Photographs Division, Washington, D.C., Reproduction Number: LC-DIG-pga-00517).

"ranche" innkeepers usually served beans and biscuits (often moldy) for meals. For overnight guests a communal hairbrush hung from a string, and there were three or four people to a bed (stuffed with corn husks usually), if there *was* a bed. There were people living at the ranches, one or two men, and occasionally a woman or even a family. Numerous ranches and the presence of so many people on the trail relieved travelers' fear of Indian attacks.

One hundred miles west of Fort Kearny, the trail divided, many gold seekers taking the South Platte "road" to Denver, others following the North Platte to Fort Laramie. Fewer trains traveled to Fort Laramie, and the trail was no longer a flowing river of people. Ranches were isolated, although there were Pony Express stations for changes of horses about every 25 miles,[38] and a "home station" every 100 miles. The horse change stations were usually lightly manned, one or two men in attendance, so they were vulnerable to attack and often were attacked, Indians driving off the reserve horses and wounding or killing the caretakers.

The Langrishes performed at Fort Kearny in May and June, until Colonel E.B. Alexander arrived with four companies of soldiers, bound for Fort Laramie. Colonel Alexander and his men provided military escort (and some mule-drawn wagon space, evidently) to the Langrishe company to Fort Laramie, where a "neat and commodious theatre" was set up for them to perform in.[39]

They had left Fort Kearny in late June[40] and arrived at Fort Laramie on July 16, 1860, Colonel Alexander taking command of Fort Laramie.[41] The Langrishes gave several theatrical performances at Fort Laramie for soldiers, civilians, travelers and the Indians who hung around the fort.

Nearly 30 years later, Mrs. Langrishe recalled that the Army gave the Langrishes wonderful accommodations, and fitted up a good performing space. Mrs. Langrishe said one chief, known as Old Smoke, nightly strode down the center of the building and sat as near as possible to the drop curtain, solemnly watching each performance. When the audience laughed, he turned around with wonder on his face, but he never cracked a smile.

One evening he entered the Langrishes' apartment just as they were finishing their supper. Langrishe used "extravagant motions" to invite him to take a seat at the table. He polished off the scraps at the table, one food at a time. The next evening, he returned, and did so for several subsequent evenings. One of those evenings, he was followed by his wife. Once he spotted her, he swept the dinner remnants into a fold of his blanket and strode out of the apartment.

A few days later, he returned again, followed by his wife. When he saw her, he abruptly left. The wife stayed behind, speaking with Mrs. Langrishe in broken English and vivid pantomime, telling her, "Smoke heap bad Indian. Smoke drink whiskey ugh! Smoke heap sick. Ugh! Ugh!" Then she said, "Then Smoke do so," giving her a push halfway across the room, "then he say, 'Go away, woman, me no want you, go away, woman!'"[42]

Fort Laramie lies about 150 miles northeast of present-day Laramie, Wyoming. About the first of August, Langrishe and George McArthur hitched mules to a wagon and started for the Cherry Creek gold diggings (Denver, Auraria and St. Charles), while the other actors continued to entertain at Fort Laramie. It took the pair about ten days of travel to reach the Denver area, seeing few white men en route, and "camping out with the red Lords of the Plains," or friendly Sioux, on several occasions.[43]

Langrishe had toured in Ohio, Pennsylvania and New York before settling in Wisconsin for eight years, so he had never seen a scenic vista like the Front Range of the Rocky Mountains: pink reticulated sandstone cliffs backed by a haze of blue evergreen-freckled mountains topped by distant snow-capped peaks, the air so clear it looked like one could reach out and touch them. Grasses were belly-high on the mules,[44] watered by frequent afternoon rain showers that quit in time for clothes to dry before nightfall. Nights were crisp and cool, humidity low.

They arrived in Denver City on August 10. By the time Langrishe visited the office of the *Rocky Mountain News* a day or two later, he had already arranged to rent Apollo Hall for theatrical presentations.[45] He bought another wagon and two mules to haul his company and their costumes, properties and sets to Denver City.

They returned to Fort Laramie, gathered their company and possessions and set out for Denver City. None of them could have imagined how this arrival would enrich and exalt them for the rest of their lives.

7

Colorado

In 1860, Jack Langrishe was a few days shy of his 35th birthday when he entered Colorado, where he'd later be regarded as the "Father of Theatre in Colorado."[1] His was not the first professional company in the Denver area, but it was the most successful, influential and longest lasting.[2]

The Colorado Rocky Mountains put on quite a show for its new arrivals, peaks opalescent with the season's first snow in the high country. The high mountains would retain their early winter dress until the summer of 1861.[3]

Langrishe's company consisted of wife Jeannette, his young leading man Harry Richmond, stagehand George McArthur, the 73-year old actor J.C. McKibbin, Mary Sullivan, Harry [E.R.] Collins, Mr. Raymond and L. Watson.[4] His Apollo Theatre was "neither ceiled nor plastered, illuminated by twelve candles, and contain[ed] rough benches for three hundred and fifty people. As it was the upper-story of a popular drinking saloon—clinking glasses, rattling billiard balls, and uproarious songs interfered with the performances. The price of admission was one dollar; receipts about three hundred dollars per night."[5] They accepted eggs and produce in season in lieu of gold dust, according to later recollections of Harry Richmond.[6]

The Langrishe company opened in Denver on September 25, 1860, with *His Last Legs* and *Fifteen Years of Labour's Lost, or The Youth Who Never Saw a Woman*.[7] It was comprised of better actors than the frontiersmen were used to, and the program was well-chosen to curry popularity with hard-working men. Women were not numerous in the Denver area, and the few respectable women in Denver, Auraria and other nearby hopeful "cities" were hesitant to attend the theatre, unsure of the respectability of the bill, the performers and the audience. Some amusement-starved ladies attended the first night, then passed the word that it was a respectable resort.

William N. Byers, editor and publisher of *The Rocky Mountain News*, Denver's first newspaper, was favorably impressed with Langrishe as a person, and his review the day after the opening augured well:

Apollo Theatre, Langrishe's first Denver venue, white building second from left. Musicians performed pre-show concerts on the balcony to attract patrons to performances (Carte de Visite Collection, Scan# 10029062, History Colorado).

> The old [less than one year old] Apollo's boards were illuminated last night and its seats and benches fairly filled with an audience of our gents and ladies, on the occasion of Mr. Langrishe's opening....
> Where well-conducted, it is generally admitted by the best cities, that the drama has exercised a civilizing influence in all new countries, and if so, in no section of the country do we wish to see an innocent and salutary state of things obtain more effectually than here. Let there be a good house to-night, as there is to be a good time there.[8]

The following day, Byers reported the theatre had "a fine assemblage last night." He opined:

> Langrishe fully equals John Drew, Chanfrau, John Owens or Billy Florence, in his interesting role.... Mrs. Langrishe is exceedingly sprightly and amusing—has a clear and commanding elocution—appears a genuine woman—a lady-like woman—that takes her audience by sympathy and surprise, as well as occasionally by not a few hard hits. Free and sparkling, naive and natural—truthful to her sex in those actions and affections which throw a grace and beauty around her renditions—she is destined to draw wherever she adorns the boards. In fine, she and her husband combine real merit of an unusual degree.[9]

The *Rocky Mountain News* assured readers that in the Apollo Theatre, "Good order and etiquette obtain, and no improper characters are to be allowed...."[10] "Improper characters" was frontier code for prostitutes, madams and pimps. In Denver, the talent, taste and polish of the Langrishe company of actors were just what Byers needed. His goal was to make Denver an economic and cultural hub for the miners in the mountains and the settlers who would populate the city and plains. Langrishe's affability encouraged his approval and Byers lavished praise upon the troupe. The company "had a rule that there should be no swearing in the theatre," according to Harry Richmond, but the "boys were real genteel with just a swear word now and then to make things lively."[11] The Langrishe Company had promised to perform for only six nights,[12] but six nights stretched into months, then years.

Like other businesses in this area, they used gold scales, accepting gold dust for admission. One man swept the box office floor and panned the sweepings, finding enough gold to buy himself a new hat,[13] especially valued in that high altitude sun.

After their first week, the *Rocky Mountain News* reported that the Langrishe troupe

> have won the good wishes and good opinions of the people in doors and out of doors. Old Langrishe himself is a host in the Dramatic line—his sterling ability, great originality, an admirable voice for Irish amusement, not lacking the essential element of the "brogue."
>
> Mrs. Langrishe commands an ease and sweetness in her acting and appearance that takes with everybody, and attracts deserved applause.... The plays last night were very finely put forth, and the Irish gems by old man Langrishe, with his shillelagh in his fist, brought down the house as a unit, fetched the putty from betwixt the boards, and knocked the spots out of every one else's rendering of the same songs....[14]

Left Hand (Niwot), chief of the Arapaho tribe camped at the edge of Denver, was in the theatre audience for *Asmodeus*. He responded to Langrishe's facial contortions with "frequent grins, as only an Indian can make...."[15] Settlers mingled with the Indians who had wintered in the Denver area for eons, as both peoples walked the new boardwalks, peered in windows and traded goods. At times the new residents laughed at the colorfully clad Indians, other times they tolerated, and later came to fear them.

The weather turned bitterly cold, and on October 12 ice formed an inch in thickness in several parts of the city.[16] Then, as if showing off its variable winter temperatures, the city enjoyed a "beautiful Indian summer" five days later.[17] Cold or warm, the theatre remained open, the company doing very good business presenting their standard repertoire of melodramas, tragedies and comedies. The *Rocky Mountain News* editor had been a theatergoer in the East, and often favorably compared the Langrishe company productions to those he'd seen in New York, Boston, Cincinnati and Chicago.[18] The *New York Clipper* reported, "In Denver City, Mr. Langrishe was the attraction, but his audiences is [sic] said to be small, owing to the high tariff charged for admission, the price being one dollar per head. At 50 cents, it is thought he would be well patronized. Mr. R.E. Collins [his name and initials are variously reported as E.R. Collins or Harry Collins] was doing Yankee business with Mr. Langrishe's company."[19]

The Apollo Theatre may still have smelled like freshly sawed wood, but that didn't stop editor Byers from referring to it as the "old Apollo" when he reported that Langrishe planned to enlarge and renovate it, "adding new stars and hosts of new attractions."[20] The following day the *News* reported, "An addition of stoves to the Apollo, renders it a very pleasant resort for the evening..."[21] indicating there had been no heat in the theatre the night the ice froze to a depth of one inch. When there was no heat for the audience, there was none at all for the dressing rooms or stage either. Apparently in December Langrishe replaced the candle lighting with oil lamps as footlights.[22] The "candle lighting" had been miners' candlesticks with holders affixed to long spikes that miners could jam into the walls of a mine. In the Apollo theatre, they were jammed between the logs of the building, casting only dim flickering light.

Windows would not have helped, as winter evenings are dark in Colorado. Audiences would have heard the performers, rather than seeing them distinctly. Oil lamps were better, but still not very effective. The oil lamps necessarily were positioned to focus on particular areas of the stage, so blocking would be dictated by which character was speaking, that character moving into light focus as the performer spoke the lines. This made "natural" acting especially difficult.[23]

A review disclosed: "Mrs. Langrishe as 'Mrs. Haller' [in *The Stranger*] drew down the house in frequent and genuine applause, and displayed a talent for pathetic and impassioned personation we have seldom seen excelled in eastern theatres."[24] This was a play that especially appealed to women, and there were some decent women in Denver. At least 48 of them served on a committee planning an Episcopal Church festival for December 20. The committee of gentlemen included most of the area businessmen.[25]

A November 14 news item said: "This well-conducted Theatre is now thoroughly warmed and made comfortable, and strict order is observed so that ladies and families may rest assured of being as comfortably secure as in any of the places of amusement East...."[26] When Langrishe produced a creditable production of *The Corsican Brothers*, the *Rocky Mountain News* remarked, "Mr. Langrishe's qualifications as an actor and manager are established beyond dispute."[27]

Mrs. Langrishe was to take her benefit Tuesday, November 20, in the play *Alice* (probably *Ernest Maltravers*, in which she played the part of Alice), but the weather turned intensely cold and attendance was light. The next night songs by Mike Dougherty were promised.[28] Dougherty, a professional actor from Pittsburgh who had come West to prospect for gold, performed a few times with the actors left stranded by Col. Thorne before Langrishe appeared.

This was the start of a beautiful friendship. Mike Dougherty was a genial Irish-American, given to poking fun at himself, like Jack Langrishe. The main difference between them was that Dougherty was a heavy drinker and Langrishe was not. The latter enjoyed a sociable "drop of the crayture" but went right back to work.

The warmth of the developing friendship was unable to dispel the extremely cold weather. They closed the theatre for two nights, intending to reopen on Saturday with *The French Spy*. Mrs. Langrishe's performance was pronounced a triumphant success. "We have never seen a better performance of the part," the *News* glowed.[29] They

Mike Dougherty, Langrishe's theatrical partner in Denver in the 1860's (Denver Public Library, Western History Division, F10092)

repeated it, then produced *Alice* (*Ernest Maltravers*), and in a rare departure from his usual roles, Langrishe played Maltravers, considered a "heavy" role. As a rule, only tragedians or "heavy" leading men played that role. There was no paper the following day (Thanksgiving), so there was no review of Langrishe as tragedian.[30]

Too many new parts for actors to learn for rapidly changing bills aroused the *News* reviewer's grousing: "One or two of the company should study their parts a little better; as the voice of the prompter heard throughout an entire play, does not fall pleasantly on the ears of the audience...."[31] The prompter was usually Jeannette Langrishe, acting as well as prompting.

Cold weather and the need for more rehearsal made a plan to temporarily close the theatre quite sensible. They announced they were to make improvements to the ceiling and improve the comfort for the audience.[32] The Apollo theatre was really a large unpainted room with benches that could seat nearly 400 people gathered closely together, but it was "fitted up in elegant and comfortable style, with extensive fixtures, new scenery, new machinery, and every auxiliary aid necessary to present ... the magnificent spectacular drama of *The Dumb Boy of the Pyrenees*." Langrishe had more stoves installed so the entire audience wouldn't have to gather around one stove, and had the walls whitened so the dim light would be amplified by the light walls.

Langrishe "courteously closed his doors" on December 20 "so that the public [could] attend the festival for the benefit of the [Episcopal] church."[33] On Christmas Day they performed the pantomime of *The Golden Axe* for a "greatly amused" audience of some 300, including many "ladies of the first order," but a succession of fights and loud quarrels in the saloon downstairs annoyed the audience until belligerents were cleared out. The audience was not aware that arms were drawn, prepared for summary vengeance (and possible tragedy in the audience), until bystanders had interfered.[34]

The year ended with a glowing review of Mrs. Langrishe in *Camille*:

> With the same surroundings and facilities afforded Miss [Matilda] Heron, in her popular and triumphant delineation of this character, we have no hesitation in saying that Mrs. Langrishe would prove no insignificant rival to this world-renowned actress.... But here, where she has so often to assume the duties of a *prompter* on the stage, in order to spare her associates the mortification of a break-down, and where she is not well-supported, the perplexities of her position must be manifest to all.[35]

On November 4 the *News* revealed: "There was a good house at the Apollo last evening. Several new faces among our first families appeared in the audience for the first time this season. The Apollo, as now managed, has become the favorite resort of our best society...."[36] Then it was time for Langrishe's benefit. The *News* printed: "The citizens of Denver owe the beneficiary a thousand thanks ... [I]t has been no small enterprise—no insignificant undertaking—to sustain well-conducted dramatic performances, in this far-off region."[37] The event called out an "unusually large and fashionable audience ... [including] numbers of the finest families and fairest ladies of Denver ... many of them for the first time."[38] Langrishe's having closed his theatre so as not to compete with attendance at the Episcopal church's affair in December was paying off. The Langrishes' regular attendance at the Episcopal church services also fortified their social status.

The following week, J.H. Wright, a former actor with Langrishe and Atwater in Wisconsin, arrived by stagecoach.[39] He was called before the curtain after his emotional performance, which "dimmed not a few eyes with tears, and made one's swallowing organs a little out of time..." and gave a speech thanking the audience and apologizing that his wardrobe had to be left behind at Fort Kearny because of the snow and he had had to wear "borrowed robes." He also said he was suffering from an indisposition "which has become rather serious."[40] That was an understatement. Wright only performed twice, his illness worsened, and the Langrishes cared for him in their home for the next nine months, at which time he left for his father's home in Pittsburgh. He died there the following month.[41]

Little more than a year after Langrishe's exodus from Wisconsin, nearly broke and in despair, he was back on his financial feet, and reported to be building a large new theatre in Denver. He was not, but competitors were. Even more ominous was what was happening in the eastern U.S. Seven southern states set up the Confederate States of America on February 8, with Jefferson Davis as president. There were southern sympathizers in Denver,[42] but they were in the minority.

Langrishe closed the season in Denver on March 9 with *Lady of the Lake* (assisted by amateur actor Edward Wynkoop) and Lord Byron's pantomime of *Don Juan*.[43] Prominent citizens offered a complimentary benefit to Mr. and Mrs. Langrishe prior to their departure for the mountains. The *Rocky Mountain News* heartily concurred in the compliment: "Since Mr. Langrishe's residence in our city, a class of dramatic entertainment has been given of a high order. Nothing to offend the most fastidious taste has ever been presented on the Apollo boards, and the utmost good order and decorum have always been maintained in the establishment...."[44] Among the spectators of one of these early productions, Albert D. Richardson, wrote, "[T]here were several ladies [in attendance], and despite the boisterousness of the house there was no gross coarseness and no profanity."[45]

The run of "six nights only" had lengthened to six months. The Langrishes and their actors had taken up residence in Denver, dressing like the settlers

Jack Langrishe as he appeared in Denver and mountain mining camps in the 1860's (Denver Public Library, Western History Collection, F5327).

when out on the street, and mingling comfortably with the residents, adding to their popularity.

The Langrishe troupe traveled by horse-drawn wagons to Central City, some 40 miles through the mountains west of Denver. Gold ore had been found in Gregory Gulch in 1859, and four towns sprang up in or near that gulch: Nevadaville, Central City, Mountain City and Black Hawk. Central City quickly became the dominant "city," and the Langrishe company planned on performing there in the upper story of Storm's Hotel.[46]

A man could be entertained there for a dollar and a half a night. Theater-going was an educational, uplifting amusement, far less expensive than attending the variety theatre saloons, drinking adulterated whisky, buying drinks for debauched women, and losing wallet and shirt at the faro table or other "games." As long as order and decorum were maintained in the theatre, the few decent women of the community could attended. And lonesome, homesick men could sit on a theatre bench and stare at decent women, reminding themselves what ladies looked and acted like, without offending them.

No newspaper had yet been established in Central City, but prospectors, businessmen and miners traveled so frequently between Denver and Central City, they kept the Denver newspapers apprised of Langrishe's success in the mountains. Their first Saturday night they had an "overflowing house."[47] The following day snow lay ten inches deep on the ground in Gregory Gulch, and it was still falling fast.[48]

In spite of the snow, reports from Central City were that the Langrishe theatre company was enjoying great success. They planned on playing a few performances in Nevadaville before returning to Denver.[49]

In Denver the paper reported: "The plays *Uncle Pat's Cabin* and *A Glance at New York* were presented [for Mike Dougherty's benefit] in such a manner as to bring down the house with frequent and prolonged outbursts of applause.... Mrs. Langrishe ... was taken ill and was unable to favor us with her presence. But Langrishe, always up to any emergency, played the character of 'Judy O'Trot' to the delight of all...."[50] At his lean six-foot height, Langrishe's Judy O'Trot undoubtedly towered over Dougherty and the rest of the cast, his much shorter wife's costume ill-fitting. Langrishe's own benefit was set for April 10. The *News* announced: "During his short sojourn in the mountains, he has earned the deserved, unanimous popularity of every lover of amusement from Gregory to Grass Valley Bar [near Idaho Springs]. His affable, unaffected and gentlemanly manners and mode of driving business with all classes of the public, have procured for him a peculiarly popular reputation...."[51] They wound up their season in Central City April 13 and moved to Nevadaville, a "thriving burg," to give a few performances.[52]

Back in the States, the South had fired on Fort Sumter, and captured it April 14, sparking the Civil War that would divide friends and families, and kill nearly 215,000 troops before it ended four years later.[53] In Colorado, hundreds of miles from the nearest state, they didn't hear about it until April 24, and then the conflict bitterly divided neighbors and even U.S. cavalrymen. Several officers and enlisted men resigned and left their posts to serve in the Confederate Army, leaving western forts undermanned.

"Gunnybags" wrote from Nevadaville that the Langrishe company had played in Maxwell Hall to an overflowing house:

> If I have seen better acting, I have often seen worse. Langrishe and Dougherty are too well known throughout the country to need a word from me. If I were sick, in the 'dumps,' or had the 'blues,' I would ask no other panacea than a song from Dougherty or a look at Langrishe.... [Regarding Mrs. Langrishe:] When we can see all that is beautiful and amiable in a woman, in the most sacred and private walks of life, combined with the ease, elegance and genius of an actress, language fails to express our feelings....[54]

Little Raven and Storm, two of the most influential chiefs of the Arapahos, visited the *News* office on April 29 requesting a meeting with Denver leaders the following day. Niwot would attend too, but that night he was to speak to the theatre audience at Apollo Theatre.[55] Amateur and professional actors joined on stage at this benefit for the poor. The paper described the event:

> Left Hand [Niwot] and a score of his brethren were present. In his vernacular, the Arapaho Chief makes a handsome speech. He wished his white brethren would stop talking about fighting with his people, because his people had no enmity against them whatever—but looked on them as brethren—that, as they came here hunting for gold, they would hunt after the gold, and let the Indians alone—that, although his white friends intruded on his antelope and buffalo grounds, it was now all right—his people could find plenty more.[56]

John Smith usually served as interpreter for the Indians and probably did so on this occasion, although his assistance was not publicly mentioned.

Perhaps it was an anniversary gift, or a substitute for salary, but on May 24, 1861, Langrishe gave his wife a house at 15th and Welton Streets.[57] The house he conveyed to her "in her own name" was sold by him alone in later years. Jeannette must have been about 45 years old, and never really had a house of her own since her marriage to Langrishe. This home was more than seven blocks from the theatre, perhaps too far to walk in the dark after completing a tiring performance. They probably had their own horse and buggy "parked" near the theatre. Having their own home also meant Langrishe could bring dogs home and have his own dog or "dogs of all degrees" [that were] found in their household. No lame, sick or emaciated canine ever caught the old man's eye in vain. He would be taken home, and to his wife's "Why, Mr. Langrishe!" he would reply "Another boarder, Jeannette."[58]

Langrishe and his company continued to perform at the Apollo Theatre. He sent to New York for new plays, and began performing those plays soon after they arrived.[59] Denver was geographically isolated but up to date dramatically. June 10 was the last night of this season at the Apollo before the company moved to Central City "where a beautiful hall of Thespis has been prepared for their reception...."[60]

Somewhere between Denver and Central City, Langrishe's theatrical company became managed by Langrishe *and* Dougherty.[61] Langrishe undoubtedly thought this would lighten his workload, and it probably did unless Dougherty was indulging in liquid conviviality. The partnership of two affable, gregarious Irishmen had to be more fun than just the one doing all of the work. The Central City theatre was crowded nightly, and "the capacity of the new Hall, solidity of the floor and firmness of the structure, was tested on Saturday night ... when there was an immense crowd assembled there..."[62] Crowded, cheering audiences warmed the managers' hearts. In the early days of Langrishe's performing in Central City, some of the "boys" in the gallery liked to disrupt the performances for fun. Some snuck a small pig into the gallery and twisted its tail, causing it to squeal at emotional parts of the play.[63]

The *News* correspondent expressed the hope that Langrishe and Dougherty would repeat *Nick of the Woods,* and "most emphatically express the wish that 'Alice' may not be up there to come down."[64] This remark referred to an incident a few nights previous, when the company performed *Ernest Maltravers*. Harry Richmond had stood on stage, tears coursing his cheeks as he looked heavenward, and agonizingly cried, "Alice, why don't you speak to me?" Between Richmond and heaven intruded the theatre's fly gallery, populated by an inexperienced stagehand who barked, "Damn it! Alice ain't up here!" The audience roared with laughter. Before dark Langrishe and Dougherty's People's Theatre began to fill, and when the curtain was raised it was just an impossibility for another person to get into the house. The comedy of *Engagements by Land and Sea* [or *Naval Engagements*] was greeted by roars of applause "as the most excellent playing justly deserved.... Langrishe sang some of his own songs in his own style, which never fails to convulse a house with laughter. When in the midst of her dance, Miss Marietta [Ravel] brought forth two national [American] flags, gracefully waving them—the rafters were fairly lifted by the thunders of applause."[65]

Shortly after the stampede to Cherry Creek and Gregory Gulch gold diggings in Colorado, prospectors had ventured further into the Rocky Mountains, discovering gold in "South Park." The *News* wrote: "We hear it is the intention of Mr. Langrishe to play an engagement in Georgia Gulch [in South Park] as soon as his new hall there is completed—after which he will return to our city, and open a theatre here this fall and winter.... Langrishe is a Napoleon in his profession—suave as a woman, yet sharp as they get 'em up."[66] Actually, Langrishe wanted to tour the whole "gold circuit," including Parkville, French Gulch, Georgia Gulch, Buckskin Joe, Fairplay and California Gulch (later the site of Leadville). Many of these towns boasted larger populations than Denver, but nearly all of their people were male adults, many in residence only in summer, moving to Denver or the States for more comfortable winters.

The *Tarryall Weekly Miners' Record* reported Langrishe and Dougherty would bring their troupe to perform either in Georgia or French Gulch, as soon as a suitable hall was ready.[67] The report continued with:

> Considerable profitable gulch and hydraulic mining is going on in the Tarryall mines.... Any quantity of Denverites, old and new settlers, of all styles, sexes and persuasions and antecedents, are to be met with here and all along the line. Denver has been a prolific settler if not civilizer of the South Park and Snowy Range country.
> Crossing the Snowy Range from Tarryall mines to the Blue River, the ascent is comparatively easy.... Breckenridge City is delightfully located along the eastern banks of the Blue—contains a few stores, saloons and hotels, and a "right smart" resident population. —The road from French gulch to Georgia, over the mountain, through the dense woods, is almost a labyrinth, and he is a lucky fellow who strays not to the right nor the left—whether mounted on mule flesh or a passenger by Foot & Walker's lines.
> Humbug and Georgia Gulches lie between two little ranges, and run into one another, something like the Gregory and Central City gulches.... Our young friend Tom Wanless is completing a large theatre building here for Langrishe & Dougherty's Dramatic troupe, who are expected here in a few weeks to present the legitimate drama for the delectation of hundreds of gold diggers in these various gulches and cities adjoining.
> Delaware Flats, like Buckskin Joe, is all the excitement these days. Claims are pretended to be bought and sold there for hundreds and thousands, and new log buildings, shanties and tents spring up there into existence by dozens every few days. They have a theatre there already, and as soon as a billiard table arrives it is prognosticated the city will be "finished."[68]

A note to the *New York Clipper* from a former actor in Denver reported:

> There is but one [successful] theatre in the Pike's Peak country, that of Mr. J.S. Langrishe, in Central City. He intends building one in this place so soon as he can see any promise of its paying, but that is very uncertain from present indications. If, however, things brighten up in the Fall, he will undoubtedly put one up here, for as soon as there is any money to be made here, Langrishe is sure to be on hand to make it, and he has means, and backers to help him.... There are some twenty actors "colonized" in these regions, who like myself have left the boards to engage in different pursuits.[69]

That correspondent also reported that Langrishe's theatre in Central City, the "People's Theatre," seated about 500 comfortably.

Langrishe and Dougherty's large theatre in Parkville, French Gulch, was nearly completed by the end of August, and the troupe was expected within days.⁷⁰ They performed wherever they could find a sufficiently large space to hold their company and a few sets, plus benches for an audience. Gold dust was cheerfully accepted for admission, the ticket seller often doubling as actor of small or "thinking" roles. They established a routine, playing Saturday, Sunday and Monday nights in Parkville, and Tuesday, Wednesday and Thursday nights at Delaware. The partners had fine large theatres in both locations.⁷¹ Other companies preceding Langrishe and Dougherty had established a pattern of performing on Sundays, so Langrishe and Dougherty followed suit. Another location they played in that summer was California Gulch, later the rich carbonate city of Leadville. In this summer of 1861, prospectors only looked for gold, cursing the heavy dark rocks and sands that interfered with their gold panning.⁷²

The length of that theatre season was to be determined by the weather, and harsh winter comes early in the high country. By October 4 there was ten inches of snow on the level at Georgia Gulch.⁷³ Langrishe and Dougherty left South Park, dropping altitude to Central City. There Langrishe received the sad news that his father had died in Madison, Wisconsin, of breast cancer.⁷⁴

As one life came to a close, another reached a milestone: The *News* announced: "Married—On the morning of Oct. 24, M.J. Dougherty to Miss Lucinda M. Converse at home of the bride's father in Denver. New York, Philadelphia and Cincinnati papers please copy."⁷⁵

In Denver the Platte Valley Theatre, built to seat 1400 people by a rival company,⁷⁶ opened to receipts of over $600, H.B. Norman starred in Shakespeare's *Richard III*, and apparently performed well.⁷⁷ Langrishe was in town October 28, his troupe in Central City. He was in the city arranging for the remodeling of the Apollo Theatre into a more attractive and competitive place of amusement. That was expected to be completed in about 12 days.⁷⁸

Workmen remodeled the whole building that housed the Apollo, eliminating the saloon and billiards from the first floor, the stage and parquette taking up much of the former main floor, the second floor cut away in a horseshoe shape to form an extensive gallery. The Apollo now had a stage 45 feet deep (ten feet deeper than any theatre west of Chicago), 30 feet wide and 20 feet high. The auditorium featured a dress circle, parquette with elevated seats, and the interior painted white and gold by "that skillful artist DeWitt Waugh." The scenery, all new, had been painted over the summer at a cost of about $2000.⁷⁹

While this was going on, the Langrishe and Dougherty company opened a short season in Central City on November 2.⁸⁰ In Central City, their company enjoyed a full house and "cordial and enthusiastic greeting given to each of the old favorites of the 'Peoples Company' as they severally appeared on stage."[81]

A frequent hazard of mountain towns is fire, and one started just above Nevadaville, then moved into that community and swept through the town. The fire was visible in nearby Central City, so businessmen and shop owners moved their wares into tunnels and prospect holes (or "glory holes") for the duration of the fire. The theatre was closed because of the fire Monday and Tuesday, until the fire burned itself out.[82]

On November 25 the *News* called the Apollo "a perfect gem of a house. Mr. Langrishe succeeded in keeping a theatre open for the space of eight months, during the dullest season of the year in Denver, when he had to contend with every disadvantage...."[83] The remodeled New People's Theatre would comfortably seat 400 to 500 people,[84] not much gain from the old Apollo that seated 400. Sight lines were undoubtedly improved and the noise from the saloon on the first floor silenced, the latter a major improvement.

Langrishe and Dougherty opened in Denver Saturday, November 30, 1861, to a crowded house. As many were turned away as were admitted, according to the *Rocky Mountain News*. The *News* remarked:

> [Some of the actors] seemed to have reached a much more faultless and finished standard of acting than when they played here before. It is the forte of Mr. Langrishe and of Mrs. Langrishe too, to influence their co-actors by a sort of silent, imitative instruction, that gradually drills them into the rules of the art, without any seeming effort and yet most successfully. They possess an ability to turn the resources of their troupe to the best advantage on every occasion.[85]

Among the "brilliant" audience were large numbers of business and professional citizens and several military officers. "His Excellency Governor Gilpin was not present, but the six or a dozen" lasses who'd like to be Mrs. Governor Gilpin were in attendance.[86] The upper tier of seats was arranged for ladies and gentlemen who wanted to have a good view of the stage and of the parquette below.[87]

The famously quixotic scholar O.J. Goldrick composed and read a lengthy poem honoring the opening of the new theatre.[88] The poem, a piece of doggerel made up of almost 50 lines of rhymed couplets, paid homage to Langrishe, Dougherty and the remodeled Apollo theatre. A brief example:

> Now stands this temple—this Dramatic hall,
> A monument of taste—a source of pride to all.
> Where Langrishe—the lion of dramatic war,
> And "Mike," the miner of Grass Valley Bar,
> Have shown by works and enterprising zeal,
> What two can do united shoulder to the wheel.

Goldrick, a native of Ireland and a close friend of Langrishe, was said to have earned his way west wearing a "glossy plug hat, a broadcloth Prince Albert, and boiled shirt but driving an ox team with a regulation bull whip." He was rumored to have cussed his team in Latin.[89]

Langrishe's competitor, the Platte Valley Theatre, closed. It was doomed by counterfeit tickets,[90] indelicate acting that drove ladies out of the theatre,[91] the death of a patron accidentally wounded in the theatre, and the reopening of Langrishe and Dougherty's "People's Theatre." The paper observed: "This institution, whose demise we, some weeks since, predicted, has succumbed to the force of circumstances, much sooner than was expected. Since the opening of the People's, it has been failing rapidly until yesterday the sheriff was called in to see its last moments."[92]

Langrishe and Dougherty's "New People's Theatre" was comfortably warm, the ushers polite, rowdy behavior controlled, and the entertainments were over at an early hour. People didn't want to be out after ten o'clock, especially when it was cold and when ladies were in their company. The theatre also employed a good orchestra.[93] Langrishe and Dougherty's coming theatre season looked encouraging.

8

Gold Circuit

The year 1862 started off auspiciously for Langrishe and Dougherty, with a packed house for *The French Spy* in spite of all of the competing balls and parties on January 1. The company continued with standard pieces, with the *News* reassuring theatergoers that the theatre was "comfortably warmed."[1] They enjoyed a "comparatively large" house the following night, even though the temperature had slipped to 10° below zero.

The weather improved in time for the production of *The Golden Axe* or *Magic Wand and Fairy Palace of Pleasure* on January 21, described as a "most magnificent and gorgeous spectacular pantomime, abounding in transformations, amusing incidents, deceptions, tricks, droll doings, unlooked-for occurrences, fancy dances, unaccountable proceedings, fun, freak, folly, farce and foibles!"[2] A reviewer wrote:

> [It] makes a body laugh till he can't help himself. The piece must be seen to be enjoyed, and the drolleries of Dougherty, Langrishe and Johnson have to be witnessed to be appreciated. ... Among the many fair and distinguished personages of the audience, we noticed Mrs. Langrishe and Mrs. Dougherty, seated in a retired part of the hall, and witnessing with much apparent interest and enjoyment the antics and actions of their liege lords on the stage....[3]

Transformations, tricks, and amusing incidents were especially treasured by Langrishe the magician.

All theatre seats were occupied and the aisles jammed for Mrs. Langrishe's benefit performance, in which she was "glorious" as Joan of Arc. A review read: "Never ... before have we [seen] so many fair and fashionable appearing ladies ... in any of our theatres. Mrs. Langrishe must have felt most particularly and highly complimented by this brilliant benefit."[4]

Langrishe and Dougherty had been producing some new plays, and the next one had recent historical significance: *Fall of the Alamo* or the *Death of Davy Crockett*.[5] They had a large audience, but some men were present who "had been at the fall of the Alamo" who "thought that one or two prominent characters of interest were not represented ... and said the church on the stage should have been painted white to resemble the real one."[6] Those who had been there must have been children at the time (1836): those of the defenders who survived were taken prisoner and executed, while the women and children were released.

Late February must have been cold, since the *News* promised the theatre would be comfortably warm.[7] Cold weather means a coughing audience, so *Camille* was suitable for the season. It was to be repeated the following night, but proverbial hell broke loose: Just before 7 p.m. on February 27, inmates of the Territorial Prison burst open the door of the jail yard and all 36 prisoners escaped, some running down the street past Langrishe's Apollo Theatre located on Larimer Street between 14th and 15th streets.[8] Two companies of cavalry and two companies of the Home Guard set out in pursuit. When the reserve guard posted beside the jail were ordered to fire, a volley of about 20 shots rang out, all missing their targets. Soldiers then became excited in the belief that citizens were shooting at them, and wanted to shoot into the crowd. The performance at the New People's Theatre was cancelled that night, and *Camille* or *The Life of a Coquette* was delayed.[9]

Langrishe and Dougherty announced they would open for a short season in Central City on April 1. The *News* announced: "All the novelties of the day will be presented.... New and magnificent scenery has been painted by DeWitt C. Waugh ... and new and elegant wardrobes have been procured from New York.... Langrishe and Dougherty, with their full troupe, will afterwards reopen at their new theatres in Georgia Gulch, and in Lauret [sic] and Montgomery cities."[10]

Long before the doors of the Central City Peoples' Theatre were due to open, a throng waited to greet the old favorites on opening night. The house was densely crowded, and "a large number of chairs had to be carried in from the neighboring hotels to accommodate the great number of ladies that graced the theatre with their presence."[11]

Pat Casey, an illiterate but lucky prospector, must have been impressed by fellow Irishman Langrishe and the supposed Irishman, Mike Dougherty (a Pennsylvania native). Casey wanted to do something to contribute to the theatrical season. He bought a horse and had it trained to ignore candles, footlights and applause, so Langrishe and Dougherty could perform some exciting horse dramas.

Their first use of the horse was in *Lochinvar* or *The Bridal of Netherby* on April 28. Many had to be turned away from the theatre that night, with the promise that the play would be repeated. A reporter described the event:

> The character of Lady Helen, as rendered by Mrs. Langrishe, was truly excellent, as was also that of Lochinvar by Mr. Richmond. The trained horse Waverly behaved himself admirably,

bearing Lochinvar and Lady Helen through the torrent, amid shouts of applause [sic] from the delighted audience.... Casey's beautiful horse Waverly appeared to great advantage and showed great care had been taken to train him for the stage and accustom him to the glare of the footlights—sound of the music and acclamations of the audience, which greeted him on every appearance, and with deafening applause in the thrilling scene of "Scaleforce Lynn," where he stemmed the current with as much ease as an animal that had been used to a theatre for years.[12]

A few days later they mounted *Mazeppa*[13] and, later, *Timour the Tartar*, both horse dramas.[14] A patron faintly recalled seeing *Mazeppa* in a Central City theatre:

owned by a friend of ours, one Jack Langrishe.... The theatre was built against the side of a mountain, the back of the theatre (which like all of the buildings in those days was of flimsy frame construction) was removable and could be shifted like the screens we shifted now when changes of stage setting are required, and thus a natural mountain scene was exposed which was used for that purpose in this play.... I remember the horse dashing up the mountain side.[15]

Langrishe was tendered a complimentary benefit by his "Brothers of the Mystic Tie," (perhaps Free Masons), for which the company performed *Nature's Nobleman*, *Lady of the Lake* and the farce *The Liquor of Life*. The company returned to Denver June 4, intending to play a short season before going on a tour of the Southern Colorado gold mines.[16] They tried the horse dramas,[17] but the stage was too small. A reporter observed: "The trained horse Waverly did not deport himself as well as his friends expected.... On the whole the play is an agreeable change from the old routine of pieces, which have been presented in Denver."[18] The following night the play went more smoothly, a mule named Maggie taking the equine behavior palm. The press noted: "To see Langrishe on that mule, will alone repay you for the investment."[19]

Evidence that the theatre was an attraction for Denver's best society lay in the "Amazonian Cavalry," described in the *News* on June 14:

Last evening after tea, a party of equestrians, consisting of some twenty-two couples, composed of our leading citizens, appeared in our streets under the leadership of the gallant Col. Leavenworth. The cortege attracted general attention, and elicited enthusiastic expressions of admiration from all who saw it. After a ride of two hours through the city and suburbs, most of the party drew rein in front of Florman's Ice Cream Saloon, dismounted, partook of ices, etc., and then visited the People's Theatre in a body [to see *Lochinvar*].[20]

The Langrishe and Dougherty company was marking time until the roads to the South Park mines were clear of snow. They stated: "Our theatre building is being remodeled and enlarged—the snow during the winter having crushed in the roof, and otherwise damaged the building...."[21]

The Langrishe and Dougherty company performed in French and Georgia Gulches, Delaware Flats and Parkville in July and August. No newspapers were printed in those areas, but intermittent letters to Denver newspapers were published about their successes. One item read: "The miners patronize Langrishe and Dougherty quite liberally, and seem to appreciate the great exertions these gentlemen have made to furnish them with rational amusements...."[22]

An item from the *Buckskin* (Colorado) *Mountaineer* reported great excitement there and in Fairplay over a rumored threat by 100 rebel soldiers or Confederate guerrillas to attack Fairplay, not many miles from Langrishe and Dougherty's enterprises.[23] Langrishe went to Denver and bought the Platte Valley Theatre. The *News* reported: "We are not at liberty to publish the price paid therefore, but it was a liberal one. They will open it about the first of October with a company equal to any west of New York City. They have already concluded engagements with a number of the best actors in the States, who will reach here by the date named and remain during the winter."[24]

When under construction the previous year, the theatre was said to be 50 by 100 feet, with a ten-foot lean-to in back to be used for a green room and ladies' dressing room. The inside height was 26 feet. It could comfortably seat 1500 people divided proportionately between orchestra and dress circles, parquette and gallery. The stage room was 30 feet, the opening 22 feet front by 30 feet deep with a proscenium height of 18 feet. The building was well-ventilated and "arrangements were very complete for thoroughly warming it in winter. On the inside the walls and ceilings were plastered, with a glittering, hard finish, and the wood work gleamed in paint and gilding."[25]

Langrishe and Dougherty's company was still playing in the high country, their new theatre at Montgomery nearly finished. Mosquitoes marred the exhilarating effects of the thin air and spectacular scenery: "They say ... that the mosquitoes on the mountains are 12 inches long, and they carry brickbats under their arms to whet their bills upon."[26] The Langrishe and Dougherty company played nearly the full month of September in their new theatre in Montgomery, then they apparently played a few days in Oro City (Sacramento City) and California Gulch. At this time (1860–61), this gulch had a population of over 10,000 people, people living in wagons attached to tents, serving meals for paying diners on boards laid across saw horses and even renting out sleeping space under or in the wagons or tents.[27]

In Denver, Langrishe had ordered the re-naming of the Platte Valley Theatre to the "Denver Theatre," and ordered it thoroughly cleaned, "a consummation devoutly to be wished," according to the *News*. The commentator also wrote, "The seats of the parquette are cushioned with soft and most comfortably stuffed cushions, upon which it is really a pleasure to sit. The whole

8. Gold Circuit

Denver Theatre, far right. Langrishe's second performance venue (Subject Collection, Scan# 10029066, History Colorado).

is comfortably warmed, and the room [may] be the most delightful in Denver in which to spend an hour or two of an evening."[28]

The company had a prosperous and cordial time in the California Gulch diggings, one of their best times in mountain settings. The main company of actors left first, Langrishe and his wife to follow in a buggy, as was their custom. They were delayed taking leave of so many new warm friends, who thrust snacks and other edibles on them for the journey back to Denver. They had the box office "take" in gold dust concealed in the apron of the buggy. They were warned that road agents infested the route they were about to take, and they might well be robbed, but Langrishe was determined to catch up to his company of actors, so on they went.

Some miles distant they saw five horsemen riding down on them at a furious gallop. Langrishe heard his name mentioned twice before the horsemen reined to a stop, greeting Langrishe and his wife in a cordial manner. After a few words of conversation, one of the men asked Langrishe if he'd take a drink with them, and handed him a bottle. The honors were done and health drunk all around. Langrishe then returned the hospitality by offering to share some of the edibles his friends had pressed upon them. After several compliments on both sides, the horsemen put spurs to horses and shouted their farewell. The Langrishes continued their journey unmolested, their gold intact.[29]

Back in Denver radiating good health, the company proceeded to open the refurbished Denver Theatre with a stream of plays new to Denver. When they got to *The Sea of Ice* in November, thrilling drama and stage effects combined to elicit several repeats of the show. The number of Union soldiers in the Denver vicinity had increased, and the soldiers proved to be lovers of drama, so Langrishe and Dougherty set out to do a show mainly for them: Dion Boucicault's *Jessie Brown* or *The Siege at Lucknow*.[30] The exciting play was based on an incident that had occurred in India in 1857, the play full of suspense and drama. When most of the British defenders in the besieged fort were dead or dying, Jessie Brown sat up and said, "Dinna ye hear them? Dinna ye hear them coming?" as the faintly heard strains of bagpipes playing "The Campbells Are Coming" rose to a crescendo in the theatre.

Soldiers made a lot of "bombs" to be used in the fort scene, officers allowed two cannons to be brought to the theatre for use in the fort, and about 50 men armed with muskets volunteered to act as the attacking army of natives. For two or three days previous to the night when the piece was to be presented there were more soldiers at work on the stage and about the theatre than helpers of any other kind. They bossed all the warlike preparations. The great night came and the soldiers filled the house. Not only were they in the gallery, but they also filled the seats and the lower floor. Mrs. Langrishe took the part of Jessie Brown. When the attack was made on the fort the firing was terrific. Then bombs began to fall into the fort. These were balls of yarn containing gunpowder. In order to produce a good effect the reckless soldiers who made these imitation bombshells had placed in each nearly half a pound of powder. They made a report as loud as the largest China bombs. The bombs made it mighty hot for poor Jessie Brown. In less than half a minute her dress was on fire in two or three places and everyone expected to see her beat a retreat. But those with her in the fort smothered her burning dress and she stood her ground.

The supposition was among the people of the Theatre that the cannons were not loaded. The priming of the pieces was to be flashed and a drum was to be struck to imitate the report. But some soldiers had slipped into one of the cannon a cartridge containing about two pounds of powder. When those in front had begun to reply to the fire of the attacking party this cannon was touched off and it blew a hole through the side of the theatre nearly eight feet square. This excited the soldiers in front, and those in the gallery began firing their revolvers up into the ceiling, while those below turned loose into the floor. In a few seconds the place was so full of powder smoke that one could hardly breathe or see. The lights presented the appearance of street lamps seen through a dense fog. The excuse that the soldiers afterward made for riddling the floor and ceiling was that all was so much like a real battle that they forgot where they were and so began firing before they realized what they were about. That night all the "boys in blue" felt that they got the full worth of their money.[31]

If this was true (it was not reported in newspapers until years later), the theatre was quickly repaired and *Jessie Brown* or *The Relief at Lucknow* was presented several more times that month. Then Langrishe and Dougherty had the theatre seats floored over on a level with the stage, for a Masonic ball just after Christmas.[32] Some 240 people were seen dancing at once in the spacious theatre, an indication that the population of women had grown.[33]

Langrishe and Dougherty's company then put *Our American Cousin* on stage, running it for several days. On Tuesday, 300 or 400 of the soldiers of the First Regiment who had returned from their victorious battles were out in force at the theatre, and they appeared to enjoy the play "muchly."[34] Sam Hunter and DeWitt Waugh then spent several days painting scenery for a new production of Dion Boucicault's *The Colleen Bawn*. The play was first staged in London in September of 1860 so it was new to most in the audiences.[35]

Langrishe and Dougherty opened *The Colleen Bawn* on February 9, 1863, and the Denver Theatre quickly became the most fashionable place to go. The opening night audience "was one of the largest and most respectable ever assembled within the spacious walls of the theatre. Everybody present was exceedingly delighted with the new play and the perfectly splendid style in which it was gotten up and performed by the several members of the company...."[36] The following night's audience was very large, comprised of "many of the most intelligent and respectable ladies and gentlemen of Denver and vicinity.... It is worth a dollar to go and see the hundreds of ladies and gents that assemble thereto...."[37]

Their next major production was Boucicault's *The Octoroon*. Premiered in London in 1859, it had been repeatedly produced in the U.S., and interest in it was renewed by abolitionist feeling during the Civil War. A reviewer stated: "Langrishe plays the heavy villain so well that everybody cordially hates him; and Dougherty's Yankee is quite as good. Mrs. Langrishe's Zoe is a very touching and pathetic piece of acting.... Dick Wilmot's Nigger is immense. Dick has added fresh laurels to his brow by his fine rendition of this old darkey. Go and see it by all means."[38]

The company was to play a short season in Central City. The press stated: "Mr. Langrishe starts soon for the States for the purpose of securing a first class company for his next theatrical season in this city. Mike Dougherty, we understand, will start in a week or two for the Salmon River."[39] Prior to their departure from Denver, the "First Regiment Band, with their excellent new instruments, came up town yesterday evening and honored Mrs. J.S. Langrishe with a delightful serenade, previous to her leaving for the States."[40]

In Central City, the Montana Theatre began to change hands, later to be bought by Langrishe, Barnes and Jones.[41] The Montana Theatre was a log structure, bark intact, and "unsealed." It must have been chinked on the outside, but perhaps it was not chinked on the inside, hence unsealed.[42] The drop curtain was rolled up by ropes around a saw log, but it had a bust of Shakespeare painted on it,[43] a touch of class.

Langrishe and Dougherty's short season in Central City was to include a benefit for Dougherty, at which he would sing his creation "Pat Casey's Night Hands." Casey, the *nouveau riche* Irishman, thought his dignity was at stake, so he primed his "night hands" at the mine to smash things up at the theatre if Dougherty sang[44] the night of April 27. Dougherty invited Capt. Frank Hall, commander of the Elbert Guard, and 50 of his men to the theatre.[45] The presence of the militia quelled all thought of violence.[46]

The Langrishes left Denver on April 29 via the Overland Stage. It was to be a five- or six-day trip across the plains. Reported the *News*: "A large number of our military officers and citizens escorted Mr. Langrishe and lady out of town yesterday."[47] The Langrishes stopped over in Leavenworth to play a star engagement at the Union Theatre.[48]

The *News* promised a "good time coming," quoting the *New York Sunday Mercury* of May 7:

> Manager Langrishe and Mrs. Langrishe are on a visit to the Atlantic States, from their own home in Colorado. Mrs. Langrishe is with her relatives and friends in Chicago, and Mr. Langrishe has been in New York for a few days, looking up talent for his Colorado campaigns, as he owns four theatres there. A man of travel, of anecdotes, of enterprise, of enlarged views, of indomitable perseverance, and, above all, with every sterling quality of nobility or endearment, we know no better or more able general at present in the service of the Drama. Langrishe is good for victory in all his campaigns. James Conner & Co., 25 West Houston street, are doing his New York business.[49]

From Chicago, Langrishe wrote the Central City editor:

> I'm leaving here tonight (June 11) for home. I am bringing with me the best artistes from New York: George Pauncefort, formerly of the Theatre Royal, Drury Lane, London, and for several years the great attraction at the New Boston Theatre, as also at the Broadway Theatre, N.Y.; M'lle Ada Laurent, premier Danseuse from the principal opera houses of Europe and now from Laura Keene's theatre, N.Y.; John Dillon, also of Laura Keene's Theatre and the greatest favorite that ever played McVicker's Chicago Theatre; Mrs. John Dillon, also of Laura Keene's and McVicker's; and Miss M. Thompson, of Grover's Theatre, Washington. We will give the good mountain people a taste of our quality as soon as we can come across the plains.[50]

Mrs. Langrishe remained in the Middle West visiting her brother, sisters, nieces and nephews. She undoubtedly also met with her daughter Rosalthe, who had been attending a school for the deaf in New York City[51] and perhaps making preparations for her late-November wedding. The existence of a daughter was still a secret from all but family members.

Langrishe and his new company were expected by July 4, but instead

George Pauncefort, a gifted but eccentric Shakespearean actor. A young star in London, he came to the New York stage; but lawsuits charging bigamy kept him moving westward. Eventually he settled in Japan and worked with Noh actors (Special Collections Department, J. Willard Marriot Library, University of Utah, P001nG078).

stopped over to perform at Fort Kearny.[52] Langrishe and his new company finally arrived in Denver July 14. The *News* greeted them: "Our people, having starved for sustenance in the way of amusements for these many months, now need a good deal of relaxation, to keep their systems in harmonious tune, and we are glad to know, or at least hope, that Messrs. Langrishe and Dougherty, in their combined wisdom and accommodation, will have their troupe tarry a short season in our city before going to the mountains...."[53] Dougherty had not gone to the Bannock rush. The company performed at the Denver Theatre on July 17 and 18, then they closed that theatre for "reconstruction and re-arrangement of the interior," the company traveling to Central City.[54] Curiously, there was no newspaper mention that Mrs. Dillon was Mrs. Langrishe's sister, but she was said to have a "fine figure, a sweet, pretty face and a voice full of harmony and music."[55]

The first mention of Mrs. Langrishe since their return was July 25, praising her performance in *Lady of Lyons*.[56] Langrishe and Dougherty's danseuse, M'lle Ada Laurent, began giving dancing (and deportment) lessons to Central City youngsters.[57]

In Denver, the *News* printed:

> The greatest managerial success, theatrically speaking, that has been seen between St. Louis and San Francisco, in the knowledge of the oldest inhabitants, has been that experienced or demonstrated by Messrs. Langrishe and Dougherty, with their peerlessly perfect and popular new company in Central City during the fortnight past. Several nights, to our personal knowledge, there were scores and scores refused tickets, on account of the mammoth theatre being already and at an early hour, crowded from the nethermost aisle to the most elevated joists and spars away above the galleries. The sturdy miners, aristocratic mill men, sharp-looking business men, polite and elegant gentlemen of leisure, official position excursionists, and this that and the other department and calling, accompanied to a very large extent with scores of the finest and most stylish-looking ladies, may be seen nightly hastening on foot and in ambulances [horse-drawn enclosed wagons] from Nevada[ville], Black Hawk and Central to see the especially able and artistic acting, dancing and singing at the "Montana," and at the same time swell up the nightly receipts of the mountain audiences, frequently to five, six and seven hundred dollars.

At the Montana Theatre, they produced the grand spectacle, *The Sea of Ice*, an undertaking the press described as "only the largest and most prosperous of the theatres of the eastern cities have ventured to undertake...."[58] Mr. Langrishe, as Horace, to those who have seen him in his regular line of business, exhibits an astonishing versatility of genius...."[59]

The company received rave reviews for *Macbeth*, which was followed by *Hamlet*. Both title roles were played by George Pauncefort. A review read: "In the latter play, that (character) of Polonius, by Mr. Langrishe, attracted our particular notice. It was as good a Polonius as we ever witnessed."[60] This may have been the production reviewed by Maurice O'Connor Morris: "There

I saw *Hamlet* performed, and though the ghost was not very spiritual, Gertrude not very queenly, and the courtiers not very courtier-like, yet the play was, on the whole, very well put on the stage; even the Prince of Denmark ... really very well rendered."[61] Then it was back to "keeping the house in a roar" of laughter, Langrishe's forte.[62]

On August 13 the Central City paper revealed: "Mr. Langrishe has purchased the residence of Mr. Johnson, nearly back of our office. He may hereafter be regarded as one of the permanent residents of Central."[63] Now Mrs. Langrishe had two homes. Their performing year had definitely been set to perform in Denver winter months, and at least some summer months in Central. Hal Sayre wrote, "Much has been written about [the Langrishes], and I will not undertake to give you an account of them, except to say that they were very estimable people and a [sic] fine actors. They lived next door to me in Central, and I found them to be excellent neighbors. Langrishe would attempt any character in the category of plays from the gayest to the gravest. He was best however as a comedian, and he could keep the house in a [sic] uproar for several minutes without uttering a work [sic]. His facial expression was truly wonderful."[64]

By September 12, the weather had cooled so nights were chilly and mornings crisp, and the aspen on the surrounding mountains had turned to gold. Langrishe and Dougherty were tendered a complimentary benefit by Central City merchants and prospectors, then they wound up their Central City season September 30. By October 17, workmen still had not installed stoves in the Denver theatre. The weather had turned cold, and so was the theatre for *Othello*. Unexpected amusement arose, however, when a Ute Indian, just in town from the South, thought it best to walk out when the conflict between Casio and Roderigo erupted. His interpreter persuaded him to sit again, and quieted his fears, although it was clear to all he didn't understand what was happening.[65]

Stoves finally were installed and the theatre interior was reported to be warm, but considering the method of heating, those nearest the stove were undoubtedly warmest, those furthest away colder. Late in October, snow began falling, melting as fast as it fell, but late in the night it began sticking. The next morning, a blanket of snow about 12 inches deep lay in Denver. Householders were caught off guard, with that much snow so "early in the season," not having laid in sufficient wood or coal for winter heating.[66]

Langrishe and Dougherty met the cold weather with a production of *The Sea of Ice*, making sure the theatre was warmed, just in time for the snow to melt, leaving a sea of mud.

The *Commonwealth* noted:

> The performances at the Denver for the past week have possessed their usual merit, but have been given, as a general thing, to but slim houses. This, to a great extent, was caused by the rough weather. The traveling, of nights, has been almost impossible for ladies; and at public entertainments of this kind, where there are but few of the angelic portion of humanity, you are sure to find but a meager representation of the masculine persuasion....[67]

Romance of a Poor Young Man elicited some damning-with-faint-praise for Mrs. Langrishe, with the comment that "she can out-cry any woman we ever saw."[68]

The weather that fall was turbulent, with cold temperatures and snows. The periodic warm Chinook winds "ate" snow and left water and mud mixed with animal manure in the streets of Denver. Theatre attendance was light as a result, but the wonder was that there was any attendance at all, considering the circumstances. Langrishe and Dougherty offered the receipts for two nights of the Denver Theatre for the relief association for the poor, raising $1090 to provide medicine, fuel and food for the poor.[69]

Langrishe and Dougherty again produced Boucicault's *The Octoroon* about the first of December. Denverites were surprised by a letter that appeared in the Denver *Commonwealth* December 23 regarding that play, signed by "an Octoroon" who had witnessed the production. "What we saw enacted in a play, we have both seen and felt in reality, and we feel it now every day of our life. The Octoroon is a sad and truthful commentation [*sic*] on the horrors of slavery and the injustice and prejudice of the people of Democratic and Christian America against all persons of color, whether they be the sable African, the Mulatto or the almost white Octoroon...."[70]

About that same time, Langrishe and Dougherty produced *Uncle Tom's Cabin*. They even ran a matinee on Christmas Day so children could see it. The *Commonwealth* engaged the "Octoroon" (William J. Hardin, an educated black man who worked in a Denver barber shop[71]) to review *Uncle Tom's Cabin*, which he did with general approval of the production.[72]

The year 1864 opened well, Langrishe and Dougherty putting on *Forty Thieves*, followed by *Richard III* and *Othello*. They must have been performing altered versions of Shakespeare's plays since there were also songs by John Dillon, dances by M'lle Laurent and a novelty act, "Red Man of Agar and his son, Master Willie."[73] The weather turned intensely cold, warming up to about zero during daylight hours. Mercury plummeted to 21° below zero early January 5. The Denver Theatre closed until Saturday night, by which time the temperatures had risen.[74] When the theatre reopened, there were large audiences.

The *News* wrote: "Messrs. Langrishe and Dougherty are entitled to great praise for the enterprise they exhibit in bringing out new plays. Not infrequently they are far ahead of St. Louis and other western cities in fresh novelties...."[75] The first production attracted a full house, but the management decided to only play three days each week for the time being. The cost of fuel for the stoves was undoubtedly eating into profits.[76]

Monsieur Zanfretta, of the celebrated Ravel troupe, came to Denver, en route to fulfill an engagement in California. Langrishe and Dougherty hired him to do the "beautiful pantomime," "The Grotto Nymph."[77] In Central City, a note appeared in the newspaper offering the Langrishes' "well-arranged and comfortable" residence on High Street for rent.[78]

The legislature for the Territory of Colorado, established in 1861, had been meeting in Golden City, but moved to Denver to continue the session, so Langrishes again had the opportunity to entertain state legislators.[79] Zanfretta and Pauncefort were both still with their large company, so the cost of doing business must have been high. Langrishe and Dougherty were putting on a new play every other night, and had their hands full.

Langrishe and Dougherty donated the use of their theatre for a fundraiser for the "Sanitary Commission." This was a relief agency for Union troops, and for a Sunday School exhibition.[80]

The Langrishe and Dougherty company concluded their Denver season April 2 and moved to Central City just in time for harsh weather there. The press lamented: "The weather is incorrigible; it is again preparing to snow. The mud is already half-knee deep and we humbly pray that we may be spared a further infliction."[81] Langrishe and Dougherty opened in Central, intending to play only one week before proceeding to the Salmon River mines. Some reports indicated there were 40,000 people in the Central City–Black Hawk area, eight times more than the population of Denver. There were large audiences, even though the weather was disagreeable. A hack transported people up the hill from Black Hawk to the theatre, where the actors were presenting a new play every night. They were enjoying full houses when one of those "bust" messages that always follows "booms" arrived in Central City: Some who went to the Bannock mines were despondent, others were returning to Colorado.[82] A "rumor on the street" was that Langrishe had sold one of his gold claims in the mountains recently for $5000 in cash.[83] Nearly everybody bought or bartered for claims during gold rushes. Lawyers arrived early and took claims or fractional interests in claims in lieu of greenbacks or gold dust. Doctors, merchants, ranchers, editors, chambermaids, farmers and mill owners all had their turns at being bitten by the gold bug.[84] It's no surprise that actors and managers were also bitten.

Business for Langrishe and Dougherty had been so good, in spite of frequent bad weather that spring, they decided they'd stay in Central City and abandon their plan to go to the Bannock or Idaho mines that year.[85] Their Central City theatre band had grown since 1861 when they had only a drum and a brass horn. Once they had more instruments, the band rode around Central, Nevadaville, Missouri Flats and Black Hawk in a horse-drawn wagon, playing their music to advertise the theatre. The musicians habitually stopped at every drinking place along the way, swigging lightning whiskey and ending the liquid afternoons at Missouri Flats playing "Dixie" as long as their wind held out.[86] O.J. Goldrick's communiqué to the *Rocky Mountain News* reported that Langrishe and Dougherty were doing good business in the Montana Theatre and they possessed some "valuable gold claims in Gregory and other developed districts."[87]

In the East the news was glorious for the Union. The telegraph brought the news that General U.S. Grant was advancing on Richmond, and General Robert E. Lee was retreating.[88] In Denver a few days later, a friendly Arapaho's warning was realized: Cherry Creek flooded. The water in Cherry Creek, normally little more than a trickle, gushed to nine feet deep at 9 p.m. Friday, May 20, carrying away houses, people and animals. The office of the *Rocky Mountain News*, constructed over the creek, was swept away, printing press and all. William N. Byers, publisher of the *Rocky Mountain News*, made arrangements to send *News* subscribers the *Commonwealth*, and quickly bought the office and equipment of the *Commonwealth*.[89]

On the plains, the month of June brought fright. Those Indians who'd been stared at, laughed at, mocked and sneered at had lost their temper. Depredations were reported from the Kansas border to Denver. Rumors flew, each voice magnifying the danger. "Gov. Evans sent a message to Major General Teller [in Central City] denying the existence of any present danger, but requesting the immediate organization of all the militia here...."[90] The attack that most frightened Colorado folks was the murder of the Hungate family—parents and two children—found with slit throats 25 miles east of Denver. Western forts were still undermanned due to the pressures of the Civil War.

Amid the turmoil, Langrishe prospered. *The New York Clipper* noted: "Langrishe and Dougherty were on the point of starting [for Bannock mines], went to Central City to play one farewell week, and finding that a large number of claims in their possession were likely to 'pan out' well, they concluded to postpone their exodus. The result was, that within two weeks they sold $8000 worth of claims, which they would probably have disposed of six months ago for less than $800...."[91]

Joe V. Baugh, a former resident of the Colorado area, wrote in his present paper, the *Nonpareil* (Council Bluffs, Iowa), that during an evening in St. Louis he saw Laura Keene and her company perform *Our American Cousin*, and was disappointed. "I have seen a 'stock company' [i.e., Langrishe and Dougherty company] play *Our American Cousin* in better style, in the Rocky Mountains!"[92]

In Denver, "people of color" celebrated the anniversary of the emancipation of slaves in the West Indies. A large delegation came from the mountains to attend the event, held in Langrishe & Dougherty's Denver Theatre.[93]

On August 8 the *News* reported: "Theatrical—For the past season and at the present, Messrs. Langrishe and Dougherty's theatrical troupe have been doing the biggest business at their Montana Theatre, Central City, that was ever known or dreamed of in this part of gold-digging creation. Three hundred dollars a night might be set down as the average for the 'houses' during the past four months...."[94]

On the plains, Indian were killing people, driving off livestock, and keeping settlers on edge. Territorial Governor John Evans made a public appeal for men to organize for the defense of their homes and families "against the merciless savages." On August 11 he authorized the raising of a regiment of "hundred day men" in Colorado.[95] Langrishe's actors Dick Wilmot and Harry Richmond signed up.[96]

The Central City theatre continued drawing large crowds until September 26, when they had to close because part of the theatre caved in, perhaps due to an excavation under the theatre.[97] The Montana was only closed one night while repairs were made. Langrishe and Dougherty had to get their actors out of the mountains before they were snowbound. By October 31 the snow was about 18 inches deep in Black Hawk, one mile below Central City.[98] Not that it was any better on the plains. It was said to be 20 inches deep on the level, snow so cold and deep that domestic livestock were dying.[99]

Dougherty had been "seriously indisposed for the last five weeks." The company presumably used the Overland stage, converted to a sled, for transportation down to the plains.[100] Dougherty recovered sufficiently to perform nightly in the Denver Theatre by late November. There was still Indian trouble on the plains, and the Colorado newspapers deplored the lack of action on the part of troops. Then came the message that there had been a big battle on Sand Creek, near Fort Lyon, and "500 Indians were reported killed and 600 hundred horses captured."[101] Colonel Chivington, a hero from the Glorieta Pass, New Mexico, battle with Confederates, had been commander at this "battle" (many called it the Sand Creek Massacre) in which Colorado Volunteers were so arranged that they were shooting toward one another. Those Indian men who escaped the dawn attack made war on settlers, emigrants and travelers with new hatred and viciousness.[102] Some of Chivington's own officers, including Sam Tappan and Silas Soule, were publicly critical of the "battle." The plains were aflame. The U.S. Congress began to look into the "attack," and Colonel (the Reverend) John Chivington's presidential aspirations evaporated.

In Denver, the company performed *Peep o'Day* with "Langrishe is a whole team in plays of this kind, every time. His facial antics and the wink of his eye can cure more people of sedentary disease than half the doctors in the country...."[103] After Christmas, they began running *Wept of the Wish-Ton-Wish*, featuring "splendid Indian costumes, trophies taken in the big battle of Sand Creek"[104] by actor-soldier Harry Richmond, who was accused of atrocities in official hearings.

9

Into Unknown Perils

While she was hosting an elaborate open house on New Year's Day, 1865, Jeannette Langrishe received word of the death of her younger (29-year-old) sister Helen Louisa Dillon, wife of John Dillon, after a "short but painful illness." Mrs. Dillon died Sunday morning, December 18, 1864, "leaving two motherless children," but severed telegraph wires had delayed notice to Mrs. Langrishe.

Helen Dillon had acted with them when Langrishe was in partnership with John B. Atwater in Wisconsin and had acted in Colorado with the Langrishe and Dougherty company until February 1864, when the Dillons abruptly left Colorado to take an engagement with Col. Woods' Museum Theatre in Chicago.[1] In remembrance of Mrs. Dillon, the Denver Theatre was closed that evening, and re-opened the following evening with *The Sea of Ice*.

Mid-January, not a good time for a dog to be lost in Denver, Langrishe's yellow bull terrier, answering to "Major," strayed off or was stolen. Langrishe offered a large reward for the return of the dog, no questions asked.[2]

Indians furious over the Sand Creek Massacre shut down stagecoach travel east of Denver, so when eminent actor James Stark arrived in Denver from California he was forced to tarry in Colorado instead of proceeding to New York City. Langrishe and Dougherty arranged for him to give a few performances in Denver.[3] Stark was a noted tragedian, so the Langrishe and Dougherty company opened with one of his best pieces, *Richelieu*. The weather was extremely cold, temperature down to minus 30° some nights,[4] but the theatre enjoyed "immense crowds" for Stark's performances.[5]

Respected officers such as Scott Anthony, Silas Soule, Sam Tappan and Edward Wynkoop were publicly critical of Colonel Chivington's Sand Creek attack. Denver citizens, including Langrishe, resented those old friends who took the Indians' side of the controversy. Langrishe apparently wrote a new song for Dougherty to sing, tune unknown: "Investigation/We are bound to raise a muss, or to have you make amends /For the 'wanton, cruel outrage' upon 'our Indian friends,'/The battle of Sand Creek has roused our indignation,/And the 'shocking bad affair' demands investigation...." Langrishe was undoubtedly relying on Harry Richmond's version of events. Richmond, recognizable and rash, was identified as one of the men who had mutilated Indian bodies.[6]

The Indian threat worsened to the extent that Samuel H. Elbert, Secretary of Colorado Territory, declared martial law.[7] Places of amusement (including the theatre) were to be closed except between the hours of two and three p.m., and each county was assigned a number of men they had to produce as volunteers. Martial law was lifted for Saturday performances at the theatre.

On March 1 the *News* announced that the dissolution of the partnership between Langrishe and M.J. Dougherty had taken place on February 25, by mutual consent. "The business will hereafter be managed by J.S. Langrishe, and all outstanding partnership accounts settled by him...."[8]

James Stark, Shakespearean actor of national fame (Houghton Library, Harvard University).

On April 7, stunning news was telegraphed to Denver: Robert E. Lee had surrendered and the bloody Civil War was over.[9] In a few days word came that President Lincoln had been shot and Secretary Seward viciously attacked. News soon followed that the president had died of his wounds.[10] Langrishe and Sam Hunter, one of his technical theatre workers, arranged a hearse and decorated the Denver Theatre for a funeral service for the president.[11] Interdenominational funeral services were held for Lincoln in both the Montana Theatre in Central City and the Denver Theatre on April 19.[12]

Langrishe's troupe was down to bare bones, so he hired more actors by telegraph. Three were due to arrive within a week, and three more later. Harry Richmond preceded the rest of the company to Central City and told the press there that he was Langrishe's new partner.[13] Mike Dougherty returned

9. Into Unknown Perils

in June and celebrated too much on July 4, dying, presumably, of alcohol consumption.

A cloudburst dumped a deluge on the Central City area July 25, filling Eureka Gulch with water, but mainly damaging homes on steep hillsides. The home of Mr. and Mrs. Langrishe was among those that were inundated, their carpets flooded with mud from higher ground.[14]

There were still many prospectors and placer miners in the area, but Central City's economy was changing from placer to lode mining, diminishing audiences. The lode miners labored strenuously underground for $2.50 to $3.50 per day, and were not as ready to spend a dollar to attend the theatre as prospectors who found their admission price in a pan and worked when they wished. Hard rock miners also tended to be married men with families.

Mrs. Langrishe played *Camille* for Mrs. Fitzwilliams' benefit on September 14, perhaps a harbinger of a stunning announcement: Mrs. Langrishe was retiring from the stage, the first of many such announcements.[15] Perhaps too many unheated dressing rooms, trying to speak when suffering from a cold or laryngitis, whatever the reason, she was said to have had a rough voice: "[H]er voice was as coarse as any I've ever heard issuing from a feminine throat."[16] This was a comment made by Samuel J. Kline over 50 years later. He termed Mrs. Langrishe a "fat, frowsy woman who was an actress" and had a "great preference for juvenile and ingénue roles."[17]

Kline was alone in this evaluation, since all contemporary writers regarded Mrs. Langrishe as a very talented actress. Kline's estimation can't be omitted, but its needless vitriol may have been revenge for a scolding he received for peeking at actresses changing clothes. A Central City paper had a more positive view of her:

> In the past years of her career upon the stage in Colorado, and always, to the present hour, the verdict of the whole people has consigned her to the leading position in the drama, and the manner in which she has sustained it has won universal admiration. On this occasion let it be remembered that to no one but to Mrs. Langrishe and her husband do we of this Territory owe the present high standard of our theatrical entertainments. Through their exertions, the play has been held aloof from all its evil influences, and rendered acceptable to all classes, the best society finding there a place of pleasant recreation....[18]

A lengthy notice, signed by the administrator of the estate of Michael J. Dougherty, announced the pending sale of Dougherty's real property including several mining claims and portions of claims, including claims on the "Jack Langrishe Lode in Gregory Mining District."[19] Langrishe probably bought claims rather than being the original filer on claims, but the "Jack Langrishe Lode" sounds as if he had done some of his own prospecting, perhaps under the tutelage of Mike Dougherty.

When the Langrishe company opened in Denver on October 24, the *News* commented, "Jack never presents his homely mug behind the footlights without receiving salvos of applause...."[20] Mrs. Langrishe made her first appearance of the season as "Sam Willoughby" in *The Ticket of Leave Man* October 30.[21] Mrs. Langrishe continued to perform, playing male roles.[22]

On February 1, Mrs. Langrishe hosted the "Ladies' Mite Society of St. John's Church" to raise funds for painting the church. Had this social gathering been held in the East, actresses would not have been welcome as guest or hostess. Mrs. Langrishe had established a reputation with the community and the church as a decorous lady, never mentioning her previous marriages nor her daughter.[23]

"Peter Pry," probably a *nom de plume* for newspaper publisher George West, wrote about his theatre experiences, and added:

> The newspaper gentry appreciate you [Langrishe] for lo! your printers bills are enormous. The druggists appreciate you, for behold, their profits on coal oil (kerosene) are the Dutchman's "one per cent." The ladies appreciate you ... for the opportunity you furnish them of showing off their fine and costly dresses, and then you know Mr. L-----, their complexions bear closer scrutiny at night. The gentlemen appreciate you, for they can ogle the girls to their hearts content; and lastly, Peter Pry appreciates you. As long as he is in funds his seat shall be in the circle, but when ingloriously strapped, he shall still be found perched on the topmost bench of the gallery.... Peter Pry.[24]

"Pry" also told about "a tall, red-faced man" (undoubtedly Langrishe) calling the "Elect" (actors) around him, and addressing them thus:

> Be Jabers, an its mesif that's spaken to ye, an I want ye to be afther listthening or I'll wallop ivery mither's son of ye, I will. Remimber ye carry *Sayser* and his fortins tonight, so listhen to my instructions. Misther B----, opin yer mouth and spake out like a man, sur. Misther M. Don't be after ringin' yer hands and shakin' yer fists in the face of Heving. He mout git mad ye know. An' as fur ye, Misther A----- ye shan't sing at all at all, ye *fly yer kite* quite too high, sur, in yer songs. Priss these here precepts on yer minds my Paddies, and if the Frademon's Burou gits locked up, an the Faynicons take the "Gim of the Ocean," *be gorra*, we'll make enough yit to spind St. Patrick's day in ould Ireland.

According to Pry, "Here the eloquent speaker turned to a gentleman, who stood near, and snatching a large black bottle from his pocket poured out a red suspicious looking liquid in a glass. Then turning to his breathless auditory, while a smile of philanthropy beamed from his countenance, he tossed it off with a grin, saying,"

> "Here's a fortin to ye all, me *b'hoys*. May ye never want for a dhrop of the craytur to warrum yerselves wid, and may ye always have a thumpin big prattle in the middle of yer throats." ... 'ye, Misther volunteer, sing sur, sing like the "Divil baten tan bark," an if the audience mistakes yer sintimintals for *comic songs*, don't ye be after gittin' mad, ye know, for begorra, it's only their way.[25]

Several prominent Denver women tendered a complimentary benefit to Mrs. Langrishe "as a testimonial of our appreciation of you as a lady, and recognizing the high position you have attained as an actress...."[26] The theatre was packed for her benefit night, every available space crowded to capacity. The *News* described the event: "Full half of the ladies present were in full dress, making an array of beauty seldom rivaled." At the close of the play, Mrs. Langrishe was called before the curtain, where she made appropriate remarks of thanks. Then the curtain rose on a table loaded with presents for the beneficiary, including household items of silver from lady friends, and a very valuable gold watch and chain. A "perfect hurricane of applause" and audience cheers rang out during the presentation. "Altogether the scene will never be forgotten by any who were present."[27]

On April 5, 1866, Jeannette Langrishe boarded a stagecoach to visit her friends east, to be absent until July or August. The press noted: "No lady in Colorado stands higher in the estimation of the public or who is more respected in private circles...."[28] Jeannette had been in Colorado since 1860, save for one brief visit to the Midwest in 1863.

Langrishe must have felt like all were abandoning him. Harry Richmond was leaving for the East to improve his acting skills[29] and Mary Rickords, the Denver lass coached by the Langrishes and added to their company, decided to do the same.[30] Then three actors passing through en route East were hired by Langrishe: George B. Waldron, tragedian and leading man, engaged for six nights, and Mr. and Mrs. N.S. Leslie for six months. Leslie was a light comedian, she a "singing chambermaid" (ingénue).[31] Langrishe raised the top price of admission from $1.50 to $2, to the displeasure of some of his audience.[32] Had Waldron overwhelmed the audience with extraordinary talent, they wouldn't have complained, but he came into Denver with a cold and his voice was hoarse.[33] Within two days, Langrishe dropped the price of admission to its usual level.[34]

The Langrishe company concluded their Denver theatre season May 19, and the *Rocky Mountain News* took the opportunity to assess the talents of individual members once they were gone. "Langrishe is, and always will be, a general favorite, outwearing, to use a western phrase, any man that ever struck the stage. In comedy, his superiors are very few indeed, and in this department of the histrionic profession, Jack Langrishe could star in the very best theatres in the world. This is no puff for Langrishe as there are but few in Colorado who do not know the man personally, and all admire him, as well for his enterprise and integrity, as for his talent in the profession...."[35]

Waldron went to Central City with Langrishe's company. There he found the Montana Theatre's stage had been "improved by alterations," new scenery painted, and canvas applied to the theatre's ceiling to catch flakes of deteriorating bark from the log roof.[36]

The *Register* reported that the theatre season had "opened as usual, with overflowing houses for a few nights, then dwindled down to the few strangers who were in town on business for a day or two...."[37] Langrishe advertised for a leading man in the July 7 *New York Clipper*: "Leading Man Wanted. For One Year, commencing August 15th, for Denver City and Central City, C.T. Season, six months at each theatre. Fare paid in coach from Missouri river, and not deducted afterwards. None but first class artists need apply. Consider silence a negative. J.S. Langrishe, Proprietor of Denver and Central City Theatres, Colorado."[38]

At the time a census of population in Gilpin County (Central City area) showed more than 7000 people, 5800 of them male adults. There were 1140 women and children and 60 colored people of all ages.[39] However, this didn't seem enough to support Langrishe's theatrical endeavors.

Soon the local press announced:

> Good bye.—The last farewell speech of our troupe of comedians was spoken last evening.... The theatrical season here has been unprecedentedly disastrous to the management, but in point of brilliant attractions, far superior to any former season. We have been favored with the latest and most popular Eastern dramas.... John S. Langrishe, a person as much in love with Colorado and her people as though he had been "indigenous to the soil," has received the plaudits of his friends (which means everybody) too often not to feel that his presence upon the stage is sufficient to create the liveliest enjoyment and appreciation of those who are there to be amused....[40]

In Denver, renovations of the Denver Theatre included installing stoves in the dressing rooms beneath the stage. The *News* expressed the hope that the stoves would "put an end to the blue noses and chattering teeth that we have noticed on that stage in previous winters."[41]

Langrishe hired other actors and actresses passing through, but occasionally a play required more actors than he had, so he cast local people as supernumeraries or extras in what some called "thinking" parts (rather than speaking). In *The Jibbenainosay* one of these supernumeraries excited merriment because of his awkward, gangling appearance, and his walking on stage waiting for a character to kill him, but when that character failed to do so, the "supe" decided to die anyhow, so leisurely laid down among the other victims.[42]

On January 7, 1867, an unusual announcement appeared in the *Rocky Mountain News*: "J.S. Langrishe, Esq.—Dear Sir: We, the undersigned, members of your dramatic company and attaches of the Denver Theatre, anxious to express in some manner gratitude for the many acts of kindness we have received at your hands, respectfully tender to you our gratuitous services for a complimentary benefit to yourself, at your earliest convenience...." Langrishe thanked the signers of the letter, naming January 9 as the date of the occasion, and added, "Hoping that our acquaintanceship, so pleasantly begun, may ripen into a lasting friendship...."[43]

9. Into Unknown Perils

On January 16 the *News* read: "A whirlwind passed over a portion of the city last evening, occasioning some alarm and doing slight damage in a few places.... The greatest consternation we heard of was at the Denver Theatre, which rocked for a moment like it was shaken by an earthquake. It would take a hurricane to damage it seriously or endanger its occupants."[44]

The cast of the Denver Theatre worked hard, rehearsing their next new production, *The Naiad Queen* or *The Revolt of the Naiads*, a romantic operatic "spectacle" in three acts. This play or opera was popular for its scenic beauty, costumes and large cast. The *News* said of the production: "Among the scenes of surpassing beauty we note the Fairy Lake, the Cavern of Riches, the Hall of the Naiads, and the closing scene, which comprises a number of magic and beautiful features—the Naiads at home, their queen rising in the magic fountain, and the Birth of the Butterfly, being the leading ones.... The martial array of the amazons was quite a feature, and their evolutions [*sic*] very military...."[45] Anyone who has been exposed to America's "first musical," *The Black Crook*, will recognize that *The Naiad Queen* was a precursor to that sequence of scenes. Langrishe's interest in magic and illusion was revived by this kind of theatricality.

Langrishe had hired Charles W. Couldock, one of the greatest actors of the time, the previous autumn, and he arrived in Denver on Monday, March 4.[46] Couldock opened with *Richelieu*, followed by *Chimney Corner*, *Othello* (Couldock played Iago) and other familiar pieces. His engagement in Denver was limited, for he and the company were to play in Central City for a time, then all wend their way to the Bannock mines, still enjoying boom status.

The weather that spring was nasty, storm following storm, laced with cold temperatures. Langrishe did have some lightly attended plays, and even shut down a few nights because of the cold weather. On March 12 the *News* observed that the thermometer "maintained its mark at two or three degrees below zero all day. As night fell, so did the mercury, until 27 degrees below zero was reached. The cracking occasioned by this excessive cold, contracting timbers in frame houses and board fences, sounded like pistol shots, in all parts of the city...."[47]

On March 13 the *Rocky Mountain News* printed an appreciation of Langrishe:

> An artist in everything he undertakes in his profession, Mr. Langrishe is the King of comedy in America, and in his delineations of Irish character has no superior. Aside from this, in his attempts at heavier parts, he has always acquitted himself creditably much superior to any one we ever heard, whose peculiar *role* like his, is comedy. As a citizen, Mr. Langrishe, by his enterprising public spirit has endeared himself to all in Denver—even those who are diametrically opposed to his peculiar profession according him honor. On every occasion he has been found ready and willing to yield up his theatre for any great public meeting for

the use of the people in giving a demonstration to their feeling, on any great national event or public enterprise.... He goes with his troupe to fill an engagement for a month in Central City. At the expiration of that time, with a chosen few of his company, including the great actor, Mr. Couldock, he makes a tour of the western Territories, his first engagement we understand, being at the Salt Lake Theatre. We, in common with all our citizens, wish that he may realize a fortune by this trip, and speedily return to his old home and friends in Denver.[48]

About Langrishe's complimentary benefit in April, the *News* wrote:

the house was crowded to its fullest capacity with the beauty and *elite* of our city.... After the play Mr. Langrishe was called in front of the curtain by a storm of applause, and George F. Crocker, Esq., appearing in behalf of the donors, presented Mr. L. with a certificate of deposit to the amount of five hundred dollars.... Mr. Crocker ... managed to get off a short, neat speech, to which Mr. Langrishe replied with an emotion that almost forbid his utterance. There was not that stereotyped sameness that is too apt to be common on such occasions, as it was plain to be seen in the broken utterance of his thanks, that the beneficiary was deeply affected with this new and substantial proof of the high place he holds in the public esteem.[49]

Langrishe's company drew very good houses in Central City, according to the *Register*. It was a strong and costly company, including Phelps and Couldock. The latter won high praise for his performances, even for his *Hamlet*.[50] They usually performed about one Shakespeare play per month, but since they had a company that could perform these plays well, they played six in about one month. The *Register* continued to crow about Langrishe's crowded theatre, but acknowledged, "The times (here) are confessedly dull; many laborers are out of employment, and prices generally yet rule high."

Couldock's daughter Eliza was going to join the company in Central City, but was apparently delayed. They stayed on, the *Register* urging people to see Couldock while they had the chance.[51] Langrishe's company was supposed to play a very short season in Denver, then proceed to Salt Lake City where they (including Couldock and his daughter) had an engagement before proceeding to the Bannock mines.[52] Langrishe solved the plight of Denver and Central City residents being without entertainment during his absence: He split his company and left some in Colorado. Charles Wilson, stage manager and actor (and sometimes billed as Langrishe's partner) would stay in Colorado, putting on plays in Central City and Georgetown for the summer. Phelps and Mr. and Mrs. Leslie were among those who would remain.[53]

Then Indian troubles renewed in force, worse northwest of Denver, along the route Langrishe and Couldock intended to travel. Langrishe and his company left Monday, June 24, 1867, by their own mule-drawn conveyances.[54] Mules were faster than oxen, and not as enticing to Indian raiders as horses. Their route was about 500 miles through Indian territory to Salt Lake City without military escort and without changing draft animals. Because of

9. Into Unknown Perils

Indian attacks from Fort Kearny to Salt Lake City, few stagecoaches were going through,[55] but Bishop Daniel S. Tuttle, the Rev. D.B. Miller, and the Rev. E.N. Goddard, all bound for Montana, planned to continue their journey by stagecoach June 24.[56] Ben Holladay, owner of the stagecoach line, traveled eastward as far as Fort Bridger, Wyoming, then turned back, intending to sail from San Francisco to Panama, thence another ship to reach New York City.[57]

The Langrishe company traveling to Salt Lake City included Richard White, L.M. Browne, Jimmy Griffith, Jimmy Martin, Mr. and Miss Couldock, the Langrishes and Mrs. Fitzwilliams.[58] They were probably hauling scenery as well as their costumes and street clothing. Travel took just over a month, but the Langrishe company did arrive safely in Salt Lake City.[59]

The weather in Salt Lake City was unpleasantly hot, "98° in the shade" amid a swarm of grasshoppers.[60] The company and Couldocks received warm praise from the press for their performances. The Couldocks were to stay on for a while in Salt Lake City, but the Langrishe company, without Langrishe, went on toward Montana on August 11, the men in the company wagons, the women via stagecoach. Langrishe stayed over a day to star in *Arrah na Pogue* Monday night. The *Salt Lake Deseret News* reported he was an "excellent comedian and an unassuming gentleman." On August 13, he was the only human passenger on the stagecoach bound for Montana. His dog rode, too, for a time.

The actors traveling toward Virginia City planned on hunting and fishing along the way. While searching for their strayed mules, they found the partial remains of a man, the skull large and symmetrical, with beautiful teeth. Looking at that skull, all property man Jimmy Griffith thought of was "Yorick." They took it with them, used the skull for *Hamlet* and carried it eventually back to Colorado. Langrishe would write more of this incident later in Deadwood.

From the Snake River, Langrishe notified the Virginia City *Montana Post* that he and his "Denver company" would open at the Peoples Theatre in Virginia City on August 31. A note appeared in the *Salt Lake Daily Telegraph* offering a $20 reward for return of a yellow bull terrier named Mose, weighing about 30 pounds, having a crooked tail. "Lost between Black Foot and Snake River. Return to C.M. Couldock, Salt Lake House, Salt Lake City."[61] Couldock could bring the dog to Montana, if it was turned in. Couldock and his daughter boarded the northbound stage for Montana September 4, 1867. There was no further mention of the dog.

Mrs. Langrishe strode into the yet-unlit Virginia City theatre, stubbed her toe on a piece of timber and dislocated a joint. She was able to play in the first piece of the evening, but had to retire from the second.[62] She recovered in a couple of days and resumed performing. The *Helena Weekly Herald* reported, "Langrishe and the Couldocks are playing with great success in

Virginia City. We understand they are soon to favor Helena with their presence, and the sooner the better, say we."[63] Such advance publicity was better than bills posted around town to whet the public's appetite for their shows. Back in Virginia City, the company and Couldocks were attracting good houses and mostly excellent reviews, although the editor and audience disliked their play *Doing for the Best*.[64]

In Virginia City, Langrishes nurtured their friendship with Daniel S. Tuttle, then First Bishop of Montana.[65] They were close friends to the end. Bishop Tuttle likely never saw the Langrishes perform.

Langrishe and his wife took a stagecoach to Helena to pave the way for the company to follow, making arrangements for a theatre. The local press reported: "The last week of Mr. Langrishe's company has been attended with unprecedented success in the theatrical history of Virginia City, and is a tribute to the merits of the company."[66]

Episcopal Bishop Daniel Tuttle, clerical friend of Jack and Jeannette Langrishe. Was the Presiding Bishop of the Episcopal Church in America from 1903 to 1923 (Utah State Historical Society, 14008).

In Helena, as at Virginia City, Langrishe's company enjoyed full houses of enthusiastic audiences, reminiscent of the early days in Colorado. Originally he had planned to journey to the Bannock mines (i.e., Virginia City, Helena, etc.) and back to perform in Colorado in the fall. Their late start due to Indian troubles plus the full month it took for his company to travel made return before winter inconvenient, if not impossible. The rolling plains of the Wyoming territory they'd have to cover are at a very high altitude subject to dangerous blizzards.

The Couldocks were coming to the end of their engagement with Langrishe's company, but Langrishe would not be without a star. George Pauncefort, former leading man from Langrishe's Denver company, showed up, and Langrishe engaged him.[67] In Helena, businessmen and officials tendered a complimentary benefit to Langrishe, and Sol Star, member of the K.S. Lodge No. 9, presented him with a Masonic keystone made of Montana gold in appreciation for favors received and the members' appreciation of him as a man and accomplishments in his profession.[68] Mr. and Miss Couldock, the

Langrishes, Jimmy Martin and Mrs. Fitzwilliams took the stagecoach from Helena to Virginia City[69] for a short season.

Storms of applause greeted the returned Langrishe company in Virginia City, and more importantly, crowded houses.[70] Early in January the roof of the theatre caught fire, ignited by a hot stove pipe. Volunteer firemen soon extinguished the blaze which might have burned the entire town had it been left to burn. The press reported:

> It was quite lively for a few minutes, in the Theatre, and quite a number of the audience had important business on the outside. Mr. Browne, the anxious lover in the play, forgot the fire raging in his bosom and turned his attention to that in the ceiling, while Martin, the diabolical, double-dyed villain (in the play), came down to the footlights and entreated the audience to not rush frantically into destruction, but stay there quietly (and be burned to death).... The audience put out at first, but after the fire was put out, they put in again. Five firemen also entered, also, about a hundred and fifty men and boys whom they had passed on the street during the day, whom the doorkeeper, in consideration of their intimate relation to the firemen, admitted on the free list....[71]

In Helena, crews working for Langrishe were busy expanding the width of the theatre and filling the walls with sawdust. This was an attempt to insulate against the cold (the temperature varied from minus 30 to minus 40).[72]

The company left Virginia City by stagecoach, intending to open in Helena on Saturday, February 1. This was George Pauncefort's first visit to Helena (other than a flying visit one day, looking over the theatre). There were probably few readers of the theatrical and sporting newspaper, the *New York Clipper*, in Helena, but if any were reading, they may have discovered Pauncefort's theatrical wardrobe had been sold at auction, probably to settle a bill for lodging. "Report says that gentleman George has embraced Mormonism, and is a 'Saint' at Salt Lake...."[73]

The sawdust insulation must have worked because their opening night was bitterly cold, but the theatre was well warmed.[74] Pauncefort allegedly was going to stay with the Langrishe troupe for several months, but Langrishe had engaged George Waldron and his new wife as guest stars, probably to replace the quixotic Pauncefort.

About April 19, the Langrishe company traveled about 50 miles to Diamond City, Montana, to perform, even though Indians were stealing horses and mules close to Helena.[75] The Helena press greeted Langrishe: "We are gratified to learn that Mr. Langrishe has been very successful in Diamond City, having been greeted with not only full but perfectly jammed houses, many on the first night of the opening of the Union Hall, failing to gain admission.... Nothing is a greater evidence of life in a town or city than the support of a Theatre...."[76]

Waldron joined them in Diamond City about May 29 to finish their run, then they returned to Helena. Since performing with the Langrishe company in 1866, Waldron had played star engagements in New York and performed at Chicago's McVicker's Theatre, where his experience included performing Iago to "the great [Edwin] Booth's" Othello, then played Othello to Booth's Iago.[77]

An item in the *Rocky Mountain News*, culled from the *St. Joseph Herald*, reported a letter from Montana Territory that said, "Times are very dull in the Territory, and many young men are out of employment. Owing to the slight fall of snow during the winter, water will be very scarce during the summer, and it will be impossible to work (placer mine) many of the gulches. Money is scarce and hard to get."[78]

Back in Helena, one evening the U.S. marshal and all of his deputies wanted to go to the theatre, and had no place to jail their Indian prisoner, so they took him along. When Langrishe's actors began "killing" one

George Waldron, leading man and co-manager of Langrishe troupes in Colorado and Montana. Later starred in McKee Rankin's *The Danites*. On a European tour of that drama, he appeared in a command performance before Queen Victoria of England (L. Tom Perry Special Collections, Arnold B. Lee Library, Brigham Young University, Provo, Utah, Mss P24, Item 115).

another in lively fashion, it was sufficiently realistic to frighten the Indian, who bolted through a window, leaped on a horse and vanished.[79]

The company fell back on some old plays,[80] then mounted the exciting melodrama *Under the Gaslight*.[81] By the end of *Under the Gaslight*, the audience was so excited "two-thirds of the audience were on their feet."[82] Madame Scheller, a German opera singer, was to leave Salt Lake City to act with the Langrishe company in Montana.[83] She was a dramatic actress, but managers selected plays that also required her sweet vocal performances.[84]

Madame Scheller opened in the "beautiful musical drama of the *Pearl of Savoy,*" earning the most enthusiastic ovation ever extended to any actress in Helena. She was called before the curtain at the end of the first act, and encored in almost every scene; "It seemed one continuous applause throughout the evening."[85] Waldron also did very well, as did most of the others in the company. Madame Scheller's husband J. Guido Methua painted scenery for Langrishe's company, adding to Langrishe's expense. The star salaries of Waldron and Scheller and the size of Langrishe's company made for a costly enterprise. When Madame Scheller joined the company, Langrishe raised the price of admission to two dollars in gold to all parts of the house.[86]

Denver newspapers nagged at Langrishe to return,[87] and his trip home would shortly be facilitated by railroad since the Union Pacific railroad was completed as far as Green River, Wyoming, about 100 miles east of the Utah border, by October 6.[88]

Montanans realized Langrishe had gone to great expense, and when they tendered him a complimentary benefit, the house was well-filled. He was presented a brick of Montana gold valued at $500.[89] (Gold was about $18 per ounce, so the "brick" would have weighed about a pound and a half.) A speaker, Colonel Woolfolk, said, "[W]e can never think of you without a smile. Your face, like that of the ancient Bacchus, will ever be associated in our memories with thoughts of mirth, laughter and joy. I know that Montanans, at

Madame Marie Scheller, German actress and singer. Appeared on London and New York stages before performing in the American West. On Broadway she played Desdemona in *Othello* opposite famed Edwin Booth as Iago (University of Washington Libraries Special Collections, UW 277940Z).

least, would prescribe 'Langrishe bitters' as an infallible cure for the blue devils.... [The brick] is intended ... as a token of our gratitude for the many, very many, delightful entertainments you have afforded us during the past year. We regret to learn that your efforts to amuse us have not been attended with profit to yourself...."[90] The *Weekly Herald* printed a thank you letter from Marie Methua-Scheller which included, "I will not close before expressing my thanks and highest satisfaction for the manner in which Mr. Langrishe has treated me, and the company have supported me, during my long engagement. I wish them health and prosperity, and a good journey...."[91]

The day Langrishe's company left Helena, a reminiscence appeared:

> We well remember when a little cub, we sat perched on the top seat in the canvas theatre of Langrishe and Atwater, in a little village of Illinois, and watched with feelings of wonder and admiration the trials and tribulations of *The Serious Family*, and we then thought Mr. and Mrs. Langrishe were two of the most wonderful people living. While age has blighted the luxuriant vegetation of our youthful opinions, we have never lost for either our admiration or respect. Celebrated throughout the land as an actor and theatrical manager, wherever he casts his lines he calls around him hosts of friends, and departs amid universal regret....[92]

A Helena correspondent of the *Frontier Index,* published wherever the railhead of the Union Pacific had reached each week, carped, "Langrishe with his theatrical troupe has just departed hence for Virginia City and hence to Denver. He claims to have made nothing here, altho' he charged $2 in gold for the privilege of sitting on a broken backed seat through the doleful miseries of *The Colleen Bawn*. Then, too, he had a thousand dollar benefit, and to cap all, a gold brick 'testimonial,' worth five hundred dollars, presentation speech included. Ungrateful! ...Only Chance."[93] (This was probably Chance L. Harris, *Chicago Times* and *Cleveland Plain Dealer* correspondent.)

The Langrishe company, with Waldron, opened a short season in Virginia City, Montana, on October 31. On November 16, the company started for Bear River City, Utah, apparently in their own conveyances.[94] They may have been hauling scenery, including the new sets painted by Methua. They would be invaluable in Denver, since word from there was that times were dull. Extravagant, spectacular shows with splendid scenery could entice audiences when mere dramas could not.

The company reached Salt Lake City about December 7. They were to fill an engagement at the U.S. Army post, Camp Douglas, then "open at the end of the railroad." That would have been at Bear River City, Utah. A few days before Langrishe and company were to appear, thugs and hoodlums formed a mob, released prisoners from jail and burned it, burned the *Frontier Index* newspaper office, had a shootout with the citizens of the town and threatened to burn the city.[95]

9. Into Unknown Perils

Wisely selecting calmer venues for his theatricals, Langrishe's company played six nights in Brigham City, then in Ogden for a few days. He intended to leave for Denver on December 17 by catching the Union Pacific train, by then close to its terminus and the hookup to the Central Pacific at Promontory Point, completion of the transcontinental railroad.

The Langrishe company's train got as far as Fort Bridger, Wyoming, where the engine ground to a stop in snowdrifts. Energetic as usual, Langrishe made the best of the stopover by entertaining the troops there. They were held up for ten days, then proceeded to Cheyenne, arriving on January 5. There they performed at the "old" theatre on Sixteenth street.[96] Cheyenne was barely a year old. They opened with *Maid of Croissey*, and the next night they were to do *The Serious Family*. According to the Cheyenne press, Langrishe's Aminidab Sleek was "enough to make a horse laugh. Go and see the play to-night by all means, and grow fat thereby."[97] (A common expression of that time was "laugh and grow fat.")

They seemed to be doing well, but the *New York Clipper* carried an item that indicated hidden expenses could be high. "An old manager, writing from the West says—'Business for traveling shows, concerts, etc., is almost at a standstill. Not that they do not draw fair houses, but expenses are frightful. Hall rents are higher than even in war times, and advertising very expensive.... Taxes and licenses have to be paid or face a row.'"[98]

The company was greeted eagerly by Denverites, having had few entertainments during the 20-month absence of the Langrishe company. The paper noted: "On the opening night the attendance was large, but it has since dwindled down fearfully, not owing to an unappreciation of the company, but because of hard times. Some claim that the falling off in attendance is due to the price of admission. Mr. Langrishe undoubtedly knows his own business best and knows whether at a lower rate of admission he could pay his expenses, and knowing it are not disposed to question his policy...."[99]

The *Rocky Mountain News* recalled Langrishe's 1860 arrival in Denver and remarked that Mr. and Mrs. Langrishe were the only two left of the original company. The paper added that he had played in Denver in winters and summers in the prosperous mining camps in the mountains in theatres he had fitted up in Central, Georgia Gulch, Delaware Flats, Montgomery, Buckskin Joe, and perhaps others.

> Mr. Langrishe is one of the best comedians in the United States and would be a star actor anywhere in that line, but he prefers to do business for himself and we believe has always done so.... Contrary to common public notions respecting theatrical people, Mr. and Mrs. Langrishe are esteemed as high socially as any in Denver.... Altogether the [Langrishe] company is far better than ordinary theatrical troupes. We never have seen as good playing

in Washington or St. Louis, and have often seen far worse in Chicago, Boston, New York and Philadelphia than is presented nightly at the Denver Theatre in this city.¹⁰⁰

Milton Nobles, a young actor whose career Madame Scheller had advanced, joined the Langrishe company.¹⁰¹ He was to enjoy a long and successful career as actor and writer, fondly remembering his days as a member of Langrishe's company. On February 11, 1869, the Langrishe company sat in a stagecoach between Denver and Cheyenne waiting for a storm to clear up. A cast member with a diamond ring etched into the Concord coach window the following names: "John Langrishe, George Waldron, Jim Griffiths, Jim Martin, George Shields, Ned Shapter, E. Brown, M. Nobles, Mrs. Langrishe, Belle Waldron, Tillie Shields, E. Fitzwilliams. On the Divide, Fby. 11-'69."¹⁰²

Years later, when that Concord coach was discovered in Denver, Milton Nobles purchased it and had it shipped to his farm on Long Island. He used it in several productions of his play *From Sire to Son* where theatres could accommodate the large coach.¹⁰³

In Central City, the editor of the *Central City Register* advised Langrishe to set the price of tickets at a dollar (he'd been charging $1.50 in Denver) and to make improvements in the "old" Montana Theatre. "Central people, though partially relieved from the deadly weight of hard times, are still poor, and can't afford to spend money for trifles in the old extravagant way, that characterized the early days when our theatre was first opened...." They advised repainting the interior and improving the seats. "All our people have suffered martyrdom upon them, and the recollection of it still lives. They should be nicely painted, and the bench part covered with carpeting or other soft, serviceable material to protect one's clothing from the grinding sand that now fills every pore of the old pine boards...."¹⁰⁴

Milton Nobles, Langrishe actor, later manager of his own theatrical company in the East. Author of *Shop Talk*, a collection of theatre anecdotes (University of Washington Libraries Special Collections, UW 36700).

On March 2 Congress passed a bill allowing construction of a railroad connecting with the Union Pacific in Cheyenne, to proceed southward, at least to Denver. Langrishe had anticipated the excitement, preparing a production of Augustin Daly's *Under the Gaslight*. In its sensational climax, an express train rushes toward the hero, who is tied to the railroad tracks. That was the bait his audiences needed.[105]

Milton Nobles later wrote that in this play he was to plunge into the "East River" to rescue the heroine, and opening night, someone awakened a dog he'd adopted and pushed him toward the stage. The dog, having been shorn except for his "mane" and a tuft on his tail and painted in vivid colors, recognized his friend and jumped into the "river," knocking over several "waves" in the process. "Of course there was an encore, during which [dog] George (named for George Waldron) succeeded in leveling the two rows of set waters, exposing the running gear of the profile boat, and finally joining me on the old mattress which constituted the turbulent waters of the East River." The audience loved it, and insisted "George" be allowed to act in all subsequent showings as well. Nobles said one night the dog showed up, cleaned of the garish colors his fellow actors had painted him, but exposing some gilded body parts when he turned his back to the audience.[106] The show ran six or seven nights to full houses.[107] When they returned to calmer dramas, the audience size diminished.

Under the Gaslight made such a hit with Denver playgoers that they re-played the scene with the train rushing into the station following the other dramas for a few nights. Then Langrishe couldn't resist parodying the play. *Under the Kerosene Lamp* or *Denver After Dark* was the afterpiece, drawing roars of laughter with its "train of local hits and jokes, songs, war dances, plots, droll doings, etc., etc.… No more amusing extravaganza was ever put upon the Denver stage."[108] The parody or burlesque was Langrishe's own creation, according to the *New York Clipper*.[109]

Then it was time for another sensational play, Dion Boucicault's *The Long Strike*, which brought the audience to a pitch of excitement. It drew large audiences for the Langrishe company. Langrishe produced this play even before it opened in New York City. It was one of Boucicault's most topical and thrilling dramas.[110] After it was repeated for a few nights, Madame Scheller arrived in town on March 21.[111] She drew large audiences, but apparently not packed houses, after her first night.

According to the Central City paper, "[Langrishe] speaks decidedly well of Montana, but says that the winter is about six months long, and that during that time little can be done in his line, for the reason that very little work can be done, and people do not have money. In Salt Lake he would do well, but for the fact that Brigham Young pockets most of the proceeds…."[112] "Little work could be done" because placer mining relies upon running streams of water, and they were frozen solid in Montana winters.

Langrishe had the old Montana Theatre in Central City spruced up, and sent Madame Scheller and his entire company there on April 18 to open a season.[113] Langrishe did not accompany his troupe, instead traveling to White Pine, Nevada, to explore mining prospects. En route he passed through Corinne, Utah. This simple act and his presence in White Pine were duly reported in city papers as far away as Montana and Wyoming. Montana papers even urged Langrishe to return for a season of theatre.[114]

Back in Central City after his Nevada trip, Langrishe and his wife appeared at the Montana Theatre May 13 for the first time in more than two years, receiving an enthusiastic ovation.[115] They performed in Central City through June 5, then split the troupe, the Langrishes, Jimmy Martin, Griffith and "one or two others" going to Georgetown to give some entertainments. Waldron was to take the rest of the company back to Denver to perform.[116]

Langrishe signed the Howson Opera troupe to perform in Colorado under his management. Later he sent most of his company, including Madame Scheller, to Cheyenne, to perform under the management of George Waldron. Mr. and Mrs. Langrishe, Griffith and Browne played small roles in the Howson Opera Burlesque and Comedy productions.[117] It was hugely popular, both reviewers and box office tills cheering. The "opera" was opera bouffe. For instance, one of the plays was *Ill-treated, Il-trovatore* or the *Mother, the Maiden and the Musicianer*.[118]

Waldron took Langrishe's company on to Laramie July 12.[119] The Howson Opera troupe, with the Langrishes, Griffith and Browne, proved extremely popular in Central City. Langrishe and the Howson troupe returned to Denver on July 19 for a limited engagement. They continued to draw good houses except for the following competition: three or four hundred Utes paraded the streets of Denver on horseback, chanting war songs, then assembled on the north side of the Platte river, celebrating a victory over Kiowas with a scalp dance. They drew a very large audience. The *Rocky Mountain News* complained, "If they had another tune the performance would be more interesting.... [This] is a fine opportunity for our Eastern visitors to see real Indians, observing their ancient customs, and they are proud to show themselves before white spectators."[120] The Utes, mountain dwellers, had not been part of the Sand Creek Massacre.

Langrishe left Denver on July 28 to catch up with his company in Laramie City. They then planned to travel further west via the newly completed railroad.[121]

10

Return to Montana

Langrishe intended for his company to play a brief season in Corinne, Utah, starting August 6, 1869. The *New York Clipper* printed:

> The town is only four months old and consists chiefly of tents. The actors live in *airy* residences on the far-stretching plains, surrounded by the impertinent sagebrush and myriads of greedy grasshoppers. Towards evening you can see them struggling across the dreary desert, through the brush, in all directions, with their wardrobe baskets on their shoulders, wending their way towards the theatre. A novel and touching sight! Board is $4 a day, with heaven for a cover and the wind whistling through every crag; everything else in proportion. Traveling expenses boundless as the sea....[1]

Langrishe and J. Guido Methua preceded the stock company to Montana, having wired friends the date of their arrival by stagecoach because in those days there was no rail connection between Utah and Montana. Impatient friends took buggies some distance out from Helena to meet the stagecoach and to bring Langrishe and Methua into town by private conveyance.[2] Townspeople cheered as they entered the city.[3] Methua was there to paint scenery and help decorate the new theatre. Most of the company was traveling under the "jehuistical" (wagonmaster) care of Billy Wilson, from Corinne to Helena.

The theatre was not completed, so the company was expected to use the old Wood Street Theatre temporarily.[4] The *New York Clipper* reported the new theatre would seat 600 and was to be lighted by gas.[5] Seats for the grand opening were sold by auction, reaping $1500. The opening bill was *The Last Man* with George Waldron and *His Last Legs* with Langrishe. The price of admission was two dollars for all parts of the house.

Mrs. Langrishe temporarily remained in Denver, where she competed in a "lady equestrienne" event at the agricultural fair. She was one of three contestants, driving a handsome pair of cream-colored horses. The *News* observed: "All three ladies managed their horses with great skill, but after a lengthy trial the prize was awarded to Mrs. W.R. Ford."[6]

Langrishe and Methua finished preparing the interior of the new theatre for its September 4 grand opening.[7] Ladies of the Langrishe company arrived by stagecoach; the males (and two musicians) arrived September 2 after an 18-day trip by wagon from Corinne, Utah Territory, after stopping to fish and hunt along the way.[8] They opened Saturday, September 4, and on Monday introduced their star player, Fanny B. Price. The house was "densely crowded" for her debut, and she received "ovation after ovation, and was called before the curtain repeatedly, to receive the acclamations of an enthusiastic multitude."[9]

The editor of the Deer Lodge *New North-West* wrote, "Happy Jack Langrishe, whose comedy acting is good for the soul, was, we are sorry to say, on the broad of his back in a narrow bed, praying for speedy deliverance from a bunion, or some horrible thing on his cheek...."[10] Mrs. Langrishe and J.C. Spencer, the Langrishe company treasurer, arrived from Corinne October 12.[11] She made her first appearance of the season a few nights later as Judy O'Trot in *Ireland As It Was*. The paper wrote of this event:

> Her reception was most enthusiastic. Good ... in many respects she is the best actress that ever appeared in Montana. But we never saw Mrs. Langrishe on the stage. We have visited Langrishe's theatre frequently, too, in the latter years. She was billed to appear, but never came—it was HELEN MC GREGOR; LITTLE TODDLEKINS; Meg Merrilies; Judy O'Trot or Lady Macbeth that appeared. Mrs. Langrishe was *always* left at the wing. Possibly that is one essential of a true actress. Versatile; appreciating with rare judgment the *spirit* of a character, representing her conception of it carefully and continuously while "on"; in a line of comedy and melodrama, truly superior, and off the stage a most estimable lady, it is no wonder that, as the *Herald* has it, "on her first appearance she was met with a perfect torrent of applause, lasting several minutes, it being some time before the play could proceed."[12]

Montana Territory was well into a snowy winter, leading residents to hope for a water-plenty summer, unlike what they had had for the past year. Water had been scarce for sluicing, but when they received an abundance of water, there was a promise of prosperous times.

Langrishe promptly paid his professional bills such as rent, board, salaries and printing, or else people wouldn't have been so enthusiastic about doing business with him. But he neglected his personal bills such as property taxes. In Denver, several of his properties were to be auctioned because of overdue property taxes.[13] Levies on 17 lots, including a house and the Denver Theatre, valued at $6,435, were in arrears, taxes owed $205.92. Apparently he had someone pay his taxes late, in time to avert confiscation of properties.

Appearing on stage in Virginia City for the first time in a year, he was accorded a crowded house and a warm reception.[14] They enjoyed good houses and enthusiastic audiences in Virginia City for about ten days, then returned to Helena March 15.[15] They presented some new plays over the next six weeks, but nothing significant enough to draw very good houses. Until mining resumed, money would be tight. Mining (i.e., sluicing and panning) was not going on because watercourses now were too high with snow melt, and mining would have to wait for creeks and rivers to subside.

In Deer Lodge, the Langrishe company performed in the Masonic Hall without, as the press observed, "a stage or the accessories of good scenery and properties, and limited to the range of pieces presentable under these circumstances, the acting has depended solely upon its own merits ... [but the company] has given universal satisfaction [and] surpassed the expectations of even those who were aware of the fact that Mr. Langrishe has one of the best stock companies in America."[16] They played in Deer Lodge for ten days, then traveled to Pioneer to perform for two nights before returning to Helena by May 15. There a new star, Jean Clara Walters, joined them.[17]

They opened the Helena season with *Lucretia Borgia* and drew lavish praise and audience acclaim.[18] The *Herald* extolled Walters as the best actress ever in specified roles, nearly all of which had been enacted by Mrs. Langrishe, evoking the same comments from the press.

On June 14, Langrishe went to Deer Lodge to see about buying a building to house a theatre there.[19] Purchase of a large building was arranged, but two of the owners were out of town. The building needed extensive alterations, so that awaited the return of the partners and the deed signing.[20]

Over 100 prominent Helena officials and businessmen tendered a complimentary benefit to Langrishe, with E.R. Collins volunteering his acting services for "old and esteemed friend Langrishe."[21] Collins was probably the "Harry Collins" who arrived in Denver in September 1860 with Langrishe, and perhaps was the "Mr. Collins" with Langrishe in 1847. Once a professional actor, he had retired to spend time prospecting.[22]

After performing in Diamond City for 11 days, they returned to Helena for two days, then traveled over the mountains to Deer Lodge.[23] They left Deer Lodge August 5 for Pike's Peak, Missoula, Frenchtown and Cedar Creek.[24]

The company was large, and Langrishe had to pay fares for all members of his company, so this was a costly venture for him. About August 15 they played in Beartown, then to Frenchtown August 16 and 17, and in the basement hall of the Louiseville Hotel the night of the 19th and the rest of the week.[25] After Missoula, they played a few days in Bear Gulch, then Beartown.[26] In Beartown, Langrishe apparently tripped on the board sidewalk, impressing locals with his "dance" to right himself.[27] One of his company, William J. Gross, later wrote that in Cedar Creek, they had performed in a cellar. Then they left their wagon at the mouth of a gulch, packed their scenery and costumes on the animals and all walked six miles to the town of Bear Gulch, where they created a "theatre" out of a butcher shop. They knocked out a partition, made bench seats out of rough boards, and used the floor for a stage. They charged two dollars per ticket, enjoyed crowded houses and played there for two weeks. There was only one woman living in the gulch at that time. When they left, hiking out of the gulch, "inhabitants turned out *en masse* and escorted the actors a long distance on the trail."[28]

A community did not have to be populous for Langrishe to make money. Theatre was such a rare treat for men in isolated locations they went to the theatre every night the theatre was open. Even in Helena, people attended the theatre at least two or three times each week. Langrishe's nightly change of bill kept them interested, too.

Charles Couldock and his daughter arrived in Helena on September 23 to begin another engagement with the Langrishe company.[29] They opened September 24 with *The Chimney Corner* to a large and appreciative audience. That night there was a vivid display of the northern lights, clearly visible as the audience left the theatre.[30] Couldocks and the Langrishe company attracted large audiences, although the plays they presented had been performed in Helena during Couldocks' previous engagement there in 1867.[31]

Even though Montana Territory was becoming more civilized, the preponderance of the population was still male. The 1870 census figures indicated about three males to one woman: 20,580 total in Helena, including 14,582 white males.[32]

Langrishe closed the Helena season November 5 and took the Couldocks and his company to Deer Lodge to perform.[33] His Deer Lodge engagement, originally scheduled for one week,

Charles Walter Couldock and daughter Eliza in a scene from their signature production of *The Chimmney Corner*. Sadly, Eliza died shortly after their western tour in 1872 (Billy Rose Theatre Collection, The New York Public Library for the Performing Arts, Astor, Lenox and Tilden Foundation, Th-05288).

expanded to two because of large audiences. Langrishe let it be known that he would be leaving the Territory, perhaps for good, and the Couldocks, too, would be moving on. The *New North-West* reported Langrishe's actual expenses were $150 per day, so he must have been making a profit to have stayed over for two weeks.[34]

The troupe returned to Helena and performed for a few nights, then left for Utah via stagecoach. They arrived in Corinne December 11 and proceeded to Salt Lake City, where they played an engagement.[35] They opened to a good house on December 14 and performed for a week with part of the resident stock company, then were joined by Couldocks about December 22, and all performed through December 31.[36]

They then backtracked to Corinne where the Couldocks and the Langrishe company performed from January 2 through 9, to large appreciative audiences.[37] Businessmen there tendered a "public benefit" to Langrishe in "evidence of their friendly regard." One of the signers of the testimonial, Adam Aulbach, would play a major part in Langrishe's life more than a decade later.[38]

Langrishe started east ahead of the troupe, on January 9.[39] They intended to open at the Denver Theatre January 16. Waldron had the "new" Langrishe company in Central City for a winter engagement.[40] Admission to the Denver Theatre was 50 cents to the gallery, one dollar to other parts of the house. A large audience greeted the reappearance of the Couldocks and the Langrishe company, the Langrishes especially warmly welcomed when both appeared in the farce.[41] They had "well-filled" houses for the rest of the month. As noted in the press:

> [Langrishe] does not forget the fact that certain classes visit the theatre more for rollicking jollity of the farces than for the pathos of melodrama or the passion of tragedy, and he consequently puts upon the boards each evening some one of his side-splitting farces in which himself and Mr. Martin conspire to wage havoc upon weak buttons and tender shirt collars.... The unities of the play [*King Lear*] were somewhat marred by the insufficient supernumerary resources; and the marching of a legion of soldiers (comprising two awkward supes) across the imaginary field, was high sport for the gallery gods ... and brought broad grins to the faces of stern critics.[42]

The Couldocks concluded their Denver engagement February 11 and moved to Central City to perform there. Marietta Ravel, a celebrated pantomimist and tight-rope performer who worked those talents into certain plays, began her Denver starring run February 13.[43]

Langrishe's benefit was set for March 8, when he'd play his "favorite role," that of John Unit in *Self* by Mrs. Bateman. The next week Langrishe and his company were to go to Central City for two weeks.[44] In Central City, they had an "immense crowd" for opening night, and "the reappearance of Jack Langrishe and Mrs. Langrishe elicited cheers from a house full of old friends, who have known and appreciated them for the last decade…"[45] The *Register* reported one man said he "got his money's worth in seeing Jack Langrishe switch his nose around like the proboscis of an elephant."[46]

McKee Rankin and Kitty Blanchard joined Langrishe's company and performed in Central City, then moved to Denver, opening April 17 in *Fanchon*. A reviewer wrote: "The stock gave [Kitty Blanchard] good support, Mr. Langrishe was sweetly angelic [sic] as Queen Catherine…. The play was by no means perfect; yet it was very well rendered considering the imperfect appointments and the hasty preparation…."[47]

Then Jack Langrishe went east on "theatrical and other business."[48]

11

Chicago

W.N. Byers, publisher of the *Rocky Mountain News,* and one of the first Denverites to meet Langrishe in Colorado, wrote letters of introduction to editors of the *Chicago Tribune,* dated June 12, 1871, to "commend to your friendship and confidence my esteemed friend, John S. Langrishe, of this city who visits Chicago on business in which the *Tribune* influence may be important. Be assured it will not be undeserved."[1] The *Chicago Journal's* Denver correspondent had already written of Langrishe:

> As an eccentric comedian, King Solomon himself could not refrain from a hearty outburst of laughter, while looking and listening to John S. Langrishe. As an Irish comedian, he has no living superior. It might safely be said that John S. Langrishe and John Collins are the only portrayers living of the Irish character, since the death of Tyrone Powers [sic]. An Irishman himself, who has carefully studied the various phases of the Irish character at home, Langrishe can "hold the mirror up to nature" in this country.... As a citizen who has lent his mite to build up Denver, he is highly respected, and no matter what demand may come for any charitable purpose, it will find his large Irish heart open.[2]

On June 18, word came that Langrishe had leased Wood's Museum in Chicago. There had been no mention of Mrs. Langrishe being with him or with the stock company in Central City, but it's likely she had accompanied him to the Chicago area. Her sister, Laurette (Mrs. J. B. Atwater), lived in Geneva, Illinois, near Chicago. Before the company opened in Chicago, the Langrishes' two-story frame dwelling on Welton Street burned down. It had been rented out, and was not insured.[3]

Langrishe's Chicago stock company consisted of Langrishe, J.K. Mortimer, Isabella Freeman, Emma Maddern, Lizzie and Annie Mahon, Mrs. Charles Walcott, Messrs. Griffith and C. H. Wilson, Mr. and Mrs. Langdon and Messrs. T.C. Howard, Richmond and Gross.[4] The cast was augmented by Charles Wells, J.M. Mason, W. Treville, C. Clements, L. Munroe and J.L. Saphore. Their opening play was to be "Sheridan's brilliant comedy in five acts, entitled the *School for Scandal*."[5]

They opened August 14, the Museum festooned with evergreens and hanging baskets filled with vines and flowers. Each lady was given a small bouquet. The Chicago *Tribune* thought *School for Scandal* was too trying for an opening test piece. The critic did conclude, however, that Langrishe was an excellent manager in that the play moved smoothly from first to last without "hitching" of scenes or mistakes on the part of anyone on the stage. Best of all, the piece moved rapidly, the waits between the acts being cut down in every instance to about a minute. The critic added: "Mr. Langrishe is evidently a fine comedian, and this fact, coupled with a purely comedy face, somewhat militated at times against his efforts to adapt himself to serious or pathetic passages. Mr. Langrishe will never be able to make his face look serious, which makes us all the more eager to see him in a purely comedy line...."[6] The *Tribune* was not favorably impressed with some of the minor players, but the Chicago *Evening Journal* thought the production "most satisfactory." That newspaper also emphasized the fact that policemen were "engaged to detect and expel any improper characters who might seek to attend either the dramatic department or the Museum.... Our ladies will find this is a time and place where they can go unattended by gentlemen, and find enjoyment without the apprehension of anything in the least to mar their pleasure."[7]

Charles Wells, a beginning actor in the company who kept a diary, reported that he started at a salary of $18 per week for performing six nights and two matinees weekly.[8] He had been recommended to Langrishe by J.B. Atwater, his brother-in-law and former business partner, who had trained Wells in an amateur theatre group in Geneva, Illinois.

After two nights, the company presented *London Assurance*, in which Langrishe played Sir Harcourt Courtly. The Chicago *Times* did not care for Langrishe's portrayal: "Chicago has been peculiarly favored in its representatives of Sir Harcourt Courtly, in the past.... We are anxious to see him in genuine low comedy, where he must be most congenially at home."[9] They repeated that play, and the Chicago *Tribune* said that "line of English comedies ... has never drawn in this city" and urged management to get out of that rut. "Mr. Langrishe played *Sir Harcourt*, but he was not *Sir Harcourt*. It was entirely out of his line of business. In low comedy we can imagine that he will prove a great success, but in such roles of genteel comedy as he has thus far been playing he is not successful, simply because nature is against him."[10] The Chicago *Evening Journal* declared: "[T]he success of Colonel Wood's Museum is now established, and since its opening ... crowded and delighted audiences have witnessed every performance.... J.S. Langrishe, the manager and comedian, has proved a great attraction in the higher walks of comedy, and when we see him, as we shall the coming week, in such characters as *Ben Bobbin* and *Dr. Ollapod*, we feel convinced he will be endorsed by the Chicago public as he has been elsewhere—one of the very best low comedians of the age."[11]

The Chicago *Times* printed a note from the Madison, Wisconsin, *Democrat* about Langrishe:

> Who of the "oldest residents in this section" would not be delighted to take by the hand their old friend—the inimitable comedian? What would not old Madisonians give to see that extremely funny "phiz" once more upon the stage. "Toodles" has not appeared upon the Madison stage since the departure of Langrishe. "Aminidab Sleek" has never appeared true to life; "Dr. O'Callaghan," "Sir Peter Teazle," a score of other first-class characters have failed comparatively, to come up to nature since the days of this great actor. With our handsome opera-house and excellent stage, Mr. L., with a good company, would prove a powerful attraction. Could he not be induced to pay our city a visit next winter, while the legislature is in session.[12]

The Chicago Times lambasted the Langrishe company when they replaced *Simpson and Co.* and *The Irish Lion* with *Speed the Plough*. "Chicago is not prepared to meekly deglutinate old English comedy without the school of the drama in reference is accompanied by something approximating to either a strong cast or handsome mounting. The first of these is out of the question with the present capabilities of the Museum company. The second does not appear to enter into the ideas of the manager of the house under any circumstances."[13]

On October 8, 1871, at about 9 p.m., Mrs. O'Leary's cow allegedly kicked over a kerosene lantern starting the fire that consumed much of Chicago, the greatest city conflagration in America. Wind blew strongly from the southwest, spreading the fire toward the center of the city. About midnight Monday, October 9, rain began to quench the fire. By then 300 Chicagoans had perished, 90,000 were homeless and property loss was estimated at $200 million.[14]

All but one theatre in the city was incinerated. The only structure usable as a theatre was the Globe, on Desplaines Street, owned by the German Workingmen's Association. All of the theatre managers competed for possession of the Globe, but Wood and Langrishe won. Nearly all of the actors in the city had lost their essential wardrobes, a loss so devastating that many had left the city. The city was under martial law, General Philip Sheridan in command.

Mr. and Mrs. Langrishe were away at the time of the fire, in "blissful ignorance of the disaster until all was over."[15] Langrishe had reportedly "lost everything." That would have been his wardrobe, sets, properties, scripts and even the Montana skull he'd been using for Yorick's in *Hamlet*. He mortgaged the Denver Theatre by wire to get re-started, and by October 21 he was ready to open the Globe Theatre. Langrishe assembled some members of his Wood's

Museum company and hired actors and actresses from other theatres to fill holes left by those who had fled. His new leading lady was Blanche De Bar, daughter of Junius Brutus Booth, elder brother of Edwin and John Wilkes Booth, and niece of Ben De Bar, who had been stage director at the Chatham Theatre when John S. Langrishe made his American debut there in 1845.[16]

In Denver, a concert was held October 31, given by St. John's choir and "the Denver band," proceeds to go to "Mr. J.S. Langrishe, who suffered extensively in the Chicago fire...."[17] The *News* assured readers: "Mr. Langrishe is not one to stay down in the world, and would be too proud to accept a charity, and as such this proposed benefit is not to be construed. It is simply a testimonial of esteem to a worthy man, or rather a part payment of a debt of gratitude to one who has done much for our city...."[18]

Langrishe presented *Who's Who* and *Won at Last* on opening evening, October 21, at Chicago's Globe Theatre,. It was well-attended, the first dramatic entertainment in the city since October 7.[19] They performed old comedies while rehearsing Augustin Daly's *Divorce*, then opened that about November 13, with new scenery painted by his old Colorado set painter DeWitt C. Waugh and J. Howard Rogers.[20] Before *Divorce* opened, the Chicago *Tribune* groused about the condition of the Globe Theatre: "It is dirty, dingy and forbidding, bare of suitable furniture or any pretense to carpets, the voice of the actors being frequently drowned in the din of scuffling boots over pine floors...."[21] Later the *Tribune* added, "We hope soon to be able to announce that the Globe has been put in condition more approaching a theatre than a rat pit."[22]

J.K. Mortimer was fired from the company for his "inevitable failing" (alcoholism) and replaced by Matt V. Lingham.[23] A German opera company was booked[24] and Langrishe left a few members of his stock company in Chicago to play between opera performance nights at the Globe, but took the rest of the company to Milwaukee and Madison for short seasons.[25] In Wisconsin, the acting company was advertised as "Col. J.H. Wood's" troupe. They opened in Milwaukee on Monday, February 12, with *Shoddy* in which Langrishe portrayed John Unit. Langrishe reportedly owned this play, but character names are those of characters in *Self* or *The Rich of New York*. *Shoddy* may have been a parody, written by Langrishe,[26] or it may have been an effort to avoid paying royalties to the playwright. Mrs. Langrishe was to enact the role of Tommy Dobbs in *The Omnibus* on February 16. "Mr. Langrishe was immense in the character of Aminidab Sleek. Indeed, we do not know as we have ever seen that character better given. His sighs and groans were terribly profound, while one look at that cunningly solemn face and those upturned eyes was enough to amply repay one for attending...."[27]

From Milwaukee they went to Madison, where the Langrishes and their company had played throughout the legislative sessions from 1852 through 1858. The local paper commented:

> The older citizens of Madison will remember as far back as 1849 [incorrect], when Messrs. Langrishe and Atwater came to our place with the first theatrical company ever brought here, and gave their exhibitions in LEWIS' HALL [sic] on Wisconsin Avenue. The company was a good one; the Hall was a bad one; but there was real enjoyment there. The company performed very well; the people were terribly crowded, but they were good natured, and made themselves happy in their discomfort.... It is now thirteen years since Mr. LANGRISHE, with his company, has been in Madison. Since that time he has been in the far West, making Denver his headquarters, and we are glad to learn, has made a comfortable fortune.... Mr. and Mrs. LANGRISHE, sustained by a first-class company, will reappear in Madison ... on Monday evening.... [W]e can assure our readers who attend, that they had better see to it, that the buttons on their garments are strongly fastened. Side-splitting may be expected. We have a good hall now, and we trust our citizens will meet this old friend with a full house, that will assure him that he is not forgotten by his early admirers. Let the capacity of the Opera House be fully tested on this greeting of an old favorite.[28]

In another item the press declared:

> Jack Langrishe—There was a time when the bare mention of this name within the range of Madison ears would almost involuntarily stir the risibles of the listeners to their very depths. Who has not heard of Jack Langrishe? What fun-loving Wisconsiner that has not tested the blessings of a round, hearty laugh at the unrivaled mimicry of Jack Langrishe? What *habitue* of the Capital in days gone by that has not been tempted to effect insurance against riven sides and loss of vest buttons, at the grotesque facial delineations of that prince of comic actors, Jack Langrishe?
>
> Since it is announced that Madison's old and best favorite, and his ensemble and talented lady are going to dispense good cheer on Madison boards, we have it from many who long since ceased to frequent theatrical delineations that they will go, just to "see" Jack once more....[29]

The company opened with *The Serious Family* and *The Omnibus*, Mrs. Langrishe to appear in the latter. The press commented: "Mrs. Langrishe ... on her first appearance, perhaps received the greatest applause of the evening. Mrs. L. was always a great favorite with Madisonians, and her many friends were glad to greet her last evening."[30]

The citizens of Madison funded a complimentary benefit for Langrishe, holding them an extra evening. "Hundreds of requests" were for him to play in *Toodles*. They started that evening with Langrishe's "favorite role" of O'Callaghan in *His Last Legs*. The next play was *Delicate Ground*, and the evening topped off with *Toodles*, Langrishe playing Timothy and Mrs. Langrishe playing Mrs. Toodles. The hall was well filled, some estimated an audience of nearly 1200 people.[31]

Glowing with success, Langrishe and his company returned to Chicago in time to perform a matinee Saturday, February 24, at the Globe. Langrishe

Jack Langrishe as O'Callaghan in *His Last Legs*, a farce he frequently presented in Colorado and Montana (Denver Public Library, Western History Collection, F4516).

11. Chicago

took his first Chicago benefit on March 30, playing Aminidab Sleek in *The Serious Family* and Pat Rooney in *Horse Railroad*, which is probably *The Omnibus* under a catchier title. Mrs. Langrishe was to play Tommy Dobbs in the latter piece, "coming out of private life, and in her first appearance in Chicago."[32]

Langrishe had a good house, but not a full house for his benefit, held the night of a heavy rainstorm.[33] The *Chicago Tribune* described the event:

> Since Langrishe came to this city he has by his good qualities made many friends. He was the first to restore the drama to an almost destroyed city. For the smoke had not yet been lifted from the blackened ruins, when the old Museum company, under his management, were playing to a trembling public.... [Mrs. Langrishe] was met with a hearty reception. At the conclusion of the first play Mr. Langrishe was called before the curtain, and after he had made a brief speech of thanks he was completely surprised by having presented to him a magnificent set of silverware. The manager, however, was for the moment nonplussed; but he expressed his thanks for the costly gift in a suitable manner. The service was presented him by the members of the company and numerous other friends.[34]

Langrishe may have seen the musical that had drawn so much attention, *The Black Crook*, and must have heard or read about its success. He had no firsthand knowledge of its power to attract until he and his players performed in support of A.M. Palmer's *Black Crook* company in late April.

Opening night, after every seat had been sold, the cashier began selling standing room, and for that the dollars continued to flow. Three weeks later, attendance was still excellent, houses still nearly full.

Langrishe's troupe ended their Globe Theatre engagement on May 4 and began an extensive tour, beginning in Green Bay.[35] Langrishe's Star Company included himself and Mrs. Langrishe, Blanche De Bar, Fanny Burt, Mrs. Stoneall, Lizzie and Annie Mahon, M.V. Lingham, J.K. Vernon, W.J. Gross, T.C. Howard, Jimmy Martin, Jimmy Griffith and Charles Wells. They played in Green Bay through May 15, performing Langrishe's standard repertoire of 16 plays, all old by then.[36] From there they went to Oshkosh, where the newspaper remarked, "With a broad-brimmed hat, a countenance of lugubrious solemnity and a dolorous voice which resembled the filing of a crosscut saw, Langrishe's conception of the character of Sleek was well portrayed. Although not as outrageously funny as the rendering of the same character by John Dillon, the Aminidab Sleek of Langrishe is more true to life, more unexceptionally dismal and forbidding, more sanctimonious, and hence more perfect."[37]

Langrishe set out to build up his finances and keep his company together while arrangements for his own *Black Crook* company proceeded in New York. They played in St. Paul, Minnesota, where two members of his cast, Lizzie Mahon and Matt V. Lingham, married.[38] The troupe opened in Minneapolis June 14, performing *Society* or *The Rich of New York* instead of *Shoddy*. The U.S.

Copyright law had been strengthened in 1870, and managers were supposed to pay royalties to authors. Many evaded royalties by changing the name of the play, and Langrishe may have been doing that too. They played in Stillwater, Minnesota, then went on to perform in the Wisconsin cities of Eau Claire, Chippewa Falls, Sparta and La Crosse before returning to Minnesota to appear at Winona,[39] Rochester[40] and Lake City. They next appeared at McGregor and Dubuque in Iowa. They probably took water transportation to Davenport, Iowa, opening there on September 23. The *Davenport Democrat* reported:

> Unheralded by any Patagonian posters in flaming colors irradiating our board fences, the Langrishe Comedy Company dropped in at our Opera House last night and took the town, or at least such portion of it as were induced by an excellent bill to attend. The fine old English Comedy of *The Poor Gentleman*, by George Colman, the younger, first played in 1802, was produced and rendered in a manner highly creditable, proving that the company as a whole is superior to any thing of its class, we have had for a very long time. Although the "cutting" especially in the first act was, to an old play goer, cruel, yet the piece went off swimmingly. Mr. Langrishe, though evidently suffering from a bad cold, gave the military apothecary with vim and humor....[41]

One of the company, Charles Wells, later wrote that the hotel had loaned them a mattress to break the fall of one of the characters in the play from a supposedly high cliff. The hotel owner, thinking he was doing them a favor, sent his softest feather bed, which proved inadequate to "break a fall." The company now had an actor with a broken ankle.[42]

The audience was small, and the editor of the *Democrat*, who might have been a former actor, or "old stager," was incensed. "We boast of our esthetic tastes, talk largely of our cultivation, of high class are the patronage of the legitimate, grumble at the lack of amusements—and when a really talented, first class company comes along with sterling pieces, and splendid actors, we leave them to play to a beggarly account of empty boxes."[43] Each night thereafter, the house was fuller than the previous evening. The company then crossed the Mississippi to open in Rock Island, Illinois, on September 30, the same day the *Davenport Democrat* printed a request for Langrishe to return to Davenport for another season. It was signed by about 300 men.[44]

In Colorado at this time, Langrishe's Montana Theatre in Central City was sold at auction to satisfy a promissory note.[45] He had taken out the loan on June 8, 1871, just before he left for Chicago.

A *New York Clipper* advertisement for 30 first class coryphées and ballet ladies for a six-month season of *The Black Crook* in New England revealed what Langrishe and his people had planned. The ballerinas were to address immediately "Herr Charles Carle, ballet master, 440 Michigan Ave., Chicago."[46] Coryphées were ranked above members of the *corps de ballet* but below soloists.

Rock Island audiences grew larger each day the Langrishe company played there.⁴⁷ They crossed the Mississippi River yet again, to start a new engagement at Davenport, Iowa. This time, the press reported, they "had a house of which any artists might be proud. Our most fashionable ladies, our best citizens and our really critical judges of dramatic excellence were present, and all were more than pleased, they were delighted...."⁴⁸ They played through October 12 in Davenport, then crossed the river again to Peoria, Illinois,⁴⁹ thence to Bloomington and Springfield,⁵⁰ and then to Terre Haute, Indiana, opening November 4.⁵¹

Langrishe was now taking a benefit every Friday evening. Then they opened in Toledo, Ohio, November 18 at Wheeler's Opera House⁵² to a less than full house. The *New York Clipper* reported that a "horse epidemic" in the Toledo area had "proved disastrous to the business of the company" because there was no public transportation to and from the theatre.⁵³ They performed through Nov. 23, then left by train for Providence, Rhode Island, to rehearse and prepare for a *Black Crook* tour of New England.⁵⁴

Theatre poster for Langrishe's Black Crook Company of tour in New England. New Bedford's Liberty Hall, May 13, 1873 (courtesy of the Trustees of the New Bedford Free Public Library).

12

The *Black Crook* Venture

The Black Crook is acknowledged to be America's first musical comedy, but the comedy was a minor part, the whole gleaned from *Faust, The Naiad Queen, Lurline* and other plays and spectacles of the time, the music from *Der Freischutz* and similar works.[1] The real attraction was scantily clad ballerinas, lavish costumes, variety show components tucked in here and there, fantastic sets, phantasmagoria, calcium lights and transformation scenes. Phantasmagoria were scenes that seemed real, dreamt or imagined.

In a day when the sight of a woman's ankle was cause for men to swoon, sheer or form-fitting costumes in theatres were scandalous. Ministers railed at the show from the pulpit, unintentionally guaranteeing larger audiences for the show. Curiously, almost identical costumes were worn by circus performers, eliciting no such outcry or audience obsession. Scantily clad ballerinas enticed the audience, the theatrical magic and audiences attracted Langrishe.

Langrishe's company had performed the comedy portion of the play in Chicago and when Dr. A.M. Palmer took his sets, costumes, ballerinas and paraphernalia back to New York, Langrishe wasted little time in planning his own production of that play. T.C. Howard, a Langrishe actor, agreed to be business manager, and Charles Carle came into the partnership as manager of the dancers.

They negotiated a contract to perform *The Black Crook* in New England for six months. Once their sets, costumes and cast were ready, they opened in Providence, Rhode Island, on December 2, at Harrington's Opera House.[2] They remained there for two weeks while they worked out the scene changes, timing and other mechanics of the production. Langrishe and his wife performed in the comedic portion of *The Black Crook* and he made sure the entire production moved briskly along.

After those first two weeks, they performed one, two or three nights in each community that had a stage large enough to accommodate at least most of their sets and machinery. It took four railroad cars to haul the company, scenery, sets and apparatus.[3] Most of the time the production was put on by a cast of 124, but variety performers came and went. They played only in very large theatres, capable of holding crowds sufficiently large to cover expenses at 50 cents per admission. Producers had to pay train fare and lodging, at a dollar to a dollar and a quarter per night, usually at least two to a bed, plus meals.[4] Expenses were said to be $500 per day.[5]

They ensured full houses by arranging for excursion trains to carry *Black Crook* fans for half-fare from towns near the main theatres.[6] They performed six nights and two matinees per week. Their first tour went to Worcester, Massachusetts; Woonsocket, and Newport, Rhode Island; Taunton and New Bedford, Massachusetts; Hartford, New Haven, Bridgeport and Waterbury, Connecticut; Springfield, Chelsea and Salem, Massachusetts; Portland and Biddeford, Maine; Manchester, New Hampshire, and again in Massachusetts, Lawrence, Lowell, Lynn, Chelsea, Taunton, Bridgewater and Pittsfield, then on to Danbury, Norwalk and Hartford, Connecticut, and back to Providence, Rhode Island, where they had started the tour.

During their first tour through New England, word spread that there was nothing objectionable (other than revealing costumes) in this production, and that the show was entertaining. But there was sufficient question in the minds of some men who had never seen the show but felt they were approaching the grave and might not get another chance, so they attended.[7]

One night Mrs. Langrishe was ill, but the show had to go on, so five-foot Jimmy Griffith, bald since youth, donned her costume and a wig and played in her stead. Charles B. Wells recalled seeing Griffith "standing back of the wings at the closing of the last act, having taken off the woman's wig, but still wearing the skirt and costume of the Old Dame, a pipe in his teeth, his bald head glistening above the lace ruff, while holding high a pan of red fire for the final tableau."[8]

They started another tour, enjoying the fruits of their reputation for reliability and inoffensiveness, going to Woonsocket, Worcester, Springfield, New Haven, Waterbury, Bridgeport, Middletown, Meriden, Lowell, Manchester, Portsmouth, Portland, Bath, Lewiston, Bangor, Augusta, Biddeford, Dover, Haverhill, Lawrence, Newburyport, Salem, Amesbury Mills, Lynn, Taunton, New Bedford, Willimantic, Hartford, Middletown, Meriden, Westfield and Pittsfield. On both tours they skipped Boston, primarily because Boston had suffered a devastating fire in November 1872. In 1873 they performed at Boston's Howard Atheneum from May 26 to June 4, drawing excellent crowds.

Two of the prima ballerinas, Emily and Betty Rigl, were devout Catholics. At "every performance while standing in the wings waiting for their entrance for the dance they were invariably telling over their beads, winding up with a hasty signing of the cross as they dashed onto the stage."[9]

The *Hartford Daily Courant* put its finger on part of *The Black Crook*'s success: "[It's] a medley of everything that is amusing. Drills of fantastically armed girls, dances of demons, learned dogs, comic ballet scenes, lightning zouave manual of arms, acrobatic feats and everything else that dazzles or entertains is put on. The whole hinges on the skeleton of a plot which nobody cares for, but the scenes of which give the performers an occasional resting spell...."[10]

When Howard, Langrishe and Carle's *Black Crook* closed in Boston, the proprietors and the cast traveled directly to Buffalo, New York. *Black Crook* playwright Charles Barras had recently died intestate, the question of ownership of the play undetermined. Two producing companies claimed to have exclusive rights, but until claims were sorted out in court, Langrishe and his partners decided to use another tactic. They wrote and copyrighted a work titled *The Magic Talisman*, had new sets painted for the show and opened it in Buffalo with their *Black Crook* company.

Critics saw *The Magic Talisman* was a slight variation on the *Black Crook* script and regarded it with some disdain. *The Magic Talisman* still had the ballerinas in tights, and that drew fairly large audiences, although not as large as *The Black Crook* drew. After their Buffalo run, they went on to Cleveland, Columbus, Dayton and Toledo, Ohio, then to Detroit, where Langrishe himself was accused of vulgarity and profanity.[11]

From *The Magic Talisman* in Detroit, they crossed the border into Canada, and the show again became *The Black Crook*, using the same cast, sets, properties and costumes. They played in Toronto, Brantford, Hamilton, London and Chatham, Ontario. They then crossed back into the U.S., performing *The Magic Talisman* at Jackson, Michigan, and Fort Wayne, Logansport, Lafayette and Indianapolis, Indiana, then to Louisville, Kentucky and Cincinnati, Ohio, for the grand re-opening of the Robinson Opera House. That coincided with the Cincinnati Industrial Exposition that attracted visitors to that city for the next month.[12]

From Cincinnati, *The Magic Talisman* continued to Hamilton, Dayton, Canton and Youngstown, Ohio; Erie, Oil City, Titusville, Corry, Meadville, Franklin, Pittsburgh, Harrisburg, Reading, Easton, Wilkes-Barre and Scranton, Pennsylvania; Binghamton, Hornellsville, Rochester, Utica and Troy, New York. Expenses were still high, but box office receipts were not as munificent as they had been when playing *The Black Crook*. Two ballerinas, owed $375, "levied upon the scenery and effects of the show."[13] The proprietors wired to New York for money and reached an amicable settlement, the sets and machinery freed for performance.

Langrishe, Carle, and T.C. Houghton (T.C. Howard's real name) copyrighted *The Banshee* and *The White Crook* on November 12. Like *The Magic Talisman*, no script was submitted to the copyright office; a printed title page sufficed.

The company went to New Haven, Connecticut, obtained new scenery and some new costumes, and performed *The White Crook* or *The Magic Talisman* in New Haven, Hartford, Meriden, Bridgeport and Winsted, Connecticut; Springfield, Massachusetts; Providence, Woonsocket and Newport, Rhode Island, and Taunton, Massachusetts. A Rhode Island paper revealed that the *Magic Talisman* company "lost forty thousand dollars this season during the panic. They have only recently commenced to put money in their purse again."[14] The troupe went on to Salem and Lowell, Massachusetts, Manchester and Portsmouth, New Hampshire; and Biddeford and Portland, Maine. For this New England tour, their advertising billed "The Black Crook Company" in large type and *The Magic Talisman* in smaller type, intending to influence editors and audiences with their reputation of inoffensive productions, while using *The Black Crook* title to draw audiences.

The tour continued to Lawrence, Massachusetts; Nashua, New Hampshire; Concord, Lynn, Chelsea and New Bedford, Massachusetts; Providence and Woonsocket, Rhode Island; and Willimantic, Norwich, New London, Danbury, Norwalk, Bridgeport, New Haven, Ansonia, Waterbury and Winsted, Connecticut. They tested the waters with *The Black Crook* in New Haven and in Meriden, then the "reconstructed" *Black Crook* in Hartford, then Springfield, Massachusetts. There the press stated: "The pecuniary value that attaches to the name *Black Crook* is really astonishing. Howard, Langrishe & Carle have been running *The Magic Talisman* this winter, their right to play *The Black Crook* having been disputed; but they found the former play unprofitable, and having ascertained that they have as good a right to the latter as anybody, they have returned to it and to prosperity...."[15]

They toured *The Black Crook* to Springfield, Worcester, Lowell, Fitchburg, Athol and Greenfield, Massachusetts; Brattleboro, Bellows Falls, Burlington and Rutland, Vermont; then Montreal, Quebec and Ottawa, before returning to the U.S. By that time Langrishe had acquired a new partner-investor, T.R. Glenn (Carle had bowed out). The company played in Ogdensburg, New York, Kingston, Ontario, Toronto and Belleville, Hamilton, London, and Chatham, Ontario, then Detroit, where Langrishe and Glenn bought sets, properties and costumes for *The Black Crook* from Dr. Palmer, the previous New York producer. Langrishe and Glenn then took most of the company and equipment to New York, to board the steamship *Acapulco* starting for San Francisco via the isthmus of Panama.[16]

Mrs. Langrishe rode on the new transcontinental railroad to Cheyenne, then the Denver & Rio Grande train to Denver, to visit friends. There she performed in *The Omnibus* for George Waldron's benefit.[17] She arrived in San Francisco one day before her husband and the company arrived August 4.

They opened in San Francisco, claiming the sets, costumes, etc., were purchased at a cost of over $25,000. The spectacular transformation scene alone cost $11,000.[18] Langrishe and his partners had also invested heavily in the dancers and variety artists so essential to *The Black Crook*'s success. Dances and some variety acts were integrated into the action of the play and others were performed between the acts. Langrishe had hired some of the best talent available. Dance portions, such as the play's famed "March of the Amazons," featured Jeanette Proscher, "Premier Danseuse Assoluta," supported by four lead dancers along with a "selected Ballet troupe of Beautiful ladies."[19] Variety artists included: "The wonderful Runnells Family, the Peers of the Arena; Chas. E. Dobson, the King Banjoist; Frank R. Clifton in his double Pirouette on the Horizontal Bar; ... Miss Frankie Etta in her Clog Hornpipe; Mr. Frank Hanchett in his curious coil of contortions; Mr. Ernst Lorenzen in his wonderful performance on wood and straw [and] Master Bonnie Runnells, the very best Dutch comedian of the age."[20]

After weeks in San Francisco they went to San Jose, Stockton and Sacramento. In Sacramento, someone realized that young hoodlums had gained access to the attic, where they could look through ventilators and see the show. Several men, including police, went upstairs to dislodge them. When the boys scattered and some making missteps, their legs passed through the ceiling and dangled in sight of the audience below. Plaster falling and the jar of the building by the scattering youth convinced the audience there was an earthquake and people started to leave. Several called upon the audience to resume their seats, and eventually calm returned.

After leaving Sacramento, Langrishe's company played a final California engagement at Marysville. The partners claimed to have cleared $15,000 in California.[21]

The company crossed over to Nevada, giving performances in Virginia City and Carson City. During the Virginia City engagement the troupe's stage hands provided extra entertainment for the townspeople. After a performance, men led by Jimmy Griffith hauled 200 pounds of calcium light equipment to the top of nearby Mount Davidson and a few minutes after midnight turned their lights on the town below to the astonishment of those who were still out on the street. Large buildings were illuminated with various colors and the lights on the mountainside resembled large, intense stars. The next day the press praised Griffith and his party for their pluck in carrying out the spectacular feat.[22]

12. The Black Crook Venture

After performing in Nevada, Langrishe's troupe returned to Sacramento, where they hired a printer who claimed to be fluent in Spanish but was not. This was a poor beginning for a tour of Mexico.

They embarked for Mexico on October 3, probably arriving at Mazatlan, and performed there for a short time, then traveled on to Guadalajara. They may have traveled this portion by sea, but a large part of their travel in Mexico was by "diligence" (stagecoach). They were traveling with three and a half tons of scenery plus railroad carloads of properties,[23] so there must have been a number of wagons in addition to the coaches carrying ballerinas, cast members and stagehands.

Langrishe later told reporters they had military guards to protect them from the banditti in the area. He stated: "It is their custom to shoot every bandit they can capture, place a strong rope around the body and hang it to a tree, as a solemn warning. On one part of the trip they saw twelve corpses hanging by the wayside, all literally riddled with bullets, and in various stages of decomposition...."[24]

In Guadalajara, they opened to a full house in a large, beautiful theatre that contained six tiers of boxes and a parquet that seated nearly 2000 people. Mexican audiences knew there would be music and dancing; they were not prepared for the comedy portion performed in English, a language few understood. Many were shocked by the dancers' revealing costumes, although single men found them enchanting. In the opinion of the local press:

> Black Crook is a hodgepodge that no one understands; one doesn't know what the actors say, pretty dancers that make one pray the "magnifica" in order not to get burned. A potbellied old man who is surely the comedian, a devil with a group of condemned people who jump like sharks; but no plot.... As one can see the plot doesn't have a beginning or an end, but the scenes are very interesting because of their sweet music; add to this a group of pretty girls with blonde hair, fantastic costumes which seem not to have the purpose of covering their magnificent figures, since they allow to be seen some superb legs, better than pickled fish and which are capable of setting all the moon on fire.[25]

They performed in Guadalajara in November and December, and opened in Mexico City about January 28.[26] It is not clear from Langrishe's telling where the following incident took place, but it was probably Mexico City: Some wealthy Mexican gentlemen fell in love with two of the ballerinas and proposed marriage. When the ballerinas accepted the proposals, their fiancés "wished them" not to appear on stage again. In Mexico a judge or director of theatres regulated everything, and "every actor and actress must ... perform to the letter every part of the *roles* assigned to them." Langrishe tried to persuade the recalcitrant dancers to perform, but they were adamant. When he explained this to a judge, the judge sent troops to the hotel to escort the most obstinate dancer to the theatre. "Shortly afterward she was marched through the streets of the city at the point of the bayonet and compelled to execute every part of her duties."[27]

They performed in the Teatro Principal in Mexico City from January 28 to February 10. They had planned to go to Orizaba, then Vera Cruz. They remained in Mexico City, however, where one of their cast members, 22-year-old Annie Mahon (Mrs. William Gross), lay gravely ill. She died in her Mexico City hotel room on March 11. "The hardships of Mexican travel, the inconveniences, the privations, the discomfort and neglect proved too much for her constitution, and just as the tour came to an abrupt termination, through financial failure and general distress, she succumbed.... [S]he was assiduously cared for by the ladies of the company, and by the Hon. Julius A. Skilton, the U.S. consul-general to Mexico."[28]

Langrishe had suffered his first complete failure in his 30-year theatrical career. He may have had to sell sets, properties and costumes to get himself, wife and over 100 others back to the U.S. For some reason his partner T.R. Glenn was imprisoned in Mexico, and Langrishe had been unable to get him released. They may also have wired friends in Denver for assistance, since they were met by a lawyer representing a Colorado client when they docked in New Orleans on April 2.[29] They signed a conveyance for Colorado property at that time, then apparently took a steamship north to take temporary refuge with family members, since they were not listed in New Orleans hotel registers.

13

Battered but Not Beaten

After Langrishe left New Orleans in early April, little or nothing about him appeared in print for almost a month. There is an indication that he returned to Madison, Wisconsin, about April 9 to contest a lawsuit filed against him by his former partner Charles Mayers over losses incurred with the failure of their floating riverboat theatre in the summer of 1858.[1]

The *New York Clipper* reported Langrishe had "just arrived in Chicago (May 7) from his recent trip to Mexico" and might establish a stock company in the city.[2] Next the Aurora, Illinois, *Beacon* revealed that Langrishe and his wife "are stopping a few days at his brother-in-law's, J.B. Atwater. They and Mr. Meyers [cq] appear next Saturday night with the [Geneva] Dramatic Club, in Charlotte Cushman's only comedy, *Simpson and Co*. No pains will be spared to make this the best bill of the season."[3]

A "very slim" audience attended a "very excellent" dramatic entertainment when Mr. and Mrs. Langrishe, assisted by the Geneva amateur dramatic company, performed. The cast included the Langrishes, Mr. Meyers, Lettie and Lillie Allen (nieces of Jeannette Langrishe, the daughters of her brother Sam) and "other members of the Geneva Amateur Company."[4]

On May 25, Langrishe wrote to an old friend from Madison, Wisconsin, F.F. Mackay, saying he had just returned from Mexico and hadn't decided what to do next. He had heard Mackay was going to manage a theatre in Philadelphia next season, and if he hadn't completed his company, could Mackay offer him a position. Or he thought he'd like to return to the West Coast and perhaps Australia, if he could get rights to do *The Shaughraun* there from Dion Boucicault, the playwright. If Mackay could speak to Boucicault about this, since he was said to be "well acquainted" with Boucicault, Langrishe would be grateful.[5] This indicated that Langrishe himself did not know Boucicault, in spite of having lived within a block of one another as children in Dublin. Boucicault was a few years younger than Langrishe.

On June 26 the *Aurora Beacon* revealed, "Mr. Atwater and Mr. Langrishe go out on a theatrical tour through Wisconsin to-morrow with a company... [T]hey have selected Miss Letty Allen, one of our amateurs, as the leading lady. They will be gone three or four weeks."[6] They started their tour in Green Bay June 23. The editor of the *Green Bay Gazette* reminisced about the old days of "Langrishe and Atwater" and predicted a well-filled house for the old favorites.[7] A reviewer stated: "Opening night was *The Miser of Marseilles* ... then *Simpson and Co.*, in which a steady-going old fellow gets involved in a maze of suspicious circumstances, and has a fine time of it in getting out. The solemn fun of Mr. Langrishe was often too much for the other actors."[8]

Next they were to perform in the Wisconsin towns of Oconto, Oshkosh, Fond du Lac, Ripon and Berlin, ending at Watertown on July 9 and 10. Their opening night in Watertown was lightly attended, but the press said that the "performers nevertheless acted their parts so cleverly and with such excellent taste, that it became the topic of conversation the next day, and their ability as actors was so favorably commented upon that a larger and finer audience greeted them on the last evening."[9]

A Madison paper disclosed: "Their agent wrote here [Madison] asking a guarantee of $400 for one night, or $600 for two nights; and no one could come to terms on that proposition."[10] They performed in Whitewater July 12 and 13, then to Beloit July 16 and 17, and wound up this tour in Freeport, Illinois, July 19 and 21.[11]

Langrishe, Atwater and the other members of the company prepared for a new tour with Lettie Allen again as leading lady, performing plays Langrishe and Atwater had performed nearly 25 years previously. The Madison *Daily Democrat* reported the company was playing to crowded houses in Illinois at Rockford, August 31,[12] Sycamore and Rochelle.[13] Returning to Wisconsin they performed some of their best comedies in Beloit September 13 to 15,[14] Monroe, September 16 to 18, and Watertown September 20 to 25.[15] They played in Ripon September 27–29, then Berlin.[16]

Langrishes and Atwater had less than a full house their opening night in Madison, but the first play, *The Sleep Walker*, went well. According to a reporter:

> When Mr. Langrishe showed his face, then the house did "come down." From first till last he kept the crowd in perfect convulsions.... The farce of *Simpson & Co.* was almost too much for the audience. We saw men and women so terribly overcome with laughter that we were frightful if they could fully straighten out again. It was all Langrishe's fault. We shall not attempt to tell what he did or how he did it. His exclamation, "I am on the ragged edge," will never be forgotten by any one present.... Mrs. Langrishe, as the jealous wife, could not speak or look without applause following, coming principally from the ladies in the audience.[17]

In a related item it was noted that Mrs. Langrishe "appeared on the street yesterday, and was greeted by many lady friends who admired her years ago; and were happy to see her appearing so well."[18]

The company was at Janesville October 12 and 13, Brodhead October 14 to 17, Dubuque, Iowa, October 21 to 26, Galena, Illinois, October 28 and 29, then back to Geneva about November 6, 1875.[19] Most, if not all, of the plays they performed were old plays under different titles.[20]

The *Aurora Beacon* reported Langrishe and Atwater had just returned from their dramatic tour, which was a "very pleasant and fairly profitable one."[21] At the end of December, the paper announced that Langrishe, Atwater and Lettie Allen would perform in Madison, Wisconsin, during the legislative session that started January 10. "They have several new pieces expressly written for them never before presented, which they will produce."[22]

They opened at Hooley's Opera House, Madison, with *The Stranger* and *Who's Who*. On January 12 they performed *The Orphan*, which was really *The Orphan of Geneva*.[23] The paper reported on Wednesday, January 12, "[T]he farce of *Simpson and Co.* came close to tearing everybody to pieces. Langrishe was 'immense.' He never was better. Some of the audience roared until they began to think something fatal would happen to them."[24]

Denver and Central City newspapers reported the Langrishes were about to return to Colorado, to bring out a company to perform in the old Denver Theatre which he had once owned, but lost title to in lawsuits. It was then owned by John Spencer (Speeney) who formerly worked for Langrishe as a stagehand.[25]

Langrishe's benefit was set for Thursday, January 27, at which time he performed the role of John Unit in *Self* or *The Rich of New York*. The largest house of the season assembled for his benefit, and those unable to attend that evening, were there when it was repeated the following night.[26] Saturday, January 29, was the last evening of the season. The press lamented, "Last night closed the amusement season at the Opera House, and many of our people feel sorry that they are to lose the familiar faces of Messrs. Langrishe and Atwater, Mrs. Langrishe, Miss Lettie Allen ... and others.... As the curtain went down, and the audience realized the fact that was the last appearance of the company, the most demonstrative approval was manifested. Mr. Langrishe took the one o'clock train this morning, for Chicago. The balance of the company will leave on Monday."[27]

Langrishe arrived in Denver February 4 from Chicago via the Kansas Pacific train with Mrs. Langrishe, Mr. and Mrs. Nate Forrester, C.H. Tyler, S. Philleo, W.A. Bowron, H. Hall, Jimmy Griffith, Adah Coleman and Minnie Edrington.[28] He was greeted in the press with: "Mr. Langrishe, than whom no Theatre manager in the western country stands more highly and honorably here and everywhere else that he has lived professionally for the past generation—will treat this people to a series of the finest dramatic entertainments which can be gotten up west of New York or Chicago. Mr. and Mrs. Langrishe made more friends in the far west, from 1859 to 1869, than any other couple who ever came here; and they honestly earned their extraordinary popularity as thorough artists."[29]

The *Rocky Mountain News* commented on their Denver opening:

> Mr. and Mrs. Langrishe appeared after the first play in the excellent farce of *Simpson & Co.*, and were received with long continued and hearty, western applause. As Mr. and Mrs. "Simpson" their capital acting brought back the "good old times" with such pleasant effect and force that the performance at times could hardly proceed by reason of the demonstrations of applause.... When the curtain fell Mr. and Mrs. Langrishe were called out and greeted with still another assurance of their welcome back to Denver and the Atheneum.[30]

Freed of their association with Atwater and neophyte Lettie Allen, the company presented newer, better plays for the Denver audiences, including *London Assurance, Divorce* and *Delicate Ground*.[31] They were playing to packed houses, and "already most of the *bon mots* [uttered on stage] have become familiar as household words on the street and in the family circle...."[32]

Shortly after Langrishe's season began, an extra train ran back and forth between Golden and Denver, carrying about 40 theatergoers eager to welcome Langrishe back to the fold. Langrishe informed the *News* that "he expects to play at least six weeks in Colorado, and then, if reports are propitious, he will take his company to the Black Hills for a short season. Wherever and whenever he goes, he will still have the best wishes of all his old and thousands of new friends."[33]

On March 1 the *Rocky Mountain News* wrote of Langrishe's last performances:

> There was the usual rush at the theatre last evening—rather more than usual, for it taxed the capacity of the dress circle and was barely comfortable in the parquette.... Every old-timer within reach of the theatre Tuesday night will no doubt feel irresistibly compelled to get inside of it, if possible, for the sake of old times.... Mr. Langrishe will appear in what many esteem his best character, that of "John Unit," in the great old comedy of *Self*. ...The present season will close on Wednesday evening, but there is hope of another one following the return of the company from the mountain towns. Denver is by no means tired of the Langrishe troupe, and, though compelled to spare them for a time, will be glad to welcome them again as soon as they find it convenient to return here.[34]

The theatre was full for his benefit, the aisles and passages blocked with chairs and standing room at a premium.[35]

The Langrishe troupe opened in Georgetown on March 2, playing through March 11 in Cushman's Opera House, drawing large audiences every night in spite of "tight times."³⁶ They went next to Central City, to perform at the "Belvedere." According to the press:

> The Belvedere, notwithstanding the heavy snowstorm prevailing, was packed last evening by representatives from nearly every part of the district, to welcome the return of Mr. and Mrs. Langrishe....
> At last the curtain rose on the *Simpsons*, the event of the evening. First appeared Mr. Langrishe, who modestly bowed his head to the storm of applause which burst from the audience, and when it was over entered with more than characteristic humor into the full spirit of the capital farce. In the next scene came Mrs. Langrishe, who likewise bent submissively to the long-continued blast which overwhelmed her from the crowded dress circle. And everybody as with one voice exclaimed, "How good it seems to see them again!" Everything intervening between the date of their departure and return was sunk in the one great joy of welcoming back their old-time favorites.... It was immensely funny, as frequent rounds of applause that shook the building attested. There never was a happier audience, and never will be....³⁷

They played just six nights in Central City, then returned to Denver, attracting large houses in spite of stormy weather.

Langrishe told newsmen his next trip would be to Colorado Springs or Pueblo, and that he believed he could establish a good-paying circuit in Colorado, including Denver, Golden, Central, Georgetown, Boulder, Greeley, Colorado Springs, Pueblo, Trinidad, West Las Animas and Del Norte.³⁸ But having been bitten by the gold bug in 1859, Langrishe couldn't help but notice the numerous accounts of people going to the Black Hills.

William J. Gross, last with their *Black Crook* tour in Mexico where his wife Annie Mahon died, joined Langrishe's company in Denver on March 21.³⁹ The *Rocky Mountain News* reported that during their recent tour of the mining towns the Langrishe troupe had played to houses that averaged $300 a night. "No troupe, strange as it may seem, has played to such average receipts in Denver of late years."⁴⁰ They performed *Streets of New York* with Langrishe playing "Badger," and repeated it two more nights. They went to Colorado Springs⁴¹ where they played from April 7 to 12, then Pueblo to open at Chilcott's Hall Thursday, April 13.⁴²

At Pueblo the paper observed: "[A] large audience composed of the elite ... assembled at Chilcott's Hall last night.... Mr. and Mrs. Langrishe, the old Colorado favorites, seem to grow younger as years roll on ... [T]his is their first visit to Pueblo...." It went on say that Langrishe has brought the "only really first-class entertainment ever given in this city."⁴³ "Mr. Langrishe, in the costume of 'Aminidab Sleek,' [stepped in front of the curtain after the close of *The Serious Family* and] delivered a short address to the audience, which, though not down on the bills, was received with roars of laughter."⁴⁴ Langrishe took his troupe from Pueblo to Boulder, performing in Union Hall, where the press noted that attendance "was not large.... Langrishe is a genius.

He can put on a look that sets the house roaring with laughter. All the acting was good, but more especially in the parts played by Mr. and Mrs. Langrishe."[45] The *Boulder County News* also noted Langrishe's troupe had given the first genuine theatrical entertainment in Boulder.[46] The troupe played in Boulder through the 22nd, then left to return to Georgetown, where Langrishe had had Cushman Opera House's stage enlarged so they could present more elaborate productions. They went to Central City May 23, where they found residents shoveling heavy snow from their roofs. They opened that night in *Self* or *The Rich of New York*.[47] They played Central City through May 27, apparently to houses that were only moderate. The Langrishe troupe returned to Denver, then boarded a train for Cheyenne, Wyoming, en route to the Black Hills. They'd be able to get to Cheyenne by train, but to go further would be far less comfortable.

14

Deadwood

The Langrishe troupe arrived in Cheyenne and opened at the Cheyenne Opera House on May 30, 1876, with *Self* or *Life in New York*.[1] Cheyenne was only eight years old, a new town created during the construction of the transcontinental railroad. In 1876 it was a jumping-off point for the Black Hills gold rush, and should have been livelier than it was. A "large and select audience" greeted their opening, but the size of the audiences quickly dwindled to "fair."[2]

Small audiences were the rule until June 12, when the Langrishe troupe formally opened McDaniel's "new" (remodeled) theatre with the play *Pique*.[3] The house was crowded for that occasion.[4] They played through June 17 at McDaniel's new theatre, renamed the 16th Street Theatre. Jeannette Langrishe wrote to her sister Laurette Atwater that they were going to the Black Hills, and weren't sure when they'd have mail service there. Laurette forwarded the message to another sister, Augusta Atwood, adding, "[The Langrishes] were full of hope, and sure of success this time.... I think they both enjoy that kind of life."[5]

On June 20 the *Cheyenne Daily Leader* announced: "The talented and popular Langrishe troupe, which has been delighting our theatre-goers for the past three weeks, will to-day take up the line of march northward ... direct to Deadwood City, where it will open the pioneer theatre of our northern Golconda.... [T]he huge tent in which the entertainments will be given has been packed, and an outfit most complete in every detail is loaded upon the wagons which are to convey the company direct to Deadwood City, the metropolis of the fabulously rich Deadwood region...."[6]

They left Cheyenne about June 20 and didn't arrive in Deadwood until July 15. Part of this 300-mile trek re-traced the route the Langrishes had taken to Denver from Fort Laramie in 1860, intending to stay a week, but staying seven years, and becoming two of the Colorado pioneers' favorite people. They may have seen few Indians on this journey northward, since most of the Lakota, Cheyenne and Arapaho warriors and their families were a few days travel northwest on the Little Bighorn river, teaching General George Custer and his troops one final lesson.

The Deer Lodge, Montana, *New North-West* printed news that the Langrishe troupe had gone to the Black Hills on their July 7 front page, and on page two ran an account of the Custer disaster that had occurred.[7] News of

Jack Langrishe in Deadwood, South Dakota. Originally printed in Annie B. Tallent's *The Black Hills* (Idaho Historical Society, Photo 79-2-20).

the Custer massacre finally reached the Deadwood *Black Hills Pioneer* on July 20.[8]

In Deadwood, men began building the frame of a theatre building, using canvas to complete some of it since there was not sufficient lumber available to enclose it. The roof was made of canvas (probably that "tent" hauled by Langrishe's wagons), the floor of sawdust. A stage was crudely constructed, and rows of benches nailed together for the audience. It was ready within a week, and a grand opening was set for July 22. The new theatre was "crowded to the doors." A "heavy sweeping rain" fell during the performance, penetrated the canvas and came streaming down on audience and actors alike, but few audience members left the house. The play was a great treat for all.[9]

The Langrishe troupe performed a great variety of pieces their first few weeks, enjoying large audiences. The Deadwood paper noted: "Mr. and Mrs. Langrishe have been greeted with immense applause.... On Sunday night the best bill of the season will be presented—the world-renowned drama in seven acts of *The Streets of New York*, with new scenery, machinery, and everything necessary to render successfully this great play, including the great fire scene, the street cars, the fearful snow storm, the tenement house, etc. Remember, Badger runs with 'der machine' and a great time may be anticipated...."[10]

Deadwood was a community without laws and without legal status. As in other western communities where law enforcement lagged far behind settlement, there were men who sought to make the community safe and law-abiding. Sometimes that took the guise of vigilantism, exercised by men who could keep a secret: Freemasons.

The notorious Wild Bill Hickok had been on both sides of the law for some time and was in Deadwood prospecting for gold, starting at the poker tables. He customarily sat facing the door of whatever saloon he was playing in, but this time the man facing

Jeannette Langrishe as she appeared while performing in Colorado and South Dakota (Denver Public Library, Western History Collection, F53372).

the door refused to move. Hickok sat, was dealt a hand of aces and eights and then Jack McCall snuck up behind him and killed him with a shot at close range. At a trial held in Langrishe's theatre, Jack McCall was found not guilty of killing Hickok. Another jury later learned he'd lied at the first trial and found him guilty, and he was hanged.[11]

Langrishe's new Deadwood theatre gave ladies a place to wear their best clothes other than church. The wife of Deadwood's first postmaster, Mrs. Adams, had a place to use her opera glasses, too. She made a display of getting them out and looking at the actors and actresses, although the theatre was so small she was undoubtedly looking at their pores. A prospector, looking on with amusement, showed up the following night in the front row. After the curtain went up, Langrishe himself on stage, the prospector raised to his eyes a small board with beer bottles sticking out of two holes, through which he peered solemnly at Langrishe. That was too much even for that seasoned professional, and he broke out in laughter. Mrs. Adams, in attendance, was also amused.[12]

Langrishe's agent in New York obtained rights to new plays for him. Even though it was difficult to produce theatre so far from suppliers, Langrishe succeeded in putting on new plays and difficult productions even here in this isolated new community. The press announced: "On next Tuesday and Thursday the citizens of Gayville ... can witness ... this excellent troupe, as Mr. Langrishe designs playing there on those evenings. The large dance hall will be appropriated, fitted up with a stage, scenery, &c., and everything necessary for a first-class performance."[13] Gayville was located about two and a half miles distant, on Deadwood Creek.[14]

Langrishe took his company to Crook City, a few miles northeast of Deadwood, for a few nights' performance while a shingled roof was being constructed over the Deadwood Theatre.[15] Langrishe's Deadwood theatre was reported to have a seating capacity of about 500, a commodious stage and dressing rooms.

General George Crook, accompanied by several officers and troops of his command, had chased off the Indians that had wiped out Custer's command, following some of the hostile Indians to within 70 miles of Deadwood, then entered that city to a hero's welcome. He was formally greeted by the mayor and as many citizens as could crowd into Langrishe's theatre.[16]

Langrishe closed that first theatrical season October 14. Four members of his troupe returned to the States, but the Langrishes, Gross and Bowron planned on staying in Deadwood.[17] Langrishe filed mining claims in the Deadwood area, and may have purchased a house. Deadwood was a raw, new town, vacant houses were non-existent, and rents high.[18] Like other new mining towns, there was frequent gunfire, ox carts rumbling through streets slick with ankle-deep mud and manure when wet, billowing choking dust when dry, numerous drunks, fistfights, dogfights, whip-cracking and rough practical jokes.

Langrishe was reported to be "taking out some beautiful gold from his hill claim, situated at the confluence of Whitewood and Deadwood creeks."[19] On December 14 there was a grand "re-opening" of the General Custer House with a ball sponsored by the Deadwood Social Club. The press reported: "The *elite* of the city were present, and many of the costumes were extremely elegant. Among the most conspicuous may be mentioned Mrs. Langrishe, richly attired in a rich polonaise of black silk, trimmed with lace and brading [sic]— underskirt of white tulle gaffeure; gold and enamel ornaments."[20]

Langrishe was making preparations for a Christmas performance in the theatre using volunteers E.R. Collins, an old friend from Montana, Colorado and perhaps New York, and Charles Aiken in *La Tour de Nesle* or *The Chamber of Death*; Fred Trusches, late of Montgomery Queen's circus, was to perform a grand trapeze act; and the Langrishes, Gross, Griffith and others in a roaring comedy. Six new stoves had been installed in the theatre, so the audience would be warm.[21] That attracted one of the largest audiences ever congregated at the Deadwood Theatre on Christmas night. They were to perform the drama of *The Drunkard* New Year's Eve, starring E.R. Collins and Mrs. Kitty Nuttall (recruited from the variety theatre in Deadwood), the Langrishes and others. They finished the evening with the farce *The Irish Lion*.[22]

Back in Wisconsin, Langrishe was "excluded" from the Freemasons, Madison Lodge No. 5, on December 21, 1876, for non-payment of dues. He had received the first three degrees in Madison in 1853, and remained a member of that Lodge for 23 years.[23]

According to a Montana paper, in 1876 there were "ten 'cities' and thirty different mining camps in the Black Hills, containing a population thought by the best informed to be about 10,000.... While some have doubtless made their fortunes, the great mass have not 'made grub,' as the expression is. The merchants and speculators in the various towns have a lively trade and big profits.... Gold dust circulates freely and greenbacks are at a discount. Pretty much all the stores, saloons, hotels and offices have scales and make their barter in 'dust' reckoning it at $20 per ounce."[24]

Jimmy Martin showed up in the Black Hills, so Langrishe scheduled a Sunday, February 4, performance of *Luke the Laborer* and the farce *A Fight for the Championship* with Martin and Langrishe assuming the characters of "The Chicken" and "Ben Bobbins."[25] In Denver, the old Denver Theatre, formerly Langrishe's, burned down, the cause thought to be arson.[26] The loss was estimated at three or four thousand dollars, only partly covered by insurance.

In Deadwood, Langrishe was not constantly occupied with his theatre, and it was too cold to do any panning, so he went to work for the *Black Hills Pioneer*. He had known how to set type since childhood, and had usually set type for his own playbills and advertisements. The *Pioneer's* description of the road between Deadwood and Gayville sounded like Langrishe: "The mud between here and Gayville is of a good quality, it is of rich quality; its adhesive properties are rare, its depth unfathomable, its color indefinable, its extent illimitable, and its usefulness unknown."[27]

The editor of the *Central City* (Colorado) *Register* warned against anyone else starting a daily newspaper there because a large proportion of the reading public had left the area. In Deadwood, the *Pioneer* editor (probably Langrishe) wondered in print whether

James "Jimmy" Martin, a utility actor with Langrishe in Colorado, Montana and South Dakota (Denver Public Library, Western History Collection, 03053).

> the Black Hills [had] enticed away the majority of the enterprising and reading people. In walking the streets of Deadwood, or Gayville, or any of our surrounding mining camps, we might be led to believe that this is the true solution of the problem. We are sometimes at a loss, when circulating 'round, to know whether we are in the Black Hills, Colorado, Montana or California, we meet so many familiar faces from each of these localities. We find ourselves in a maze, and when informed there are hundreds and thousands more on the road from the same directions, we can only ask, for Heaven's sake, who are left behind?[28]

Who, indeed? The Deer Lodge *New North-West* reported "the Hon. William H. Clagett has gone to the Black Hills. The stampede there is enormous." The editor, James H. Mills, was appointed Secretary of Montana in early April, and "among the pleasantest incidents of last Thursday was a telegram of congratulation from Sol Star and Jack Langrishe, Deadwood. We feel very near Deadwood ourself."[29] Not long afterward, "Jack Langrishe, Esq., of happy memory in Montana, is editor of the *Black Hills Pioneer* during Al Merrick's absence. Welcome to the ranks, Jack."[30]

Editor Langrishe met with famed author Mark Twain at the *Pioneer* office on June 25, 1877.[31] Twain was writing articles for national publication and occasional books, probably gathering material for *Roughing It*, published in 1880.[32]

The editor of the *Daily Pioneer* (probably Langrishe) suggested the community needed more swine in town to clean the kitchen refuse in the back alleys, although he acknowledged it wasn't a good idea generally to let hogs run at large. "We never noticed but one hog running at large in the city limits, and he was so fat that his eyes were almost useless...."[33]

The *Pioneer* reported that Deadwood at night had changed. No longer did the constant firing of pistols disturb sleep, and "late frequenters of the streets are as orderly as can be found in any Eastern city and people can travel at all hours without fear of molestation. Contrast the quiet night with the busy appearance of our city during the day...."[34]

The new variety theatre, the Bella Union, was leased by Langrishe for use as a legitimate theatre.[35] Harry J. Norton, former Montana journalist, reported:

> The moral strata of [Deadwood] is upheld by two churches, the orders of A.F. & A.M. [Freemasons], I.O. of O.F. [Oddfellows] and the Knights of Pythias, and at least 200 families who, if not unexceptionably God-fearing, are all that is required in a moral way.... At first glance a visitor is more likely to see the scum and froth of society.... The *nymph du pave* here flaunts her burnished charms as boldly and unrestrainedly as the hawker does his wares.... Old Montanians are met here by the score, and I am told that, as a class, they have done better financially than any others.... The only Montana ladies I have met are Mrs. J.S. Langrishe, Mrs. Scott and her pretty and amiable daughter, Miss Frankie.... Mr. J.S. Langrishe is temporarily the managing editor of the daily *Pioneer,* and without endeavoring to bring the blush of modesty to his tender cheek, I feel like complimenting him on the journalistic tact and ability displayed in its columns. It is by odds the largest and best newspaper in the Hills, and must be making a good salary for its proprietor, Mr. A.W. Merrick....[36]

The Deer Lodge *New North-West* republished an item by Langrishe, the article entitled "Yorick's Skull." Langrishe wrote:

> In casting plays for a short company, there are more things in heaven and earth than are dreamed of in philosophy. We have seen the ghost, after retreating to the realms of shade, reappear as the fiery Laertes, and the fair Ophelia caper nimbly as the affected Osric. We have also detected a remarkably striking family resemblance between Polonius and the first grave digger. Characters may be doubled or scenes omitted, but Yorick's skull must be forthcoming or the show can't go on. In the absence of the real article we have seen queer substitutes.... Without the pumpkin head in the burlesque, Hamlet's soliloquy would be solemn,

indeed. But your true property man will never rest until he has a genuine skull. The skull that for several years counterfeited Yorick in Montana and Colorado, has a queer history.

A party of theatricals on the road to Montana encamped on Blacktail Deer creek. While searching in the willows that fringe the creek, for horses, one of the party discovered the skeleton of a man. Fire had consumed the trunk, leaving only the head and leg intact.... The head was finely shaped and contained the most perfect set of teeth we ever saw. The skull helped to play Hamlet many a night in Colorado and Montana, and at last was taken to Chicago, where it was cremated in the great fire. It is somewhat singular that a portion of his body should be reduced to ashes in the wilds of the far West, while the conflagration of a great city destroyed the remainder.—Jack Langrishe in *Deadwood Pioneer*.[37]

Langrishe completed arrangements for an opera house at Central City (Dakota), nearly two and a half miles from Deadwood, to be run alternatively with Deadwood's Bella Union theatre. The Central City building was to be 100' × 25' and "furnished in the most approved style."[38] The Bella Union was 125 feet long by 25 feet wide, the stage 25' × 20' and the height to the ceiling 30 feet. It had a seating capacity for 1000 people, 17 private boxes and a large private reception room. Five sets of scenes and two drop curtains were painted before its opening. It featured three large entrances and a balcony at the front of the building which was to hold a brass band that would play to entice audiences.[39] Langrishe had the gallery boxes removed, and chairs were placed on the lower floor. The public was assured: "No bar and nothing that can offend will be tolerated in the new institution...."[40]

He opened this new season with *A Gentleman from Ireland* and *The Soldier of Warsaw*.[41] His company now consisted of himself, his wife, Jimmy Martin, W.J. Gross, Jimmy Griffith, Mrs. Nuttall and Miss Rogers.[42] The following week, when they were to perform *Ten Nights in a Bar-Room*, they added a local child, Julia McCutcheon, to portray "Mary Morgan."[43] The paper reported: "Manager Langrishe must feel greatly encouraged by his repeated large and fashionable audiences.... The company 'wears' well; in fact, shows greater ability at each entertainment. Additional members will arrive from New York this week, when strength sufficient for *London Assurance*, and latter-day society plays will be at the command of enterprising Jack."[44]

Even though Indians were attacking stagecoaches within ten miles of Deadwood,[45] Langrishe's new actress Augusta Chambers arrived safely in Deadwood November 22.[46] She proved instantly popular with her "fine form, pretty face,...clear, musical voice, and an archness and vivacity, which, coupled with an evident thorough knowledge of her 'business,' captivated the audience at once."[47] Langrishe's company was just performing Wednesdays and Saturdays at this point. The company then produced *Trodden Down* and *Who's Who* for the grand opening of the Central City Opera House Monday,

December 10.[48] A very crowded house opened that theatre, standing room was taken, and would-be audience members turned away.[49]

In Deadwood, a guest artist was to sing "Adeste Fideles" Christmas evening, accompanied by notes tapped on tuned drill steels. Shortly after midnight, Christmas morning, theatre workers hauled the steels on a bobsled up to a small hill at the head of the valley, and set them up. A xylophonist working for Langrishe awakened residents of the gulch, tapping out clear carrying notes of "Adeste Fideles" on the drills. Langrishe had intended it as a surprise in his theatre, but instead he made it his Christmas gift to all Deadwood residents.[50]

Later in the morning, Christmas Day was ushered in by the discharge of firearms "from a demonstrative few" and at the theatre, "jollity reigned supreme. The house was crowded and the audience sat through a very long bill, but that they did remain, attests the excellence of the three plays presented.... [I]t seemed that everybody was present, and enjoyed the best laugh of the season."[51] New Year's Day was observed with a ball at Spearfish, the miner's ball at Central City, the debut of Viola Porter at Langrishe's Theatre (the Bella Union) and the traditional calls upon the ladies of Deadwood.[52] The last day of the year, the *Black Hills Daily Times* reported that Langrishe had just completed negotiations for May's Hall, "which will be at once transformed into a first-class opera house."[53]

E.R. Collins, "retired" actor and old friend of Langrishe, made a brief comeback to perform *The Stranger* with the Langrishe company January 5 in Deadwood. They performed in Deadwood at the Bella Union, which owner Billy Nuttall was remodeling to serve again as a variety theatre.[54] Even though it was winter, the ground must have been sufficiently bare for Langrishe to find and file on a new lode, the "Courincopia lode" (probably Cornucopia Lode) in Black Tail gulch.[55]

Although Langrishe now had two young leading ladies, Mrs. Langrishe played the female lead, Mrs. Haller, in *The Stranger*, a part she had mastered when much younger. She also starred in *The Dumb Boy of the Pyrenees*.[56]

Maude Dennee, a Deadwood child, was recruited to portray Little Eva in *Uncle Tom's Cabin*. She suffered stage fright at every appearance; Augusta Chambers told her she'd get over it, but she never did.[57] During one matinee performance, just after Little Eva had "died," Langrishe "turned on all of the storm and hail in the thunder-box and rang the curtain down with a big old-fashioned dinner bell. He kept ringing that bell like a man at a railroad eating house." Maude Dennee said she didn't know what was happening, but she "stayed dead" until the curtain came down. Jimmy Martin, later reminding Maude of that performance, explained, "Langrishe said he wanted to give

Little Eva a good send-off, and he asked Mrs. Langrishe if she didn't think the effects helped the scene. It was a poor house anyway. We never got good matinee houses."[58]

The Langrishe company continued to perform at Central City, where they presented *The Serious Family* and *Frightened to Death*.[59] In Deadwood, work on the foundation for "Langrishe's new theatre on Sherman street" was begun on February 25. The theatre was to be 35' × 100' and be ready for occupancy about April 1. It had a 30-foot (deep) stage and a gallery in the auditorium.[60]

Three men were appointed from each of 11 nearby camps to form a committee to plan a St. Patrick's Day ball. Langrishe was one of the representatives from Deadwood, and others served from Central City, Gayville, Golden Gate, Lead City, Montana City, Spearfish, Galena, Crook City, Bear Gulch and Anchor City.[61]

The weight of a wet spring snow crushed some roofs in Deadwood, but when the sun emerged, everyone, including many merchants, came out and started throwing snowballs. All had had quite enough of winter. Some windows were broken in the glee.[62]

The theatre foundation was complete and work proceeded inside on the tormentor wings sets, and scenery of Langrishe's new theatre, but work on the exterior had to wait "until the snow was tramped down a little."[63] Jimmy Martin and W.J. Gross were painting the scenery.[64] The press observed: "The ladies of the theatrical profession in the Hills all wear soft felt hats, just like the men."[65] After the snow came a thaw, rendering the roads impassable by heavy wheeled vehicles. The men in Langrishe's troupe had to walk to Deadwood from Central City after their performance Saturday night.[66]

The *Black Hills Daily Times* editors delighted in light-hearted, racy and sometimes libelous stories. The *Daily Times* reported that three broncos stampeded the previous evening, just as Mr. and Mrs. Langrishe were crossing the street, and "probably the Colonel never did as good acting as upon that particular occasion. He wanted to stop the frightened animals and at the same time prevent them from running over Mrs. L. It was fun to see him spread himself. But he accomplished both objects all the same."[67] The *Daily Times* was calling Langrishe "Colonel Langrishe," an honorary title given to mine owners. Langrishe and partners had filed a claim on the "Tecumseh" lode in the Ida Grey district.[68]

Langrishe's new theatre was nearing completion, the work of calcimining and painting begun now that the building was "sealed" (ceiled, probably). New scenery had been painted by Gross and Martin. The press found it to be "an elegant temple of amusement and a credit to our city."[69]

Laurette Atwater wrote to her sister Augusta Atwood on April 28, 1878, that she had received a letter from Jeannette saying they "are well, and are playing again, to get money to work their mines. She is as full of hope as ever, and writes of the good times we are to have visiting you, when she comes again. I do hope they will be successful...."[70]

Under the headline "Things Theatrical," the *Daily Pioneer* reported, "The new theatre for Langrishe in Lead City is rapidly approaching completion, and will be ready for the inaugural performance about the first of May. The new building in this city is nearly completed, and will be opened in about ten days. There has been no performance in the Central City Opera House for nearly two weeks, on account of the horrible weather." This was the first reference to a theatre under construction in Lead City.[71] A plank walk was to be built between the new Langrishe theatre and the Odd Fellows' hall by the street commissioner as soon as the ground settled.[72]

Langrishe's acting style depended mostly on his line readings and, secondarily, on facial expression. He undoubtedly mastered the latter many years before, but Annie Tallent was the first to write about his facial expressions, having seen him in Deadwood: "An occasion is now recalled when the part required that he fail to grasp a point that was plain as noonday to everybody else, and to follow his changing expression which [went] from that of the densest stupidity gradually brightened, as the light of comprehension began to dawn upon his benighted mind, until his broad good-natured face beamed with the effulgence of supreme intelligence, was truly a rare treat. We do not often see his equal as a comedian...."[73]

There was a scramble for seats for the grand opening of Langrishe's new Deadwood theatre, so Langrishe had them auctioned off. His company, now augmented by Frank Perkins, was to perform in George Colman's great comedy *The Poor Gentleman* and close with *The Obstinate Family*.[74] The theatre opening was a gala occasion, with Deadwood society dressed in their finest. Even though it was May, the nights were cold. The press complained: "Manager Langrishe has lost at least the price of ten stoves since opening his new theatre, because he has not had one up and booming in his place of amusement...."[75] The following day, the note that the theatre would be well warmed was included in a puff for *Rip Van Winkle* that night at the theatre.[76] One of Langrishe's leading ladies who had left Deadwood returned; his other leading lady, Augusta Chambers, left the following day for Chicago.[77] A later report said she'd been fired.

In Lead it was announced, "Brokaw's new building, 25 × 75, on Main Street ... will soon be finished. The upper story will be occupied by the Langrishe troupe, and the lower story by C.P. Greenley, as a saloon and billiard hall."[78]

Fanny B. Price, a celebrated young actress who had performed with Langrishe's company in Montana in 1869, arrived in Deadwood June 3 for an engagement with the Langrishe troupe.[79] As of June 5, it was the thirty-fifth day straight that it had either rained or snowed in Deadwood.[80] June 18, Langrishe and company were to be back in Deadwood, to present *Life and Times of a Factory Girl*.[81] That was the day the mosquitoes came out, described as "full grown; some of 'em as big as bats, and musical as a buzz saw."[82]

Years later, Jimmy Martin, an actor with the Langrishes since 1863, told a young Estelline Bennett:

> Mrs. Langrishe was one of the greatest dramatic geniuses this or any other country ever produced. But she would always be unappreciated and unknown to fame because she would live and die on the frontier.
>
> She loved the stars above the mountains better than any on the boards, and western sunshine more than bright white lights. She was one of the greatest of character actresses and far ahead of her day and generation.... Those who saw Mrs. Langrishe in the Black Hills did not know her in her prime. They saw a lady well advanced in years who even in her youth had never been beautiful. Her voice, once round, full and musical, was worn out through illness and excessive use, and often was beyond her control. When you remember that for years she not only played the heaviest of heavy parts in five-act tragedies or melodramas nightly but also wound up the performance with a farce, the wonder is that she had any voice at all left. With all this she still was a great actress.[83]

These mining camps were frontier towns, many "buildings" being tents, and foundations a luxury for many of the buildings. Langrishe's "Opera House" in Central City was one with piles of rocks here and there for the foundation. Anything could wander under the Opera House and take up residence. During a performance, Miss Price's character enticed an actor to walk toward her, where he stepped upon a trap door and was plunged below the stage. Ordinarily he would have crawled out, brushed himself off and re-entered the house through a back door. This time he landed on a sow and her piglets, all old enough to squeal, which they did as they ran in every direction.[84] Straight faces were scarce in both the audience and the cast.

Langrishe's Lead theatre opened about July 27 with Price appearing in *Fanchon, the Cricket*.[85] His plan then was to perform two nights a week in Deadwood, Wednesdays and Saturdays. Langrishe and his company presented *The Celebrated Divorce Case*, described by a reviewer as having been presented

> far more acceptably than it has been rendered by some more pretentious companies in high-toned theatres in the large cities of the East.... Beside being a finished and versatile actor of the old-time school, Mr. Langrishe is a gentleman of keen discrimination in his profession. Where others fail, he succeeds, and this is because he has within him the elements of a general. That is, he knows how to handle his company. He has all the members thoroughly drilled to graceful methods of action. Where they happen to be a little remiss as to style, like a good, apt tutor, he kindly gives them timely and valuable suggestions, which, at once,

disrobes the crude diamond of its roughness and dresses it with exquisite polish and effulgent brilliancy."[86]

Varying the theatrical fare and probably drawing a crowded house, the Langrishe company performed *The Bullion Racket*, a play written by a "gentleman" of Deadwood that was a "rich and racy hit at the times...." Those kinds of plays usually involved hits at local people, too, arousing hearty laughter.[87] A variety combination started the same circuit that Langrishe was using, on alternate nights, attracting good-sized audiences.[88]

By the fall of 1878 Deadwood had a population of about 5000, housed in precarious locations on the sides of the steep hills. Stairs, not roads, led to many houses in the gulch. Reporters from outside newspapers reported that the region "has rude theatres, dance houses, gambling halls and uncounted bar-rooms; yet ... there is far less ruffianism than might fairly be expected in a new mining place. There are banks, churches, a school house, three daily newspapers and good hotels."[89]

A competing legitimate theatre, the Metropolitan, opened in Mechanic's Hall, Deadwood, and the company was comprised of all or nearly all of Langrishe's company. The *Daily Times* wished them well, but "the best wishes of the world won't do them any good. If our people were unable to sustain the Langrishe troupe in a manner it deserved, that ought to settle the business..."[90] Langrishe's leading man, Frank Perkins, had formed the group to compete with Langrishe.

The *Daily Times* implied Langrishe had an interest in the "Old Lexington mine,"[91] the subject of a lawsuit over ownership. "The best evidence ... that a mine is valuable is the amount of litigation it creates. The owners of the Old Lexington mine in Spruce Gulch are getting ready for a lawsuit" because J.D. Russell had a deed which conveyed to him several hundred feet of that mine, and now it was claimed that the deed was a forgery.[92]

Langrishe discovered that living next door to a newspaper office was not a good idea, if one wanted privacy. The *Daily Times* observed: "It is refreshing to see with what care Col. Langrishe takes the washing off the clothes line these cold afternoons. The Colonel is a most exemplary husband. He does all the light work usually allotted to women, such as chopping wood, carrying water, etc."[93]

Langrishe brought together his wife, William Gross, Jimmy Martin, vocalist-actress Anna Mahr, Marie Connors and Little Julia McCutcheon (who had performed with the Langrishe company in other plays) to present *Maid of Munster* and *Ireland as It Was* on March 18. They attracted a large audience "of a fashionable exterior."[94] A school exhibition to raise money to pay for seats in the new schoolhouse took in $187.50, "including $50 for rent of the theatre."[95] Langrishe may have had to pay that much in rent when he used the theatre, too, since it was owned by businessmen who had paid for the construction.

Starting around April 20, three days of steady rain washed out bridges and building foundations. "A ten thousand pound rock last evening started down the hill from the Boulder flume straight for the Langrishe theatre, but fortunately lodged between two large stumps, and thus the utter demolition of that institution, and probably the loss of life, was averted."[96]

Langrishe brought in more new actors to augment his company. The first to arrive was his former leading lady Augusta Chambers,[97] recently involved in a scandalous shooting scrape in Chicago. Crowded and fashionable audiences warmly greeted her return.[98] Behavior considered scandalous in Chicago was shrugged off in Deadwood. A report from Leadville, Colorado, published in the *New York Clipper*, undoubtedly caught Langrishe's eye. His former partner T.C. Howard had produced *The Black Crook* with success in Denver, then produced it in Leadville to crowded houses.[99]

The Langrishe company played occasionally through April and May, Mrs. Edwards and Misses Mahr and Connors improving with each performance.[100] Jimmy Griffith was back, too. Deadwood had changed in one or two short years. Now citizens were complaining about the number of hogs running loose and fast driving through city streets by "fast men and fancy women."[101] Perhaps taking advantage of Miss Chambers' notorious reputation, Langrishe scheduled his company to do *Six Degrees of Crime*, then *Jack Sheppard* with Chambers playing the title role.[102] His company was further augmented by the arrival of Emma Whittle and J.P. Clark from the New York theatres.[103]

Langrishe leased the "old" Tremont house in Central City and had it remodeled for a theatre, doubling its size. The press noted: "New scenery and other stage property are now en route for the same."[104]

Many Deadwood prospectors were leaving for Leadville, Colorado. Rich silver-lead ore was attracting men from all over the nation. The *Black Hills Daily Times* reported that crime was rife in Leadville at that time, as well as a lot of sickness and death attributed to the altitude.[105]

The other legitimate theatre company was attracting audiences from Langrishe, so he planned to present *Othello* in Deadwood June 12, the first presentation of Shakespeare in the Black Hills.[106] Mrs. Langrishe had been "seriously ill with fever for the past week," but was convalescing thanks to Dr. Miller.[107] Langrishe was appointed to plan amusements for Deadwood's Fourth of July celebration with Jim Wardner and others, and Mrs. Langrishe to decorate the "Car of State" with Mrs. Jim Wardner and other ladies.[108] A few years hence, they'd meet up with the Wardners again.

Othello was repeated Saturday night. Rains on the nights his company performed were so regular the *Daily Times* suggested a committee deter him from having his company play on July 4 to ensure nice weather. Deadwood residents had an exhausting July 4, with a salute fired at sunrise, a grand parade featuring the Seventh Cavalry band, the "Car of State, the Knights of Pythias, the E Clampus Vitus hoodoo and our resident capitalists in carriages. After marching around until 'busting' a wheel on the Car of State, and overturning the hook and ladder truck onto Tom Bently, the column headed toward the school grounds, where everything was arranged for the convenience of the orator of the day, Dr. Chas. W. Meyer...."[109] The brass bands associated with the three theatres (i.e., Langrishe's, Metropolitan and a variety theatre) joined forces and paraded through the city, little boys accompanying them carrying banners for the theatres.[110]

By July 8, Emma Whittle and J.P. Clark had been fired from the Langrishe company[111] and joined the Metropolitan company. Eight days later the *Daily Times* reported: "There will be music in the air at Fort Meade the balance of this week. Col. Langrishe's company, the Metropolitans, the Gem troupe, Ida Livingstone and a company of itinerants from Bismarck, are all there, or will be to-day or to-morrow."[112] All of the actors had been idle, the soldiers lacking funds for admission, until the arrival of the paymaster. He finally arrived at the Fort July 28.[113]

The idleness proved too much for two veterans of Langrishe's company: Jimmy Martin and W.J. Gross, who had acted together for years and lived together in Deadwood, got into a fight, Gross getting the better of Martin. According to a source, "Martin then drew a knife and went for blood in dead earnest, but bystanders interfered, one of them being accidentally cut." Another item revealed, "Martin returned from Meade last evening, with the evidence of the struggle upon his optics, but as to the cutting we have no corroborative evidence.... It was also reported that the commanding officer had issued an order prohibiting the troupe from further performing within the limits of the post."[114]

James and Belle Gilbert moved from the Metropolitan to begin performing with the Langrishe company August 4.[115] The Gilberts left Deadwood in late August to fill an engagement in the South, and Langrishe contemplated leaving too. He apparently thought about going to Montana,[116] and made arrangements for other combinations to play at the Langrishe theatre.[117] Then on September 13, the *Daily Times* reported, "Col. Jack Langrishe left for Denver, Colorado, yesterday morning, to play an engagement there during the week of the Colorado State Fair, commencing about the 20th inst. (September). He intends to bring a company back with him."[118] Four days later, the *Denver Times* reported Langrishe in Denver, and commented:

[His appearance has] excited a desire among his legion of friends here to see him before the footlights again for the sake of revival of a multitude of old memories. Mr. Langrishe is one of the finest comedians in the United States, as all who have seen him will attest. Though a trifle more portly, he has lost nothing of his old heartiness and vigor, and don't [sic] look a day older than when he conducted the theatrical amusements of Denver in the earliest times.... No actor who has played before our people is more popular or interesting, and he would be certain to have crowded audiences.[119]

Mrs. Langrishe had not accompanied him to Colorado, but she may have traveled eastward by stagecoach to visit family. There is no evidence she was in Deadwood on September 25 when a fire gutted downtown Deadwood, destroying 500 buildings.

15

High in the Rockies

Langrishe was in New York City hiring new actors as of October 11, 1879, according to the *New York Clipper*. He returned to Denver with the Misses Phosa McAllister, Clara Rainford, Sarah Goodrich and Julia Parker, and Edwin F. Knowles, Charles Norris, Murdoch, Duignan, Nalod, Watson and W.J. Gross.[1] The company was to open in Denver October 22 in *London Assurance*.[2] He changed his mind at the last minute and instead presented *Serious Family* and *Gentleman from Ireland*.[3]

Langrishe's company drew "very fair" houses their first week. The *Rocky Mountain News* held:

> Outside of *London Assurance* and *The Serious Family*, however, Mr. Langrishe has presented nothing that has called for special commendation.... The public appreciating his worth inwardly sigh for more of the old English comedies—more of the character of Boucicault's *London Assurance*.... It is said that during his sojourn east Mr. Langrishe secured the right of presenting many of the late eastern successes.... His repertoire is complete enough without having to resort to a class of drama distinguished mainly for its insipid sentiment and its mock heroics....[4]

Langrishe hadn't made money with this engagement but his old Denver friends set up a complimentary benefit for him, at which time he presented *Man of the World* and *Naval Engagements*.[5] A large audience attended his benefit, Langrishe appearing "to excellent advantage and infused life and animation into the evening's entertainment...."[6]

Langrishe actress Phosa McCallister, leading lady in his Leadville, Colorado, company. She later headed her own troupe in tours of the Pacific Northwest in the 1880's (University of Washington Libraries Special Collections, UW36701).

Friends in Golden expected him to

play a few nights there, but he went on to Central City to play three nights in the then new Teller Opera House. His opening night there drew a "very fair audience" on short notice. The press related: "Mr. Langrishe is a show within himself, one crook of that nose of his being worth the price of admission."[7] Followed by: "Mr. Langrishe is just as young as he used to be. His right arm is out of joint shaking hands with old friends and admirers."[8] Several of his "dear 500 friends" tendered him a complimentary benefit, and again he chose to perform *Naval Engagements* and *Gentleman from Ireland*.[9] Langrishe telephoned the editor of the Golden, Colorado, *Transcript* from Central, his first reported use of that device, telling the editor that "he must proceed at once to Leadville on the close of his engagement" in Central, and he promised to appear in Golden the first time he returned to the valley.[10]

Langrishe took his company to Leadville to adapt to breathing thin air for a few days before they opened. Leadville, sometimes called "Cloud City," sits at an altitude of 10,350 feet, nearly twice Denver's altitude and about 2000 feet higher than Central City's 8500 feet. Some were already calling Langrishe the "father of Colorado theatre," and as an old favorite of Coloradans, it was appropriate that his company was chosen for the grand opening of the Tabor

Tabor Opera House, Leadville, Colorado. The opera house still stands and is a popular tourist attraction (Wakely and Clements Collection, Scan# 20004790, History Colorado).

15. High in the Rockies

Opera House in Leadville. He had been quite near the future city of Leadville in 1862 in California Gulch, where prospectors were panning gold and cursing the heavy black stuff in their pans. The heavy black stuff turned out to be silver, sparking the Leadville boom 16 years later.

Langrishe hired T.C. Howard, his former *Black Crook* partner, as business manager for his Tabor Opera House engagement.[11] He set up *The Serious Family* and *Who's Who* for the grand opening November 20, 1879. He played Aminidab Sleek in *The Serious Family*.[12] It was only fitting that he promote himself on this occasion, since his name would be the draw, the other members of his company unknown to prospective audience members.

The theatre was lighted with 72 gas jets, a luxury Langrishe had only lately encountered in western theatres,[13] although the home he left in Dublin 34 years previously had gas lighting, too. The theatre interior was comfortable and well decorated. The Leadville *Weekly Herald* declared, "[T]he opening of the opera house will be the commencement of a new era in the social life of Leadville."[14] The opera house seated about 850, 450 on the main floor, 400 in the dress circle above.[15] The aura of the city's cultural event was shaken

Interior of Leadville Tabor Opera House. Setting is for Langrishe's production of *Self*, one of the first plays to be presented in the opera house (Denver Public Library, Western History Collection, X180).

when two "footpads" (holdup men) were taken from the jail (neither were locked in a cell) a day or two later and lynched by a mob of black-masked men.

After the grand opening on November 30, the newspaper reported that Langrishe, "Colorado's favorite actor, was never more successful...." Reserved seats had been sold at a premium price every evening since the opening, and even standing room was occupied long before the time for the curtain to rise. Langrishe changed the bill every other day, attracting full houses, even though it had been predicted that the house could not be filled for a single night with a first-class audience.[16] Langrishe had evidently shaken the black rain clouds that had appeared on every occasion the previous summer, for Indian summer prevailed in Leadville in November.[17]

The *Black Hills Daily Times* reported Langrishe was making "b'rls of money" at Leadville, his theatre crowded every night and large audiences for matinees; "We hope the colonel may make more money than he can count in six months."[18] Leadville *Weekly Herald* reported a "late census" taken at Deadwood revealed a population of 2794, "quite a tumble from the 10,000 of three years ago."[19]

Christmas Day, Langrishe tried to entice people of every taste, and performed five different characters during the day. Performances began with *Fox and Goose*, starting at 2 p.m., then *Day After the Wedding* and *What's Become of the Women?* In the evening, the company put on *The Life and Trials of a Factory Girl* with Langrishe as Toby Twinkle and *The Irish Lion* with the whole company in a lively dance. Langrishe sang "the hero of Ballingcrazy" with a "hundred voiced (more or less) chorus of accompaniment...."[20]

New Year's Day, Langrishe set up a matinee of *Orphan of Geneva* and *Dutch Lovers*, then in the evening it was *Flower Girls of Paris* and *Two Gregories*. He was to appear in all four plays that day.[21] The *Leadville Daily Democrat* reported theatrical actors in Leadville were paid from $20 to $75 per week.[22]

One of the things that set Langrishe apart from other theatrical managers in the West was knowing when to change the bill and what plays would please his audience, constantly drawing in more people.[23] On Monday, January 5 he produced a show that had been weeks in preparation with elaborate scenery: *The Sea of Ice* or *The Wild Flower of Mexico*.[24] Phosa McAllister was not able to act in this production, having collapsed after performing on January 2 and confined subsequently with pneumonia.[25] She returned to star in *Sea of Ice* January 7,[26] and about a day later, T.C. Howard fell ill with inflammatory rheumatism.[27]

Colorado's favorite actress, Jeannette Langrishe, left Deadwood on the

15. High in the Rockies

stagecoach January 14,[28] bound for Leadville to join her husband. She probably had not been in Deadwood those four months since Jack left, but it's likely she had been in the Midwest visiting sisters, nephews and nieces, her brother and her daughter Rosalthe. She may have returned to Deadwood to sell property before proceeding to Leadville. The Langrishes owned some mineral claims and perhaps lots, although their home there probably burned in the great fire on September 25, 1879.

The Tabor Opera House in Leadville had been built by Horace A.W. Tabor, who years before had owned a grocery store in California Gulch. He had "grubstaked" some prospectors with an estimated $17 worth of food, for a share of their findings, findings that made him fabulously rich.

The *Black Hills Daily Times* reported, "Jack Langrishe is piling up another fortune, but it's no sure thing that he will keep it. He has piled up several during his long years as manager, but allowed them all to slip."[29] Mrs. Langrishe arrived in Leadville on January 18, after several days of travel from Deadwood. The press suggested: "It would be a rich treat to see herself and husband in one of their favorite comedies in which they are so famous."[30]

Langrishe was preparing to present another ambitious play to Leadville: *The Long Strike*. New scenery had been built, Langrishe had engaged T.C. Howard's current partner, E.P. Sullivan, to portray Noah Learoyd, and arranged for telegraph apparatus and Manager Hood of the Western Union Telegraph company to be set up on the Tabor stage for the run of this play.[31] *The Long Strike* ran for two nights, then was to give way to two comedies Saturday night, starring Langrishe and his wife, *The Simpsons* and *The Omnibus*.[32] That drew one of the "largest, most brilliant and fashionable houses of the season."[33] They planned to present *Ireland as It Was* and *Where Did the Money Come From?* Monday night.[34] That night there was a terrible snowstorm, so much snow falling that in Tennessee park where the coal and lumber gatherers had been working, they had to stop, since the snow lay four to five feet deep on the level. Lightly traveled summer roads to other camps were traveled only by "snow shoe" (skis). The lack of coal meant lights out for Leadville residents, because their municipal lighting came from coal-produced gas.[35] The theatre apparently was furnished gas for lighting a few more nights.

The Langrishe company performed *Toodles*, *Poor Pillicoddy* and *The Omnibus* January 28, a performance relished by four patrons who had made an extraordinary effort to see the Langrishes. The newspaper explained: "Among the audience on Saturday night at the Tabor Opera House ... two ladies and gentlemen who had [traveled 30 miles on skis to witness a dramatic performance] and enjoyed the performance as much as those who alighted from a coupe at the door. They left upon Sunday morning expressing their delight and gratification and declared that their transit over the snow was equal in its enjoyment to the evening's entertainment."[36]

They ended the month with a play in which Mrs. Langrishe performed especially well: *The Dumb Boy of the Pyrenees* or *The Broken Sword*. She portrayed the boy who lost his power of speech after witnessing an awful crime. They wound up that evening with *Poor Pillicoddy*.[37]

Frank Roche joined the company, so having a leading man again, they could expand their offerings.[38] According to the *Leadville Democrat*: "They were going to repeat *Ingomar* another night, but Manager Langrishe met audience members at the door, telling them the theatre would be dark that night, and offered them their money back. Few, if any, took it. For want of coal (buried beneath several feet of snow), there was no gas to light the theatre."[39]

W.H. Bush, manager of the opera house, rounded up a quantity of coal, so theatres could open and the city could once again be lit.[40] The Langrishe company then presented *Romance of a Poor Young Man*, *Don Cesar de Bazan*, and *Richelieu*.[41]

Langrishe's actors fell ill, one by one: Norris, then Howard, then Mrs. Langrishe. On February 18, Langrishe himself took to his bed. The cold plus the altitude and prevalent germs took their toll. In spite of illness, the company opened Joaquin Miller's *Danites* February 16[42] and it drew full houses for several nights, ending February 21.[43]

During the church service in the Tabor Opera house Sunday evening, vandals broke into one of the boxes used by the Tabor company as a dressing room and did considerable damage to the costumes and equipment stored there.[44] The Langrishe company continued to attract good audiences to the Tabor Opera house. Langrishe was convalescing, and T.C. Howard, acting manager in Langrishe's absence, was doing a good job.

Langrishe appeared on the streets for the first time Friday, February 27.[45] Lewis N. Tappan, a very prominent pioneer in Colorado, passed away in Leadville earlier that day, and a number of pioneers, including Langrishe, met in the parlor of the Clarendon hotel to pass resolutions showing their appreciation of Tappan. They also agreed to escort the remains out of the city as a token of respect.[46] Langrishe returned to the stage March 1 for the first time since the onset of his illness.[47] The *Daily Democrat* puff for that play, *Money*, reported, "Jolly Jack has had a close call, but is yet ready to start another theatre in the next new city of consequence that is founded...."[48]

On March 3 the paper printed: "The first thirteen weeks' engagement of Mr. Langrishe at the Tabor, proved so successful that at the close of the term, ten days ago, a new engagement was made to terminate on the first of

May. At this time the house is to be placed under the sole management of Mr. Knowles, formerly of the Langrishe troupe, but now in New York selecting a company for the summer season in Leadville."[49] Langrishe was to take over again in the fall, but he did not.[50]

Langrishe followed *Money* with *The Stranger*, then *Led Astray*. Bad weather reduced the audience size the first night, but the second night a good-sized audience enjoyed the play.[51] Then a new team arrived in Leadville to enliven Langrishe's company: James and Belle Gilbert, with whom he had worked in Deadwood. They opened with *The Hidden Hand*[52] and followed with *Joshua Whitcomb*.[53]

The Gilberts were just what the city needed. Leadville was tired of tragedy and turned out in droves for the comedies. Belle Gilbert was young, beautiful and vivacious, with a pleasing musical voice. James was a good comedian, and they were supported by Langrishe's excellent stock company.[54] March 6 was payday for miners and employees "of various kinds," so that influx of money bolstered the box office of the Tabor.[55]

On the 100th night of Langrishe's management of the opera house, they presented *Joshua Whitcomb*, followed by a farce new to Leadville: *Grimshaw, Bagshaw and Bradshaw*. A critic observed:

> In these modern days the style of public amusement catering has so changed that the old-time farce which used to convulse audiences with merriment, is seldom presented at our metropolitan theatres.... [T]here are few comedians living who have versatility and humor to make the old-fashioned farce attractive. But John Langrishe is one of that few, and it would be hard for any man or woman living to refrain from inordinate laughter while he is indulging in his comicalities—and his repertoire seems inexhaustible ... [H]e has caused the oldest and youngest inhabitants alike to laugh and cry for more. This faculty of his has been one reason of the success of the past season....[56]

Their next Tabor production, Boucicault's *The Shaughraun*, was a scenically complex play for which T.C. Howard happened to have Boucicault's original scenery models. Stage carpenters built scenery based on them.[57] This play featured a dog, Tatthers, as protagonist, biting the right people at the proper time. They didn't use a trained dog, but reached offstage to pet and talk to "Tatthers" from time to time and talk about him. He usually only appeared onstage for the curtain call, receiving a very big hand.[58]

The Shaughraun ran March 15 through 18 (covering St. Patrick's Day), then gave way to the operatic drama *The Child of the Regiment*,[59] starring the Gilberts. The "regiment" evidently was formed by the local "Highland Guards," who proved a popular addition. Among the notables attending was Colorado's Lieutenant Governor H.A.W. Tabor, owner of the opera house, who expressed pleasure regarding the production.[60]

A Shakespearean actor appeared in Leadville with his wife, so Langrishe immediately set up *Othello*, the first Shakespeare play produced in Leadville. C.H. Thompson as Iago, Frank Roche as Othello, Mrs. C.H. Thompson as Desdemona and Mrs. Edmonds as Emilia performed on March 22.[61] *Othello* drew a very large house, and was repeated two successive nights.[62]

Othello gave way March 25 to *The Marble Heart*, in which Frank Roche starred and dazzled Leadvillians with his acting ability.[63] About this time Mr. and Mrs. Thompson left the company and the Gilberts rose like cream to star again at the Tabor Opera house.

On March 29 they opened Boucicault's *Jessie Brown* or *The Relief of Lucknow*, with new scenery painted by an accomplished artist, Lieutenant St. George Stanley, who had been in this 1857 siege as a child.[64] In the performance the last tableau in the third act aroused the audience to "an intense degree of excitement."[65] *Jessie Brown* ran through April 1, then was replaced by Madame Morlacchi, ballerina and pantomimist, in *The French Spy*.[66] The Gilberts acted in afterpieces, sending the large audiences home in good humor.[67] Roche, the Gilberts and Langrishe's company performed in support of Madame Morlacchi.[68]

Jimmy Martin, the actor who was fired after he pulled a knife on Gross, had worked for the *Deadwood News* since his dismissal. On April 11 he showed up in Leadville, where he was appointed stage manager at McDaniels' rival New Theatre on State street,[69] although the *Deer Lodge New North-West* reported he had gone to "join Langrishe in Colorado."[70] T.C. Howard left the Langrishe company on amiable terms, to prepare a new production of *The Black Crook*.[71] Howard had wanted to put it on at the Tabor, but when he calculated production costs, he found the Tabor's seating capacity was too small to make the production pay. E.P. Sullivan, then working as the Langrishe company's mechanic, left with Howard.[72]

Langrishe presented a new production of *Uncle Tom's Cabin* that started a run Monday, April 19.[73] *Uncle Tom's Cabin*, augmented by the "New Jubilee Singers," ran for six nights, through April 24.[74] That was followed by J.H. Haverly's Church Choir company performing *H.M.S. Pinafore*, opening Monday, April 26, the same night that *Black Crook* was to open at the Grand Central theatre.[75] "Nearly every seat was taken" at the Tabor Opera house, which seated about 850; and at least the first three nights of *Black Crook*, they had to turn crowds away from the 3000-seat Grand Central.[76]

Late in the spring of 1880, the *Rocky Mountain News* published numerous stories of mineral discoveries in the vicinities of Gunnison, Buena Vista and Idaho Springs. Idaho Springs had been worked over from 1858 to 1860, but apparently some areas had been overlooked. William J. Gross and his new wife, Julia Parker, left Langrishe's company and headed for the Gunnison

15. High in the Rockies

Giuseppina Morlacchi, famed dancer and a featured player in Langrishe's Colorado company. Married Texas Jack Omohundro (Jerome Robbins Dance Division, The New York Public Library for the Performing Arts, Astor, Lenox and Tilden Foundation, 5238023).

country in a wagon and team of their own.[77] The Tabor was dark from May 3 through 5, then opened May 6 for a benefit for Langrishe, for which he and Mrs. Langrishe acted in *Naval Engagement* and *The Irish Doctor*. Three volunteers filled out the program with vocal and violin selections.[78]

Langrishe's term as manager of the Tabor Opera house was coming to an end, and he seemed to be tired of it. He engaged Charles L. Davis and his stock company to perform *Alvin Joslin*.[79] They were to play for a week, then E.F. Knowles would take over the management. Mr. and Mrs. Langrishe reportedly intended to go to the Gunnison.[80]

Eighteen eighty was a census year, and the census taker listed Langrishe as age 40 (he was 55) and born in New York, as were his parents (all were born in Ireland). Jeannette Langrishe was listed as 38 (she was over 55), born in New York (Thetford, Vermont, was usually identified as her birthplace), with parents born in New York (possibly true, but not verified).[81]

The Langrishes may have gone to the Gunnison area, to look over the mineral properties and perhaps to relax or fish. By July 14, he was reported doing a good theatrical business in Kokomo,[82] located near Climax, Colorado.[83] Apparently they opened there on Monday, July 12,[84] and intended to perform there for a week. The town's residents, and the residents of neighboring towns, thought their appearances were a "delightful treat."[85] They next opened in Breckenridge, enjoying a very successful season. There the press recalled how the Langrishes "regaled the citizens of this camp twenty years ago, when our only source of wealth were the placer mines."[86] From Breckenridge they journeyed to Georgetown opera house.[87] Gradually lowering their altitude, they next traveled a short distance down the canyon to perform at Idaho Springs.[88]

The Georgetown paper noted: "[The Langrishes] deserve well at the hands of our theatre-loving people, for they never fail to put upon the boards pieces of undoubted merit, and, what is better, render them in a style that cannot be bettered, everything considered. They have a painstaking company who strive, and succeed, in pleasing their patrons."[89] Their next engagement was in Golden, having skipped Central City. At Golden the press lauded them: "Mr. and Mrs. Langrishe were always favorites in Colorado, and Golden especially, and they were greeted on this occasion by a large number of old-timers who would as soon play Dr. Tanner for a week [i.e., go without food][90] as miss seeing them play."[91] They performed August 9 in Golden, then north along the foothills for an engagement in Boulder August 10, playing through August 15 at Boettcher's Hall.[92] A large frame-and-canvas structure was erected at 16th and Lawrence streets in Denver, to be called the "Democratic wigwam." Langrishe planned to use it as a theatre as soon as scenery, stage and proper fittings could be arranged.[93]

The Langrishe company opened the new Wigwam theatre August 21 with *The Serious Family* and the "new comedy of *Obstinacy*." Frank Roche was leading man in a company that included Mrs. Langrishe and Jimmy Martin. Admission was 50 cents to all parts of the house.[94] The theatre, equipped with gas fixtures and chairs, could seat 1000 or 1200.[95] This was the same location as the old Denver Theatre owned and operated by Langrishe years before.[96] On Monday, August 23, they performed *Father and Son*, but the *Rocky Mountain News* revealed some deception: *Father and Son* was really *Naval Engagements*, "but they had a very fair house."[97] They played through Thursday, then the structure was taken over for political meetings.[98]

About two months previous, the *News* disclosed that Langrishe and one of his actors, Charles A. Cook, bought "an old prospect hole on Chicago Creek, a few miles above Idaho [Springs]. Men were put to digging and today the happy comedians are taking mineral from a 43-foot shaft that yields them $100 per ton. The pay streak is 18" wide."[99] A few days later, Langrishe took the train to Idaho Springs and told a *Rocky Mountain News* reporter that he had passed up this creek a thousand times long before a railroad in Colorado was ever thought of, and witnessed the many changes since he had first visited those rocks 22 years ago. "Then after a few moments' pause the old comedian began in a low sad voice and sang, 'and I turn with a sigh to the days gone by and the hearts that shall greet me no more.'"[100] The mine that Langrishe and Cook owned was called the Great Eastern, and in early October it was yielding $78 per ton in silver, the "vein gradually widening and increasing in strength." The partners planned to work the mine the entire winter.[101] On October 8, the Great Eastern mine was said to be producing $150 ore.[102]

The following day, there was an attempt to "jump" the mine, but the parties were driven off by employees of Langrishe and Cook. Several shots were fired, but no one was harmed. Langrishe and Cook were in possession October 11.[103] More trouble was reported at that mine October 21.[104] "Jumping" claims or mines or lots was a common occurrence in the early West. People would wrest possession of a claim or mine or lot from others or take possession of any of the three if the owner was absent, and claim to be the owner. The true owner could only establish his claim by going to court unless the jumper would accept money instead.

A number of warrants and counter-warrants were issued by local justices for the arrest of parties implicated in the jumping of the Great Eastern mine.[105] By the end of October, the Great Eastern was reported to be shipping ore that runs from $90 per ton, and upward. One lawsuit contesting ownership was decided in favor of Cook and Langrishe.[106]

16

Mining, Managing and Acting

Langrishe and Cook's Great Eastern mine was still producing good ore in early January 1881, notwithstanding the litigation over ownership.[1] Langrishe met with a number of other "barnacles" in Denver on January 11 to plan a pioneers' banquet for January 25. They called themselves "barnacles" because they had arrived prior to 1861, and "hung on" or remained.[2]

Charles Leichsenring had just completed construction of a Denver "opera house" on 16th Street,[3] so Langrishe leased it and left Denver to engage a new company of actors in the East. The theatre had all new scenery, and during Langrishe's absence the floor was raised, elevating some of the seats.[4] One paper said the theatre would seat 600,[5] another reported 800.[6]

The *Denver Republican* mentioned Langrishe's leaving and added, "He is familiar with the tastes of the people, and has never yet failed to entertain and delight them.... To the perplexed and the wearied, the sight of Jack Langrishe, as he walks across the stage and turns up his eye to the audience, is forgetfulness of trouble and relief from fatigue. A place of genuine, refined amusement is a necessity in a city...."[7]

Mrs. Langrishe attended the Pioneer Banquet at the Windsor Hotel January 25.[8] Langrishe himself was in New York at that time, undoubtedly attending a special benefit for Matt V. Lingham, who was very ill.[9] Lingham had acted with the Langrishe company in Chicago and the Midwest and married one of the company's actresses, Lizzie Mahon. Langrishe probably felt a special obligation to Mahon, since she and her sister Annie had been with the Langrishe company in Mexico when Annie died.[10] Their father had been a New York City newspaper man for many years, perhaps one of Langrishe's old friends.

Langrishe returned to Denver February 17 with his new company: Misses Rose Lisle, Lillian Joyce, Agnes Wood, Jessie Deagle, Mrs. Robinson, Ogden Stevens, R. Eldridge, Joe Hazelton, P. Brooks, Mr. Everett and the "well-known

16. Mining, Managing and Acting

comedian and fine vocalist, Mr. Wilson." Hazelton and Langrishe chatted on the train trip west, Langrishe offering to give him an extra $100 at the end of the season if he'd perform comedy and act as stage manager.[11]

They planned to open Monday, February 21, with Marsden's five-act play *Devotion*.[12] The theatre was "comfortably filled" for the opening. The *Rocky Mountain News* was favorably impressed by the production, but not the play. "It belongs to a class of plays known as 'Emotional' ... where the actor's art is employed in the delineation of physical suffering, dealing with the sorrows rather than the foibles of humanity.... Langrishe [who played Professor Muggs] was welcomed on his first appearance with round after round of applause and by his broad humor fully deserved the approbation given to him in advance...."[13] Obviously the Denver audience didn't like emotional drama, and that was what Rose Lisle was hired for. She refused to play anything except leading lady, so Langrishe had to pay her to do nothing for weeks.[14]

They put on some old favorites, adding Mrs. Langrishe to the cast.[15] Then they revived *Jessie Brown* or *The Relief at Lucknow*, starting March 21. They probably used the scenery painted in Leadville for this play by St. George Stanley, who had been at Lucknow during the siege in 1857.[16] Langrishe was paying a leading lady, but didn't have one to act the plays he and the audience wanted. Langrishe gave Hazelton a $20 bill to locate and engage Maud Granger by telegraph.

Langrishe took his company to Pueblo to perform at the Pueblo Opera house, opening with *Devotion* with Rose Lisle.[17] The *Pueblo Chieftain* commented: "Mr. Langrishe, as Prof. Muggs, was the very life of the play, and upon his appearance before the footlights was greeted with loud huzzas by his many old-time friends in Pueblo. Years seem to add to his power as a comedian, and without any thought of contradiction, we unhesitatingly state that he is the finest comedian who ever stood upon the boards before a Pueblo audience...."[18] Langrishe wrote to a Denver friend, "We have played to the biggest business ever done in this city. The first night we turned many away, and last night the house was crowded to the doors...."[19]

Langrishe's new leading lady, Maud Granger, was a beautiful woman with an opulent wardrobe, all that was required of a star. Her acting was praised, although reviewers acknowledged the roles she essayed were lightweight, such as in *Frou Frou*.[20] The Sixteenth Street Theatre advertisement on April 6 identified Langrishe alone as manager[21]; on April 7 the advertisement read "Langrishe and Pierce, managers."[22]

Actor Hazelton said "Cap" Pierce ran a faro bank at 16th and Larimer Streets and he was responsible for paying cast members Monday mornings.

Hazelton said Monday afternoons, "we all went down and played faro, and either doubled our money or, as was more often the case, gave our salaries back to the management."[23] In Denver, following the last performance of *Forbidden Fruit*, Miss Granger and the Langrishe company took the train to Colorado Springs to open the new opera house there.

Camille was not an appropriate opening play for a community of consumptives sent to Colorado Springs for their health, but Granger and the "Langrishe Metropolitan Company" opened the new opera house with that play.[24] Perfumed programs printed on satin partly made up for that gaffe. The audience was overwhelmed with the magnificence of the house and the excellence of the performance.[25]

Granger and Langrishe's company also performed *Forbidden Fruit* for the rest of the week.[26] In this play, Langrishe played Sergeant Buster. The *Daily Gazette* reviewer was one of few western newspapermen not acquainted with Langrishe, calling him "William Langrishe": "Mr. William Langrishe was wonderfully funny as Sergeant Buster. He showed himself to be a comedian of the greatest ability. His command of facial expression is truly remarkable and his comical glances are irresistible. His reception last night was warm and cordial and his playing was greeted with frequent and hearty laughter. It would be difficult to speak too highly of Mr. Langrishe as the sergeant and those who like to laugh ought to see him in this character."[27]

Langrishe leading lady, Maud Granger (also known as Ann Brainard Follen). A favorite with Western audiences (University of Washington Libraries Special Collections, UW 36699).

From Colorado Springs, Granger and the company traveled to Leadville to perform at the Tabor Opera house for a

16. Mining, Managing and Acting

week.[28] A rich mine owner's son had fallen in love with Granger, and when they traveled to Leadville, they traveled in a private car arranged by the suitor. He also filled the theatre aisles with baskets of champagne.[29] At the conclusion of that engagement, Langrishe and his troupe stayed in Leadville to support Rose Lisle at the Academy of Music,[30] but they drew only slim audiences.[31] On May 9, Langrishe and company appeared in Cañon City, supporting Lisle. The *Fremont County Record* said they would be in Cañon City Monday through Wednesday,[32] but they apparently played there all week. He had evidently played Cañon City before, since the *Fremont County Record* reported his reception "this time has been very flattering...."[33] The company returned to Denver where they "disbanded, their three months' engagement having expired."[34]

Langrishe left for Leadville June 8 to "assume one of the principal characters in a new play entitled *The Brothers of Pisa*, written by Mr. L.N. Cella" of Leadville. The play was to debut in Leadville.[35] Cella had written the part of Sampson for Langrishe.

Then Langrishe had good news and bad. The good news was that he and Charles Cook had won their lawsuit against mine claim jumper Robert Olds. The bad news was that the judgment wasn't as much as the lawyers' fees. The lawyers immediately filed a lien against the damages awarded ($132.25) and the Great Eastern lode for $300 for their legal services.[36]

Langrishe and Pierce were still managing the Sixteenth street theatre, booking combinations of stars with their traveling stock companies, but audiences were dwindling in size due to hot weather and a lack of ventilation in the theatre.[37] When the partners succeeded in engaging the Madison Square Company for Denver, performing *Hazel Kirke*, they drew very large audiences to see Langrishe's old friend Charles Walter Couldock star in this long-running play. A reviewer commented: "At the matinee the audience had to witness it under umbrellas, as the house let in the rain to an alarming extent, and at one time it was thought that boats would have to be resorted to by the audience...."[38]

A cloudburst struck in the mountains west of Denver, flooding Central City, Black Hawk and Idaho Springs, washing out roads and bridges.[39] On September 2 the *Denver Tribune* reported Langrishe traveling to Idaho Springs to "organize his forces for a fall campaign in his silver mine.... His expectations of fabulous wealth know no bounds."[40] Langrishe was involved with his silver mine and managing a theatre in Pueblo, so was out of newspaper mention much of the time. Langrishe and Pierce had leased Turner Hall in Pueblo, and set out to fit it up as a place of amusement, making arrangements to book all of the entertainments that would play at the Tabor Opera house in Denver, following those engagements. The remodeled hall in Pueblo was renamed the Turner Opera house, and seated 600 to 800 patrons.[41]

The *Denver Times* published a list of the officers of the new Pioneer Society, including John S. Langrishe as one of the directors.[42] The *Rocky Mountain News* reported that Langrishe and Cook's mine, the Great Eastern, "was one of the largest silver bearing fissures in Burns' Gulch. The vein carries a solid body of galena three feet and over in width, yielding from fifty to one hundred ounces of silver per ton. The vein also carries a large body of white iron, which is said to be even richer in silver than the galena."[43]

Celebrating silver in art, Stanley Wood, former city editor of the *Colorado Springs Gazette,* wrote the libretto for *Brittle Silver* and W.F. Hunt, formerly of Colorado Springs, then a Pueblo resident, wrote the music. The Colorado Opera Club in Denver determined to perform this original opera, and did so to acclaim in that city. Langrishe and Pierce then took the company on a tour of the state, to Pueblo for two nights and a matinee, thence to Colorado Springs and other communities.[44]

Langrishe was among the volunteers for a February 14 benefit for Alf Bouvier, manager of the Tabor Opera house box office. He was "quite his old self and was most heartily received by his many admirers."[45] In Pueblo, the *Chieftain* reported, "[O]ur people are anxious to see Manager Langrishe in a comedy again, and if he should at any time see fit to bring a company to Pueblo, he would be accorded a reception such as few people have ever received here. His reception in Denver on Monday night at Bouvier's benefit was a perfect ovation."[46]

James Mills, editor of the *Deer Lodge* (Montana) *New North-West,* was undoubtedly the author of this item:

> There are perhaps no people better or more kindly remembered by old-time Montanians generally than Mr. and Mrs. John S. Langrishe. Their lives have been full of vicissitudes—victories and vanquishments—since leaving Montana, "Jack" having twice achieved competence and twice had everything swept away. At present he is opening a mine in Colorado and has good prospects. As Mr. Langrishe's business is not such as to demand his constant attention we may have the pleasure of seeing him in Montana this winter, and there would be none other so competent and popular in establishing a Montana dramatic circuit.[47]

Langrishe's close friend and fellow Irishman, O.J. Goldrick, died of pneumonia November 25, 1882. A pioneer of Denver, Goldrick was as eccentric as he was beloved. He was the most extraordinary bullwhacker folks had ever seen, having crossed the plains driving an ox team while wearing a dress coat, lavender trousers, kid gloves and a beaver hat.[48] His fastidious habits were still evident as he lay dying, and Langrishe came to see if there was anything he could do for his friend. Goldrick asked that he make sure that the barber who would shave him before the funeral didn't leave shaving cream in his ears.[49] Members of the Pioneer Association, undoubtedly including Langrishe, attended the funeral in a group.[50]

Before and during the Civil War, theatres had stock companies in residence or were visited by traveling stock companies. After the Civil War, stars toured, performing with the local stock companies. About 1880, theatrical fashion changed to "combinations," a star touring with his own stock company, performing a single play that he or she had the sole right to perform. This change in theatrical production was facilitated by the transcontinental railroad and the railroads' customary discounted fares to theatre groups.

In spite of his lifelong preference for being his own boss, Langrishe went to work for M.B. Leavitt, one of the most successful managers of traveling combinations. As a business agent for Leavitt, he accompanied the combinations to the West Coast from Denver from February 1883 to autumn of that year. Among the shows he handled for Leavitt were *My Sweetheart* with Lily Palmer, *Fogg's Ferry* with Minnie Maddern Fisk and Leavitt's *Cheek* company with Roland Reed.

Langrishe, temporarily back in Denver, was called to testify in a trial of Tabor Theatre manager W.H. Bush. Owner Tabor had accused Bush of embezzling $2000 from his Denver opera house. When asked what pay a manager ought to get, Langrishe said he thought five percent of the gross receipts would be proper, or $125 per week. Gross receipts of the Tabor theatre since its opening in 1881 was about $274,000.[51] That would have paid Bush considerably more than $2000 per year. Bush testified that after the first year as manager of the opera house, he asked Tabor what his compensation would be, and Tabor said $2000 per year. Upon advice of counsel, Bush withheld that amount from opera house funds and told Tabor he had done so. The jury was out only nine minutes before they returned with a verdict of not guilty of embezzlement.[52] It's doubtful that Langrishe had ever made five percent of gross receipts of his companies.

Not surprisingly, Langrishe tired of serving actors and actresses of little merit. Early in the fall of 1883, he determined to resume acting, in a piece he concocted and called *Man in a Maze*. He quickly assembled a company comprised of Harry Richmond, Charles Fox, George Stevenson and the Misses Lizzie (Mahon) Lingham, Josie Bascomb, and Ada Stevenson, plus George Staley to sing and take on some comedic roles.[53] Mahon's husband Matt Lingham had died March 5, 1882,[54] and, to honor him, she changed her surname to his. Langrishe and his new company were to appear in the Tabor Opera house, Leadville, after Henry Ward Beecher, and before Dion Boucicault, on September 17 and 18.

Langrishe's opening night in Leadville was not a stunning success, thanks to a storm. His second performance there, September 18, drew a very crowded house and an "audience that fairly roared ... from rise to fall of curtain."[55] A few days before that, when Langrishe spoke before the Quarter-Centennial (of gold discovery) banquet of pioneers, he said he could "truly say that the hearty cheer and generous applause bestowed upon my efforts, and those of my co-laborers, were the most cheering sounds that ever dropped upon my ear or fell within the sound of my hearing."[56] He was about to get more cheering news: The management of the Tabor Opera house in Denver was swamped with inquiries for tickets for Langrishe's appearance Monday, September 24. This was his fifty-eighth birthday, and one day before the twenty-third anniversary of his debut in Denver. Management of the Tabor had planned to put tickets on sale September 20, but orders for groups ranging from 12 to 20 tickets were piling up. As the *Rocky Mountain News* observed, "The remembrance of the olden days of Langrishe and Dougherty have still a charm which no present performance can ever efface, and the new generation will join with the old in doing honor to one, who has done so much public and private good when Denver was struggling in its infancy."[57]

The *Denver Republican* reported: "Among the pioneers of Colorado, none achieved greater popularity, both in public and private, than John S. Langrishe and his estimable wife. 'Genial Jack,' as he was termed by those to whom his house and purse were ever open, 'Honest Jack,' by those who had business connections with him, and 'Jolly Jack,' as he was styled by the thousands who have laughed at his comical stage impersonations." The *Republican* added that he was giving up management for acting. G.H. Pierce would manage his company and T.C. Howard would be general representative. He would be starring in a combination of two comedies (*The Simpsons* and *The Skeptics*) he called *The Man in a Maze* because the plots bewildered his character, as he traveled from trouble to trouble, until the curtain was to fall amid a "perfect roar of laughter." His supporting company was new to Colorado except for Harry Richmond, an old-time Denver favorite.[58]

Attendance was poor in Colorado Springs for *Man in a Maze*. A review stated: "While we recognize Langrishe's merits as a comedian of the standard school, he cannot expect a very enthusiastic reception in any community with the poor support that he has, and the presentation of *Man in a Maze* last night more reminded one of a country school exhibition than anything that has been given in the opera house since it opened. There was not a single person in the cast outside of Langrishe that has a single redeeming quality."[59]

Langrishe and his company were greeted by a large and enthusiastic audience in Denver at the Tabor Grand Opera house Monday, September 24. The

16. *Mining, Managing and Acting*

Exterior of the Tabor Grand Opera House in Denver in the 1880's (Denver Public Library, Western History Collection, WHJ 1208).

reception given to him was a testimonial to the high esteem in which he was held. The surprise in the play's review was that, in spite of Langrishe's often-repeated statement that there would be nothing to offend the most fastidious, the *Times* reviewer suggested: "*The Simpsons* might be toned down a little to meet the requirements of the present taste which objects to that frankness of the past that persisted in calling a spade a spade. There were not a full half-dozen objectionable phrases uttered during the evening and those could be easily eliminated without injuring the comedy in the least...."[60] The *Republican* wrote that Langrishe "is one of the comedians of the old school that are funny in voice and delivery, and who can cause the heartiest laugh by a well-delivered witticism without resorting to baboonish grimaces or high-kicking gyrations."[61] Langrishe's engagement was extended to the end of the week.

On September 26, General William T. Sherman arrived in Denver from Leadville. Following a large reception for him, he attended Langrishe's play with other dignitaries. Sherman was so pleased with the Langrishe performance that he purchased a private box to see *The Serious Family* the next night.[62]

Interior of Tabor Grand Opera House in Denver. Langrishe filled the house in his last Denver engagement (Denver Public Library, Western History Collection, X24784).

Mrs. Langrishe emerged from retirement to portray Mrs. Sowerby Creamly in that play.

The Langrishes performed in Greeley, Colorado, on October 1, then Cheyenne, Wyoming, bidding adieu to Colorado forever, whether they intended to or not. They did draw a "good-sized audience" their first night in Cheyenne, but the plays "did not meet with unqualified approval, and were, in fact, somewhat weak and lacking in interest.... Mr. Langrishe himself is an excellent comedian, with an enviable facility of facial expression, and has the power of calling forth laughter at will...."[63]

They traveled west to Laramie, where the Langrishe company dedicated the hall in the Masonic building which had been fitted up for entertainments.[64] They may have played in Rawlins, Wyoming,[65] and Corinne, Utah, before arriving in Salt Lake City to perform October 12 and 13. The Salt Lake Tribune wrote, "Among the pioneer actors of Utah, none have been held in more esteem than Mr. and Mrs. Langrishe, and none left more genuine friends among all classes when they took their departure...."[66] Bills posted in Salt Lake City bore Langrishe's picture and the press commented that these were the "first pictures of Mr. Langrishe that have been engraven or published, and but one glance at them is needed to convince the beholder of the wonderful mirth-provoking powers possessed by the original. Mr. Langrishe was the first man who brought a regularly organized dramatic company to Salt Lake in the old-time days of ox team and 'prairie schooners.'"[67]

Throughout his career, Langrishe had been praised for having an excellent stock company supporting his efforts. This tour was quite different. Correspondent after correspondent remarked on the poor acting of his supporting players. The *New York Dramatic Mirror's* Cheyenne reporter said, "This company ... is composed of as poor a lot of actors as I ever saw...."[68]

The Denver correspondent of *San Francisco Music and Drama* wrote: "Jack Langrish, a sixty-niner [sic], appears in a new version of the antique English comedy, *The Man in a Maze* [actually two old English comedies combined and re-named by Langrishe]. He plays north and west, and you will probably see him in Spring time. The whole thing is an imposition.... Zephyr."[69] The October 20 issue of *San Francisco Music and Drama* carried a note from their Salt Lake City correspondent agreeing that Langrishe's "whole thing" was an imposition, signed by "Mormon."[70]

From Salt Lake City, they traveled north, performing at Bullion, Hailey and Blackfoot, Idaho; and Dillon and Deer Lodge, Montana. A Deer Lodge paper revealed: "The old favorites were received with a storm of applause, and whether they felt it or not their reappearance took a dozen years off from half their auditors and recalled 'the good old days' when 'Jack Langrishe' played to Montana audiences with a company that has never been equaled since...." The article went on to mention Couldock and his daughter Eliza; Pauncefort, George Waldron and wife, Jimmy Martin, Gross, Griffith and Shields.[71]

17

On the Last Tour

All over Helena the talk centered around Langrishe on October 29, 1883. "Have you seen Langrishe?" "Is he here?" Throngs of Montanans who waited in hotels, eager for the first handshake, were disappointed. Members of his company arrived the evening before on a freight train, but Langrishe and their entire luggage were to follow on the regular train. An accident delayed his reaching Helena until late Monday morning. News of his arrival spread fast, and prominent businessmen rushed to grasp the oldtimer by the hand. The *Helena Daily Herald* reported, "[The] President of the United States never received a more cordial greeting than has been given to this genial comedian. Time has dealt gently with him, and there is no perceptible difference between his present appearance and that which he presented thirteen years ago...."[1]

He was undoubtedly heavier. The Deer Lodge *New North-West* had reported Langrishe weighed 170 pounds in 1871.[2] That's a lean weight for a six-footer, but photos taken of him about 1875 show his build as portly.[3] Mrs. Langrishe was also very popular with Montanans, but the furor in the newspapers centered on her husband. Instead of performing their "signature" piece *Man in a Maze*, they opened with *Self* or *The Rich of New York* (they called it *Self* or *The New York Merchant*) so that Mrs. Langrishe, portraying Mrs. Apex, would appear on opening night. She was not in the *Man in a Maze* plays. The evening closed with *The Skeptics*, the bill giving Langrishe an opportunity to display his "wonderful versatility, as his various portrayals range from the loftiest sentiment and the most tearful pathos to the most extravagant comedy."[4]

Tickets sold quickly for the evening's performance, and "a magnificent audience" greeted[5] the first appearance of Jack Langrishe and his company at Ming's Opera house. The press noted: "Parquette, dress circle and gallery were crowded and the fellow so unlucky as not to have secured a reserved seat was fairly entitled to sympathy.... Among the 'old-timers' present, who were patrons of Langrishe's theatre thirteen years ago, our reporter caught sight of the following familiar faces: [names occupy the next seven inches of the column]." Langrishe, called before the curtain following *Self,* expressed pleasure "in finding himself once more surrounded by the old friends of Last Chance Gulch." *The Skeptic* provoked roars of laughter and thunderous applause.[6]

Langrishe and his company performed *Man in a Maze* or at least the *Simpsons* part of it on October 31. Following *The Simpsons*, they performed *The Gentleman from Ireland*. The audience had enjoyed the first part of the program, but in the second piece the "audience smiled, then laughed, then shouted and roared, for nearly an hour. It is safe to say he has had no equal in this character."[7] The next day they presented *Father and Son* (*Naval Engagements*) and *Fight for the Championship*.[8] The *Helena Daily Herald* reported on the audience's reactions to *Man in a Maze*: "[I]f mirth is conducive to health, then Langrishe is certainly one of the best physicians in the world...."[9] Friday night they presented *Trodden Down* or *The Days of '98*, a sensational play, somewhat different than the previous offerings.[10]

The *New York Clipper* printed the names of Langrishe's troupe and said they were to play in Helena, Bozeman and Butte for a week each. Cast members were the Langrishes, George C. Staley, Harry Richmond, James E. Fox, Mr. and Mrs. Henry O. Davison, Lizzie Lingham, Nellie Pixley and Ada Stevenson, and Gilbert H. Pierce was proprietor and manager.[11]

They repeated *Trodden Down* Saturday night, and the *Helena Daily Herald* waxed sentimental:

> Langrishe's Adieu Tonight. As merry an audience should assemble to-night to bid goodbye to "Jolly Jack" and his wife as that which greeted them on their arrival in Helena. As regards himself personally, he is the same fun-provoking comedian as of yore, and has given the same satisfaction in the present as in the past—and as old Father Time seems to be particularly lenient toward him, it would not be a matter of surprise should this perennial favorite reappear many years hence, as fresh as ever, with not a hair faded, and not another wrinkle around that roguish mouth, not a muscle of that wondrously movable nose weakened, and cause our children's children to laugh as heartily as our parents did before us. Mrs. Langrishe is the same estimable woman and excellent actress as ever.
>
> Adieu, old friends, and may you speedily return. May you both have as many happy hours as you have bestowed on others.[12]

On Monday, November 5, the Helena *Daily Herald* printed a letter dated November 2, tendering Langrishe a complimentary benefit, signed by over 160 prominent officials and businessmen. Langrishe responded that he was "really surprised and correspondingly pleased at being so remembered by the friends with whom I have associated in earlier days.... My heart is full, so full that I cannot express my gratitude, and I can only say that I will select next Saturday night, and arrange as amusing a programme as possible. J.S. Langrishe"[13]

Meanwhile, Langrishe took his company to Bozeman, to perform November 6, 7 and 8. A delegation from Townsend, Montana, visited him and guaranteed a large audience if he would perform in that community for one night, so he relented and performed there November 9.[14] The following day, Saturday, the company returned to Helena for Langrishe's complimentary benefit.

Langrishe's countenance was said to be especially beaming at his immense reception in Townsend the night before. "The great bulk of the inhabitants of that town and the surrounding country are well-acquainted with the jovial actor, and the attendance is most due to the efforts of Mr. J.D. Beary, who took a team and notified the population far and near, in a sort of Paul Rever [sic] ride. Long before night vehicles of all kinds began to gather until the place looked like a camp meeting gathering. The hall was too small to contain the anxious spectators, and many had to content themselves with simply listening on the outside."[15]

The *Helena Daily Herald* reported that James Allison, an Australian manager, had made overtures to Langrishe to star there on his circuit, and John R. Rogers, manager of the Minnie Palmer company touring in England, had made an offer to star him in England in summer, support to be provided by an English company.[16]

For his complimentary benefit in Helena on Saturday, November 10, Langrishe played Sir Charles Coldstream, for whom the Coldstream guards are named, in *Man of the World*. Several amateurs and professionals volunteered to participate in the entertainment. He had a full house. The show, with added volunteer attractions, ran late, and the audience was happy until the end of the evening.[17]

They traveled on to Butte City to perform November 12 through 17. John Maguire, manager of the Ming's Opera house in Helena, told *Butte Daily Miner* editors that he "never saw a more enthusiastic audience than that which greeted this old-time actor [Langrishe] at Ming's Opera house on his opening night there."[18] On that night in Butte, a "tremendous burst of applause [came] from Jack's friends who gathered in full force on this occasion.... Langrishe has not lost any of the comical force with which he used to delight Montanians years ago, in fact he has rather improved, in as much as there is an unctuous mellowness about his comedy which, like good port, improves with age."[19] In Helena, all evenings the Langrishe company performed were to full houses; in Butte, audience sizes slipped a little, from "crowded" to "good-sized."[20]

From Butte, the company went on to Missoula, to perform November 19 and 20. Arthur Hall was reportedly packed their opening night, because residents expected an extraordinary company, and because of Langrishe's reputation, but the editors of the *Missoula County Times* found the company inferior, and felt even Langrishe could have been better. "Mrs. Langrishe, as far as her limited part went, was very good, but there was not enough of 'Sarah' to really determine the ability of the actress."[21]

Once they were beyond the reach of Butte, the *Butte Weekly Intermountain* turned on the Langrishe company: "The Langrishe company have gone and the people of Butte still live. Each is a matter for congratulation. It is now sincerely to be hoped that Jolly Jack and the aged and lugubrious females who accompanied him will accept that six months' engagement in Honolulu and there be received with such acclamation and give such immense satisfaction that they will extend their engagement ten or fifteen years."[22] Obviously the *Butte Weekly Intermountain* received none of the advertising or printing money from the Langrishe appearance. While the company was in Butte, the reviews from the other newspaper were enthusiastic.

Later Langrishe company members laid claim to having been the first theatrical troupe to travel the Montana route via the Northern Pacific Railroad.[23] Their next performance was apparently in Spokane Falls, Washington, on November 24. Because of the miserable weather, the size of the audience was smaller than the company was worth, according to the *Spokane Falls Review*.[24] Next they were to play one-night stands in Cheney and Sprague, Washington, then to Colfax November 28 through 30. They then performed in Lewiston, Idaho, December 3 through 6, to full houses at Grostein and Binnard Hall.[25] After that, they performed in Dayton, December 7 and 8, and Waitsburg, Washington, December 10,[26] thence to Pendleton, Oregon, December 11 through 13.[27] They had to get to the Dalles by Friday, December 14.[28] They performed twice there and had a day of rest before going to Portland Monday morning; they were to open in the New Market Theatre that evening, December 17.[29]

In every community where they performed, there were residents who had seen and/or known Langrishe in Montana, Colorado, Minnesota or Wisconsin, so he had a core of an enthusiastic and friendly audience wherever he went.

His "general agent" (advance man) T.C. Howard had joined a Langrishe company in 1871 in Chicago and had been told a number of things, some of which he related to the press in advance of Langrishe's appearance, weren't true. Langrishe himself was not precise with time periods, but he surely would not have claimed that Charles and Ed Thorne had ever been members of his company, but that was one of the stories newspapers printed to heighten interest in Langrishe's company.[30] In another questionable yarn, he took his company west to Colorado in 1860 and defended his company "twice from Indian attacks."[31]

When the company reached Portland, they reported they had had a "very unpleasant trip from storms and difficult traveling for several weeks past," but their business had been good all along.[32] Belle Douglas left the Grismer troupe in Portland and joined the Langrishe company there.[33] According to the *Portland Daily Oregonian*, "Langrishe is a broad comedy actor of the old school of which Ben DeBar and Charles Burke were the famous exponents forty years ago. He went to Denver, Colorado, some twenty years ago, and was one of the great favorites of that place for many years. So long as he remained there he made money; but his starring tours into Utah, Nevada and California [no, Montana] did much toward depleting his exchequer."[34]

The Langrishe company had a full house for their opening night in Portland. "As both plays are only farces and do not call for high order of character acting, it would not be just to pass criticism on Mr. Langrishe's ability. ... [H]e has a way of keeping his audience constantly in roars—and a quiet, neat way, too—and accomplished what is most to be desired in a comedian."[35] The audience was smaller for the second presentation of *Man in a Maze*. The Langrishe troupe was to perform *Self* or *The Rich of New York* December 19, and their afterpiece was usually something different, but by request of a large theatre party, they repeated *The Skeptics* following *Self*.[36] The first night of *Self* drew a fair-sized audience, the second night a large audience. They were to perform *Father and Son* (*Naval Engagements*) and *A Gentleman from Ireland* Friday and Saturday, at matinee and evening performances.[37]

After the company left, the *Portland Oregonian* reported that like most of the combinations coming through Portland, the Langrishe troupe was not very "well balanced." They judged Langrishe himself a good actor, but his support weak. The reviewer especially admired his rendition of *The Gentleman from Ireland*, saying that actors of greater fame had tried in vain to portray such characters, but Langrishe did it with ease and "thorough breeding" they had not seen since the days of the "lamented Hudson." The reviewer expressed the hope that when Langrishe came back through Portland he would play Sir Patrick O'Plenipo in *The Irish Ambassador* or Sir Hector O'Dougherty in *St. Patrick's Eve*. "With all the fame achieved by Barney Williams, Billy Florence and John Drew, they paused at mediocrity in this line of business, in which Mr. Langrishe reminded us more than once of dear old John Brougham and achieved success in a very clear-cut bit of acting."[38]

They performed at the Alpha Opera hall, Tacoma, Washington, December 24 and Christmas Day, the Tacoma newspaper claimed the company was one of the best that had visited Tacoma.[39] Whereas the Portland *Oregonian* had referred to Langrishe's productions as "thoroughly clean in their witty sentiment,"[40] the Tacoma *Daily Ledger* objected to the "profane words, and jokes of a very questionable character" that had been introduced into their plays.[41] They went on to Seattle, arriving just in time for a day of dismal weather, rain leaving dirty, muddy water flowing in all directions. The audience was small, but those who braved the elements to get to Yesler Hall were amply rewarded. Their opening night, December 26, they performed *Self* and *The Skeptics*, the latter keeping the audience screaming with laughter. The *Seattle Post-Intelligencer* thought the whole company good.[42]

One item in the *Post-Intelligencer* December 28 about the Coeur d'Alene mines undoubtedly caught Langrishe's eye. The item included an estimation that the Coeur d'Alene gold discoveries were "among the most important discoveries that have been made for years."[43]

They performed in Seattle through December 29, before traveling on to Victoria, British Columbia, December 31 through January 3.[44] On December 29, the *San Francisco Music and Drama* published a note from their Montana correspondent "Shaun the Post," reporting that Langrishe's Montana business was bad throughout, except his opening night in Helena and his benefit night reaching upwards of $500. "Langrishe, who is a popular actor in Montana, would have done a bigger business than any one else had he a company of average ability, but taken as a whole, they were below par...."[45]

Nor was this publication about to let up: "The Langrishe company, after a wretched week's business, closed their unsuccessful engagement [in Portland].... The company is entirely composed of incapable performers, and thoroughly incompetent to appear before a first-class audience...."[46]

In Victoria, the Langrishe company drew a full house each night until their last, when bad weather encouraged people to stay home. Langrishe and his company proved very popular in that community.[47] They crossed the Sound to appear in Port Townsend next, on January 5. They drew a fairly filled house and kept the audience in "uproarious laughter during the greater part of the evening."[48] They may have crossed the Sound to Bellingham, home to Beriah Brown, who had been editor of the *Madison* (Wisconsin) *Argus and Democrat* when Langrishe's father worked there; he had recently served a term as Seattle's mayor.[49] They were undoubtedly playing in that vicinity.

They next appeared in Vancouver, Washington, on January 10, for a three-night run.[50] Their first night they presented *Man in a Maze* at Vancouver Barracks. The following evening they were to present *Matrimonial Oddities* and *The Gentleman from Ireland* in Marsh's Hall.[51] The editor of the *Vancouver* (Washington) *Independent*, J.J. Beeson, called Langrishe "the only comedian in America who can boast of 35 years uninterrupted success on the stage... [In Vancouver] the houses were good, and all who attended went away well pleased. Langrishe is the same laugh-making man that he was in 1850, when we first saw him,[52] and seems hardly a day older. Many old friends have greeted him on this coast, and he would be welcomed again."[53]

From Vancouver, they traveled to Astoria, Oregon, to perform on January 14 and 15 at Occidental Hall where their performance of *Man in a Maze* elicited a continuous roar from beginning to end. In the estimation of the local press: "Mr. Langrishe is an admirable comedian; we were prepared to see a good performance, for he comes to Astoria heralded by high praise, but last evening's performance far surpassed anything in the humorous line seen in Astoria since the Occidental was opened.."[54] A large audience gathered for *Self* the following night, and a light afterpiece left the audience convulsed with laughter. "Should Mr. Langrishe return to Astoria he will fill the Occidental by the announcement."[55] They were to go on to Salem, but apparently performed somewhere between, since they next showed up in Albany, Oregon, on January 23.[56] By now the press was printing that the "strike" in the Coeur d'Alenes was the "greatest since the Comstock Discovery."[57] Whether or not this strike coincided with a national economic downturn, the *San Francisco Music and Drama* reported, "Ten combinations recently went to pieces on the Western circuit within two weeks, and the prospects are that the number will shortly be doubled."[58]

The Langrishe company continued to draw good houses. From Albany they apparently went to Salem. That would have been backtracking for them, but the Salem notes of January 25 in the *Portland Oregonian* of January 26 reported that the "Langrishe Comedy Company have arrived in the city and are stopping at the Reed house."[59] Occasional backtracking was necessary because a hall had been reserved for other events, as Langrishe learned when he toured New England with his *Black Crook* company. They went on to Eugene, performing on January 28 and 29,[60] then to Roseburg January 30 and 31.[61] They had a large audience at Lane's Hall their first night and a small audience their second night in Eugene.[62] Prior to their performance in Eugene, the *Eugene State Journal* reported there were "many residents of this place who knew [Langrishe] in Colorado, Montana, etc., and all speak of his abilities as a laughmaker in the highest terms."[63] The *Portland Oregonian* reported the Langrishe troupe playing in "the interior with indifferent success. They go hence to Denver [incorrect]. Miss Belle Douglas recently left the troupe to accept an engagement at Helena, Montana...."[64] The hall in Roseburg was well-filled for the two nights the Langrishe company performed there. "Mr. and Mrs. Langrishe are very fair comedians, in fact above the average of strolling players. The rest of the company members were young and ambitious, while the women were pretty. They will probably make their mark hereafter, although we failed to discover any original genius among them...."[65]

They traveled to Jacksonville, Oregon. February 4 to 7, and on to Phoenix, Oregon, February 8 before appearing in Ashland, Oregon February 11 through 13.[66] "The only reason that a combination of such high metropolitan standing visits this burgh, is that they decided on the overland route to San Francisco, thinking that our public halls were equal to those of the small towns in the East, which are nearly all well appointed with stages and scenery. It is quite evident that such a treat will not again be offered for years, if ever, as the difficulties of traveling will continue a bugbear to all good troupes in the future as in the past...."[67] The Portland *Oregonian* reported that the Langrishe Dramatic players "have gone to California by the overland route, which is a severe journey at this season, and we hope they will make money on the trip. Mrs. Jane Tennant has taken the place made vacant by the departure of Miss Belle Douglas."[68] Over three feet of fresh snow fell on the Siskiyou mountains on January 19, and the ensuing bad roads had delayed stagecoach travel "from the south" to Ashland for a week.[69]

18

End of the Last Tour

Langrishe's company was engaged in San Francisco for April of 1884 and the journey toward that city would have been easier by steamship, but to keep his company together he needed to continue playing, so he took the inland route south.[1] Langrishe had been in San Francisco and Sacramento in February when he was a business agent for M.B. Leavitt's Minnie Palmer Company, but perhaps was not aware of the size of the state or the wintry weather that could prevail in the far north of California.

They drew full houses in Yreka, then traveled on to Fort Jones, Etna and Callahans, California, where houses were also full.[2] They were supposed to open in Red Bluff on March 1, but Langrishe telegraphed the *Red Bluff Sentinel* that they were stuck in Trinity Center, California, by "fifteen or sixteen feet of the 'beautiful.' Yours in a snow bank, John S. Langrishe."[3] The editor of the *Marysville Weekly Appeal* wrote that Langrishe had contracted with "Grant and Evans of Etna" to take them through to Redding. "Should they find it impossible to make the journey with their extensive company and great quantity of baggage, scenery, etc., we may anticipate their return this way again to go down the Sacramento river road, which is also rough for travel, though covered with much less snow to plow through."[4]

His company was supposed to open the new Zumwalt Hall in Anderson on February 29, then go to Red Bluff, Chico, Biggs and Oroville, en route to Marysville and Sacramento.[5] The *Red Bluff Sentinel* reported there are "several citizens of Red Bluff who have seen Langrishe in the East and speak in excellent terms of his impersonations. He holds a high social position as well as a professional standing and has an undoubted capacity for making firm friends of the public wherever he appears...."[6]

A crowded house greeted the company in Red Bluff in a very large hall, so instead of the usual one dollar admission, admission here was 50 cents.[7] The *Oroville Weekly Mercury* quoted the *Astoria* (Oregon) *Daily Independent*: "[Langrishe] appeared last night as 'John Unit, the Banker.' [H]is soliloquy after making his will is one of the finest pieces of character acting ever witnessed on any stage, and he was almost interrupted by the frequent applause, while at other times the audience hushed to the proverbial pin drop silence. His Irish Gentleman kept the audience in a roar...."[8] In Oroville, he "produced a fit of laughter every time he opened his mouth, and he opened it very frequently. He can assume an expression of idiotic simplicity and dumbfounded amazement that will provoke a laugh from the most cynical...."[9]

The company traveled on to Grass Valley via four-horse coach.[10] After opening on March 17, they saw no empty benches over a five-night season.[11]

Prior to their arrival in Nevada City, the *Transcript* reported:

> In 1857 the *Transcript* scribe attended a theatrical performance at Madison, Wisconsin, and the star of the splendid company occupying the boards that night was John S. Langrishe, the great comedian who is now delighting Grass Valley with his comicalities and will next week hold forth in Nevada City. Mr. Langrishe's wife at that time came in for a large share of the honors awarded to the company by the enthusiastic people of Madison. She was not only a remarkably beautiful woman, but a most powerful actress. The writer does not remember these things, as he was only about four years old then; but his parents have a distinct recollection of them.[12]

There were still ten in Langrishe's company, but according to hotel arrivals, there were some new names: Frank Cleaves and J. Rush Bronson. The troupe now consisted the Langrishes, Nellie Pixley, G.C. Staley, Mrs. E. Tennant (and son), Lizzie Lingham, James E. Fox, J. H. Richmond, Cleaves and Bronson.[13]

The weather turned nasty once they arrived in Nevada City, and it stormed at least three days running, discouraging many from attending Langrishe's performances.[14] They went on to Auburn, then Galt.[15] Initially they were to perform in San Francisco in April, but in March there was a major uproar in that city over tickets for a concert by Adelina Patti, one of the world's first superstars. Her managers let speculators buy most of the tickets prior to their sale to the general public, infuriating prospective ticket-buyers: "[T]he crowd [mashed] in the glass in the front doors of the opera house and tore down the pictures and decorations along the sides of the entrance."[16]

The Langrishe company did well in Galt with large enthusiastic audiences from April 5 to 7, then went to Modesto, Merced, Fresno,[17] Visalia,[18] Bakersfield[19] and Los Angeles, where they had crowded houses April 30 through May 13.[20] They went on to San Bernardino,[21] Riverside,[22] and Anaheim May 14 to 16, delighting audiences who attended in only "fair" numbers.[23] Until Anaheim, houses had been reported full.

Rail lines were not completed linking San Diego with Anaheim so the troupe boarded the famous old side-wheel steamer, the *Orizaba*, the "Mayflower" of the West Coast. The ship had plied the waters of the West Coast from 1865 to 1884, but was old by then in shipping terms.[24] This was the same steamer that Langrishe's Black Crook Company used when they began the ill-fated tour of Mexico in 1874.

In San Diego, the company's arrival was eagerly awaited, and Langrishe became the talk of the town, or would have been had everyone known how to pronounce his name. "Numberless arguments are hourly being held as to the proper pronunciation of the somewhat peculiar name of the comedian who is to appear at Horton Hall next week. It is 'Lan-grish,' with the accent on the first syllable, and the final 'e' at termination is silent. His agent avers that he has to answer the query 'How do you pronounce that name?' fully a hundred times daily."[25]

Their opening night in San Diego, the audience was large and appreciative.[26] According to the *San Diego Union*, "Everyone should go and hear him before he leaves, particularly 'those who do not laugh, that they may learn the art; and those who do, that they may laugh the louder'...."[27] After the company's last performance the *Union* remarked, "[W]e consider Mr. Langrishe one of the very best comedians that has ever come to this place ... his conception of the ridiculous is simply perfect.... [T]he company will leave for Santa Barbara by the steamer *Santa Rosa* this evening."[28]

In contrast to the aged *Orizaba*, the *Santa Rosa* was a brand new, handsome ship built for Pacific Coast destinations. The Langrishe company arrived in Santa Barbara on Monday, May 26, in time to open that evening in Loberos's theatre. The press noted: "Mr. Langrishe, as Mr. Skeptic, was quite irresistible. When he turned his eyes on the audience and said nothing, everybody went into convulsions...."[29] The productions were augmented by the Santa Barbara Orchestra, performing between the acts.[30] On Saturday, May 31, the *Daily Independent* reported, "The more one sees of the Langrishe company the better he is pleased with them...."[31]

The company traveled south to Ventura for the grand opening of the new Ventura Public Hall on June 2. The press reported: "The sale of seats the first and also the second nights of his stay here far exceeded that of any other occasion, with one exception.... Langrishe is ... a rare exception as manager of a theatrical troupe, for he is liberal and believes in paying a fair price for work done for him."[32] They played in San Luis Obispo, where they enjoyed "phenomenal" success,[33] then Santa Maria and Arroyo Grande and then back to San Luis Obispo to catch a northbound passenger ship.[34] They landed in the Monterey area and then traveled inland a few miles to reach Salinas,[35] Santa Cruz, then Oakland for an extended engagement at the Tivoli Opera house.[36]

In Oakland, tickets at the Tivoli theatre were only 25 cents, reserved seats 50 cents.[37] Langrishe was drawing "large and fashionable" audiences who appreciated his comedy, but admission prices were so low and his expenses high that he was not clearing much, if any, money.[38]

Langrishe's advance agent, T.C. Howard, had been in San Francisco since about June 20,[39] apparently arranging for new scenery and machinery and a cast for a new *Black Crook* company. Langrishe cancelled his company's dates for the "Humboldt county circuit" and released his troupe for vacation. Then he and Harry Richmond joined the cast of Howard's *Black Crook* company at the Grand Opera house in San Francisco, opening August 6.[40] They ran through August 17 and toured some inland cities before heading east without Langrishe.[41]

Langrishe reorganized his troupe and started the next tour September 8, mainly offering *Divorced*, *The Octoroon* and *Waiting for the Verdict*, plus humorous afterpieces.[42] This was to be Langrishe's first appearance in Sacramento since he had brought his *Black Crook* company through California nine years previously. For their productions of *The Octoroon*, they augmented the cast with local "Jubilee Singers."[43]

They moved on to Nevada City, where of the plays they performed was *That Terrible Telegram*, reportedly written for Langrishe.[44] Actually it was a play entitled *Confusion* by Joseph Derrick, based on a farce called *The Blessed Baby*.[45] It probably was not written for Langrishe, but he may have obtained exclusive rights to perform it. He and the playwright used the same talent agency in New York.

On Tuesday, September 9, the Nevada City paper reported that during the Langrishe production of *Divorce*, when the "wronged wife comes to take her final leave of her husband ... asked him imploringly to forgive her if she had failed in her duty as a wife. He stood unmoved, a cold, heartless wretch. Not so a certain '49er in the audience, who, in his whole-souled honesty, smote his hands and cried out, 'D–n the man!' It is needless to say it 'brought down the house.'"[46] The "unmoved" actor was not Langrishe.

After a tiring rail journey, they arrived late in Nevada City, then went on to Grass Valley, Auburn and Marysville, to perform four nights. There a reporter recalled: "Twenty-three years ago we knew John S. Langrishe when he was the favorite in the mountains with all classes of people. During all that time he has remained a favorite, and there is no company in the trans-Missouri country that can draw so large a house as any troupe that Langrishe brings around."[47] They traveled on to Oroville and Chico, where "[t]wo persons at Bidwell Hall last evening unhinged their jaws laughing at Langrishe."[48] From Chico they proceeded further north, to Red Bluff, performing from October 6 to 11. The company traveled back south, performing in Tehama,[49] Colusa, Stockton[50] and Galt.[51]

They worked northward and, after playing in Eureka, they performed in Ferndale, Hydesville, Rohnerville and Arcata before returning to Eureka for two more performances.[52] They missed the steamer they were to take November 19, so continued to perform in Eureka through November 29.

The *Eureka Times-Telephone* remarked: "[L]et us say that of all the actors who have amused us here, none so forcibly present the difference between the school of actors who grew up under the old stock system, and that school which is the growth of the modern innovation system. The former educated actors; the latter makes specialists."[53]

After a short sea voyage on the next steamer they docked at Coos Bay, Oregon, and performed at Marshfield, Oregon, on Tuesday, December 2. The newspaper remarked: "The advent of a troupe to the bay, possessed of merit, is of rare occurrence. Being at present out of the line of travel usually taken by the professionals, we have to be contented with such 'shows' as the De Moss family and other bilks, who 'take in' the bay as well as the people. The Langrishe company is good, and if they ever visit the bay again, they can rest assured of having large houses."[54] The company arrived at Astoria on December 7 aboard the *Coos Bay*. The ship had been "bar bound" all along the coast, and delayed by rough weather.[55] They opened their Astoria season with *Man in a Maze* on December 8. The press commented, "Though insufficiently advertised by reason of delay in coming by sea ... the house last night was a creditable one, and to-night will be overflowing. They played *That Terrible Telegram* Thursday, complete with live dog and live baby."[56] They deserved a better house than they received, according to the *Daily Astorian*.[57] The Langrishe company then probably caught a steamship, traveling north to Seattle, there performing December 16 through 18.

Langrishe and his company toured under difficult circumstances. The 1884 winter was an exceptionally cold one, with deep snows in the Pacific Northwest. In Walla Walla, Washington, the walls of Small's Opera house collapsed, killing a man.[58] In Murray, Idaho, site of the Coeur d'Alene gold rush, heavy snows crushed four large buildings, the largest the Theatre Comique, a variety theatre.[59] In southern Oregon, the Columbia river froze solid above the mouth of the Willamette, and several trains en route for Portland were snowbound near the Hood River, including a train carrying cattle. Since the cattle were in danger of perishing, they were turned loose. Snow at the Dalles was eight feet deep on the level. Even the Willamette Valley suffered deep snows.[60]

From Seattle, the Langrishe company traveled further north, to Victoria, British Columbia, to perform December 19 through 25.[61] Langrishe had had small audiences in Seattle, and Victoria was as bad, if not worse. As the paper said: "[The Langrishe company] have met with heavy loss during their stay in this city, as the audience, on no occasion, was large enough to pay expenses. They left this morning for Port Townsend."[62]

Suffering heavy financial losses ran counter to Langrishe's intention to raise sufficient money for retirement. Life was difficult for actors at that time, as the business of theatre was changing. In the East, theatre owners had to slash admission prices to attract audiences. Even though they only charged ten cents admission, some of the theatres were large enough to make substantial profits, paying actors well. Other theatres cut salaries, as they had cut admission prices. To remain financially viable, combinations (star and company) needed places to perform, theatres needed to rent their facilities, and to cut transportation costs, booking agents formed circuits enabling combinations to travel only short distances between theatres.

The Langrishe company apparently did not perform for several days before they turned up in the Willamette Valley, Oregon.[63] The troupe performed at Salem from January 16 to 26, admission to all parts of the house 25 cents.[64] The *Statesman's* reviewer confessed he laughed until he cried at the production of *That Terrible Telegram*.[65] They reduced admission prices, drew larger audiences, and then concluded to remain in Salem rather than traveling south in the valley as they had planned.[66] The *New York Dramatic Mirror* printed a note: "Dramatic agents report that they have never had a worse season. Business is almost at a standstill."[67]

The Langrishe company crossed the Columbia to perform at the garrison hall of Fort Vancouver, Washington, and then moved to the city of that name to perform.[68] They opened the remodeled Tivoli theatre in Portland,[69] its seating capacity enlarged to "allow the adoption of a low scale of prices, viz.: dress circle, 35 cents; orchestra, 25 cents; parquette 15 cents."[70]

Langrishe's troupe was trimmed down a little when they opened in Portland with a new play, *The Serpent on the Hearth*. The company was accustomed to a nightly change of bill, but now they were playing in a more "modern" style, performing the same play several days in a row. The Langrishes, T.C. Howard, Lizzie Lingham, J. Harry Richmond, C.M. Grey, Herbert O. Neil, W.O. Neill and E.M. Juvell were the cast members, plus a native newcomer to the stage, Katie Dalgleish.[71] This play ran for a week, plus Wednesday and Saturday matinees, drawing good to crowded houses. On Saturday night, they changed to *That Terrible Telegram*.[72]

On Saturday night, February 28, they performed *The Streets of New York* after adding some actors to the cast, including Frank Cleaves.[73] They drew very good houses, then changed the bill March 7 to *The Galley Slave* or *The Dumb Boy of the Pyrenees*.[74] This was an old play, the Langrishes having performed it since 1853 in Wisconsin, but it was new to Portland, and Portland playgoers found it "one of the most interesting and exciting dramas presented in Portland for years."[75] They introduced an entirely new play, *Heart of the Siskiyous* or *The Early Days of California*.[76] This was a play about frontier life that exhibited manly sentiments with a "moral calculated to render mankind better and happier."[77] The company withdrew from the Portland Tivoli Theatre for a week, since another attraction had been booked for one week.[78]

The *Chicago News Letter*,[79] *New York Dramatic Mirror*[80] and *New York Clipper*[81] reported that the Langrishe company was playing to "splendid business" in Portland. The *Clipper* correspondent said the Langrishe company had "done much to make the place [the remodeled Tivoli theatre] a success."[82] Langrishe and his company again crossed the Columbia to Vancouver, to play four nights.[83] The troupe crossed back to Portland to open with *Hearts of Oak* or *The Mariner's Compass*, one of the most successful plays of that day. It proved popular with Portland theatergoers, and the Langrishe company had excellent houses through April 19, ending a nine-week engagement. The following week the theatre owner was going to feature variety entertainment, "Hindoo" jugglers, Berlin lady orchestra and the California marvels.

19

Another Gold Rush

The lure of gold was irresistible, drawing Langrishe to the new gold rush as a magnet attracts iron filings. He and his company left Portland, Oregon, April 20, 1885, headed straight for the Coeur d'Alenes, where gold had been discovered over a year before. His troupe could take the train to Rathdrum, Idaho, then a stagecoach to Coeur d'Alene city (about 11 miles) and then board the steamship *Coeur d'Alene* across the lake and up the South Fork to Kingston, on the Coeur d'Alene river. A toll road from Kingston to the mines, about 30 miles, was finished shortly before the company arrived, enabling them to take wheeled vehicles to Murray, the main settlement serving the gold mines.

Mines were reported to be very rich. Claims filed on gulches and on high bars were paying well.[1] Langrishe's first claim, filed May 25, 1885, was apparently filed on one of those "high bars," that lay much earlier in geological history on the valley floor, but became a ridge well above river level[2] when the floor washed away.

Langrishe was 59 years old, probably too old himself to haul rock and gravel down to the river for panning, but if it were a rich claim, he could have someone else do that heavy work. The claim covered about ten acres in the Beaver Mining District, in White's gulch. He also filed a placer mining claim, called "Langrishe," on about eight acres between Accident Gulch and Prichard Creek, in the Coeur d'Alene District.[3]

His troupe was still intact, playing in Murray a few days per week.[4] Few Murray newspapers from that time are extant, but the June 25, 1885, issue of the *Coeur d'Alene Sun* carried an ad for the Langrishe theatre performing every "Wednesday, Saturday and Sunday evenings, a new program each night."[5] That rare issue carried news of the Langrishe company performing *East Lynne* to a fair house. Another item in the same issue promised that the company would produce *The Streets of New York* on Saturday.[6] Back in Portland, the Tivoli, opened so grandly by the Langrishe company, closed because of "hard times."[7] The Murray theatre where Langrishe and his company were performing was not identified.

In November, Langrishe and a partner, William McKay, hired a man to build a two-story structure on Main Street, just east of the Bank of Murray.[8] That probably would have been a theatre building, but a later comment indicated it might have been a saloon. Charles Hussey, a prominent mine owner, sold Lot 6, Block D, north side of Main Street, to McKay for a dollar on November 20, 1886. The Shoshone County assessor's list indicated that the owners of Lot 6, Block D, Main Street, were "McKay and Langrishe." The assessed value of the property was $600. They must have built on the property before actually buying it from the rightful owner. About the time of this remarkable land sale, there was a Shoshone County election for justice of the peace. There were three candidates, two of whom would be the justices of the peace for the county. Joseph Kline got 269 votes, Langrishe 244 and H. McCorkindale 196. Kline and Langrishe became justices of the peace of Shoshone County, Murray precinct.[9]

The *Black Hills Daily Times* reported, "Jack Langrishe, well known in the Hills, is pleasantly located in the Coeur d'Alene country. He was elected justice of the peace at the late election, and we venture to say will preside with dignity and ability. He is also interested in a popular resort at Murray."[10] "Popular resort" usually meant a saloon. If Langrishe were in the saloon business, it didn't last long.

On October 25, 1885, a friend of the Langrishes from their 1867 Montana tour, Bishop Daniel S. Tuttle, conducted the first Episcopal service in Murray in the "old" (perhaps one year old) courtroom.[11] Langrishe probably knew nearly all of the prospectors and merchants in Murray from acquaintance in Colorado, Montana or Dakota. There were few women in the camp, and not many were "ladies." It would not be long before some of the men would send for their wives and families, as Mrs. Langrishe knew, and her presence would embolden more ladies to come.

According to *Field and Farm,* an agricultural periodical published in Denver, "Jack Langrishe, the old time Coloradan and frontier comedian, is at Murray City, in Idaho Territory…."[12] Before the month was out, they reported, "Mrs. Jeannette Langrishe is residing at Murray City, in the mountains of Idaho Territory, retired from the stage after thirty years' devotion to the dramatic profession."[13]

Like other new mining towns, Murray was raw, houses built of resin-oozing, sharp-smelling wood roofed with canvas, all close together, clinging to the slopes in the narrow portion of Prichard Valley. There was one main street, fronted by business houses, residences located behind them. Prospecting was in such a frenzy that some were digging up the main street and sluicing that.

By the end of 1886 Langrishe's acting company had broken up, and the character of the Coeur d'Alene mining area was changing. Initially the "boom" stemmed from discovery of gold on a tributary of the North Fork of the Coeur d'Alene river, Murray becoming the main community. Prospecting was still lively on the North Fork when Noah Kellogg stumbled onto rich outcrops of silver on a tributary of the South Fork of the Coeur d'Alene river. Legend has it that he was trying to catch a borrowed burro carrying his tools and food, when he saw surface veins of mineral. Kellogg didn't know what it was (he was looking for gold), but Philip O'Rourke did: It was galena and silver, even richer than the carbonate ores that had enriched many in the vicinity of Leadville, Colorado, O'Rouke's former residence.

O'Rourke, his partner Con Sullivan and Kellogg posted location notices on the entire seam, naming the site on one side of the valley the Bunker Hill and on the other side the Sullivan. As in all mineral booms, small communities popped up, grew, then disappeared, almost as ephemeral as flushes of mushrooms. Towns called Beaver and Eagle had been quickly abandoned in the rush to Murray. A few mining towns survived, but many did not. One of the communities that survived near the Bunker Hill and Sullivan mines was originally called "Kentuck or Kentucky," later changed to Wardner in honor of Jim Wardner, who had a stake in the mining operations.[14] Wardner and Langrishe had served on an amusement planning committee in Deadwood for the July 4, 1879, celebration, and their wives had worked on decorating the "car of state" for the July 4 parade that year.[15]

About May 1886, Adam Aulbach, publisher of the *Coeur d'Alene Sun* in Murray, had started a newspaper in Wardner, the *Wardner News*.[16] He apparently turned the editorship of the *Coeur d'Alene Sun* in Murray over to Langrishe. Aulbach had met Langrishe in the late 1860s in Utah, where he published the *Corinne Reporter* until he was "'frozen out' by the Mormons [in 1871]."[17]

Through December 1886, snow was scarce, too thin on the ground to permit sled transport of ore. Then winter arrived in earnest. "Miner," a correspondent of the Spokane Falls *Morning Review* from Murray, wrote the "beautiful" snow began falling January 10, and "is still falling" [February 18].[18] Sounding like Langrishe, he continued:

> The road to Thompson is in a dangerous condition and freighters have been warned that they travel it at their own risk, for the untold millions of Shoshone County are not yet available for taxes and the county is now too poor to repair its roads.
> The snow is between five and six feet deep on a level; it has drifted to twenty and thirty feet in many of the gulches, and report says to even a greater depth.... The snow that now causes so much inconvenience will prove a boon to the miners next summer, for the unprecedented snow fall will undoubtedly provide water enough for a long and prosperous (sluicing) season.
> Our sister city, Wardner, was shut off from all communication with the outside world for only twenty days, but it seemed to her anxious citizens like so many months.... The mas-

querade ball given by the Murray orchestra on St. Valentine's Day was quite a success, and was well attended. Our fire laddies will give a dance Washington's birthday, it being the last of a series of very pleasant social hops that have relieved the monotony of our hermit life during the winter.... Miner.[19]

By March 1, 1887, Murray had received 17'5" of snow. The nearly abandoned community of Eagle received 22 feet. This snow was not all on the ground as of March 1, the depth usually about five feet at Murray, much deeper higher on the mountains.

As the snow receded, more prospectors moved into the Coeur d'Alenes, and so did some capitalists. Simeon G. Reed of Portland represented a syndicate of capitalists who bought the Sullivan and Bunker Hill mines for over a million dollars.[20]

About June 1887, Langrishe moved to Wardner and began working on that paper.[21] Jeannette bought a lot and had a home built in Wardner. She paid $100 for lot #1, Block #2, situated in the town of Wardner, and it was home for the Langrishes for the rest of their lives. The transaction was done in Murray, the county seat, on May 17, 1887.[22] Walter McKelvey, son of a Deadwood hotel landlady, was editing the *Wardner News* when Langrishe started there. It must have been irritating to have to work "for" the fellow you formerly knew as hotel dishwasher in Deadwood. The *Wardner News* became a tri-weekly June 16, 1887, but about a year later changed back to a weekly. (The *Wardner News* is in the poorest condition of any newspaper studied for this biography, thanks to an arsonist who burned the *News* office in 1914. The archived newspapers folded to octavo size, all edges burned, columns rent asunder one from another.)

It had been said that Mrs. Langrishe loved the beauty of the mountains and the starry skies in preference to the bright lights of a city. They had seen and lived in beautiful mountains, but the town where they made their new home was far from beautiful. A forest fire had burned all but one of the trees in the narrow valley, blackened snags and stumps attesting to the fire's fury. There was a preponderance of man's—not God's—handiwork in that narrow gulch, about one-half mile below the entrances to the Bunker Hill on the one side, the Sullivan mine on the other side of the gulch, other mines opening into the gulch as it climbed and narrowed even further. The valley was so narrow that the sun only shone for a few hours each day, the main street so steep there was a drop of nearly 100 feet in its one-mile length.[23]

Narrow Milo creek tumbled through the new town, some residents building outhouses or other structures on stilts over the creek, contaminating the water. The water was not potable anyway, since the concentrator company used the water in the reduction of ore, rendering it muddy. It emptied at last into the South Fork of the Coeur d'Alene river, flowing toward Lake Coeur d'Alene. In

19. Another Gold Rush

less than six months from founding, Wardner had 1200 residents, two banking houses, ten stores, two first-class hotels, two drug stores and about 300 buildings. It had one street, curving southward through the town toward the mines, then back north, out of the gulch. There was no municipal organization, the town dependent on county officials for enforcement of law in its early days.[24] The red light district was fenced off, a sign proclaiming "This Way to Hell."[25]

The narrowness of the gulch limited the population for the future, but at the mouth of the gulch, it widened onto a plain cut through by the South Fork of the Coeur d'Alene river. There lay the embryonic town of Milo, the name changed to Kellogg in June 1887 in honor of Noah Kellogg.[26]

Wardnerites soon built wooden sidewalks which reverberated like approaching thunder when miners wearing hobnail boots trod those boards, headed for home or their favorite saloon.[27] The narrow valley held and magnified those reverberations; everyone in town could hear the men were finished for the day. Due to the steep slope in the narrow valley, every several yards there were stairs built into the wooden sidewalks that extended along the principal business street to the mines. The sidewalk was lethal to pedestrians when it was icy, but the steep road was fair game for tobogganers and sledders of all ages. Townspeople delighted in snowballing sledders as they passed.[28] Toboggans and sleighs picked up so much speed it was hazardous to those on the sleds, stray dogs and horses, and of course people.

Langrishe continued to work for the *Wardner News* and as a justice of the peace in Wardner. Justice of the peace was not a well-paying position; the County Commissioners usually awarded him less than $20, a small cost per case, and it cost over $10 for him to travel to Murray to make his report.

A reporter wrote in the October issue of *Northwest Magazine*,

> Whom should I meet in the wilds of the Coeur d'Alene mining region last month but old Jack Langrishe, who, years ago, was one of the best all-round actors in the country, and who in his time supported the elder Booth, Forrest, Davenport, Wallack, Keene and many other dramatic stars of the first magnitude. Langrishe has turned editor in his old age, and is writing for the Wardner, Idaho, *News*. I spent a delightful hour jobbing [sic] his memory of old times on the stage. Charles Kean was his ideal *Hamlet*; Edwin Booth he thinks too sentimental and effeminate. Forrest he greatly admires, and he said that only fools who never heard him, speak of his magnificent virile declamation as rant. There are no great actors now, said the old man, because everyone tries to make a hit in some special part and, if he succeeds, plays it year after year. In former times a good actor had to be equally good in many parts. Much harder study was required and a much higher grade of artistic power. "An actor makes no lasting reputation," said Langrishe, sadly; "His fame is writ in water. It dies with the generation that witnesses his triumph. Of all artists he alone leaves no mark behind. Nothing commemorates him but a fading tradition."[29]

In Wardner, the Langrishes helped a group of amateurs give a dramatic performance, their first play *The Ticket-of-Leave-Man*.[30] A number of Wallace residents engaged a special excursion train to Wardner (so the trip wouldn't take two days) to see the production. Their reasons for going were that they knew they'd see a good show, and that a number of Wardner residents had attended a play put on by Wallace residents.[31]

The *Wardner News* was being published by McKelvey and Philip O'Rourke, Aulbach having sold his two-thirds interest to O'Rourke. The Langrishes were settled in Wardner, Jack doing the writing and perhaps the typesetting one letter of type at a time for the paper. Once it had cut back to a weekly, he had more time to work on stories, so he began traveling in the valley to report on the other mines. In August he visited the settlements of Burke and Wallace, both east of Wardner and Kellogg. "This was his first trip above [east of] Osburn, and he expressed himself as much pleased with this section."[32] The following week he spent several days in the Mullan area (nearly on the border of Montana Territory), looking over some of their "famous mines in the interest of [the *Wardner News*]."[33]

Walter McKelvey covered the territorial Republican convention for the *Wardner News*.[34] The election was to be held November 6. Langrishe was a candidate for re-election as justice of the peace.

Under "Local Miscellany," the *Wardner News* carried this item: "Lost— Between Kellogg and Wardner Junction, a dark-grey overcoat with chinchilla collar and pockets containing hair brush and pair of gloves. The weather is getting cold now, and if the finder will please leave it at this office he can have the use of it next summer."[35] This was a typical overcoat popular among male actors, apparently Langrishe's own coat.

An intact copy of the November 3, 1888, *Wardner News* survives. It was by then published by "P. O'Rourke, W.E. McKelvey and C. Sullivan." It contained a review of the "Plantation Minstrels," favorable because they "performed all the acts announced on their program," and an announcement that the *Wardner News* had a "steam book and job printing press."[36]

Feelings were still running high after the election, as evidenced by the *Wallace Free Press*' vicious attack on McKelvey, one of the owners of the *Wardner News*, and Langrishe, an editor of that newspaper. It was probably written by Adam Aulbach, then the editor-publisher of the *Free Press*. The attack was in retaliation for the *Wardner News*' wanting the county seat to be moved closer to Wardner. They first wanted the county seat moved from Murray to Kellogg, and then campaigned to get it moved from Murray to Osburn. Aulbach undoubtedly wanted it moved to Wallace, since the newspaper in the county seat received the legal advertising money,[37] and he was publishing the *Wallace Free Press*.

The year ended with the publication of the delinquent tax list. Mrs. Langrishe, residence on Mill St., Wardner, owed $2.65. *Wardner News*, printing outfit, owed $106.50.[38]

The year 1890 opened with a note in the *New York Dramatic Mirror* that the Miacos were playing *The Magic Talisman* in New Orleans. Langrishe, Charles Carle and T.C. Houghton (T. C. Howard's real name) had copyrighted it in 1873,[39] but all the copyright office obtained was the title page (a legal copyright at that time). Perhaps the Miacos obtained a script from Howard or Carle, or made up their own script, having learned it was a way to evade lawsuits and royalties, yet still put on an extravaganza such as *The Black Crook*. It's extremely doubtful they were paying royalties to Langrishe.[40]

Shoshone County commissioners approved the bonds of newly elected officials, including "J.S. Langrishe, justice of the peace, Wardner, $500."[41] The economic pinch was felt by all in a small mining town such as Wardner when the principal mines shut down and most of the townspeople were thrown out of work. Litigation succeeded in shutting down the Bunker Hill and Sullivan mines in mid–September 1889.

On January 1, 1890, V.M. Clement and George McAulay secretly bought the *Wardner News*,[42] but their names did not appear in the paper as publishers. Clement was general manager of the Bunker Hill & Sullivan mines, McAulay owner-manager of the Granite mine. "Publisher" Walter McKelvey served as business manager and Langrishe continued as editor.[43] The Shoshone County commissioners received a report from justice of the peace Langrishe and paid him $16.50 in fees on January 25, 1890.[44]

It was a snowy winter, so the Wardner *News* published, "We heard a Wardnerite exclaim yesterday, 'Oh! For a sight of something green—if it is only a grass widow [divorced woman].'"[45] Some of the residents of the Coeur d'Alenes were beginning to understand why that area had not been winter home to any Native Americans who summer there.

July 4, 1890, was truly special for the Langrishes and the residents of all of Idaho Territory, for Idaho had become a state the day before. In the Coeur d'Alenes, the "Grey Eagle of the North," Judge W.H. Clagett, gave an oration; men in tubs tried to race across the river; scrub horses raced; boys raced in a 100-yard dash; men raced for 100 yards; men vied in a sack race (won by a one-legged man); fire companies raced each other; a gun club held a marksmanship contest; and a grand ball wound up the day in Wallace. A strawberry and ice cream stand raised money for a new schoolhouse. People from all over the valley traveled to Wallace for festivities that day.[46]

20

A New Career and Reflections

Some professional actors—old friends of Langrishe—came to Wardner on July 14, 1890, performing one of Langrishe's favorite plays, *Naval Engagements*, under the title *Father and Son*. His promotion of the piece revealed his thinking about this play and the purposes of drama:

> [*Father and Son*] is one of those delightful dramatic pictures of everyday life in which the sentiments are manly and pure, and the moral calculated to make mankind better and happier. In the part of Old Phil Stapleton, Mr. [Felix A.] Vincent has a character that requires his best efforts. In following him through the various scenes of the play, tears and laughter take their turn, tears of joy and sorrow, laughter, not at idle buffoonery but genuine humor and well-seasoned wit, while often a sentiment touches the tenderest chord of charity, calling forth bursts of emulation, that proclaim the stage a legitimate school "to raise the genius, and to mend the heart." Eva Vincent has a dashing high comedy part in Marion Hardrose, and she plays it to perfection, while in the afterpiece of the "Bonnie Fishwife" she fairly captivates her audience and takes the house by storm. We hope to see the Coliseum crowded to its fullest capacity and our citizens welcome those genuine artists, in a truly cordial manner.[1]

In late July, George L. Shoup, governor of the new state of Idaho, issued a formal proclamation calling for statewide elections on October 1, 1890.[2] Shoup probably had known Langrishe in Colorado, since Shoup, too, was a '59er. He had served as a colonel in the Colorado 100-day volunteers, participating in the Sand Creek Massacre, although that scandal and odium apparently had not tainted his political future.[3]

In spite of a disastrous fire July 27,[4] Shoshone County Republicans convened in charred Wallace on August 11 to nominate candidates for the legislature and county officers, and also to elect delegates to the state Republican convention at Boise. "Philip O'Rourke was unanimously elected temporary chairman.... The following county ticket was nominated: State Senators—John A. Finch and John S. Langrishe; Representative—J.F. Cameron. The convention was most harmonious throughout. Most of the nominations were made by acclamation...."[5]

20. A New Career and Reflections

Langrishe later maintained he had not sought the nomination, and did not want it.[6] The Shoshone County Commissioners appointed election judges and registrars for the various precincts, including Wardner Registrar J.S. Langrishe.[7] Being registrar precluded his traveling in the county to campaign for the State Senate seat for which he'd been nominated, but he was paid $77.50 for his registrar work, much more than the small amounts he'd earned as a justice of the peace.[8]

Even though becoming involved in politics, Langrishe did not entirely abandon the stage. On September 3, the citizens of Wardner tendered a benefit to Eva Vincent, and her benefit performance of *The Man in a Maze* featured Mr. and Mrs. Langrishe.[9]

An editorial in the Wallace, Idaho, *Coeur d'Alene Miner*, praised the Republican candidates for the legislature for knowing the importance of good mining laws. Langrishe and James F. Cameron "are men of more than ordinary talents and will go to Boise with no other purpose in view than securing the passage of laws advantageous to all our people...."[10]

Then the Wallace *Coeur d'Alene Miner* quoted the Deadwood, South Dakota, *Black Hills Times*:

> The *Spokane Falls Review* of recent date says: "John S. Langrishe, who has been nominated by the Republicans of Shoshone County, Idaho, for state Senator, is widely known throughout the west. He is better known, however, as Jack Langrishe, the actor. Within the past thirty years he has played in nearly every mining camp in the West." The subject of this sketch is well known in the Black Hills, particularly to old-timers, and the miners of the Coeur d'Alene country have performed a fitting and graceful act in nominating Jack for the state senate. He has followed the miner through all his varying fortunes. When diggings panned out rich, he shared their prosperity, and when they became exhausted without a murmur he accepted the common misfortune, and at all times, either on or off the stage endeavored to entertain and amuse the public. Jack is one of the few remaining of the old school of actors that thirty years ago, when stock companies only catered to the public, contained the most popular men in the community. Jack was a pioneer to the West when that portion this side of the Missouri was terra incognita indeed, and has lived in the West ever since, appearing with a theatre simultaneously with the establishment of every new mining town of importance. Thus he appeared with [sic] Deadwood early in '76, remaining with varying fortunes till early in the eighties [he left in '79], when he proceeded to Colorado, and gradually drifted into Idaho. Although the stage and the press are closely allied, Jack seeded to the press gang with more than ordinary kindness [sic], and when not on the boards was, as a rule, in the editorial room of a friendly paper devouring exchanges, playing cribbage or lending a graceful hand preparing copy. The old boy must be well along in years, but we almost hear him repeat in reality the line of a certain part he took so well, "I feel as young as I used to do." If elected to the Idaho senate, that [sic] will be sure of at least one honest, faithful, accomplished member.[11]

The election was to be held October 1, so nearly 200 men became citizens September 29.[12] The *Coeur d'Alene Miner* published an editorial note Langrishe had been unable to canvass the county because he was serving as registrar, although it "would have given him much pleasure to have done so, and it would have been a great pleasure to his hundreds of friends in every canyon to meet the veteran of many camps."[13]

Langrishe and most other Republican candidates in Shoshone County were elected.[14] The first state legislative session was to begin December 8, in Boise. Langrishe had to line up someone to take his place temporarily on the *Wardner News*. His last acting tour had not left him with a sufficient nest egg on which to retire, nor had his mining claims enriched him. The rate of taxation had gone up in the county, but Mrs. Langrishe's house was still valued at $100 (there was no separate listing for him), her delinquent taxes being $3.55.[15]

The *New York Clipper* printed portions of a private letter Langrishe had sent to Jimmy Martin, an old friend and actor in Langrishe companies for several years:

> My friend, Felix Vincent, erred in supposing I was the nominee of all parties for State Senator in Idaho. I did receive the nomination on the Republican ticket, and was elected by a majority of over 200 in a hotly contested struggle. I can honestly say I sought no such honor, and positively refused to have my name go before the convention; but, in spite of all remonstrance, that body nominated me, and the first intimation I had of their action was a telegram stating the fact. Your reminiscence of days gone by (the senate scene in *Damon and Pythias*), when, wrapped in sheets of questionable cleanliness, we sat on wooden stools "incorporate with the marble," and lustily ejaculated words in condemnation or approval of the mighty matters being weighed by ourselves and other Syracuseans, recalled strange and not unpleasant memories, causing me to doubt very much whether I did not then feel more at home than I am likely to feel when I "stand a Senator in the Senate house" at Boise.[16]

Legislators from North Idaho were charged with getting a U.S. Senator acceptable to that region. In those days, and until passage of the Seventeenth Amendment to the Constitution (May 31, 1913), state legislators elected U.S. Senators. The Republican state convention had conceded one U.S. Senator to North Idaho, and that resolution was seen as "just as binding as any portion of the platform upon which the party stood...."[17] Since most of the people in the Coeur d'Alene region depended on mining for a living, directly or indirectly, they supported the free coinage of silver and a protective tariff on lead, and intended to rely on a North Idaho Senator to work for such legislation.

Langrishe, James F. Cameron and other newly elected state officials left for Boise City on Tuesday, December 2. They had to take the train to the head of navigation on Lake Coeur d'Alene, a ferry across the lake, then probably a stagecoach to Rathdrum, where they could catch the Northern Pacific train.[18] After using a variety of conveyances over the several legs of the journey, Langrishe registered at the Overland Hotel in Boise and met a number of old friends and admirers, as was usual in any community in the West.[19]

20. A New Career and Reflections

The legislature convened on December 8, 1890, organized committees and elected officers on that date and December 9.

Langrishe's service as the first Shoshone County Senator to be elected to the Idaho state legislature was respectable but undistinguished. Although his oratorical skills were equal to any other Senator, he spent most of his time listening to others debate.[20] He did introduce a bill to regulate medical practice but it failed to pass. During discussion of an anti-gambling bill he offered this sarcastic-sounding amendment: "Provided, however, that it shall not be a crime to win, but it shall be considered a crime to lose." Surprisingly, his amendment was adopted. Then the entire section was struck out and the bill killed.[21] On the positive side, Langrishe served on the committee that selected designs for the Idaho state flag and seal. The designs were the only state flag and seal in the nation created by a woman.[22] The legislature also made use of Langrishe's knowledge of printing and appointed him to the committee that approved bills for printing.

John S. Langrishe after being elected Senator to serve in the first Idaho state legislature. Photo taken in the 1890's and is included in a composite picture of Idaho's first state senate that is on display in the Idaho State House in Boise (Idaho Historical Society, Photo 3363-218).

Only a few other items pertained to Langrishe's term in the Idaho Senate. On December 22, 1890, he was paid $179 for his travel and living expenses.[23] This included a five dollar per diem.[24] In another instance, he and the entire Shoshone County delegation returned home for Christmas and came back to Boise on January 2 of the New Year to reconvene the legislative session.[25]

Langrishe joined the rest of the legislature in attending a performance by the Home Dramatic Company in February.[26] The play, Derrick's comedy

Confusion, featured a baby and a pug dog, also key elements in Langrishe's former production *That Terrible Telegram*.[27] It may have been the same play.

All the state Senators, including Langrishe, devoted most of the session to the important Constitutional task of selecting two men to become members of the United States Senate. The process turned out to be complicated, confusing and eventually as absurd as any farce ever presented by Langrishe in his theatre days. U.S. Senators for each state serve staggered terms, so the Idaho legislature was faced with electing one Senator for a full term, the other for a short term. Legislators representing mining areas feared their choice would get the short term, then be replaced by a person not committed to preserving mining interests. Squabbling escalated until they agreed they'd elect three Senators, one to serve a full term beginning March 4, 1891, another a short term, two to four years (depending on which paper the elect would draw), and the third would serve only until March 4, 1891.

First choice of the northern Idaho legislators was William Clagett, lawyer and mine owner (and carpetbagger, having served in legislatures in other states), but Clagett refused to participate in the "three Senators" scheme. After Christmas recess, the legislature buckled down and elected three Senators, the "north Idaho" representative a merchant from Lewiston. None would represent mining interests, so the north Idaho legislators managed to elect Clagett as a fourth Senator anyway. The Secretary of State refused to certify his election.[28]

The legislative impasse came under ridicule in the local and regional press, Senator Langrishe bearing the brunt. The *Spokane Falls Review* editorialized: "Idaho is young, but she has a faculty for turning out United States Senators that must make the slow coaches of the East turn dizzy with surprise. It takes New York, Pennsylvania and the other eastern states six years to groom and elect one Senator, but little Idaho has turned out four in as many weeks. If this thing goes on, United States Senators will be thicker in the Gem of the Mountains than colonels in Kentucky."[29] The (Boise) *Idaho Statesman* quoted the *Helena* (Montana) *Journal*: "Idaho evidently goes on the principle that electing United [sic] Senators is like courting a widow—it can't be overdone."[30]

Langrishe was not a candidate in the controversy, but his reputation as an actor and his stance on mining led the press to use theatrical metaphors and references in describing the legislative antics. The *Idaho Statesman* labeled the efforts of the Northern Idaho delegation to get a full-term Senator as a "coup" and wrote:

> We regret to be obliged to announce that it was absolutely necessary to postpone the coup. A dress rehearsal was held last night but things didn't go "smooth"—the property man

20. A New Career and Reflections

couldn't be found. Some of the flats wouldn't work, and the ballet was deficient in some respects. Mr. Langrishe thinks there must be "a yellow clarionet" in the band....

Following the successful performance of the coup there will be given some afterpieces. Several county farces are in active preparation by the same performers. One tickts [sic] admits to all.... The Third House is to be organized at once and four Senators elected, one from each N.N.E., S.W. by W., N.W. by N., S.E. by E., a few points either way. These will immediately proceed to Washington and play Tiddledy Winks for seats.[31]

The "yellow clarionet" reference alludes to a belief among theatre folks that a yellow clarinet in the orchestra is bad luck..[32]

After the legislature elected four men to serve in the Senate, Clagett's election was declared invalid and, as the mining faction had feared, the North Idahoan drew the six-week term. So much time had been spent on the election controversy that many bills were postponed to the next session and "sharp work" was in store before the present session ended.

The Idaho state legislators voted for the most popular man in the assembly, and that honor went to J.M. Wells. Surprisingly, Langrishe didn't get a single vote from his peers.[33] He was there out of a sense of duty, not there having sought the position. Known for his honesty, he'd been foiled by unexpected conniving of politicians. The man renowned for his popularity and affability had become a curmudgeon. When the Legislature adjourned, legislators turned souvenir hunters, stealing "everything moveable in the Capitol building except the yellow clarionet...."[34]

21

Shattered Peace

The Langrishes, after a long, adventurous and peripatetic life, wanted to retire quietly in a peaceful mountain setting. They couldn't have chosen a worse location.

They spent a summer as peaceful and quiet as possible, except for the daily rumble of hobnail boots on board walkways and the regular passage of heavily laden ore buckets thundering on the overhead tramway to the concentrator.

Summer also brought a change in ownership of Langrishe's *Wardner News*. On Saturday, July 4, 1891, a "dissolution notice" appeared in the *Wardner News,* announcing the partnership of Philip O'Rourke, W.E. McKelvey and Cornelius (Con) Sullivan, as publishers of the *Wardner News* was dissolved by mutual consent. Sullivan was leaving the partnership, his place to be taken by J.M. Kennedy of Butte, Montana.[1] Those were the names on the masthead, although the paper was secretly owned by V.M. Clement and George McAulay, managers of mines in the Wardner valley. Langrishe remained as editor.

Other events marked the summer. By early July, Wardner finally had the "arc light" (i.e., electricity)[2] and the *Wardner News* reported that Langrishe declaimed the Declaration of Independence as part of Wardner's July 4 celebration in the pavilion.[3]

The great tragic actress, Sarah Bernhardt, was to give performances in Spokane Falls on September 23 and 24. The Northern Pacific railroad sold excursion tickets at reduced fare for round trips.[4] Bernhardt, 46 years old, was probably in her prime. The Langrishes apparently went to see the far-famed tragedienne, for this headline appeared in the *Wardner News*: "Seeing Sarah, The Great French Actress Succeeded in Drawing—Crowds a Hundred Miles And More to Behold Her—Wardner Well Represented and Truly Appreciative" and was followed by:

> Sarah Bernhardt who has starred with unqualified success in almost every part of the world appeared one night last week in Spokane and as a consequence drew crowds of people, who

live hundreds of miles distant, to see her. The disappointment that usually exists in hearing an artist speak his or her lines in a foreign tongue was not wanting on the occasion referred to, but generally speaking the majority of those in attendance were satisfied with seeing the woman if they failed to appreciate the true quality of her acting....[5]

On October 3, 1891 Langrishe announced a change for the *Wardner News*:

> The office of the *Wardner News* has been moved to its former quarters on upper Main Street where our old friends and the public are cordially invited to call. In assuming the management of the oldest established journal in the South Fork the undersigned, encouraged by past favors while holding the position as its editor, hopes for a continuance of same. In doing so I beg to assure the patrons of the paper and the public generally that it will be my constant aim to forward, as far as within my power, the interests of the Coeur d'Alene country and conduct the *News* in a manner that will prove creditable to myself and deserving the support of the people. J. S. Langrishe[6]

This was probably the location remembered by Earl B. Crane, who lived in an apartment on the second floor of the *Wardner News* office as a child. He regarded their apartment location as somewhat unfortunate because Langrishe could not concentrate on his editorials if there was the least sound on the floor above him. It seemed that he always was working on an editorial of great importance, in spite of three children cooped up for the winter in a small apartment above. Crane recalled:

> Mr. Langrishe was a stout florid man, an ex-actor of the old Shakespearian school. He would be called a ham, now, but in Wardner his stage background lent him great prestige. His language was stagy and commanded respect. Daily, and sometimes twice a day, he would stalk up the stairs and knock at our door. "Madam," he would say, "can you not keep your children quiet? It is impossible for me to concentrate with that bedlam overhead." One time Mother invited him to come in and see what was making the noise. And there was Marguerite on the floor, smoothing a little piece of tinfoil on the carpet with her toy flatiron. Mr. Langrishe made a stately exit without a word.[7]

Wardner had a theatre called "The Coliseum." When the Chicago Comedy Company came to play in Wardner, Langrishe renewed acquaintance with his two of old friends Lizzie Lingham and Frank Cleaves,[8] who had met and married in Langrishe's last theatre company.

The *Wardner News* was allegedly sold to R.E. Brown, a civil engineer from Wallace, although the complaint in J.S. Langrishe v. George B. McAulay *et al.* indicated Clements and McAulay still owned the newspaper.[9] A Wallace paper disclosed: "For the present, Mr. Langrishe will continue to be its editor, assisted no doubt by the new proprietor. The *News* has been under the weather for some time and made a steady call for 'more sinews' on its proprietors...."[10] The name of the newspaper was changed to the *Coeur d'Alene Barbarian*, a name hard to associate with the gentlemanly Langrishe.[11]

Winter arrived, and Langrishe could see that the main street of Wardner "affords as fine a place for coasting as can be found anywhere."[12] He and his wife escaped the winter doldrums by taking part in the Wardner Social Club's "mask ball" on February 15. Many Wallace people arrived in sleighs, the Wallace band occupying the lead sleigh. They stopped in Osburn for whiskey, then on to Wardner. "It was growing dark when they arrived, and the Wallace band played a 'staring time' as it passed through the business district. The band went first to the office of the *Barbarian*, where they were heartily received by that genial gentleman, J.S. Langrishe. From there they played at various places down the street. The ball took place in the old 'Coloseum' [sic] theatre. The main room was crowded with dancers, while the stage and boxes were literally packed with spectators." The ball lasted until almost 4 a.m.[13]

The ladies of Wardner hosted a leap year ball February 29, breaking winter's isolating grip on the residents of Wardner and Wallace. Among those attending were Langrishe and Adam Aulbach, without their wives.[14] Langrishe and his wife attended the Wardner miners' union St. Patrick's Day ball fundraiser. The dance was held in the large storeroom under the Odd Fellows' Hall, decorated with stars and stripes and "occasional green banners in honor of Erin. A canary bird in a cage suspended midway of the hall mingled his pretty notes with those of Tilley's orchestra and added cheerfulness to the scene."[15] The canary bird, of course, was significant in mining as its silence served as the toxic air alarm in mines.

Festivities continued to the end of March. Langrishe ran an item in the *Coeur d'Alene Barbarian* promoting a March 31 "sheet and pillow case" party, for which all attending had to be costumed in sheets or pillow cases. He wrote: "Herein lies the chief amusement of such an entertainment, and the difficulty in discovering the identity and in many cases, the sex of your partner, adds additional fun to the affair. The festivities will be appropriate—at the hour of twelve when the sheets and pillow slips will be discarded, April Fools will be found in abundance. Remember the date, and assist in fooling your neighbor."[16]

Perhaps Langrishe had forgotten about his early days in New York when he or his representative claimed he had performed before all of the crowned heads of Europe, but on March 26 he lambasted the Cosgrove Concert Company who, "after having played before all the crowned heads of Europe, played this week before the equally distinguished heads of the Coeur d'Alene camp. The people of the Coeur d'Alene camp extend their sympathy to the crowned heads."[17]

Festivities and entertainments could not mask the animosity between labor and management in the region's mining camps. Strife between miners and the Mine Owners' Association prompted an attack on Langrishe by Adam

Aulbach, editor of the *Wallace Press*: "The *Wardner Barbarian*, aptly named, is termed the tin-whistle of the Mine Owners' Assn."[18] Langrishe retorted in the *Barbarian* that although he seemed supportive of the union, Aulbach's own employees at the *Wallace Press* were not union members, but "bleary-eyed, humpbacked and decrepit" boys.[19] Aulbach responded that the Irish lads were filling apprentice positions and when they had three years' experience they could go to a metropolitan area and join a union.

As labor tension continued, the Mine Owners' Association announced they would pay all underground workers $3.50 for ten-hour shifts, but they "wouldn't hire a union man under any circumstances." Rumors flew they were bringing in strike breakers.[20] Aulbach's attacks on Langrishe and the *Wardner Barbarian* were unceasing. He knew there was a link between the *Barbarian* and the Mine Owners' Association, but he apparently didn't know what it was.[21] The conflict continued to build, the Mine Owners' Association obtaining injunctions and striking miners stocking up on guns and ammunition.[22] On May 20 a special train arrived in Wallace bringing 75 strike-breaking miners guarded by about 50 men.[23]

Towns on the South Fork of the Coeur d'Alene River are close together, three to five miles separating them. Anything that affects one affects all. Owners of the Bunker Hill, Sullivan and Helena and Frisco mines obtained restraining orders against the miners' union in early June,[24] and by June 18, 267 non-union men were working at the Bunker Hill & Sullivan mines.[25] The stage was set for violence. Langrishe, stung by the incessant barbs from Aulbach, wrote, "Adam is running amuck in the political arena. Rope and room, gentlemen, for the editor of the Wallace Press, no hangman is needed."[6] A week later, July 9, under the headline "The Lying Barbarian," Aulbach retorted, "The Barbarian (circulation 60 copies) made one of its spasmodic kicks at the union again last week...."[27]

Then members of the miners' union turned violent, putting non-union miners on a train to leave the country, and fighting left five dead and many injured. Members of the Miners' Union put a ton of "giant powder" under the Bunker Hill and Sullivan mill and told the manager to either get the scabs out of the country or they'd blow up the mill.[28] Idaho Governor Norman B. Willey, recognizing the danger facing the Coeur d'Alenes, asked President Benjamin Harrison for troops from Fort Sherman or some other military encampment be dispatched to quell violence, since the state did not have the militia necessary.[29] The troops got as far as the Cataldo Mission, ten miles short of Wardner, when they stopped because the Miners' Union threatened to blow up the Bunker Hill and Sullivan mill if they proceeded toward Wardner.[30] Members of the Miners' Union discovered the Mine Owners had had a spy in the Union, and then blew up a mill and went after scabs waiting for a ferry to transport them away from the Coeur d'Alene valley, shooting and wounding or killing all in their sights. The governor proclaimed martial law and about 600 union men were arrested, at least 350 of whom were held in a stockade dubbed the "bullpen."[31] As the valley resounded with gunshots, Jeannette Langrishe's sister and brother-in-law, Augusta and E.H. Atwood of St. Cloud, Minnesota, arrived in Wardner for a visit.[32]

R.E. Brown "severed" his connection as editor of the *Barbarian* as of July 23, leaving Langrishe "of the editorial staff [to] assume full charge."[33] Brown then moved to Wallace and bought Aulbach's newspaper, the *Wallace Press*.[34] Aulbach's prickly defenses of the Miners' Union had irritated Generals Curtis and Carlin, so he was better off away from them, but still in the Coeur d'Alene region where he took over the *Mullan Tribune,* which he already owned.[35]

By the end of July, 127 Wardner men were incarcerated, including five sent to Boise to stand trial. Between 400 and 500 troops remained in the Coeur d'Alenes, stationed at Wardner, Osburn, Wallace, Burke and Gem.[36] In Wardner, General E.J. Curtis ordered the town cleaned up. "[T]he fact that [the clean-up] was brought about by a military order has had a wholesome effect upon the minds of indifferent people, and reminds them that cleanliness is a part of good order and good citizenship...."[37]

Life for Langrishe and his fellow citizens became more normal, although some bitterness from the recent labor confrontation remained. Wardner residents complained that the electric light service was turned on late in the evening, and that the current was weak.[38] The town was well supplied with banks, however—faro banks. Seven were in operation, plus nine crap games and a roulette table.[39] Then the Republican County Convention selected candidates for election, including Langrishe for justice of the peace.[40] Work began on a new Knights of Pythias building in Wardner, to be 40 × 100 feet in size and three stories high. The first floor was to be occupied by businesses, the second for a public hall and the third a hall for secret societies.[41] Adam Aulbach returned to Murray, publishing the *Murray Sun*.[42]

Duties as justice of the peace occupied Langrishe's days. One man threatened to kill another if the latter attempted to go to work at the Sierra Nevada mine, for which he was arrested and brought before Justice Langrishe.[43] A Wallace paper revealed: "Petty offenders are becoming more numerous every day and Judge Langrishe is kept busy.... Al Quackenbush was bound over in $500.00 bonds, by Judge Langrishe, to await the action of the grand jury. Quackenbush is charged with an assault with a Bowie-knife upon two soldiers."[44] Another item reported that a masked man held up the faro dealer at

Justus Loeber's saloon, took over $1000 dollars, but the man who was in the "look-out" chair grabbed the thief. The robber was taken before Judge Langrishe, where he pled guilty.[45] Martial law was withdrawn at noon on November 19, allowing all soldiers to be withdrawn.[46]

Langrishe enjoyed some diversion from his various duties. In Wardner, the Knights of Pythias building was nearly complete and a grand ball was planned for its formal opening December 26. "[The] local Knights thought the floor should be settled before it was subjected to the strains of the immense crowd expected on the 26th and a small dancing party was given during the week. Only a few of the heavy weights were invited."[47] The Langrishes also attended a December 2 social held by the Columbian Social Club at the Odd Fellows Hall with dancing, entertainment and refreshments.[48] Also in attendance was Aaron Frost, an old friend of Langrishe. A newspaperman in Georgetown, Colorado, during the early 1880s, he was currently the "authorized agent" of the *Coeur d'Alene Miner*.[49]

Holiday festivities and bad weather marked the end of the year. Officers of the Bunker Hill and Sullivan Co. gave a "sumptuous banquet" for V.M. Clement, general manager of the company, who left for California December 21, leaving F.G. Bradley in charge of the mine operations.[50] Also that week the weather turned nasty, with blizzards, snow drifts and wind sufficient to blow a large cedar tree over the railroad tracks, partially disabling the engine. In Wardner itself, water pipes froze and burst, and the flume that carried water to the electric plant froze so no water could get through. Thus there was no electricity for lights.[51] The day after Christmas, the grand ball for the opening of the Knights of Pythias Hall was held, Mr. and Mrs. Langrishe attending.

Langrishe's duties continued even during the holiday season. Wardner was lively with several fights breaking out, including one that involved the discharge of a firearm. The shooter appeared before Judge Langrishe, who "bound him over in $250 bonds to appear on Monday afternoon for a primary examination."[52] On New Year's Eve, Justice Langrishe conducted a wedding ceremony.[53]

Justice of the Peace Langrishe was tucked into an isolated, snow-choked corner of America, but Comedian Jack Langrishe was warmly remembered by members of the dramatic profession. The Christmas edition of *Dramatic News* published a poem by Eugene Field about Langrishe, "Soldiers with Brutus in St. Jo." By that time Field was a noted newspaper columnist and poet, known especially for his children's poems, which included "Wynken, Blynken and Nod." He had spent 1881 and 1882 in Denver as managing editor of the *Denver Tribune*, and would have met Langrishe at that time. Field may have acted in one of Langrishe's productions, but they were not "soldiers with Brutus in St. Jo." Denverites read the poem with fond reminiscence when it was published in the Denver *Rocky Mountain News* Christmas Day, 1892. The poem, some ten stanzas long, began with:

> To-day while walking in the square, Jack Langrishe says to me:
> "My friend, the drama nowadays ain't what it used to be!
> These farces and these comedies—how feebly they compare
> With that mantle of the tragic art that Forrest used to wear!
> My soul is warped with bitterness to think that you and I—
> Coheirs to immortality in seasons long gone by—
> Now draw a paltry stipend from a Boston comic show,
> We, who were Roman soldiers with Brutus in St. Jo!"
> —Christmas Dramatic News[54]

22

The Last Act

News of Langrishe in January of 1893 included both official duties and his social life. Shoshone County commissioners "approved the official bond of J.S. Langrishe, justice of the peace, and approved his report," then paid him $60 out of the general fund.[1] For diversion, Mr. and Mrs. Langrishe attended the third Columbian social dance held in the Pythian Home January 2, "a grand success, socially and financially."[2]

Later in the month, Langrishe was ill. He explained in his paper: "Indisposition has prevented the editor of the *Barbarian* from attending to his duties this week—hence the lack of usual matter in these columns."[3] The editor of the *Coeur d'Alene Miner,* in Wallace, reported, "Our genial friend, J.S. Langrishe, of the *Barbarian,* was seriously indisposed last week with an attack of the grippe, being confined to his bed for five days. This week, however, he has resumed his editorial and judicial duties."[4]

A swift-moving fire struck Wardner's Cosmopolitan Hotel, some residents barely escaping with their lives. "Bernard Arnold, the printer at the *Barbarian,* who slept the sleep of the just and innocent and was, therefore, rather hard to awaken, had an extremely close call. The flames had already reached his bedroom before he waked. He seized such of his raiment as was handiest at the moment and made his way to the street clad only in a suit of underclothing and a wild look of surprise...."[5]

George B. McAulay, a prominent banker and mine owner in Wardner (and the secret owner of the Wardner *Coeur d'Alene Barbarian*), treated Langrishe unfairly. It was reported that McAulay sat down at a faro table in Josh Collins' place Friday at 1 p.m. and did not close out until Monday. Friday night, he lost several thousand dollars, then Saturday he complained the limit was too low for him so "the limit was removed entirely, and George piled up $1000 and $1200 at a time and won or lost it as nonchalantly as he refuses Irishmen work...." When he closed out, he had won back all but $1500 of the money he had lost.[6] An interesting aspect to this is that, as owner of the *Coeur d'Alene Barbarian,* he was not paying Langrishe for his work putting out the newspaper.[7]

Early in 1893 Langrishe and his lady made a brief return to acting. At the February 22 meeting of the Ladies' Columbian society, they decided to put on an entertainment about March 15. The entertainment would be a three-act play starring the Langrishes, but they were not ready to announce the title. Langrishe wrote, "It will, if well received, make Rome howl with envy, and the quartzite rocks that abound on the South Fork will be turned to lava. Mortals will break the necks of their fellows in their anxiety to secure seats for the first act. They assure their patrons that the arrangements will be ample on the evening of the entertainment to protect life, and also a large supply of sabers, cutlasses, cimeters [scimitars], tomahawks and slingshots will be ready for those who wish to make challenges on the spot."[8]

Hard times awaited Langrishe and Wardner. The U.S. was in an economic slump, but the Panic of 1893 was yet two months in the future. Locally, the Bunker Hill & Sullivan mines shut down on March 4 and paid off 380 men, injecting $42,000 into circulation in the South Fork area on that date. Yet there was some levity. As one paper reported: "One of the miners, late a soldier in the Queen's own, a man who boasts of having fought in the Zulu war, created a sensation by sliding down the street, sitting astride his trunk, playing 'The Girl I Left Behind Me' on a flute, the sled going at a high rate of speed."[9]

Mr. and Mrs. Langrishe announced they'd star in *Naval Engagements* April 15 in the Pythian Home, supported by local talent, to raise funds for the purchase of new scenery for the Pythian Home, sometimes referred to as the Knights of Pythias Hall. Mrs. Langrishe was to play the male role of "Dennis."[10] The *Wallace Democrat* noted the coming performance in a column headed "Wardner Items" and added that the appearance of the Langrishes should be a guarantee of a full house. "To the old-timers they need no introduction. Our people should demonstrate, by their presence that these people are as dear to them now as they were in the past."[11] (The performance did not occur at that time, being delayed until July 1.[12]) The July 8 *Coeur d'Alene Miner* called it the "best performance ever given in Wardner."[13]

At 1:30 a.m. April 20, a fire consumed a substantial part of Wardner. More than 80 buildings were destroyed; very few of them were insured. No lives were lost and no injuries reported. Several dwellings were lost in addition to meat markets, lodging houses, restaurants, a dry goods and clothing store, a millinery, the Odd Fellows' building, the Miners' Exchange bank building, the central station of the telephone company, a hotel, a stationer, tailor shops, another lodging house, a wallpaper store, drugstores, the post office building, barber, a three-story hotel and the board sidewalks.[14] The newspaper office of the *Coeur d'Alene Barbarian* and the Langrishes' home were spared the flames.

22. The Last Act

Rebuilding started the next day, but the scarcity of lumber and general discouragement made it a slow process. A bright spot, as reported in the press, lay in the fact that "since the fire Main street [had been] accurately surveyed and staked so that hereafter a grade may be established that will avoid the numerous steps on the sidewalks that have been such a nuisance and menace in the past...."[15] Later in the month, the trickling stream that ran through Wardner, Milo Creek, became a howling torrent for a couple of days, and Wardner people turned out en masse to keep it within its bounds. Some unspecified damage was done; in that area, people built outhouses over such creeks, and some of those may have washed away.[16]

On June 6, 1893, Langrishe, through his attorney W.B. Heyburn (later a Senator), filed an action for assumpsit in district court against George B. McAulay and V.M. Clement. This was an action filed to recover money owed the plaintiff by the defendants.[17] The defendants failed to show up, and the judge issued a declaratory judgment in Langrishe's favor on August 28. The execution was filed on October 7. The outcome was that Langrishe "bought" the newspaper and its equipment at a sheriff's auction in lieu of back salary. It was probably a pre-arranged default on the parts of the manager of the Bunker Hill & Sullivan mines (Clement, no longer in Wardner) and the banker-mine owner (McAulay), in exchange for Langrishe's editorial support of the mine owners during the labor troubles of the previous years. Adam Aulbach's outrage at Langrishe and the newspaper's support of the mine owners had been right on target. Langrishe changed the newspaper name back to *Wardner News*.

With the return of winter in late 1893, Langrishe would enjoy viewing the antics of his fellow citizens. As described in a Wallace paper, Wardner's main street, through the middle of the business district, is straight and steep. A good pack of snow made "coasting ... the amusement that ranks above all others in Wardner and is shared in by persons of both sexes, old and young, and will continue to be, as it is both exciting and exhilarating.... A few days ago three boys, mounted on a long coaster, took a horse off its feet and for a few moments the surprised animal and the three lads were all prostrate together. Fortunately they all escaped without serious injury."[18]

The year 1894 started off quietly with little of interest happening in Wardner. The Langrishes were active with a group of amateurs in the Wardner Dramatic Club. They went to Wallace to perform on March 8, "A.E.A." (perhaps Adam Aulbach) reporting that the "amateur actors performed their parts in a very commendable manner. As for the old stagers, I think they acted with as much vim and vigor as they did 30 years ago when I heard them 'back in the states.'"[19]

In April, Governor William J. McConnell appointed Langrishe to represent Idaho at the annual convention of railroad commissioners to be held in Washington, D.C., on May 8.[20] Langrishe politely declined.

Throughout his life, Langrishe had enjoyed the camaraderie and respect of diverse people, from poor to rich. He had been a Republican, perhaps sharing President Abraham Lincoln's negative view of slavery; throughout his travels Langrishe had avoided performing in the South which was fertile ground for theatre. Now his political views began to create enemies. An editorial in the *Idaho State Tribune* of October 29 attacked him: "Vile epithets and indecent personal abuse of men, Mr. Wardner *News,* whom are your peers in every respect by common consent of their respective communities might be considered reason and argument by you, but only lick-spittles of soul-less corporations will stoop to cast such slurs upon the representatives of the wealth producers of this community—unworthy the efforts of a newspaper man."[21]

The new Populists nearly swept the election, an exception in Shoshone County being that of Republican Langrishe, re-elected justice of the peace.[22] The *Idaho State Tribune's* crowing over their party's successes included some slams at Langrishe: "Barry Murphy sends love to Grandma Langrishe.... Another extra of Grandma's paper, and there would not have been a grease spot left of the Republican party.... If necessary, we will send our office devil down to sit up with the Wardner News man, and endeavor to console him. Poor old Langrishe.... Now, then, let us give the county the best business administration it has ever had. Make the Wardner News man even ashamed of himself for having called us such horrid names...."[23] The *Tribune* diatribe continued: "The stranded barn stormer [sic] who edits the News (better known as the Wardner Bladder) tried to injure the election of the candidate for the legislature on the populist ticket from this town, by telling the people that he had jumped a lot here (which everybody knows is a lie) must feel like a whipped boy, not a word had he to say in his last issue about the brilliant victory of the above-mentioned candidate for the legislature...."[24]

The vitriol spilled over into December, when an *Idaho State Tribune* editorial stated, "The *Tribune* believes in peace, in fixing up matters.... We most emphatically believe in a free press but when an editor [Langrishe] continues to malign the very men, in season and out of season, whom he expects to make his living of (cq), it is time to call a halt. It is too apparent this particular paper and its editor is [sic] owned body, soul and breeches by the Bunker Hill & Sullivan Mining Company, he dare not say his soul is his own...."[25]

Away from the political arena, Langrishe revealed some of his attitudes toward the drama in his critique of *The Clemenceau Case*, performed at

Pythian Hall by the Charles Riggs Co.: "The morale [sic] of the play may be said to be rather questionable. With but few exceptions, in the list of Sardou's and Dumas' dramas, there is the unending iteration of the one theme—that of the realism of the improbable. Sardou revels only in sensual sensationalism and is never more in his element as a playwright than when his subject is the glorification of a cardinal sin. His works are to the stage what Zola's novels are to the literature of fiction...."[26]

The Lord Rooney Comedy Company came to Wardner and drew a "well-filled house," but Langrishe sharpened his pen for his review, calling it "The Rooney Monstrosity" and remarking: "In days of yore, we used to laugh at Pat Rooney, who was not an actor, but a most admirable comic vocalist; his 'Solid Muldoon' was so natural and mirth-provoking his fun was infectious and it easily spread throughout the length and breadth of the land. On the strength of his reputation the party that inflicted us with their presence on Monday night are touring..." He added that the costumes were tawdry, "the performers unable to sing or dance [and] the attempts at acting were unlike anything hitherto seen and can be set down as positively idiotic...."[27]

In March of 1895 arrangements were completed for the building of an Episcopal church at Wardner, for about $1000. It would seat 100 and be built of Oregon lumber, with 15 large stained glass windows. A.J. Holworthy was pastor.[28] The Langrishes attended that church.

Langrishe and his fellow citizens welcomed the easing of tension between miners and owners. Officials of the Bunker Hill & Sullivan mines wanted a businessmen's declaration supporting their right to pay what they wished made public. By the time the declaration was made public, there were 186 names on the list, including Langrishe's.[29] The Bunker Hill & Sullivan Co. resumed operations after a nine-month shutdown[30] and the Last Chance mine, also above Wardner, reopened in early July.[31] The people of Wardner were euphoric, buoyed by the organization of two companies of state militia who arrived July 8, with 140 Springfield rifles and 10,000 rounds of ammunition. Their presence "has had a decidedly cooling effect on those who are disposed to trample on the laws."[32]

Langrishe's former brother-in-law, John Dillon, had finally defeated his "failing" (alcoholism) and was enjoying great popularity. In late July he was performing in Boise, and traveling in the direction of Wardner. Langrishe wrote: "We hope the genial John will appear in Wardner, as there are many here who know him well, have seen him often and would be more than pleased to see him again. Mr. Dillon is the very personification of fun, his methods are entirely original, his manner so easy and his acting so natural, he captivates his audience on his first appearance and keeps them in a continual roar of laughter the whole evening. Come this way, John, Wardner will be glad to greet you."[33] Langrishe was letting Dillon know he'd be welcomed by the Langrishes as well, now that he was sober.

Langrishe had given Dillon his start on the stage, but after Dillon's first wife, Helen Allen (Mrs. Langrishe's sister) died, Dillon's drunken bouts became more notorious; he showed up when the Langrishes were in Deadwood and other remote places but they did not hire him, leaving him to work in variety theatres. Now that he was sober, they'd be happy to see him and hear news of their two nieces (Dillon's daughters). Whether Dillon did see them or not is not known. Dillon performed in Hamilton, Montana, on July 29, and Missoula on July 30, and then the company was to take a vacation in "the National Park" (Yellowstone) from August 2 through 10.[34]

Given the details of the event, Langrishe evidently attended a party as described in his paper on September 14:

> A grand ball was held at Pythian Hall in early September, closing a most delightful season of both instruction and amusement. The Pythians and their friends evidently left their Quaker legs at home and brought their dancing pumps with them. The ball room presented a brilliant sight; pleasure prevailed and smiles of satisfaction gleamed on every countenance. Supper was served at Page's hotel, where the worthy proprietor fairly surpassed himself in the excellence of the service and the profusion of good things and delicacies on the menu. Twice the tables were reset and everybody pronounced the repast the best ever offered in Wardner—in fact a banquet fit for the gods. The guests were determined to prolong the festivities and the dancers followed the matchless strains of the superb orchestra until after 4 o'clock Friday morning.[35]

"Our doctors report considerable sickness among our citizens," noted the *Wardner News* November 9. The *Wallace Miner* reported on November 16, "Judge Langrishe has been confined to his home by sickness for the past two weeks, but is now greatly improved."[36] A later report said he'd suffered from a heart ailment at that time.[37]

Langrishe probably wrote the review of the Johnnie Pringle and Edna May dramatic company engagement: "Considering the number of combinations that have appeared here in almost rapid succession recently, they played to good average houses nightly. Mr. Pringle is a most admirable actor and was seen to much advantage in the various characters he assumed. Miss Edna May is a very attractive and accomplished young lady and fairly captivated her audience by her inimitable Kaleidoscope dance."[38]

On Wednesday, November 20, Langrishe performed a wedding ceremony in Kellogg. He united Postmaster M.J. Sinclair of Kellogg to Mrs. E.J. Thwaite of the same place, in the presence of the father and mother of the bride and a few intimate friends of the family.[39]

On Saturday, November 30, 1895, Langrishe went to his *News* office and

22. The Last Act

John Dillon in his maturity and still on tour in the 1890's (authors' collection, donated by Mrs. Catherine Barth, granddaughter of John Dillon).

spent a few hours working, then walked home, chatting pleasantly with several old friends on the way. A Wallace paper reported: "Between 7 and 8 o'clock, he was reading to Mrs. Langrishe, when he suddenly took a notion to lie down on the bed, but did not manifest any serious illness. He asked Mrs. Langrishe to sit where he could see her, and a short time later said, 'I believe I will get up again.' His wife set the armchair for him and took hold of his hand to assist him as he attempted to rise, when he suddenly fell back on the bed and expired instantly without a struggle or a sigh."[40]

The Rev. A.J. Holworthy wrote to Bishop Daniel S. Tuttle on December 4, 1895; Tuttle included the letter in his "Reminiscences":

[I]t is with a deep personal feeling of regret that I write to tell you of the passing away of your old and dear friend, Judge Langrishe, who died very suddenly at his home in Wardner on Saturday last.... Mr. Langrishe had been quite sick for several weeks but was feeling much better during the ten or fifteen days preceding his last and fatal attack. He had heart trouble and suffered very much, always hiding his pain whenever possible for his dear wife's sake.... Poor soul, it was really heart-rending to see her for several hours afterwards, but she finally became calm and bore up wonderfully well on the day of the funeral. While she spent the last few moments looking for the last time on earth on the face of him who had for half a century been her faithful companion and protector it was my privilege to be alone with her, and try to comfort her as well as my own deep sorrow would allow, for he was one of my warmest friends and more like a father in his attachment to me. Grand old man, he is sleeping the sleep of the just (for he had so many, many virtues that if he had any faults they were more than covered by his noble qualities) up on the lonely hillside where he has toiled many a time to pay the last tribute of respect to a brother man, more than once reading the beautiful service for the burial of the dead, where no minister could be had....

When I went East a few months ago, he said to me one afternoon in the church, where he was regularly to be found, 'Mr. Holworthy, you may see Bishop Tuttle while you are away and if you do, tell him,' and then he broke down and cried like a child. I soothed him and told him I knew what he wanted me to say—for he had read me a letter some months ago which you had written him, and which he wanted to answer so much. He had told me that several times he took out the letter from the drawer where he kept it, intending to sit right down and reply to it, but each time he was so very much affected that he had to give it up and it worried him so much for fear you might think him unkind and unappreciative of your thoughtfulness of him and the kind sentiments expressed in the letter. During his last sickness, while sitting with him and talking of you, we agreed that as soon as he was quite well again he should tell me what to say and I would write the letter for him. Now, I am writing to tell you how much he loved you, and that he, poor fellow, will never be able to tell you so himself.[41]

Tuttle was Presiding Bishop of the Episcopal Church in America from 1903 to 1923. It was unusual for any church official to remember an actor so kindly in his memoirs. He was not the only one to so remember Jack Langrishe. Bishop Ethelbert Talbot, Presiding Bishop from February 18, 1924, to January 1, 1926, also wrote about Langrishe, but not by name:

Among the interesting experiences of my life in the Far West was the meeting from time to time, in some remote and isolated corner of that vast hiding place, a striking personality.... In Wardner, when the camp was new, I met a man who impressed me as a person of unusual culture. He had a striking face, and his grace of manner and a certain elegance and dignity of bearing convinced me that he was no ordinary individual.... Were I to mention his name, those of my readers familiar with the American stage forty years ago would recognize him as a noted actor of that day.... Though very poor, and compelled, with his invalid wife, to live in a little log cabin and practice the most rigid economy, he was highly esteemed. He eked out a precarious living by writing for the newspapers; for he had good literary taste, and was the master of a polished and graceful style. It was always a privilege to meet the old man. He was a lover of good books, a student and interpreter of Shakespeare, and possessed brilliant conversational gifts.... He became deeply interested in the church, and admired enthusiastically the dignity and beauty of the Book of Common Prayer. In his early days, simply as an act of friendship, he had given several prominent clergymen lessons in elocution, with special reference to the proper reading of the service, which he could render with an impressiveness and appreciation rarely found. It was to the credit of the people of that mining-camp ... that they ministered with lavish and unremitting kindness to the needs of this aged couple, and did not suffer them to lack any of the simple comforts of life in their declining years....[42]

Langrishe's funeral, under the auspices of the Odd Fellows, was held at 1 p.m. Monday, December 2, at the new Episcopal church, the Rev. A.J. Holworthy officiating. The hearse was preceded by a body of Odd Fellows members and followed by a long line of vehicles and citizens afoot, the largest funeral held in the Coeur d'Alenes by that time. Only one-half of the persons present could get into the church to hear the service. The broken-hearted widow insisted on following the remains to the grave in the Kellogg cemetery.

According to the *Coeur de'Alene Miner:* "Mrs. Langrishe will remain in Wardner and will continue to occupy her home back of the American house, where kindly neighbors will give her such attentions as her age and condition require. She has a sister in St. Cloud, Minnesota, and one in St. Paul, but she

22. The Last Act

Grave marker of Jack Langrishe in the Kellogg, Idaho, cemetery. Wind, weather and time have all but erased the inscriptions on the stone (authors' collection).

prefers to remain with her friends and associations of the past few years, for the present at least.... [S]ome of her nearest friends advise her not to dispose of the property [the *News*], but to retain it as a source of revenue in her declining years."[43]

At the time of his death, Langrishe was 70. Perhaps even he didn't realize his birth year was 1825, not 1830 as most sources reported (his tombstone reads 1860).[44] Time seemed to be a relative term to him; for instance, he sometimes reported that he spent "nearly two years" in Mexico City when he had spent about two months there. As stated in his Wallace, Idaho, obituary:

> He was brusque, hearty, genial, whole-souled and popular, but withal easy in manner and courtly as a knight when occasion required it. "Jack Langrishe" was extended a cordial welcome wherever and whenever himself and his meritorious company appeared. At that time he was possessed of means that would today be considered an ample competency, and to a person of less generous impulses would have constituted the foundation for a princely fortune, but successive fires in Denver, Deadwood and other places ... swept away his possessions and seriously curtailed his financial resources....

> In his private, social and business relations Judge Langrishe was characterized by such uniform courtesy and kindness as one rarely meets in these days, but only those who have seen him at home with his life partner can fully appreciate his kindly character and genial manners. Age had not robbed him of the numerous little acts of graceful tenderness which emanate only from a generous disposition and a heart full of sympathy for the frailties of mankind....[45]

In Wisconsin the *Madison State Journal* printed the most accurate obituary:

> "Jack Langrishe," the inimicable [sic] comedian, is dead.... John S. F. Langrishe ... was one of the most famous men in western history, and once appeared in Mark Twain's *Roughing It*, as a type of theatrical manager. Langrishe was known as the proprietor of the first theatre built in Denver, and also as the first man with daring enough to essay Shakespearean roles in the wild mining region of the west when the dance hall was the most exalted form of amusement.... "Jack" Langrishe was as well known in Madison in early times as any man in the state. He, in company with J.B. Atwater, opened the first theatre in the place, then a village, and it was in a building belonging to Jehu Lewis, on the corner of Wisconsin Avenue and Johnson Street, opposite the spot where the Masonic Temple now stands. The name of the theatrical company was Langrishe and Atwater. This company played in every city in the state in the early days. Mr. Langrishe was a great favorite with all classes. His 'Toodles,' his 'Aminidab Sleek,' 'John Unit,' 'Sir Peter Teazle,' 'Paul Pry,' 'William' in *Black Eyed Susan*, and many other characters, will never be forgotten. Mr. Langrishe's name until changed by an act of the legislation [sic] of this state in the fifties, was Folds. He took the name Langrishe—his mother's maiden name [not true]—when he first went on the stage in London.[46] His father, John S. Folds, was the founder of the Dublin magazine, and he was government printer in Dublin for several years, when he came to Madison and worked in the old Argus office.... Mr. Langrishe was a cousin of George Folds, who conducted a dry goods store so many years where Ogden now keeps.... He was about 73 years old.[47]

Obituaries blossomed from San Diego to New York City, reporting the sad news. In Montana, where Langrishe had been especially popular, he was described as "a large man with a big nose and homely face, and a poor actor, but was very popular among the rough miners."[48] Critics in the largest cities in the Midwest and East apparently thought highly of his acting abilities, especially after 1870 when he performed in those areas. The *Leadville* (Colorado) *Herald-Democrat* wrote in his obituary:

> Jolly, tireless Jack Langrishe, "everybody's friend," has gone to his last rest and a great throb of anguish strikes the heart of every one of the myriad of western people who knew this noble man for so many years. The pioneer manager in every mining camp in the west for nearly half a century, he won the lasting friendship of people in every walk of life. Full of ready wit, at home alike in the prospector's cabin, or the banker's parlor, he upheld at all times the dignity of his profession and strove steadily to elevate the drama. Hundreds of beginners on the stage who enjoyed his friendship and benefitted by his teachings, will grieve over his loss as that of a foster father. Sincerely mourning his death and revering his memory, we can only turn to his beloved Shakespeare and quote: "What! Old acquaintance! Could not all this flesh keep in a little life? Poor Jack, farewell! We could have better spared a better man."[49] (*Henry IV, Part 1*, Act V, Scene 3)

Epilogue

Lincoln J. Carter's *Defaulter* company was performing in western Montana in December 1895. A member of the company was Lettie Allen, Jeannette Langrishe's niece, originally introduced to acting by Jeannette and Jack Langrishe. She may have been able to get to Wardner to console her aunt following her bereavement,[1] since she would have had December 24 off, as the company traveled from Missoula to Spokane, Washington, Wardner situated in between.[2] The *Wardner News* was published November 30, there was no issue for December 7, and on December 14, the masthead read "Mrs. J.S. Langrishe, Proprietress, Aaron Frost—Lessee and Publisher."

Frost had been a Langrishe friend since the 1870s, when he worked for the Georgetown, Colorado, *Miner,* and lately had been working in Spokane. He too would draw the ire of the Miners' Union, but before he did, the *Coeur d'Alene Miner* lashed out at the *Idaho State Tribune,* editors of which retorted, "So, Mr. *Miner,* we did the late Jack Langrishe an unpardonable wrong, and should be classed with the natives of the infernal region, and all this for simply stating a few facts. How about the man that has used him up to his last moment and then refusing [*sic*] to bury him? Where does he belong, among the angels of course?"[3]

George West, editor of the (Golden, Colorado) *Colorado Transcript*, published a portion of a letter he received from Langrishe's long-term leading man, Harry Richmond:

> "Jack Langrishe is dead!" To thousands upon thousands in Colorado, Montana, Idaho and Wyoming those few words will fall with mournful cadence. But how mournful, how pregnant with desolation and woe to that lone widow amid the hills of Idaho. No ray of sunshine irradiates the gloom that shrouds her heart. Surrounded by sympathetic friends no doubt she is, but they are not her "lover husband," for such he was from the beginning to the end. Associated with them for years, I can truthfully say no married couple ever lived more in harmony, or more fully demonstrated "each for the other and in that other for their dearer self" than Jack Langrishe and his most worthy wife.
>
> "Jack" Langrishe built his own monument. The outgoing, present and rising generations will cry with one accord "requiescat in pace." "He was a good man." And I, who worked

by his side for years, can say "God is with you, Jack. I shall never look upon his like again." His co-worker, Harry Richmond.[4]

Since many had been unable to enter the church for the Reverend Holworthy's funeral sermon, he repeated it December 15.[5] The citizens of Wardner realized they needed a justice of the peace, so signed a petition, asking the county commissioners to appoint A.B. Wood to that office.[6] Mrs. Langrishe notified the townspeople: "Good people of Wardner: I wish to sincerely thank you one and all, for your kind assistance given, and tender sympathy expressed in my great bereavement. Many friends have asked as to my future plans. I shall remain in Wardner, where I have formed ties that bind me closer than any other earthly ties, where I have friends who have been tried and not found wanting. I cannot leave you. I sincerely thank you. Mrs. J. S. Langrishe."[7]

All knew Langrishe could write, set type and print, but few knew he was careless about the business of his newspaper. His circulation records were completely inadequate. Subscribers were listed by name, not the date they subscribed or the date their subscription would need renewal. Frost ran a "Notice to Subscribers" on page one:

> Notice is hereby given to all persons who are in arrears for subscriptions that all back subscriptions which are paid into this office on or before January 1, 1896, will be for the sole benefit of Mrs. J.S. Langrishe, or if more convenient, the same may be handed to Mrs. Langrishe personally. It is hoped that all delinquents will avail themselves of the privilege thus offered of showing a substantial testimonial of respect for Mrs. Langrishe and appreciation of her late husband. Many of the subscriptions as shown on the books are without date, so that those who have been receiving the News will be better able to judge of the obligations incurred than any other person, and we trust that each one will respond promptly and in full.[8]

Langrishe had said his acting art was ephemeral, his fame "writ on water." In February 1895, less than a year before he passed away, he ran an article in the *Wardner News* about "Edison's Latest," a kinetoscope being exhibited on Salt Lake City's Main street, that showed a prize fight, "every move just as natural as life" that was drawing big crowds.[9] Whether he or his readers realized that from that time on, acting could be a permanent art rather than an ephemeral one, is not known. Six months after his death, an article appeared in the *New York Dramatic Mirror* about Edison's Vitascope, and an exhibition in New York of what this recorder could do, showing "the Leigh Sisters in their umbrella dance ... the breaking of waves on the seashore ... a burlesque boxing match between Walton and Mayon, the long and short comedians; a scene from Hoyt's 'A Milk White Flag'; and a serpentine dance with all the colored calcium [light] effects, and an amusing picture showing an argument between John Bull and Uncle Sam."[10] Thus they inched toward theatrical motion pictures, a form capable of capturing the once ephemeral art of acting.

After Langrishe's funeral, Pythian Hall finally received the scenery they'd needed for some time and that Langrishe had helped to raise money for. It cost nearly $400, but for that sum Sosman & Landis, scene painters in Chicago, supplied an elegant drop curtain and 35 scenic drops and set pieces.[11]

A couple new to Wardner moved in with Mrs. Langrishe soon after she was widowed. Mr. and Mrs. Parish had just moved from Oregon. The husband was a music teacher.[12] Bishop Ethelbert Talbot, an old friend of the Langrishes, arrived in Wardner on January 29, just in time to hold services at St. Peter's Church. After the sermon, Jeannette and Lila Johnson presented themselves at the communion rail and received the rite of confirmation.[13] A few days later Jeannette received the sad news that her nephew, B.A. Atwater of Chicago, had been murdered in St. Louis, Missouri. He was working for leading eastern magazines as a photographer. Both of his parents, J.B. Atwater and Jeannette's sister Laurette, were listed as survivors.[14]

Jeannette Langrishe as she appeared in the 1890's (Subject Collection, Scan# 10044753, History Colorado).

Mrs. Langrishe rode in a carriage "plentifully decorated with bright yellow color" with three other women in the July 4 parade in Wardner, representing the Equal Suffrage Club.[15] On July 17, the Ladies of St. Peter's Guild put on a program for their friends, including Jeannette's recitation of "The Switchman's Story." The press noted: "While all the numbers were excellently rendered, yet especial mention must be made of the recitation by Mrs. Langrishe. It was not she who told us the story but the switchman himself, and the speaker, and the audience were lost to all but the touching tale of heroism. Mrs. Langrishe's power is more than art, it is not acting, it is being."[16]

The *Wardner News* published the delinquent tax list on December 19, 1896. Mrs. Langrishe owed taxes on a dwelling house on the upper side of Mill Street, and the News printing outfit on upper Main Street, total of

$32.25.¹⁷ Even if Aaron Frost paid the taxes on the *News* office, Mrs. Langrishe apparently couldn't afford the taxes on her house. In a special term of the Shoshone County commissioners, they cancelled her property taxes for the year 1895, and that may have removed her property from the books, since she did not have to re-petition the commissioners after that.¹⁸

By 1898, she wrote her brother-in-law E.H. Atwood (husband of her sister, Augusta) that she had been so busy writing business letters that she hadn't had time for personal correspondence. She said she was "very well, but Oh? So lonely." She wished she had people near with whom she could talk about the past, "and of those we have loved, and lost..." She also mentioned the excitement over the Spanish-American War.¹⁹ The treaty ending that war was signed on February 10, 1899.

However, there was no peace for Mrs. Langrishe and the citizens of Wardner. In Minnesota a paper reported that on April 29, 1900, shortly after noon,

> 1000 masked men from towns in the eastern Coeur d'Alenes stole a mail train and proceeded to Wardner on a mission of riot and destruction of property. A powder house had been looted, and the same train that brought the men brought 3000 pounds of dynamite. Arriving at Wardner ... the men marched directly to the Bunker Hill property where the dynamite was placed beneath the office and mill, all this taking place in broad daylight. The torch was applied and a terrible explosion followed which fairly made the hills groan....²⁰

The noise must have been ear-splitting in Wardner, sound waves funneled up the narrow canyon. Again, martial law was declared. In response to her brother-in-law's query, Jeannette responded:

> I am safe for the present, but have had a dredful [*sic*] time, for a number of nights, I did not dare to take off my dress, part of the time I slept at some neighbors house, but could not rest, fearing my little home would be destroyed while I was absent. I think I know how you felt during the Indian trouble. I am worried for fear my heart will stop, if it does, I do not know what I shall do.... There are Troops placed all through the mining camps. Martial law has been proclaimed so I begin to feel safe, great numbers have been arrested and are in a pen like so many swine.... [W]ith love to you all, ...I am your affectionate sister Jeannette Langrishe.²¹

January 18, 1900, Jeannette executed a quitclaim deed to Urias Landes for the rear 50 feet of her small lot. The front 50 feet fronted on Mill Street, the rear on High Street. The amount she gained from the transfer was not stated.²² On June 12 and 13, 1900, the census was taken in Wardner, and in house number 206 resided Jeannette Langrishe, head of household, born May 1834 (incorrect), no age reported, widowed, number of years married 33 (crossed out), no children. Born in Vermont, father born in Massachusetts, mother born in Connecticut. Occupation, variety actress (very incorrect). Months not employed, 12. No figure for having attended school. Can read, can write, can speak English, owns her home free of mortgage. At the same house, a boarder was identified as George Maitland, white male, born 1850, age 49, widowed, occupation saloonkeeper.[23]

On Wednesday, August 15, 1900, Jeannette Allen Langrishe died after a brief illness at the age of 84, according to the Spokane *Spokesman-Review*. She had been a resident of Wardner for 14 years and "was well known in Spokane." "The funeral services were held at Pythian Hall under the auspices of the L.O.T.M. [Ladies of the Maccabees] of which organization she was a member. The Rev. T.W. Walters of Colfax preached the funeral sermon."[24] There was no mention of her daughter Rosalthe Allen Stewart, who passed in 1917, in Grove City, Ohio, age 77.

Thus were the eventful lives of Jack and Jeannette Langrishe ended. The American frontier where they had entertained thousands had closed by 1890. Time would erase memory of their adventures and exploits, their lives written upon water.

Chapter Notes

Chapter 1

1. *Boston Evening Transcript*, Sept. 19, 1845.
2. Folds family lore.
3. Registry of Baptisms, Marriages and Burials in Saint Peter's Parish, Dublin, Ireland, book 7, 48.
4. "Death of John S. Folds, Printer," *Madison Wisconsin Daily Patriot*, Oct. 21, 1861.
5. *Dublin Freeman's Journal*, Sept. 16, 1844.
6. *Oshkosh (WI) Daily Northwestern*, Aug. 14, 1917.
7. "Private Theatricals—Moore—Miss O'Neil—Chief Justice Bushe" *Dublin University Magazine*, vol. XXXV, No. CCX, June, 1850.
8. *New York Dramatic Mirror*, April 13, 1895.
9. *Dublin Freeman's Journal*, May 8,1844.
10. Ibid., Aug. 7,1844.
11. "Death of John S. Folds, Printer," *Madison Wisconsin Daily Patriot*, Oct. 21, 1861.
12. William Boulger Folds, "Sketch of the Life of William Boulger Folds," p 8 typescript, n.d.
13. His Tribune refused theatre ads first few years.
14. Playbill, copy owned by author. From Boston Public Library.
15. *New York Herald*, June 17, 1846.
16. Odell's *Annals of the New York Stage*, vol. V, p. 222.
17. *Pittsburgh Daily Morning Post*, Aug. 6, 1846.
18. Leman Thomas Rede, *The Road to the Stage*, New Ed. (London: J. Onwhyn, 1835).
19. *New York Dramatic Mirror*, May 16, 1885.
20. *New York Reformer*, Oct. 10, 1850.
21. *New York City Spirit of the Times*, January 3, 1846.
22. *Utica Daily Gazette*, July 4, 1846; *Syracuse Daily Star*, July 18, 1846; *Syracuse Onondaga Standard*, July 22 1846; *Syracuse Daily Star*, July 27,1846; *Buffalo Morning Express*, Sept. 22, 1846.
23. Ibid., *Syracuse Daily Star*, March 6, 1847.
24. Playbills observed at the American Antiquarian Society library, specifically some printed for Howard & Fox co. by A.C. Greene. Thus deprived of printing revenue, newspapers were not inclined to encourage attendance or to give a favorable review of the production.
25. *New York Dramatic Mirror*, Dec. 17 1887.
26. *Utica Daily Gazette*, Sept. 14–16, 1847.
27. *Rochester (NY) Daily American*, Oct. 15, 1847; *Syracuse Daily Star*, Nov. 2 1847.
28. Ibid., Nov. 3, 1847
29. *Utica Daily Gazette*, Dec. 23, 1847.
30. The identity of "Mr. Collins" is unknown, but he's possibly the same "old friend" E.R.Collins who later occasionally performed with Langrishe's companies in Colorado, Montana and Deadwood, S.D.
31. *Rochester (NY) Daily American*, Nov. 10, 1847; Phyllis Hartnoll, ed. *Oxford Companion to the Theare*, 2nd ed. (London: Oxford University Press, 1962), p. 822.
32. *Rochester (NY) Daily American*, Nov. 30, 1847.
33. *New York Clipper*, Dec. 28 1895.
34. *Utica Daily Gazette*, Nov. 10, 1848.
35. *Rochester (NY) Daily American*, Aug. 16, 1848.
36. *Rochester (NY) Daily Advertiser*, Aug. 21 1848.
37. *Fredonia (NY.) Censor*, Dec. 5, 1848.
38. *Erie (PA) Observer*, Dec. 23, 1848.
39. Hartnoll, p. 822.
40. *Meadville (PA) Crawford Democrat*, Dec. 30, 1848.
41. Ibid.
42. *Youngstown (OH) Republican*, Mar. 28, 1849.
43. Jeannette Allen Langrishe's name was frequently spelled "Jennette," even by her sisters, although in her only extant letters, written late in life, she spelled it Jeannette. *Pittsburgh Daily Gazette*, May 1, 1849

44. *Pittsburgh Daily Morning Post,* March 15, 1849.
45. Unidentified, undated clipping of Jeannette Langrishe obituary, given to author by Harry E. Atwood, great grand-nephew of Jeannette Langrishe.
46. Notes by Mrs. E.H. Atwood (Augusta Allen Atwood) in box 5, A.A. 887, Atwood papers, Minnesota Historical Society. Bela Allen and Susan Fenton Allen were identified as parents of Augusta Allen Atwood, younger sister of Jeannette Langrishe, in the E.H. Atwood family papers. Their mother, Susan Fenton Allen, was a cousin of Governor Reuben E. Fenton of New York.
47. 1880 U.S. Census, Franklin County, Ohio, 6th ward Columbus, p. 16. Rosalthe A. Stewart, age 40, deaf and dumb (1900 census says she's deaf only), born in New York.
48. *Pittsburgh Daily Gazette,* May 1, 1849.
49. John Miller, *History of Erie County, Pennsylvania.*(Chicago: Lewis Publishing Co., 1909), p. 845.
50. *Sandusky (OH) Daily Sanduskian,* July 7, 1849.
51. *Buffalo Daily Republican,* July 28, 1849.
52. "Cholera at Sandusky," *Buffalo Daily Republican,* Aug. 1, 1849.
53. *Sandusky (OH) Clarion,* Oct. 27 1849.
54. Nancy S. Pollak, "Traveling Nineteenth-Century Ohio," *Ohio Historical Society Echoes,* v.20, No. 1, p. 1.
55. *Oswego (NY) Daily Commercial,* Sept. 20, 1849.
56. Ibid., Sept. 24,1849.
57. Ibid.
58. *Corning (NY) Journal,* Feb. 13, 1850.
59. *Ithaca Journal and Advertiser,* March 20, 1850.
60. *Utica Daily Gazette.,* May 24, 1850.
61. Ibid., May 29, 1850.
62. *Oswego (NY) Daily Commercial,* June 4, 1850
63. *Oswego (NY) Commercial Times,* June 10–July 3, 1850.
64. Ibid., June 17, 1850.
65. Ibid., June 28, 1850.
66. *Syracuse Daily Star,* July 8, 1850.
67. Ibid., summer, 1850.
68. Ibid., July 19, 1850 .
69. *Syracuse Standard,* Aug. 10, 1850.
70. U.S. Census, Syracuse, Onondaga County, New York, p. 194.
71. *Corning (NY) Journal,* Jan. 15, 1851.
72. Ibid., Jan. 22, 1851.

Chapter 2

1. *Jackson (MI) American Citizen,* March 26, 1851.
2. *Dublin Freeman's Journal,* July 5, 1845.
3. This was Laurette Allen, soon to be Mrs. John B. Atwater.
4. Charles Hume, *The Sacramento Theatre, 1849-1885,*Ann Arbor, MI: University Microfilms, p. 18.
5. Pension War 1812 papers, Philadelphia, PA, March 2, 1871, clerk of the Orphans court. His service was from September, 1814 as a private of Capt. Jacob Cash's PA Volunteers to January 3, 1815.
6. *Milwaukee Sentinel and Gazette, Milwaukee Daily Free Democrat,* July 7–23, 1851.
7. *Milwaukee Sentinel and Gazette,* July 12, 1851.
8. *Racine Advocate,* July 30, 1851.
9. Ibid., Aug. 6, 1851.
10. *Kenosha (WI.) Telegraph,* Aug. 8, 1851.
11. Ibid.
12. Ibid., Aug. 15, 1851.
13. *Racine Advocate,* Aug. 27,1851.
14. *Kenosha (WI) Telegraph,* Aug. 22, 1851.
15. *Sheboygan (WI) Journal,* Aug. 27, 1851.
16. Ibid., Sept. 3, 1851.
17. *Watertown (WI) Chronicle,* Sept. 24, 1851.
18. Ibid.
19. *Janesville (WI) Gazette,* Oct. 9, 1851.
20. Ibid., Oct. 2, 1851.
21. *Waukegan (IL) Gazette,* Nov. 8 1851.
22. *Kenosha (WI) Telegraph,* Nov. 21,1851.
23. *Racine Advocate,* Nov. 26, 1851.
24. *Kenosha (WI) Telegraph,* Nov. 28, 1851
25. *Racine Advocate,* Dec. 3, 1851.
26. Ibid., Dec. 10, 1851.
27. Quoted from the *Janesville (WI) Democrat Standard,* Dec. 17, 1851; (*Milwaukee Standard,* Dec. 23 1851. Curiously, there was no mention of this event in the *Janesville (WI) Gazette,* Dec. 18, 1851.
28. *Janesville (WI) Gazette,* Dec. 25, 1851.

Chapter 3

1. Henry C. Youngerman, 1946-47,"Theatre Buildings in Madison, Wisconsin, 1836–1900," *Wisconsin Magazine of History,* 1946–47, 30:274.
2. Ibid.
3. *Madison Daily Argus,* Jan. 8, 1852.
4. *Beloit (WI) Journal,* Jan. 8, 1852.
5. *Madison Daily Statesman,* Jan. 14 1852. The state legislature session started this date.
6. *Madison Daily Wisconsin Argus,* Jan. 19, 1852.

Notes—Chapter 3

7. *Madison Daily Statesman,* January 19–24, 1852.
8. Ibid., Feb. 9, 1852; *Madison Daily Wisconsin Argus,* Feb. 10, 1852.
9. *Madison Daily Statesman,* March, 15, 1852.
10. Ibid., March 19–20. 1852, passim; *Madison Daily Wisconsin Argus,* March 20, 1852.
11. *Mineral Point Wisconsin Tribune,* April 1, 1852.
12. *Galena (IL) Daily Jeffersonian,* April 7, 1852.
13. *Galena (IL) Daily Jeffersonian,* April 29, 1852.
14. *St. Paul The Minnesotian,* May 22, 1852.
15. *St. Paul Minnesota Pioneer,* May 20, 1852.
16. Ibid., May 27, 1852. Winnebago, Chippewa and Sioux (Lakota) were much in evidence, mingling with settlers along the river. (*St. Paul Minnesota Pioneer,* April 8, 1852.)
17. Ibid., June 10, 1852.
18. *Fort Winnebago (WI) River Times,* February 23, 1852.
19. Ibid., June 22, 1852.
20. Ibid., June 28, 1852.
21. *Fond du Lac (WI) Journal,* June 24 and July 8, 1852.
22. *Green Bay Advocate,* July 22, 1852.
23. *Kenosha (WI) Telegraph,* Aug. 6, 1852.
24. *Waukegan (IL) Gazette,* Aug. 14, 1852.
25. *Kenosha (WI) Tribune,* Aug. 5, 1852.
26. *Kenosha (WI) Democrat,* Aug. 19, 1852.
27. *Kenosha (WI) Tribune,* Aug. 19, 1852.
28. *Grand Rapids (MI) Enquirer,* Sept. 1, 1852.
29. Ibid., Sept 8, 1852.
30. *Janesville (WI) Gazette,* Oct. 23, 1852.
31. Ibid., Nov. 6, 1852.
32. *Freeport (IL) Journal,* Nov. 19, 1852.
33. *Galena (IL) Daily Jeffersonian,* Nov. 26, 1852.
34. Ibid., Dec. 4, 1852.
35. *Madison Argus and Democrat,* Dec. 16, 1852,
36. *Mineral Point Wisconsin Tribune,* Jan. 13, 1853.
37. *Madison Daily Argus and Democrat,* Jan. 17, 1853.
38. Ibid.
39. Ibid., Jan., 1853.
40. Ibid., Jan. 27 1853.
41. *Kenosha (WI) Telegraph,* Feb. 11, 1853. The reference to the "Tiger" is to playing Faro, a gambling game. The box holding the cards had a tiger painted upon it.
42. *Madison Daily Argus and Democrat,* Feb. 11, 1853.
43. Ibid., Feb. 19, 1853.
44. *Madison Wisconsin State Journal,* March 30, 1903.
45. Letter, Dec. 7, 1979, Doyn Inman, P.G.M., Grand Secretary, Grand Lodge Free and Accepted Masons of Wisconsin, to Dr. Charles Lauterbach.
46. *Galena (IL) Daily Jeffersonian,* May 5–7, 1853.
47. *Mineral Point Wisconsin Tribune,* May 19, 1853.
48. Ibid., May 26, 1853.
49. *Madison Daily Argus and Democrat,* June, 6, 1853.
50. Ibid., June 6–30, 1853.
51. Ibid., June 20–21, 1853.
52. *Fond du Lac (WI) Fountain City Herald,* July, 26, 1853.
53. *Fond du Lac (WI) Union,* July 28, 1853.
54. *Racine Daily Advocate,* Aug. 31, 1853.
55. *Kenosha (WI) Tribune,* Aug. 25, 1853.
56. Ibid., Sept. 8, 1853.
57. Ibid.
58. Ibid.
59. *Watertown (WI) Chronicle,* Sept. 14, 1853.
60. *Racine Daily Advocate,* Sept. 15–30, 1853.
61. *Waukesha (WI) Chronotype,* Oct. 12, 1853.
62. *Green Bay Advocate,* Oct. 20, 1853.
63. *Janesville (WI) Gazette,* Oct. 29 - Dec. 31, 1853.
64. *Madison Daily Argus & Democrat,* Jan. 9 and 11, 1854.
65. Ibid., Jan., 13–31, 1854.
66. Ibid., Feb. 8, 1854.
67. Ibid., Feb. 11, 1854.
68. Ibid., March 2, 1854.
69. Ibid., March 29, 1854.
70. *Janesville (WI.) Standard,* April, 15, 1854.
71. *Milwaukee Daily Sentinel,* April 24, 1854. After this start Dillon became one of the most popular comedic actors in the Middle West and in New York for the next four decades, in spite of a "failing" that usually extinguished acting careers: he was an alcoholic, and was not dependable. Details in typed reminiscences of Dillon, gift to this author by Dillon's granddaughter, Catherine Barth.
72. *Milwaukee Daily Sentinel,* April 28, 1854.
73. Ibid., May 1, 1854.
74. Ibid., May 2–13, 1854.
75. *Kenosha (WI) Telegraph,* May 19, 1854.
76. Ibid., May 12, 1854. The Calladine company "sloped" a few days later without paying their bills. *Kenosha* (WI) *Tribune,* May 18, 1854.
77. Ibid., May 25, 1854.
78. Ibid., June 1, 1854.
79. Ibid., June, 8, 1854.
80. *Waukegan (IL) Gazette,* June 10, 1854.

81. Ibid., June 17, 1854.
82. *Green Bay Advocate,* Aug. 10. 1854.
83. *Oshkosh (WI) Daily Courier,* Aug. 28, 1854.
84. *Madison Daily Argus and Democrat,* Sept. 30, 1854.
85. *Janesville (WI) Gazette,* Oct. 21, 1854.
86. Ibid., Aug. 12, 1854.
87. *New York Clipper,* Dec. 23, 1854. This weekly newspaper was devoted to news of theatre, games and sports.

Chapter 4

1. *Madison Daily Argus and Democrat,* Dec. 23, 1854.
2. Ibid., Dec. 10, 1854.
3. Youngerman, p. 276.
4. Ibid.
5. *Madison Daily Argus and Democrat,* Jan. 6, 1855.
6. Ibid., Nov. 3, 1855.
7. *Chicago Tribune,* Jan. 23, 1855.
8. *Madison Daily Argus and Democrat,* March 1, 1855.
9. Ibid., March 10, 1855.
10. Ibid., March 17, 1855.
11. *Mineral Point (WI) Tribune,* April 18, 1855.
12. *Portage, (WI) Badger State,* May, 19,1855.
13. *Portage (WI) Independent,* May, 17, 1855.
14. *Fond du Lac (WI) Union,* June 21, 1855.
15. Ibid., July 5, 1855.
16. *Green Bay Advocate,* Aug. 23, 1855.
17. Ibid., Sept. 13, 1855.
18. *Janesville (WI) Gazette,* Oct. 13, 1855.
19. *Green Bay Advocate,* Sept. 27, 1855.
20. *Fond du Lac (WI) Union,* Oct. 25, 1855.
21. *New York Clipper,* Feb. 23, 1884.
22. *Ripon (WI) Home,* Nov. 2, 1855.
23. *Janesville (WI) Gazette,* Dec. 1, 1855.
24. *Madison Daily Argus and Democrat,* Dec. 12, 1855.
25. Ibid., Jan. 8, 1856.
26. Ibid., Jan. 24, 1856.
27. Ibid., Jan. 24, 1856.
28. Ibid., Jan. 26, 1856.
29. Ibid., March 17, 1856.
30. Ibid., March 25, 1856.
31. *Fond du Lac (WI) Union,* July 5, 1855.
32. Wisconsin General Laws (1856), p. 16.
33. Hartnoll, pp. 629–630.
34. *Madison Daily Argus and Democrat,* March 31, 1856.
35. Ibid., April 5, 1856.
36. Ibid., April 21, 1856.
37. Ibid., April 16, 18, 1856.
38. *Sheboygan (WI) Journal,* April 22, 1856.
39. *Monroe (WI) Sentinel,* April 23, 1856.
40. *Beloit (WI) Journal,* April 17, 1856.
41. *Waukegan (IL) Gazette,* May 3, 1856.
42. *Kenosha (WI) Tribune and Telegraph,* May 1, 1856.
43. *Madison Daily Argus and Democrat,* May 14, 1856.
44. Ibid., May 16, 1856.
45. *Whitewater (WI) Gazette,* May 15, 1856.
46. Ibid., May 22, 1856.
47. *Beaver Dam (WI) Dodge County Citizen,* May 23, 1856.
48. *Portage (WI) Independent,* May 29, 1856.
49. *Oshkosh* (WI) *Weekly Courier,* June 11, 1856.
50. *Fond du Lac* (WI) *Fountain City Herald,* June 18, 1856.
51. *Green Bay Advocate,* June 19, 1856.
52. Ibid., June 19, 1856.
53. "Yankee Bowman" appears out of nowhere. He may in fact be Atwater (John Bowman Atwater) who allegedly used the name "John Bowman" when he was a violin player and dance master, prior to the start of his acting career. Hume, p. 18.
54. *Galena (IL) Daily Courier,* June 24, 1856.
55. *Prairie du Chien (WI) Courier,* July 10, 1856.
56. Ibid., July 17, 1856.
57. *Davenport (IA) Daily Gazette,* Jul 24, - Aug. 15, 25, 1856.
58. *Mineral Point (WI) Tribune,* Sept. 23, 1856.
59. *Baraboo (WI) Republic,* Sept. 27, 1856.
60. *Portage (WI) Independent,* Oct. 16, 1856.
61. *Baraboo (WI) Republic,* Oct. 4, 1856,
62. *Madison Daily Argus and Democrat,* Oct. 20, 1856.
63. *Portage (WI) Independent,* Oct. 23, 1856.
64. *Janesville (WI) Free Press,* May 2, June 7, 1856.
65. *Madison Daily Argus and Democrat,* Dec. 30, 1856.
66. Ibid., Jan. 15, 1857.
67. Ibid., Jan. 23, 1857.
68. Ibid., Jan. 31, 1857.
69. Ibid.
70. *Kenosha (WI) Tribune and Telegraph,* Feb. 5, 1857.
71. *Madison Daily Argus and Democrat,* Feb. 6, 1857.
72. Ibid., Feb. 7, 1857.
73. Ibid., Feb. 8–10, 1857.
74. Ibid., Feb. 9, 1857.
75. Ibid., Feb 20,, 1857.
76. Ibid., Feb. 24–26, 1857.

Notes—Chapter 5

77. Ibid., Feb. 26, 1857.
78. Ibid., Feb. 25, 1857.
79. When the cast's photos were taken (ambrotypes), we believe Langrishe was costumed as one of the characters.
80. *Madison Daily Argus and Democrat,* Feb. 28, 1857.
81. Lillian Krueger, "Social Life in Wisconsin, Pre-Territorial through the Mid-Sixties." *Wisconsin Magazine of History,* 1938, v. 26, p. 418.
82. *Madison Daily Argus and Democrat,* March 18, 1857.
83. Ibid., April 6, 1857.
84. *Janesville (Wis.) Gazette,* Oct. 13, 1855.
85. *Watertown (WI) Democrat,* April, 9, 1857.
86. Ibid., April 30, 1857.
87. *Beaver Dam (WI) Dodge County Citizen,* May 5, 1857.
88. *Horicon (WI) Argus,* May 8, 1857.
89. *Beaver Dam (WI) Dodge County Citizen,* May 12, 1857.
90. *Watertown (WI) Democrat,* May 21, 1857.
91. *Shullsberg (WI) Lafayette County Herald,* June 5, 1857.
92. *La Crosse (WI) National Democrat,* June 30, 1857.
93. Ibid., July 7, 1857.
94. *St. Paul Daily Minnesotian,* July 16, 1857.
95. *Madison Daily Argus and Democrat,* July 18, 1857.
96. *Mantorville (MN) Express,* July 30, 1857.
97. *McGregor (IA) North Iowa Times,* Sept. 11, 1857.
98. Ibid.
99. *Madison Daily Argus and Democrat,* Sept. 25, 1857.
100. Ibid., Sept. 26, 1857.
101. Ibid., Oct. 5, 1857.
102. Ibid., Oct. 17, 1857.
103. Ibid., Oct. 22, 1857.
104. Ibid., Nov. 2, 1857.
105. Ibid., Nov. 12, 1857.
106. Ibid., Dec. 7, 1857.
107. Ibid., Dec. 8, 1857.
108. Ibid., Dec. 9 1857.
109. Ibid.
110. Ibid., Dec. 18, 1857.
111. Ibid.

Chapter 5

1. *Prairie du Chien (WI) Leader,* Feb. 6, 1858.
2. *Madison Daily Argus and Democrat,* Feb. 2, 1858.
3. Ibid., Feb. 6–11, 1858.
4. Ibid., Feb. 12, 1858.
5. Ibid., Feb. 15, 17, 1858.
6. *Prairie du Chien (WI) Leader,* Feb. 13, 1858.
7. *Madison Daily Argus and Democrat,* Feb. 18–26, 1858.
8. Ibid., March 1, 1858.
9. Ibid., March, 18, 1858.
10. Ibid., March 19–20, 1858.
11. Ibid., March 23, 1858.
12. *Monroe (WI) Sentinel,* March 24, 1858.
13. *Madison Daily Argus and Democrat,* April 19, 1858.
14. Ibid., April 22, 1858 .
15. Lloyd Morris, *Curtain Time, the Story of American Theater* (New York: Random House, 1953), p. 144.
16. *Madison Daily Argus and Democrat,* March 7, 1853.
17. Richard Moody, ed. *Dramas from the American Theatre, 1762–1909* (Boston: Houghton-Mifflin Co., 1969), p. 352.
18. *Madison Daily Argus and Democrat,* April 23, 1858.
19. Ibid., April 24, 1858.
20. Ibid., April 30, 1858.
21. Ibid., May 3,1858.
22. *La Crosse (WI) National Democrat,* June 1, 1858.
23. Ibid., June 8, 1858.
24. Charles George Mayers v. John S. Langrishe, Dane County (WI) Circuit Court, v. 4, p. 70.
25. Ibid.
26. *La Crosse (WI) National Democrat,* June 15, 1858. Contemplated appearances in Chippewa and St. Peter make no geographical sense, according to modern atlases; perhaps this was a fatal flaw in the success of this partnership.
27. *La Crosse, (WI) Independent Republican,* June 9, 1858.
28. *Pepin (WI) Independent,* June 18, 1858.
29. *Prairie du Chien (WI) Courier,* July 8 and 10, 1858.
30. *McGregor North Iowa Times,* July 14, 1858.
31. *Galena (IL) Daily Courier,* July 14, 1858.
32. *Prairie du Chien (WI) Leader,* July 17, 1858.
33. *St. Paul Pioneer and Democrat and Daily Minnesotian ,* June-August, 1858.
34. *Guttenburg (IA) Clayton County Journal,* July 1, 1858.
35. *Prairie du Chien (WI) Leader,* July 17, 1858.
36. The Albert O. Barton papers, notebook #1, held by the Wisconsin Historical Society, claims that John S. Folds, Langrishe's father, traveled with Langrishe at times, especially in 1857 and 1858, performing as a minor actor.

37. *New York Clipper*, Sept. 4, 1858.
38. *Madison Daily Argus and Democrat*, Sept. 3, 1858.
39. *Madison Daily Patriot*, Sept. 3, 1858.
40. *St. Paul Daily Minnesotian*, Sept. 4, 1858.
41. *Madison Daily Argus and Democrat*, Oct. 1, 1858.
42. Ibid., Oct. 5, 1858.
43. Ibid., Oct. 6, 1858.
44. Ibid., Oct.7, 1858.
45. Ibid., Oct. 16, 1858.
46. Ibid., Nov. 1, 1858.
47. *Madison Wisconsin Daily Patriot*, Nov. 1, 1858.
48. Ibid., Nov. 6, 1858.
49. *Madison Daily Argus and Democrat*, Nov. 8–13, 1858.
50. *Madison Wisconsin Daily Patriot*, Nov. 17, 1858.
51. *Madison Daily Argus and Democrat*, Nov. 26, 1858.
52. Ibid., Nov. 29, 1858.
53. Ibid., Dec.2, 1858.
54. Ibid., Dec. 15, 1858.
55. *Madison Wisconsin Daily Patriot*, Dec. 31, 1858.
56. Ibid., Jan. 12, 1859.
57. *Madison Daily Argus and Democrat*, Jan. 20, 1859.
58. *Madison Wisconsin Daily Patriot*, Jan. 24, 1859.
59. Ibid., Jan. 25, 1859.
60. *New York Clipper*, Jan. 29, 1859.
61. *Madison Wisconsin Daily Patriot*, Feb. 1–12, 1859.
62. Ibid., Feb. 14, 1859.
63. Ibid., March, 19, 1859.
64. *Madison Daily Argus and Democrat*, April 5, 1859.

Chapter 6

1. Marc McCutcheon, *Everyday Life in the 1800s* (Cincinnati: Writer's Digest Books, 1993), p. 152.
2. Caroline Bancroft, *Gulch of Gold* (Boulder, Colorado: Johnson Publishing, 1958).
3. Robert L. Perkin, *The First Hundred Years* (Garden City, N.Y.: Doubleday Publishing, 1959) p. 13.
4. Melvin Schoberlin, *From Candles to Footlights* (Denver, Colo.: Old West Publishing, 1941), p. 42.
5. *Wisconsin General Laws, General Acts Passed by the Legislature of Wisconsin*. Madison; Calkins & Proudfit, 1856, p. 15.
6. Langrishe's uncle, George Folds, emigrated from Ireland in 1848 and settled in Janesville, Wisconsin with his wife and children. *Beloit (WI) Journal*, Jan. 13, 1853.
7. *Prairie du Chien (WI) Leader*, March 12, 1859.
8. John Allen may have been related to Jeannette Allen Langrishe, but there's no mention of that relationship in his obituary printed in theatrical newspapers.
9. Charles A. Krone, "Recollections of an Old Actor," *Missouri Historical Society* (1908-11):3–3, pp.. 287–291.
10. Ibid.
11. Ibid., p. 295.
12. "Overland Trip to Pike's Peak and Back," *Madison Wisconsin Daily Journal*, June 6, 1859.
13. Elbert R. Bowen, *Theatrical Amusements in Rural Missouri Before the Civil War*. Missouri: 1959 p. 60.
14. *Kansas City (MO) Western Journal of Commerce*, July 8, 1859.
15. Ibid. July 7, 1859.
16. Ibid., July 6–14, 1859.
17. Ibid., Aug. 7, 1859.
18. Ibid., Aug. 9, 1859.
19. Ibid., Aug. 12, 1859.
20. *St. Joseph Weekly Free Democrat*, Sept. 24, 1859.
21. *Leavenworth Daily Times*, Oct. 11–31, 1859.
22. Ibid.
23. Ibid., Oct. 31, 1859.
24. Ibid., Dec. 21, 1859.
25. *New York Clipper*, Dec. 31, 1859.
26. *Lecompton (KS) National Democrat*, Nov. 24, 1859.
27. Schoberlin, p. 41.
28. *Lecompton (KS) National Democrat*, Nov. 24, 1859.
29. *Atchison (KS) Weekly Champion*, Dec. 17, 1859.
30. Reprinted in the *Manhattan (KS) Express*, April 14, 1860.
31. Raymond W. Settle and Mary Lund Settle, *Saddles and Spurs, the Pony Express Saga* (Lincoln, Nebraska: University of Nebraska Press, 1955), pp. 56–57.
32. Dr. C.G. Coutant, *History of Wyoming and the Far West* (New York: Argonaut Press, for University Microfilms, Ann Arbor, Mich. P.) p. 370.
33. *Nebraska City News*, April 14, 1860.
34. *New York Clipper*, Aug. 28, 1869.
35. *Field and Farm*, v.10, #16 Oct. 18, 1890 p.6.
36. Schoberlin, p. 41.
37. *Wood River Center (NE) Huntsman's Echo*, June 14, 1860.

38. Settle, p. 23.
39. "Frontier Footlights," *Denver Tribune,* Jan. 1, 1881.
40. Vol. 72, Fort Kearny, N.T., Letters Sent, Jan. 1856-Sept. 1860 National Archives, Tape MC3, Side 1.
41. LeRoy R. Hafen, *Fort Laramie and the Pageant of the West, 1834-1890* (Glendale: Arthur M. Clark Co., 1938).
42. "Reminiscences," *Field and Farm,* v. 8 #14, Oct. 5, 1889, p. 6. Old Smoke was an Oglalla chief who had attracted the attention of Francis Parkman, author of "The Oregon Trail," when he was invited to partake of puppy stew (prepared by that wife, apparently) in Old Smoke's lodge. Francis Parkman, The Oregon Trail, Garden City, NY: Doubleday & Co., 1948, pp. 95-96.
43. "Frontier Footlights, *Denver Tribune,* Jan. 1, 1881.
44. Verbal communication to author from Boulder valley pioneer Mart Parsons, ca. 1953.
45. *Denver Weekly Rocky Mountain News,* Aug. 15, 1860.

Chapter 7

1. Schoberlin, Frontis.
2. "Col." Charles R. Thorne had brought a small troupe to Denver about a year earlier, and left after about a week, abandoning some actors. Schoberlin, pp. 24-25.
3. *Denver Rocky Mountain News,* Sept. 14, 1860.
4. Schoberlin, p. 42.
5. Albert D. Richardson. *Beyond the Mississippi; From the Great River to the Great Ocean* (Hartford, Conn.: American Publishing Co., 1867), p. 306.
6. "First Actor to Cross the Plains," *Denver Republican,* Oct. 12, 1902.
7. Schoberlin, p. 43.
8. *Denver Rocky Mountain News,* Sept. 26, 1860.
9. Ibid., Sept. 27, 1860.
10. Ibid., Sept. 28, 1860.
11. "First Actor to Cross the Plains," *Denver Republican,* Oct. 12, 1902.
12. *Denver Rocky Mountain News,* Sept. 24, 1860.
13. Libeus Barney. *Letters of the Pike's Peak Gold Rush.* Reprinted from the *Bennington* (VT) *Banner,* 1859-1860 (San Jose, California: The Talisman Press, 1959).
14. *Denver Rocky Mountain News,* Oct. 6, 1860.
15. Ibid., Oct. 8, 1860. Prejudice against Native Americans was often expressed in print in the early days.
16. Ibid., Oct. 23, 1860.
17. Ibid., Oct. 18, 1860.
18. Ibid., Oct. 19-23, 1860.
19. Ibid., Oct. 27, 1860.
20. Ibid., Nov. 5, 1861.
21. Ibid., Nov. 6, 1860.
22. Schoberlin, p. 46.
23. Ibid., pp. 46-47.
24. *Denver Rocky Mountain News,* Nov. 6, 1860.
25. Ibid., Nov. 26, 1860.
26. Ibid., Nov. 14, 1860.
27. Ibid., Nov. 15, 1860.
28. Ibid., Nov. 21, 1860; Dec, 2, 1864.
29. Ibid., Nov. 26, 1860.
30. Ibid., Nov. 28, 1860.
31. Ibid., Dec. 12, 1860.
32. Ibid., Dec. 14, 1860.
33. Ibid., Dec. 19, 1860. Note: The Episcopal church was Langrishe's church, having belonged to the Church of Ireland before emigrating. He was accustomed to "higher church" than is usual in America, according to his cousin, William Folds. Ancestors had been members of the clergy, and a number of cousins were priests in Ireland.
34. Ibid., Dec. 26, 1860; *Denver Weekly Rocky Mountain News,* Jan. 2, 1861.
35. Ibid., Dec. 31, 1860.
36. Ibid., Jan., 4, 1861.
37. Ibid., Jan. 8, 1861.
38. Ibid., Jan. 9, 1861.
39. Ibid., Feb. 9, 1861.
40. Ibid., Feb. 13, 1860.
41. Ibid., Dec. 31, 1861.
42. Ibid., Feb. 20, 1861.
43. Ibid., March 8, 1861.
44. Ibid., March 12, 1861.
45. Albert D. Richardson. *Beyond the Mississippi: From the Great River to the Great Ocean* (Hartford, Conn.: American Publishing Co., 1867).
46. Schoberlin, p. 57.
47. *Denver Rocky Mountain News,* March 19, 1861.
48. Ibid., March 20, 1861.
49. Ibid., April 5, 1861.
50. Ibid., April 6, 1861.
51. Ibid., April, 8, 1861.
52. Ibid., April 13, 1861.
53. *World Almanac and Book of Facts,* 2005, p. 227.
54. Ibid., April 25, 1861.
55. Ibid., April 29, 1861.

56. Ibid., April 30, 1861.
57. Book H, p. 366 Arapahoe County, real estate transfers.
58. *Leadville (CO) Herald Democrat,* Dec. 22, 1895, Ice Palace edition.
59. *Denver Rocky Mountain News,* May 17, 1861.
60. Ibid., June 10, 1861.
61. Ibid., June 15, 1861.
62. Ibid., June 18, 1861.
63. Lynn Perrigo "*A Social History of Central City, Colorado, 1859-1900.* Unpublished Ph.D. thesis, University of Colorado, 1936, p. 304 (note).
64. *Denver Rocky Mountain News,* July 1, 1861.
65. Ibid., July 8, 1861.
66. Ibid., July, 10, 1861. Georgia Gulch was situated east of the road between Breckenridge and Dillon. The town serving that rich area was Parkville, which may have had a larger population than Denver in 1861.
67. *Tarryall (CO) Weekly Miners' Record,* Aug. 17, 1861.
68. Ibid.
69. *New York Clipper,* Aug. 3, 1861.
70. *Tarryall (CO) Weekly Miners' Record,* Aug. 24, 1861.
71. Ibid., Sept. 14, 1861.
72. Rodman Wilson Paul *Mining Frontiers of the Far West, 1849-1880* (Albuquerque, NM: University of New Mexico Press, reprint, 1974), p. 127.
73. *Denver Rocky Mountain News,* Oct. 4, 1861.
74. *Madison Wisconsin Daily Patriot,* Oct. 21, 1861.
75. *Denver Rocky Mountain News,* Oct. 24, 1861.
76. *New York Clipper,* July 27, 1861.
77. *Denver Weekly Rocky Mountain News,* Oct. 30, 1861.
78. *Denver Colorado Daily Republican and Rocky Mountain Herald,* Oct. 29, 1861.
79. *Denver Rocky Mountain News,* Oct. 31, 1861.
80. Ibid., Nov. 1, 1861.
81. *Denver Weekly Rocky Mountain News,* Nov. 6, 1861.
82. *Denver Rocky Mountain News,* Nov. 7, 1861.
83. Ibid., Nov. 25, 1861.
84. Ibid., Nov. 29, 1861.
85. *Denver Weekly Rocky Mountain News,* Dec. 7, 1861. (From daily of Dec 2.)
86. Ibid.
87. *Denver Rocky Mountain News,* Dec. 4, 1861.
88. *Denver Weekly Rocky Mountain News,* Dec. 7, 1861.
89. Robert L. Perkin, *The First Hundred Years.* (Garden City, NY: Doubleday & Co., 1959), p. 147.
90. *Denver Weekly Rocky Mountain News,* Nov. 23, 1861.
91. *Denver Colorado Republican and Rocky Mountain Herald,* Nov. 22, 1861.
92. Ibid, Dec. 12, 1861.
93. *Denver Rocky Mountain News,* Dec. 12, 1861.

Chapter 8

1. *Denver Rocky Mountain News,* Jan. 13, 1862.
2. Ibid. Jan. 21, 1862.
3. Ibid., Jan. 25, 1862, (From daily of Jan. 22.)
4. Ibid., Feb. 4, 1862.
5. Ibid., Feb. 12, 1862.
6. Ibid., Feb. 13, 1862.
7. Ibid., Feb. 19-20, 1862.
8. Perkin, p. 145.
9. *Denver Rocky Mountain News,* Feb. 28, 1862.
10. *Denver Weekly Rocky Mountain News,* April 5, 1862. (From daily of April 3.)
11. *Denver Rocky Mountain News,* April 8, 1862.
12. Ibid., April 28 -May2, 1862.
13. Ibid., May 6-10, 1862.
14. Ibid., May 27, 1862.
15. Samuel J. Kline. *Recollections and Comments* (Los Angeles, [no publisher], 1924), pp. 11-12.
16. *Denver Rocky Mountain News,* June 5, 1862.
17. Ibid., June 11, 1862.
18. Ibid., June 12, 1862.
19. Ibid. June 13, 1862.
20. Ibid. June 14, 1862. (From daily of Fri. 13.)
21. Ibid., June 11, 1862.
22. Ibid., July 26. 1862.
23. Re-published in the *Denver Weekly Rocky Mountain News,* Aug. 7, 1862.
24. *Denver Rocky Mountain News,* Aug. 28, 1862.
25. Ibid., Oct. 8, 1861.
26. *Denver Commonwealth & Republican,* Sept. 4, 1862.
27. Don and Jean Griswold, *Colorado's Century of Cities* (Denver, Colorado: Smith-Brooks, 1958), p. 67.
28. *Denver Commonwealth and Republican,* Oct. 16, 1862.

Notes—Chapter 8

29. *Denver Tribune*, Jan. 1, 1881.
30. *Denver Weekly Rocky Mountain News*, Dec. 18, 1862.
31. *Fort Benton* (MT) *River Press*, May 5, 1886.
32. *Denver Commonwealth and Republican*, Jan. 1, 1863.
33. Ibid.
34. *Denver Weekly Rocky Mountain News*, Jan. 15, 1863, (From dailies of Mon., 12 and Wed., 14.)
35. Ibid., Jan. 22, 1863. (From daily of 20.)
36. Ibid., Feb. 12, 1863. (From daily of Tues, 10.)
37. Ibid., Feb. 12, 1863. (From daily of Wed., 11.)
38. *Denver Commonwealth and Republican*, March 5, 1863.
39. *Denver Weekly Rocky Mountain News*, April 16, 1863. (From daily of Sat., 11.)
40. Ibid., April 30, 1863. (From daily of Wed., 29.)
41. James Burrell. *History of Gilpin County, History of Colorado: Clear Creek and Boulder Valleys* (Chicago: O.L. Baskin Co., 1880).
42. Frank Hall; "Favorite of the Footlights," *Denver Post*, Oct. 12, 1902, section II.
43. Ronald L. Davis. *"They Played for Gold: Theatre on the Mining Frontier."* Southwest Review, Spring, 1966, p. 172.
44. Hall, Oct. 12, 1902, section II.
45. Letter, M.J. Dougherty to Capt. Hall, April 27, 1863, Henry M. Teller papers, University of Colorado Historical Collections
46. Hall, Oct., 12, 1902, section II.
47. *Denver Weekly Rocky Mountain News*, May 7, 1863. (From daily of Thurs., 30.)
48. *Denver Commonwealth and Republican*, June 11, 1863.
49. *Denver Weekly Rocky Mountain News*, June 25, 1863.
50. *Denver Tri-Weekly Miners' Register*, June 25, 1863.
51. Rosalthe Riddell, daughter by a previous marriage. Mrs. Langrishe would undoubtedly not have enjoyed the esteem of society had those ladies known Mrs. Langrishe had been previously married, so Rosalthe's existence was never mentioned in any public sources. She had learned to speak before she suffered the high head fever that left her deaf, probably about age 7 or 8. Information from family letters in the Edwin H. Atwood and family papers, held by the Minnesota Historical Society, and from U.S. Census, 1880, Ohio, Franklin County, p. 229D.
52. *Denver Weekly Commonwealth and Republican*, July, 9, 1863.
53. *Denver Weekly Rocky Mountain News*, July 16, 1863. (From daily of Wed., 15.)
54. Ibid., July 23, 1863. (From daily of Thurs., 16.)
55. Ibid., July 23, 1863.
56. *Central City* (CO) *Tri-Weekly Miners Register*, July 25, 1863.
57. Ibid., July 30, 1863.
58. Ibid., Aug. 4, 1863. The production was postponed, due to Mrs. Langrishe's illness.
59. Ibid., Aug.13, 1863.
60. Ibid., Aug. 20, 1863.
61. Maurice O'Connor Morris , *Rambles in the Rocky Mountains: with a visit to the Gold Fields of Colorado* (London: Smith, Elder & Co., 1864).
62. *Denver Tri-Weekly Miner's Register*, August 22, 1863.
63. *Central City* (CO) *Tri-Weekly Miners' Register*, Aug. 13, 1863.
64. Hal Sayre MSS 1-a VIII, Colorado State Historical Society Library.
65. *Denver Commonwealth*, Oct. 22, 1863.
66. Ibid., Oct. 28, 1863.
67. Ibid., Nov. 4. 1863.
68. Ibid., Nov. 7, 1863.
69. Ibid., Dec. 17, 1863.
70. Ibid., Dec. 23, 1863.
71. Robert G. Athearn. *The Coloradans* (Albuquerque: University of New Mexico Press, 1976).
72. *Denver Daily Commonwealth*, Dec. 30, 1863.
73. *Denver Rocky Mountain News*, Jan. 2–4, 1864.
74. Ibid., Jan. 6–8, 1864.
75. Ibid., Jan. 18, 1864.
76. Ibid., Jan. 20, 1864.
77. Ibid., Feb. 3, 1864.
78. *Central City* (CO) *Daily Miners' Register*, Feb. 1, 1864.
79. *Denver Rocky Mountain News*, Feb. 8, 1864.
80. Ibid., Feb., 1864.
81. *Black Hawk* (CO) *Daily Mining Journal*, April 5, 1864.
82. *Central City*, (CO) *Daily Miners' Register*, April 9, 1864.
83. *Denver Daily Commonwealth*, April 13, 1864.
84. Bayard Taylor, *Colorado: A Summer Trip* (New York: G.P. Putnam & Son, 1867), p. 59.
85. *Central City* (CO) *Daily Miners' Register*, April 26, 1864.
86. "Colorado Theatricals," *Central City* (CO) *Daily Miners' Register*, Feb. 8, 1876.
87. *Denver Rocky Mountain News*, April 30, 1864.

88. Ibid., May 9, 1864.
89. Perkin, pp. 219–221.
90. *Central City (CO) Daily Miners' Register,* June 16, 1864.
91. *New York Clipper,* July 9, 1864.
92. *Black Hawk (CO) Daily Mining Journal,* July 25, 1864.
93. *Denver Rocky Mountain News,* Aug. 2, 1864.
94. Ibid., Aug. 8, 1864.
95. Ibid., Aug. 10–11, 1864.
96. Ibid., Aug. 26, 1864.
97. *Central City (CO) Daily Miners' Register,* Sept. 27, 1864.
98. *Black Hawk (CO) Daily Mining Journal,* Oct. 31, 1864.
99. Ibid., Nov. 10, 1864.
100. *Denver Rocky Mountain News,* Nov. 9, 1864.
101. Ibid., Dec. 7, 1864.
102. Robert Perkin, "Sand Creek," In *A Colorado Reader,* Ed. by Carl Ubbelohde (Boulder, Colo.: Pruett Press).
103. *Denver Rocky Mountain News,* Dec. 22, 1864.
104. Ibid., Dec. 28, 1864.

Chapter 9

1. *Chicago Tribune,* Dec. 19, 1864; *Chicago Times,* Dec. 20, 1864.
2. *Denver Rocky Mountain News,* Jan. 18, 1865.
3. Ibid., Jan. 23, 1865.
4. Ibid., Jan. 25, 1865.
5. Ibid., Jan. 26–31, 1865, passim
6. Sam Tappan's notebook, January 1st, 1865, at Colorado Historical Society.
7. *Denver Rocky Mountain News,* Feb. 7, 1865.
8. Ibid., March 1, 1865.
9. Ibid., April 7, 1865.
10. Ibid., April 15, 1865.
11. Ibid., April 15–20. 1865.
12. *Central City (CO) Daily Miners' Register,* April 19, 1865.
13. Ibid., May 18, 1865.
14. Ibid., July 26, 1865.
15. Ibid., Sept. 30, 1865.
16. Samuel J. Kline, *Recollections and Comments* (Los Angeles, Calif.: 1924), p. 61. The author was not an admirer of Mrs. Langrishe, on or off stage.
17. Ibid., pp. 60–61. His opinions were his own, not shared by any other writer who was contemporary with the Langrishes.
18. *Central City (CO) Daily Miners' Register,* Oct. 3, 1865.
19. Ibid., Oct. 6, 1865.
20. *Denver Rocky Mountain News,* Oct. 25, 1865.
21. Ibid., Oct. 30, 1865.
22. Ibid., Nov. 11, 1865.
23. *Denver Weekly Rocky Mountain News,* Feb. 7, 1866. (From daily of Wed., Jan. 31.)
24. *Denver Rocky Mountain News,* March 13, 1866.
25. Ibid., March 13, 1866.
26. Ibid., March 20, 1866.
27. Ibid., March 28, 1866.
28. Ibid., April 4, 1866.
29. Ibid., April 17, 1866.
30. *Central City (CO) Daily Miners' Register,* May 3, 1866.
31. *Denver Rocky Mountain News,* May 1–3, 1866.
32. *Central City (CO) Daily Miners' Register,* May 4, 1866.
33. *Denver Rocky Mountain News,* May 1, 1866.
34. Ibid., May 3, 1866.
35. Ibid., May 21, 1866.
36. *Central City (CO) Daily Miners' Register,* May 20, 1866.
37. *Ibid.,* June 10, 1866.
38. *New York Clipper,* July 7, 1866.
39. *Central City (CO) Daily Miners' Register,* July 12, 1866.
40. Ibid., Sept. 16, 1866.
41. *Denver Rocky Mountain News,* Sept. 20, 1866.
42. Ibid., Oct. 20, 1866.
43. Ibid., Jan. 7, 1866..
44. Ibid., Jan. 16, 1867.
45. Ibid., Jan. 25, 1867.
46. Ibid., March 5, 1867.
47. Ibid., March 13, 1867.
48. Ibid., April 6, 1867.
49. Ibid., April, 8, 1867.
50. *Central City (CO) Daily Mining Register,* April, 1867.
51. Ibid., April 18, 1867.
52. *Denver Daily Rocky Mountain News, Central City (CO) Daily Mining Register,* April-May, 1867.
53. *Denver Daily Rocky Mountain News,* May 9, 1867.
54. *New York Dramatic Mirror,* May 21, 1892.
55. *Denver Rocky Mountain News,* June 12, 1867.
56. Ibid., June 18, 1867.
57. Ibid., June 12, 1867
58. Ibid., June 26, 1867.

59. *Salt Lake City Daily Union Vedette*, July 30, 1867.
60. Ibid., Aug. 6, 1867.
61. *Salt Lake Daily Telegraph*, Aug., 25, 1867.
62. *Virginia City Montana Post*, Sept. 14, 1867.
63. *Helena (MT) Weekly Herald*, Sept. 26, 1867.
64. *Virginia City Montana Post*, Sept. 14, 1867.
65. Daniel S. Tuttle, "Early History of the Episcopal Church." *Contributions to the Historical Society of Montana*, vol. V, (Helena,: 1904) p. 294; Daniel S. Tuttle, *Reminiscences of a Missionary Bishop* (New York: Thomas Whittaker, 1906), pp. 170–171.
66. *Virginia City Montana Post*, Sept. 21, 1867.
67. Ibid., Nov. 2, 1867.
68. *Helena (MT) Weekly Herald*, Nov.14, 1867.
69. *Virginia City Montana Post*, Nov. 26, 1867.
70. Ibid., Nov.-Dec., 1867.
71. Ibid., Jan. 11, 1868.
72. *Helena (MT) Weekly Herald*, Jan. 23, 1868.
73. *New York Clipper*, Feb. 8, 1868.
74. *Virginia City Montana Post*, datelined Helena, Feb. 8, 1868.
75. *Denver Rocky Mountain News*, April 2, 1868.
76. *Helena (MT) Rocky Mountain Gazette*, May 23, 1868.
77. *Helena Montana Post*, May, 2, 1868.
78. *Denver Rocky Mountain News*, May 30, 1868.
79. William S. Greever. *Bonanza West, The Story of the Western Mining Rushes 1848-1900* (Moscow, ID: University of Idaho Press, 1993).
80. *Helena Montana Post*, June, 1868.
81. *Helena (MT) Weekly Herald*, July 2, 1868.
82. *Helena Montana Post*, July 3, 1868.
83. *New York Clipper*, Aug. 8, 1868.
84. Ibid., Nov. 23, 1863.
85. *Helena Montana Post*, Aug. 21, 1868.
86. *New York Clipper*, Sept. 12, 1868.
87. *Helena (MT) Weekly Herald*, Sept. 24, 1868. (Quoting the *Denver Herald*.)
88. *Denver Rocky Mountain News*, Oct. 6, 1868.
89. *Helena Montana Post*, Oct. 23, 1868. (From Tues., Oct. 20).
90. *Helena (MT) Weekly Herald*, Oct. 22, 1868. (From daily Oct. 20).
91. Ibid., Oct. 19, 1868.
92. *Helena Montana Post*, Oct. 30, 1868. (From daily Oct. 26).

93. *Frontier Index*, Nov. 17, 1868.
94. *Helena (MT) Weekly Herald*, Nov. 19, 1868. (From *Virginia City (MT) Democrat* of Nov. 14.)
95. *Central City (CO) Daily Register*, Nov. 21, 1868, (Dateline Salt Lake, 20) and *Denver Rocky Mountain News*, Nov. 27, 1868.
96. *Cheyenne Leader*, Jan. 5, 1869.
97. *Cheyenne Leader*, Jan. 8, 1869.
98. *New York Clipper*, Jan. 9, 1869.
99. *Denver Daily Colorado Tribune*, Feb. 21, 1869.
100. *Denver Rocky Mountain News*, Feb. 24, 1869.
101. Ibid., March 29, 1869.
102. *New York Dramatic Mirror*, July 28, 1894.
103. Ibid.
104. *Central City (CO) Register*, March 3, 1869.
105. Frank W. Zern, "Early Day Show Houses and Actors," *The Trail*, vol. III, No. 5, Oct. 1910, pp. 17–18.
106. Milton Nobles, "George," *New York Mirror*, Dec. 24, 1887.
107. *Denver Rocky Mountain News*, March 4, 1869.
108. Ibid., March 16, 1869.
109. *New York Clipper*, April 3, 1869.
110. Philip V. Allingham, Contributing ed., *The Victorian Web*. www.victorianweb.org/mt/boucicault/pva233.html
111. *Denver Daily Rocky Mountain News*, March 22, 1869.
112. *Central City (CO) Register*, April 1, 1869.
113. *Denver Daily Rocky Mountain News*, April, 19, 1869.
114. *Daily White Pine (NV) News*, Apr. 28, 29, 1869; *Cheyenne Daily Evening Leader*, May 8, 1869; *Helena (MT) Post*, May 14, 1869.
115. *Central City (CO.)Register*, May 14, 1869.
116. *Denver Daily Colorado Tribune*, June 6, 1869.
117. *Denver Daily Rocky Mountain News*, June 26,1869; June 6, 1869.
118. *Central City (CO) Register*, July 7, 1869.
119. Ibid., July 11, 1869.
120. *Denver Rocky Mountain News*, July 22, 1869.
121. Ibid., July 28, 1869.

Chapter 10

1. *New York Clipper*, Aug., 28, 1869.
2. *Denver Rocky Mountain News*, Sept. 1 1869.

3. *New York Clipper,* Sept. 25, 1869.
4. *Deer Lodge (MT) New North-West,* Aug. 20, 1869.
5. Ibid., Aug. 27, 1869.
6. *Denver Rocky Mountain News,* Sept. 27, 1869.
7. *Deer Lodge (MT) New North-West,* Sept. 3, 1869.
8. *Helena* (MT) *Weekly Herald,* Sept. 9, 1869. (From daily of Sept. 2.)
9. Ibid.
10. *Deer Lodge, (MT) New North-West,* Oct. 8, 1969.
11. Ibid., Oct. 15, 1869.
12. Ibid., Oct. 22, 1869.
13. *Denver Rocky Mountain News,* Feb. 16, 1870.
14. *Helena (MT) Daily Herald,* March 5, 1870; *Capital Times,* March 2, 1870.
15. Ibid., March 15, 1870.
16. *Deer Lodge (MT) New North-West,* May 6, 1870.
17. *Helena (MT) Daily Herald,* May 11, 1870.
18. Ibid., May 23, 1870.
19. *Deer Lodge (MT) New North-West,* June 17, 1870.
20. Ibid., June 24, 1870.
21. *Helena (MT) Daily Herald,* July 7, 1870.
22. Ibid., July 9, 1870.
23. *Deer Lodge (MT) New North-West,* Aug. 5, 1870.
24. Ibid., Aug., 5, 1870.
25. Ibid., Aug. 26, 1870.
26. Ibid., Sept. 16, 1870.
27. *Helena (MT) Rocky Mountain Gazette,* Sept. 26, 1870. (From Tuesday's daily.)
28. *New York Dramatic Mirror,* March 25, 1893.
29. *Deer Lodge (MT) New North-West,* Sept. 23, 1870.
30. *Helena (MT) Daily Herald,* Sept. 26, 1870.
31. Ibid., Sept.-Oct., 1870.
32. Ibid., Oct. 25, 1870.
33. Ibid., Nov. 5, 1870.
34. *Deer Lodge (MT) New North-West,* Nov. 25, 1870.
35. *Corinne (UT) Daily Utah Reporter,* Dec.12, 1870.
36. *Salt Lake City Deseret Evening News,* Dec. 31, 1870.
37. *Corinne (UT) Daily Utah Reporter,* Jan., 1871.
38. Ibid., Jan. 6, 1871.
39. Ibid., Jan. 9, 1871.
40. *Denver Rocky Mountain News,* Jan. 12, 1871.
41. Ibid., Jan. 17, 1871.
42. *Ibid.,* Feb. 5, 1871.
43. Ibid., Feb. 12, 1871.
44. Ibid., March 8, 1871.
45. *Central City (CO) Daily Register,* March 14, 1871.
46. Ibid., March 17, 1871.
47. *Denver Rocky Mountain News,* April 23, 1871.
48. Ibid., June 10, 1871.

Chapter 11

1. William Byers' Letter: University of Colorado Manuscript Collection.
2. *Denver Rocky Mountain News,* May 26, 1871.
3. *Denver Rocky Mountain* News, Aug. 10, 1871. Unpaid insurance added to his father's financial woes when his printing plant had burned in Dublin.
4. *Chicago Tribune,* July 22, 1871.
5. Ibid., Aug. 12, 1871.
6. Ibid., Aug. 15, 1871.
7. *Chicago Evening Journal,* Aug. 15, 1871.
8. Charles B. Wells. *Memoirs of a Mummer.* Privately printed, 1924, p. 7. Portions given to author by Wells' grand-niece, Mrs. Helen June Hamlin.
9. *Chicago Times,* Aug. 18, 1871.
10. *Chicago Tribune,* Aug. 18, 1871.
11. *Chicago Evening Journal,* Aug. 19, 1871.
12. *Chicago Times,* Aug. 27, 1871.
13. *Ibid.,* Sept. 29, 1871.
14. www.chipublib.org/004chicago/timeline/greatfire.html and www.chicagohs.org/fire/conflag
15. *Deer Lodge* (MT) *New North-West,* Dec. 23, 1871.
16. Wells, p. 50.
17. *Denver Rocky Mountain News,* Oct. 17, 1871.
18. Ibid., Oct. 31, 1871.
19. *Chicago Times,* Oct. 21, 1871.
20. Playbill owned by Chicago Historical Society.
21. *Chicago Tribune,* Nov. 2, 1871.
22. Ibid., Nov. 5, 1871.
23. Wells, p. 10.
24. *Chicago Tribune,* Feb. 10, 1872.
25. *Chicago Times,* Feb. 11, 1872.
26. *Milwaukee Evening Wisconsin,* Feb. 8, 1872.
27. *Daily Milwaukee News,* Feb. 16, 1872.
28. *Madison Wisconsin State Journal,* Feb. 17, 1872.
29. *Madison Daily Democrat,* Feb. 19, 1872.

30. *Ibid.,* Feb. 20, 1872.
31. Ibid., Feb. 23, 1872.
32. *Chicago Tribune,* March 30, 1872.
33. *Chicago Times,* March 31, 1872.
34. Ibid.
35. *Chicago Tribune,* May 5, 1872.
36. Wells, pp. 56–57.
37. *Oshkosh (WI) Weekly Northwestern,* May 23, 1872.
38. *St. Paul Daily Pioneer,* June 14, 1872.
39. *Winona (MN) Daily Republican,* Aug. 17, 1872.
40. Ibid, Aug. 19, 1872.
41. *Daily Davenport (IA) Democrat,* Sept. 24, 1872.
42. Wells, pp. 58–59.
43. *Daily Davenport (IA) Democrat,* Sept. 25, 1872.
44. Ibid., Sept. 30, 1872.
45. *Daily Central City (CO) Register,* Sept. 21, 1872.
46. *New York Clipper,* Sept. 28, 1872.
47. *Rock Island (IL) Argus,* Oct. 3–5, 1872, passim; *Rock Island (IL) Daily Union,* Oct. 3–5, 1872.
48. *Daily Davenport (IA) Democrat,* Oct. 8, 1872.
49. Ibid., Oct. 14, 1872.
50. *Peoria (IL) Daily National Democrat,* Oct. 20, 1872.
51. *Terre Haute Gazette ,* Nov. 5, 1872.
52. *Toledo Blade,* Nov. 18, 1872.
53. *New York Clipper,* Nov. 30, 1872.
54. Wells, p. 59.

Chapter 12

1. Myron Matlaw, ed. *The Black Crook and Other Nineteenth Century American Plays* (New York: E.P. Dutton & Co., 1967), p. 319.
2. *Providence Evening Press,* Dec., 3, 1872.
3. *Danbury (CT) Evening News,* Feb. 26, 1873.
4. Wells, p. 56.
5. *Providence (RI) Evening Press,* Dec. 9, 1872.
6. Ibid., Dec. 14, 1872.
7. *Danbury (CT) Evening News,* March 5, 1873.
8. Wells, p. 61.
9. Ibid., p. 54.
10. *Hartford Daily Courant,* Jan. 2, 1873.
11. *Detroit Daily Post,* July 15, 1873.
12. *Cincinnati Enquirer,* Sept. 3, 1873.
13. *Troy (NY) Daily Times,* Dec. 9, 1873.
14. *Providence (RI) Evening Press,* Feb, 2, 1874.
15. *Springfield (MA) Republican,* March 31, 1874.
16. *New York Clipper,* July 18, 1874.
17. *Denver Rocky Mountain News,* July 26, 1874.
18. *San Francisco Daily Alta California ,* Aug. 10, 1874.
19. Ibid.
20. Ibid.
21. *Sacramento Daily Union,* Oct. 3, 1874.
22. *Virginia City (NV) Daily Territorial Enterprises,* Sept. 16, 1874.
23. *San Francisco Daily Alta California ,* Aug. 10, 1874.
24. *Daily Central City (CO) Register,* March 13, 1876.
25. *Juan Panadero* (Guadalajara, Jalisco, Mexico), Nov. 26, 1874.
26. *Two Republics* (D.F. Mexico City), January 26, 1875.
27. *Daily Central City (CO) Register,* March 13, 1876.
28. *New York Clipper,* May 15, 1875.
29. Arapahoe county district court, second judicial district. Solomon Hexter v. John S. Languishe, *(sic)* Thomas Clifford and Michael D. Clifford.

Chapter 13

1. *Madison Democrat,* April 11, 1875.
2. *New York Clipper,* May 15, 1875.
3. *Aurora (IL) Beacon,* May 19, 1875.
4. Ibid., June 12, 1875.
5. Letter from Langrishe, Geneva, Ill., to F.F. Mackay, held in Rare Book and Manuscript library (801 Butler Library), Columbia University.
6. *Aurora (IL)Beacon ,* June 26, 1875.
7. *Green Bay Gazette,* June 21, 1875.
8. Ibid. , June 25, 1875.
9. *Watertown (WI) Democrat,* July 15, 1875.
10. *Madison Daily Democrat,* July 13, 1875.
11. *Freeport (IL) Journal,* July 21, 1875.
12. *Madison Daily Democrat,* Aug. 31, 1875.
13. *Aurora (IL) Beacon,* Sept. 1, 1875.
14. *Beloit (WI) Free Press,* Sept. 9, 1875.
15. *Watertown (WI) Democrat,* Sept. 23, 1875.
16. *Berlin (WI) Courant,* Sept. 25, 1875.
17. *Madison Daily Democrat,* Oct. 7, 1875.
18. *Madison Daily Democrat,* Oct. 7, 1875.
19. Ibid., Oct. 12, 1875; *Galena (IL) Daily Gazette,* Oct. 21, 1875.
20. *Madison Wisconsin State Journal,* Oct. 9, 1875.

21. *Aurora (IL) Beacon,* Nov. 6, 1875.
22. Ibid., Dec. 29, 1875.
23. *Madison Daily Democrat,* Jan. 12, 1876.
24. Ibid., Jan. 13, 1876.
25. *Central City (CO) Daily Register,* Jan. 18, 1876; *Denver Rocky Mountain News,* Jan. 19, 1876.
26. *Madison Wisconsin State Journal,* Jan. 18, 1876.
27. *Madison Daily Democrat,* Jan. 30, 1876.
28. *New York Clipper,* Feb. 5, 1876.
29. *Denver Rocky Mountain News,* Feb. 6, 1876.
30. Ibid., Feb. 9, 1876.
31. Ibid., Feb. 10-16, 1876.
32. Ibid., Feb. 17, 1876.
33. *Golden (CO) Transcript,* Feb. 16, 1876.
34. *Denver Rocky Mountain News,* Feb. 27, 1876.
35. Ibid., March, 1, 1876.
36. *Georgetown Colorado Miner,* March 11, 1876.
37. *Central City (CO) Daily Register,* March 14, 1876.
38. Ibid., March 20, 1876.
39. *Denver Rocky Mountain News,* March 21, 1876.
40. Ibid.
41. *Colorado Springs Gazette,* April 8, 1876.
42. *Pueblo (CO) Chieftain),* April 12, 1876.
43. Ibid., April 14, 1876.
44. Ibid., April 15, 1876.
45. *Boulder (CO) County News,* April 21, 1876.
46. Ibid., April 28, 1876.
47. *Central City (CO) Daily Register,* May 23, 1876.

Chapter 14

1. *Cheyenne Daily Leader,* May 28, 1876. This may have been an alternate title to *Self* or *The Rich of New York.*
2. Ibid., June 1, 1876.
3. Ibid., June 11, 1876.
4. Ibid., June 13, 1876.
5. Letter, Laurette Atwater to Augusta Atwood, Aug 8, (1876), E.H. Atwood Family Papers, Box 1, Minnesota Historical Society.
6. *Cheyenne Daily Leader,* June 20, 1876.
7. *Deer Lodge (MT) New North-West,* July 7, 1876.
8. *Deadwood Black Hills Pioneer,* July 15-22, 1876.
9. Annie D. Tallent, *The Black Hills or Last Hunting Grounds of the Dakotahs* (Brevet Press, Sioux Falls, SD: 1974).
10. *Deadwood Black Hills Pioneer,* July 29, 1876.
11. Ibid., March 3, 1877.
12. Watson Parker, *Deadwood the Golden Years* (Lincoln, NE: University of Nebraska Press, 1981), p. 174.
13. *Deadwood Black Hills Pioneer,* Sept. 2, 1876.
14. Parker, p. 174.
15. *Deadwood Black Hills Pioneer,* Sept. 23, 1876.
16. Ibid., Sept. 23, 1876.
17. Ibid., Oct. 14, 1876.
18. *Deer Lodge (MT) New North-West,* Dec. 1, 1876.
19. *Deadwood Black Hills Pioneer,* Dec. 9, 1876.
20. Ibid., Dec. 16, 1876.
21. Ibid.
22. Ibid., Dec. 30, 1876.
23. Letter from Doyn Inman, P.G.M. Grand Secretary, Grand Lodge Free and Accepted Masons of Wisconsin, to Dr. Charles E. Lauterbach, Dec. 7, 1979.
24. *Deer Lodge (MT) New North-West* , Dec. 22, 1876.
25. *Deadwood Black Hills Pioneer,* Feb. 3, 1877.
26. *Denver Rocky Mountain News,* March 20, 1877.
27. *Deadwood Black Hills Pioneer,* March 24, 1877.
28. Ibid., April 28, 1877.
29. *Deer Lodge (MT) New North-West,* April 13, 1877.
30. Ibid., April 27, 1877,
31. *Deadwood Black Hills Daily Times,* June 26, 1877.
32. Ibid.
33. Ibid.
34. Ibid., July 13, 1877.
35. Ibid., Aug. 24, 1877.
36. *Deer Lodge (MT) New North-West,* July 20, 1877.
37. Ibid., Sept. 14, 1877.
38. *Deadwood Black Hills Daily Times,* Oct. 23, 1877.
39. *New York Clipper,* June 2, 1877.
40. Ibid., Oct. 27, 1877.
41. Ibid.
42. Ibid., Nov. 5, 1877.
43. Ibid., Nov. 6, 1877.
44. Ibid., Nov. 12, 1877.
45. Ibid., Nov. 23, 1877.
46. Ibid.
47. Ibid., Nov. 26, 1877.
48. Ibid., Dec. 11, 1877.

49. *Deadwood Black Hills Daily Pioneer,* Dec. 11, 1877.
50. *Denver Times,* Dec. 24, 1899.
51. *Deadwood Black Hills Daily Times,* Dec. 26, 1877.
52. Ibid., Dec. 31, 1877.
53. Ibid.
54. Ibid., Jan. 5-7, 1878.
55. Ibid., Jan. 7, 1878.
56. Ibid., Jan. 8, 1878.
57. Estelline Bennett. *Old Deadwood Days* (Reprint, Lincoln, Nebraska: University of Nebraska Press, 1982), pp. 123-124
58. Ibid., pp. 126-127.
59. *Deadwood Black Hills Daily Pioneer,* Feb. 14, 1878.
60. *Deadwood Black Hills Daily Times,* Feb. 25, 1878.
61. Ibid., Feb. 28, 1878.
62. Ibid., March 14, 1878.
63. Ibid., March 12, 1878. "Tormentor wings" were flats that obscured the wings from the audience.
64. *Deadwood Black Hills Daily Pioneer,* March 7, 1878.
65. *Deadwood Black Hills Daily Times,* March 14, 1878.
66. Ibid., March 18, 1878.
67. Ibid., April 25, 1878.
68. *Deadwood Black Hills Daily Pioneer.* April 9, 1878.
69. *Deadwood Black Hills Daily Times,* April 24, 1878.
70. Letter, Laurette Atwater to Augusta Atwood, Apr. 28. Box 1, E.H. Atwood Family Papers, Minnesota Historical Society.
71. *Deadwood Black Hills Daily Times,* April 25, 1878.
72. Ibid., April 30. 1878.
73. Tallent, p. 206
74. *Deadwood Black Hills Daily Times,* May 6, 1878.
75. Ibid., May 17, 1878.
76. Ibid., May 18, 1878.
77. Ibid., May 23, 1878.
78. *Deadwood Black Hills Daily Pioneer,* June 1, 1878.
79. *Deadwood Black Hills Daily Times,* June 3, 1878.
80. *Deadwood Black Hills Daily Pioneer,* June 6, 1878.
81. Ibid., June 18, 1878.
82. *Deadwood Black Hills Daily Times,* June 18, 1878.
83. Bennett, pp. 125-126.
84. *Deadwood Black Hills Daily Times,* June 29, 1878.
85. *Deadwood Black Hills Daily Pioneer,* June 25, 1878.
86. Ibid., July 25, 1878.
87. *Deadwood Black Hills Daily Times,* Nov. 2, 1878.
88. Ibid., Nov. 12, 1878.
89. Ibid., Nov. 11, 1878.
90. Ibid., Jan. 6, 1879.
91. Ibid., March 14, 1879.
92. Ibid., March 15, 1879.
93. Ibid., March 18, 1879.
94. Ibid.
95. Ibid., March 31, 1879.
96. Ibid., April 23, 1879.
97. Ibid., April 29, 1879.
98. *Deadwood Black Hills Daily Pioneer,* May 4, 1879.
99. *New York Clipper,* May 3, 1879.
100. *Deadwood Black Hills Daily Times,* May 9, 1879.
101. Ibid., May 11, 1879.
102. Ibid., May 14, 16, 1879.
103. Ibid., May 21, 1879.
104. Ibid., May 22, 1879.
105. Ibid., spring, 1879.
106. Ibid., June 10, 1879.
107. *Deadwood Black Hills Daily Pioneer,* June 11, 1879.
108. *Deadwood Black Hills Daily Times,* June 15 and 17, 1879.
109. Ibid., July 6, 1879.
110. Ibid., July 4, 1879.
111. Ibid., July 8, 1879.
112. Ibid., July 16, 1879.
113. Ibid., July 29, 1879.
114. Ibid.
115. Ibid., Aug. 3, 1879.
116. *Deer Lodge (MT) New North-West,* Aug. 8, 1879.
117. *Deadwood Black Hills Daily Times,* Sept. 9, 1879.
118. Ibid., Sept. 13, 1879.
119. *Denver Times,* Sept. 17, 1879.

Chapter 15

1. *Denver Rocky Mountain News,* Oct. 19, 1879.
2. Ibid., Oct. 21, 1879.
3. Ibid., Oct. 22, 1879.
4. Ibid., Oct. 26, 1879.
5. Ibid., Nov. 9, 1879.
6. Ibid., Nov. 11, 1879.
7. *Central City (CO) Register-Call,* Nov. 12, 1879.
8. Ibid., Nov. 12, 1879.

Notes—Chapter 15

9. Ibid., Nov. 15, 1879.
10. *Golden, (CO) Transcript,* Nov. 19, 1879.
11. *Leadville (CO) Weekly Herald,* Nov. 29, 1879.
12. Evelyn E. Livingston Furman, *The Tabor Opera House, a Captivating History* (Privately printed, 1972), p. 53.
13. Ronald L. Davis, "They Played for Gold: Theatre on the Mining Frontier," *Southwest Review,* v. LI, no. 2 (Spring, 1966), p.172.
14. *Leadville (CO) Weekly Herald,* Nov. 22, 1879.
15. Ibid., Nov. 15, 1879.
16. Ibid., Nov. 29, 1879.
17. Ibid.
18. *Deadwood Black Hills Daily Times,* Dec. 9, 1879.
19. *Leadville (CO) Weekly Herald,* Dec. 20, 1879.
20. Ibid., *Leadville (CO) Weekly Herald*, Dec. 27, 1879.
21. *Leadville (CO) Daily Democrat,* Jan. 1, 1880.
22. Ibid., Jan. 2, 1880.
23. Ibid., Jan. 3, 1880.
24. Ibid., Jan. 4, 1880.
25. Ibid.
26. Ibid., Jan. 7, 1880.
27. Ibid., Jan. 9, 1880.
28. Ibid., Jan. 14, 1880.
29. *Deadwood Black Hills Daily Times,* Jan. 18, 1880.
30. *Leadville (CO) Daily Democrat,* Jan. 20, 1880.
31. Ibid., Jan. 21, 1880.
32. Ibid., Jan. 24, 1880.
33. Ibid., Jan. 25, 1880.
34. Ibid.
35. Ibid., Jan. 25, 1880.
36. Ibid. Feb. 5, 1880.
37. Ibid., Jan. 31, 1880.
38. Ibid., Feb. 1, 1880.
39. Ibid., Feb. 5, 1880.
40. Ibid., Feb. 6, 1880.
41. Ibid., Feb. 6–11, 1880.
42. Ibid., Feb. 15, 1880.
43. Ibid., Feb. 21, 1880.
44. Ibid., Feb. 24, 1880.
45. Ibid., Feb. 27, 1880.
46. *Leadville (CO) Weekly Herald,* Feb. 28, 1880.
47. *Leadville (CO) Daily Democrat,* Feb. 29, 1880.
48. Ibid.
49. Ibid., March 3, 1880.
50. Ibid., March 7, 1880.
51. Ibid., March 6, 1880.
52. Ibid., March 7, 1880.
53. Ibid., March 10, 1880.
54. Ibid., March 9, 1880.
55. Ibid., March 6, 1880.
56. Ibid., March 13, 1880.
57. Ibid., March, 14, 1880.
58. These authors had a wire fox terrier cross we named after this protagonist.
59. *Leadville (CO) Daily Democrat,* March 19, 1880.
60. Ibid., March 20, 1880.
61. Ibid., March 21, 1880.
62. Ibid., March 24, 1880.
63. Ibid., March 26, 1880.
64. Ibid., March 30, 1880.
65. Ibid., March 31, 1880.
66. Ibid., April 1, 1880.
67. Ibid., April 7–9, 1880.
68. Ibid., April 11–17, 1880.
69. Ibid., April 11, 1880.
70. Ibid., April 16, 1880.
71. Ibid.
72. Ibid., April 11, 1880.
73. Ibid., April 21, 1880
74. Ibid., April 24, 1880.
75. Ibid., April 25, 1880.
76. Ibid., April 28, 1880.
77. Ibid., April 28, 1880.
78. Ibid., May 6, 1880.
79. Ibid., May 9, 1880 .
80. Ibid.
81. 1880 U.S. Census, Colorado, Lake county, Leadville, June 9, 1880 p. 12, enumeration district #81.
82. *Leadville (CO) Daily Democrat,* July 14, 1880.
83. Muriel Sibell Wolle, *Stampede to Timberline* (Self-published: Boulder, CO, 1957).
84. *Georgetown Colorado Miner,* Aug. 7 1880.
85. *Leadville (CO) Daily Democrat,* July 14, 1880.
86. *Breckenridge (CO) Daily Journal,* July 22, 1880.
87. *Georgetown Colorado Miner,* July 31, 1880.
88. Ibid., Aug., 7, 1880.
89. Ibid.
90. *Central City (CO) Daily Register-Call,* July 31, 1880. Dr. Tanner, in N.Y., proposed to fast for forty days.
91. *Golden Colorado Transcript,* Aug. 11, 1880.
92. *Boulder, (CO) News and Courier,* Aug. 15, 1880.
93. *DenverRocky Mountain News,* Aug. 15, 1880.
94. Ibid., Aug. 21, 1880.
95. *New York Dramatic Mirror,* Sept. 4, 1880.
96. *Denver Daily Tribune,* Aug. 19, 1880.

Notes—Chapter 16

97. *DenverRocky Mountain News*, Aug. 24, 1880.
98. Ibid., Aug. 27, 1880.
99. Ibid., Sept. 15, 1880.
100. Ibid., Sept.21, 1880.
101. Ibid., Oct. 2, 1880.
102. Ibid., Oct. 8, 1880.
103. Ibid., Oct 12, 1880.
104. Ibid., Oct. 21, 1880.
105. Ibid., Oct. 22, 1880.
106. Ibid., Oct. 30, 1880.

Chapter 16

1. *Denver Rocky Mountain News*, Jan. 13, 1881.
2. *Denver Times*, Jan. 11, 1881.
3. *Denver Rocky Mountain News*, Jan. 20, 1881.
4. *Denver Republican*, Jan. 24, 1881.
5. *Denver Rocky Mountain News*, Jan. 25, 1881.
6. *Denver Daily Colorado Tribune*, Dec. 21, 1880.
7. *Denver Republican*, Jan. 24, 1881.
8. *New York Dramatic Mirror*, Feb. 5, 1881.
9. Ibid.
10. *New York Clipper*, Feb. 5, 1881.
11. *Denver Times*, June 26, 1897.
12. *Denver Rocky Mountain News*, Feb. 18, 1881.
13. Ibid., Feb. 22, 1881.
14. *Denver Times*, June 26, 1897.
15. *Denver Rocky Mountain News*, Feb. 26, 1881.
16. Ibid., March 22, 1881.
17. *Pueblo (CO) Daily Chieftain*, March 27–31, 1881.
18. Ibid., March 29, 1881.
19. *Denver Rocky Mountain News*, April, 1, 1881.
20. Ibid., April 5, 1881.
21. Ibid., April 6, 1881.
22. Ibid., April 7, 1881.
23. *Denver Times*, June 26, 1897.
24. *Colorado Springs Daily Gazette*, April 19, 1881.
25. *Denver Rocky Mountain News*, April 19, 1881.
26. *Colorado Springs Daily Gazette*, April 21, 1881.
27. Ibid., April 21, 1881.
28. *Denver Rocky Mountain News*, April 24, 1881.
29. *Denver Times*, June 26, 1897.
30. *Denver Rocky Mountain News*, May 1, 1881.
31. *New York Clipper*, May 14, 1881.
32. *Cañon City (CO) Fremont County Record*, May 7, 1881.
33. Ibid., May 14, 1881.
34. *New York Dramatic Mirror*, May 28, 1881.
35. *Denver Rocky Mountain News*, June 8, 1881.
36. Transcript of Judgment docket, Book 56 p. 17, Clear Creek county records.
37. *New York Dramatic Mirror*, July 9, 1881.
38. *New York Dramatic Mirror*, Aug. 13, 1881.
39. *Denver Rocky Mountain News*, Aug. 9. 1881.
40. *Denver Tribune*, Sept. 2, 1881.
41. *Pueblo (CO) Daily Chieftain*, Jan. 26, 1882.
42. *Denver Times*, Jan. 25, 1882.
43. *Denver Rocky Mountain News*, Jan. 6, 1882.
44. *Denver Republican*, Feb. 4, 1882.
45. *Denver Rocky Mountain News*, Feb. 14, 1882.
46. *Pueblo (CO) Daily Chieftain*, Feb. 16, 1882.
47. *Deer Lodge (MT) New North-West*, Sept. 15, 1882.
48. *Denver Times*, Nov. 27, 1882.
49. *Field and Farm*, July 3, 1886.
50. *Denver Rocky Mountain News*, Nov. 28, 1882.
51. Ibid., May 20, 1883.
52. Ibid., May 22, 1883.
53. *New York Dramatic News*, Sept. 25, 1883.
54. *New York Dramatic Mirror*, March 18, 1882.
55. *Denver Rocky Mountain News*, Sept. 21, 1883.
56. *Denver Times*, Sept. 13, 1883.
57. *Denver Rocky Mountain News*, Sept. 19, 1883.
58. *Denver Republican*, Sept. 20, 1883.
59. *Colorado Springs Daily Gazette*, Sept. 23, 1883.
60. *Denver Times*, Sept. 25, 1883.
61. *Denver Republican*, Sept. 22, 1883.
62. *Denver Times*, Sept. 27, 1883.
63. *Cheyenne Daily Leader*, Oct. 3, 1883.
64. *Laramie (WY) Journal*, Oct. 6, 1883.
65. *Denver Tribune*, Sept. 21, 1883.
66. *Salt Lake City Daily Tribune*, Oct. 12, 1883.
67. *Salt Lake City Deseret News*, Oct. 12, 1883.
68. *New York Dramatic Mirror*, Oct. 13, 1883.
69. *San Francisco Music and Drama*, Oct. 6, 1883.
70. Ibid., Oct. 20, 1883.
71. *Deer Lodge (MT) New North-West*, Nov. 2, 1883.

Chapter 17

1. *Helena (MT) Daily Herald,* Oct. 29, 1883.
2. *Deer Lodge (MT) New North-West,* Feb. 17, 1871.
3. Schoberlin.
4. *Helena (MT)Daily Herald,* Oct. 29, 1883.
5. Ibid., Oct. 30, 1883.
6. Ibid.
7. Ibid., Nov. 1, 1883.
8. Ibid.
9. Ibid.
10. Ibid., Nov. 2, 1883.
11. *New York Clipper,* Nov. 3, 1883.
12. *Helena (MT) Daily Herald,* Nov. 3, 1883.
13. Ibid., Nov. 5, 1883.
14. Ibid., Nov. 9, 1883.
15. Ibid., Nov. 10, 1883.
16. Ibid., Nov. 9, 1883.
17. Ibid., Nov. 12, 1883.
18. *Butte Daily Miner,* Nov. 9, 1883.
19. Ibid., Nov. 13, 1883.
20. Ibid., Nov. 14, 1883.
21. *Missoula County Times,* Nov. 21, 1883.
22. *Butte Weekly Intermountain,* Nov. 22, 1883.
23. *Seattle Daily Post-Intelligencer,* Dec. 19, 1883.
24. "Good Show," *Spokane Falls Review,* Dec. 1, 1883.
25. *Lewiston (ID) Teller,* Dec. 6, 1883.
26. "Routes Ahead," *New York Clipper,* Dec. 1, 1883.
27. *Pendleton Semi-Weekly East Oregonian,* Dec. 4, 1883.
28. Ibid., Dec. 11, 1883.
29. "Routes Ahead," *New York Clipper,* Dec. 1, 1883.
30. *Tacoma Daily Ledger,* Dec. 18, 1883.
31. Ibid., Dec. 18, 1883.
32. *Portland Daily Oregonian,* Dec. 13, 1883.
33. Ibid., Dec. 16, 1883.
34. Ibid., Dec. 16, 1883.
35. Ibid., Dec. 18, 1883.
36. Ibid., Dec. 19, 1883.
37. Ibid., Dec. 21, 1883.
38. Ibid., Dec. 23, 1883.
39. *Tacoma Daily Ledger,* Dec. 25, 1883.
40. *Portland Daily Oregonian,* Dec. 22, 1883.
41. *Tacoma Daily Ledger,* Dec. 27, 1883.
42. *Seattle Post-Intelligencer,* Dec. 27, 1883.
43. Ibid., Dec. 28, 1883.
44. *Victoria Daily British Colonist (British Columbia),* Dec. 27, 1883.
45. *San Francisco Music and Drama,* Dec. 29, 1883.
46. Ibid., Jan. 5, 1884.
47. *Victoria Daily British Colonist (British, Columbia),* Jan. 3, 1884.
48. *Port Townsend (WA) Puget Sound Weekly Argus,* Jan. 10, 1884 (From Saturday's daily)
49. *Vancouver(WA) Weekly Independent,* Jan. 17, 1884.
50. Ibid., Jan. 10, 1884.
51. Ibid.
52. Possibly in 1851 at Fond du Lac, Wisconsin where Beeson was raised
53. *Vancouver (WA) Independent,* Jan. 17, 1884.
54. *Daily (OR) Astorian ,* Jan. 15, 1884.
55. Ibid., Jan. 16, 1884.
56. *Albany (OR) State's Rights Democrat,* Jan. 25, 1884.
57. *Portland Oregonian,* Jan. 15, 1884.
58. *San Francisco Music and Drama,* Jan. 26, 1884.
59. *Portland Oregonian,* Jan. 26, 1884.
60. *Eugene City Guard,* Jan. 26, 1884.
61. *Roseburg (OR) Douglas Independent,* Jan. 26, 1884.
62. *Eugene City Guard,* Feb. 2, 1884; *Eugene State Journal,* Feb. 2, 1884.
63. *Eugene State Journal,* Jan. 26, 1884.
64. *Portland Oregonian,* Jan. 27, 1884.
65. *Roseburg, (OR) Douglas Independent,* Feb. 2, 1884.
66. *Ashland (OR) Tidings,* Feb. 1, 1884.
67. Ibid., Feb. 8, 1884.
68. *Portland Oregonian,* Feb. 9, 1884.
69. *Ashland (OR) Tidings,* Feb. 22, 1884.

Chapter 18

1. *Chico (CA) Weekly Butte Record,* Feb. 23, 1884.
2. *Ashland (OR) Tidings,* Feb. 29, 1884; *Marysville (CA) Weekly Appeal,* March 7, 1884. (From Saturday's daily.)
3. *Marysville (CA) Weekly Appeal,* March 7, 1884.
4. Ibid.
5. *Red Bluff (CA) Weekly Sentinel,* Feb 23, 1884.
6. Ibid., Feb. 23, 1884. (From Friday's daily.)
7. Ibid., March 1, 1884.
8. *Oroville (CA) Weekly Mercury,* March 7, 1884.
9. Ibid., March 14, 1884 (From March 12 daily.)
10. *Grass Valley (CA) Union,* March 18, 1884.
11. Ibid., March 15, 1884.
12. *Nevada City (CA) Daily Transcript,* March 20, 1884.

13. Ibid., March 25, 1884.
14. Ibid., March 30, 1884.
15. Ibid., April 5, 1884.
16. *Grass Valley (CA) Union*, March 16, 1884.
17. *Fresno Evening Expositor*, April 17, 1884.
18. *Visalia (CA) Weekly Delta*, April 17, 1884.
19. *Bakersfield Kern County Californian*, April 26, 1884.
20. *Anaheim Gazette*, May 10, 1884.
21. *New York Dramatic Mirror*, May 24, 1884.
22. *Riverside (CA) Press and Horticulturist*, May 10, 1884.
23. *Anaheim Gazette*, May 17, 1884.
24. Jerry MacMullen, "The *Orizaba* and Johnson Heights," *Journal of San Diego History*, vol. 5, No. 3, July, 1959.
25. *San Diego Union*, May 17, 1884.
26. Ibid., May 20, 1884.
27. Ibid., May 22, 1884.
28. Ibid., May 23, 1884.
29. *Santa Barbara Independent*, May 27, 1884.
30. Ibid., May 29, 1884.
31. Ibid., May 31, 1884.
32. *Ventura Free Press*, June 6, 1884.
33. *San Luis Obispo Daily Republic*, June 11, 1884.
34. *Santa Maria (CA) Times*, May 31, 1884.
35. *Salinas (CA) Weekly Index*, June 26, 1884.
36. *Oakland Times*, June 19, 1884.
37. Ibid., June 28, 1884.
38. *Ibid.*, June 29 - July 20, 1884 passim.
39. *New York Dramatic News*, June 28, 1884.
40. *New York Dramatic News*, Aug. 9, 1884.
41. "California—San Francisco, *New York Clipper*, Aug. 23, 1884.
42. *Sacramento Daily Record Union*, Sept. 3, 1884.
43. Ibid., Sept. 10, 1884.
44. *Nevada City (CA) Daily Transcript*, Sept. 16, 1884.
45. *New York Dramatic Mirror*, Apr. 23, 1887.
46. "Deeply Interested," *Nevada City (CA) Daily Transcript*, Sept. 12, 1884.
47. *Marysville (CA) Daily Appeal*, Sept. 20, 1884.
48. *Chico (CA) Weekly Butte Record*, Oct. 11, 1884. (From Fri., Oct. 3 daily.)
49. *Red Bluff (CA) Tehama County Democrat*, Oct. 11, 1884.
50. *Stockton (CA) Mail*, Oct. 24, 1884.
51. *Galt (CA) Weekly Gazette*, Oct. 25, 1884.
52. *Eureka (CA) Daily Times-Telephone*, Nov. 13, 1884.
53. Ibid., Nov. 22, 1884.
54. *Marshfield (OR) Coos Bay News*, Dec. 10, 1884.
55. *Astoria (OR) Daily Astorian*, Dec. 9, 1884.

56. Ibid., Dec. 11. 1884.
57. Ibid., Dec. 12, 1884.
58. *Walla Walla Union*, Dec. 27, 1884.
59. *An Illustrated History of Northern Idaho*, (Spokane, WA : Western Historical Publishing Co., 1903), pp.1042–1043.
60. *Ashland (OR) Tidings*, Dec. 1884–Jan., 1885.
61. Craig Clifford Elliott, "Annals of the Legitimate Theatre in Victoria, Canada, from the Beginning to 1900." Ph.D. diss., University of Washington, 1969.
62. *Seattle Post-Intelligencer*, Dec. 20, 1884.
63. *Ashland (OR) Tidings*, Jan. 16, 1885.
64. *Salem (OR) Weekly Statesman*, Jan. 20–23, 1885.
65. Ibid., Jan. 16, 1885, (From Thursday's daily)
66. Ibid., Jan. 16, 1885, (From Sunday's daily)
67. *New York Dramatic Mirror*, Jan. 31, 1885.
68. *Vancouver (WA) Independent*, Feb. 5, 1885.
69. Ibid., Feb. 12, 1885.
70. *Portland Oregonian*, Feb. 12, 1885.
71. Ibid., Feb. 14, 1885.
72. Ibid., Feb. 28, 1885.
73. Ibid.
74. Ibid., March 7, 1885.
75. Ibid., March 9, 1885.
76. Ibid., March 15, 1885.
77. Ibid., March 25, 1885.
78. Ibid., April 3, 1885.
79. "Oregon—Portland," *Chicago News Letter*, April 4, 1885.
80. "Oregon—Portland," *New York Dramatic Mirror*, March 28 and April 4, 1885.
81. "Oregon—Portland," *New York Clipper*, April 4, 1885.
82. *New York Clipper*, April 4, 1885.
83. *Vancouver (WA) Independent*, April 2, 1885.

Chapter 19

1. "Coeur d'Alene," *Portland Oregonian*, April 14, 1885.
2. Hazel Kirke claim, filed by John S. Langrishe May 25, 1885 (filed for record May 29, 1885), Book I, p. 410, Beaver District.
3. Book I, p. 484, Coeur d'Alene District, recorded Oct. 3, 1885, name of claim: Langrishe.
4. Letter from Laurette Atwater to her sister, Augusta Atwood, Apr. 28th (NY), Box 1, E.H. Atwood Family papers, Minnesota Historical Society.
5. *Murray (ID) Coeur d'Alene Sun*, June 25, 1885.

6. Ibid.
7. *New York Dramatic Mirror,* June 6, 1885.
8. George W. Fuller v. J.S. Langrishe and William McKay, Shoshone County Court, Idaho Territory, exhibit A for mechanics' lien.
9. Proceedings of Shoshone county commissioners, Murray, Idaho, Nov. 17, 1886.
10. *Deadwood Black Hills Daily Times,* Dec. 8, 1886.
11. Robert Wayne Smith, "History of Placer and Quartz Mining in Coeur d'Alenes," typescript, p. 53, University of Idaho Library.
12. "Personal and Impersonal," *Field and Farm,* Jan. 2, 1886.
13. Ibid., Jan. 30, 1886.
14. *Spokane Falls Morning Review,* April 7, 1886.
15. *Deadwood Black Hills Daily Times,* June 15-17, 1879.
16. Dorothy Whiteman. *History of the Kellogg-Wardner News,* typescript, 1935-36, University of Idaho Library, p. 2.
17. *Missoula County Times,* Nov. 14, 1883; J. Cecil Alter, *Early Utah Journalism* (Salt Lake City, Utah: Utah State Historical Society, 1938,) p. 54.
18. J. W. Watson's great poem, "Beautiful Snow," created something of a sensation in the literary world, and made a national reputation for the author, inasmuch as it was copied into nearly all the leading publications and received the praise of the press generally.)
19. *Spokane Falls Morning Review,* Feb. 22, 1887.
20. *Spokane Falls Morning Review,* April 24, 1887.
21. *Field and Farm,* June 4, 1887.
22. Shoshone County Recorder, grantee index.
23. William T. Stoll, *Silver Strike; The True Story of Silver Mining in the Coeur d'Alenes* (Reprint, Moscow, ID: University of Idaho, 1991), p. 78.
24. *Spokane Falls Morning Review,* Oct. 20,1886.
25. "With Our Pioneers," *Kellogg (ID) Shoshone Tribune,* Jan. 26, 1951.
26. George Hobson, ed. "Gems of Thought and History of Shoshone County." *Kellogg Evening News Press,* 1940.
27. "With Our Pioneers," *Kellogg (Idaho) Shoshone Tribune,* Jan. 16, 1951. (Additional oral information from old resident.)
28. Ibid., Aug. 31, 1951.
29. Smalley's *Northwest Magazine,* Oct., 1887. Langrishe's acting with those named stars has not been supported by evidence.
30. *Wallace (ID) Free Press,* Feb. 18, 1888.
31. Ibid., Feb. 25, 1888.
32. Ibid., Aug. 11, 1888.
33. "Mullan." *Wallace (ID) Free Press,* Aug. 18, 1888.
34. *Wallace (ID) Free Press,* Sept. 22, 1888.
35. *Wardner (ID) News,* Nov. 3, 1888.
36. Ibid., Nov. 3, 1888.
37. *Wallace (ID) Free Press,* Dec. 7, 1888.
38. Ibid., Dec. 29, 1888.
39. "Magic Talisman"—an original operatic spectacular play, by J.S Langrishe, Charles Carle and Thomas C. Houghton, Boston, 1873. *Dramatic Compositions Copyrighted in the U.S., 1870 to 1916.* Washington: Government Printing Office, 1918.
40. *New York Dramatic Mirror,* Jan. 5, 1888.
41. *Wallace (ID) Free Press,* Jan. 19, 1888.
42. J.S. Langrishe v. George B. McAulay, No. 993, District Court of First Judicial District, state of Idaho, County of Shoshone.
43. N. Avon Wilson, "The Pack Mule Press of the Coeur d'Alenes." Typescript, n.d. University of Idaho holdings.
44. *Wallace (ID) Free Press,* Jan. 25, 1890.
45. "Local Miscellany," *Wardner (ID) News,* March 29, 1890.
46. *Wallace (ID) Coeur d'Alene Miner,* July 5, 1890.

Chapter 20

1. *Wardner (ID) News,* July 12, 1890.
2. *Wallace (ID) Coeur d'Alene Miner,* July 26, 1890.
3. Robert L. Perkin, "Ten: Sand Creek." *A Colorado Reader* (Carl Ubbelohde, ed. :Pruett Press: Boulder, CO. 1962.)
4. *Wallace (ID) Coeur d'Alene Miner,* Aug. 2, 1890.
5. "Shoshone County," *Boise Idaho Statesman,* Aug. 16, 1890.
6. *New York Clipper,* Nov. 8, 1890.
7. *Wallace (ID) Coeur d'Alene Miner,* July 19, 1890.
8. *Wallace (ID) Press,* Nov. 15, 1890.
9. "Benefit to Mrs. Eva Vincent," *Wallace (ID) Coeur d'Alene Miner,* Sept. 3, 1890.
10. "Our Legislative Candidates," *Wallace (ID) Coeur d'Alene Miner,* Sept. 28, 1890.
11. "Jack Langrishe," *Wallace (ID) Coeur d'Alene Miner,* Sept. 30, 1890.
12. *Osburn (ID) Coeur d'Alene Statesman,* Sept. 30, 1890. Authors haven't found where or whether Langrishe became a U.S. citizen.
13. *Wallace, (ID) Coeur d'Alene Miner,* Sept. 31 [sic] ,1890.

14. Ibid., Oct. 3, 1890.
15. "County Taxpayers," *Wallace (Idaho) Coeur d'Alene Miner*, Oct. 25, 1890.
16. *New York Clipper*, Nov. 8, 1890.
17. *Wallace* (ID) *Coeur d'Alene Miner*, Oct. 18, 1890 editorial.
18. Barbara Perry Bauer, "The Main Line Comes to Boise." *Idaho Yesterdays*, v. 44, #1 Spring, 2000.
19. "Gossip of the Hotels," *Boise Idaho Daily Statesman*, Dec. 6, 1890.
20. *Salt Lake Herald*, March 8, 1891.
21. "Local Intelligence," *Boise Idaho Daily Statesman*, Feb. 21, 1891.
22. *Journal of the Senate of the State of Idaho: First Session* (Boise City, ID: Statesman Printing Co., 1891), p. 20.
23. *Boise Idaho Daily Statesman*, Dec 23, 1890.
24. Ibid.
25. *Wardner* (ID) *News*, Dec. 27, 1890.
26. *Boise Idaho Daily Statesman*, Feb. 26, 1891.
27. Ibid., Feb. 18, 1891.
28. Margaret Lauterbach, "A Plentitude of Senators," *Idaho Yesterdays*, v. 21, no. 3, Fall,1977, 1.
29. *Osburn (ID) Coeur d'Alene Statesman*, Feb. 13, 1891.
30. *Boise Idaho Daily Statesman*, Feb. 14, 1891.
31. *Boise Idaho Daily Statesman*, Feb. 4, 1891.
32. Lauterbach. [See note 28.]
33. Ibid., March 16, 1891.
34. "Editorial Brief," *Boise Idaho Daily Statesman*, March 16, 1891.

Chapter 21

1. *Wardner (ID) News*, July 4, 1891.
2. *Wallace (ID) Press*, July 11, 1891.
3. Ibid., July 11, 1891.
4. *Wallace (ID) Coeur d'Alene Miner*, Sept. 19, 1891.
5. *Wardner (ID) News*, Oct. 3, 1891.
6. Ibid.
7. Earl B. Crane, "Wardner in the Glory Days; Lively Account of a Man Who Was A Youngster in This Bunker Hill and Sullivan Boom Town" n.d., Unknown newspaper, clipping from Idaho Cities and Towns, Wardner, Pamphlet File, University of Idaho.
8. *Wardner (ID) News*, Oct. 24, 1891.
9. J.S. Langrishe v. Geo. B. McAulay et al, District Court, First Judicial District, County of Shoshone, #993.
10. "A Newspaper Purchase," *Wallace (ID) Press*, Jan. 23, 1892.
11. *Wallace (ID) Coeur d'Alene Miner*, Jan. 23, 1892.
12. Ibid., Feb. 6, 1892.

13. Ibid., Feb. 20, 1892.
14. *Wallace (ID) Press*, March 5, 1892.
15. *Wallace (ID) Coeur d'Alene Miner*, March 19, 1892.
16. *Wardner (ID) Coeur d'Alene Barbarian*, March 26, 1892.
17. Ibid.
18. "Editorial," *Wallace* (ID) Press, April 23, 1892.
19. Richard G. Magnuson, *Coeur d'Alene Diary* (Metropolitan Press: Portland, OR, 1968), p. 186.
20. *Wallace (ID) Coeur d'Alene Miner*, May 7, 1892.
21. *Wallace (ID) Press*, May 14, 1892.
22. *Wallace (ID) Coeur d'Alene Miner*, May 14, 1892.
23. Ibid., May 21, 1892.
24. Ibid., June 4, 1892.
25. Ibid., June 18, 1892.
26. *Wardner (ID) Coeur d'Alene Barbarian*, July 2, 1892.
27. *Wallace (ID) Press*, July 9, 1892.
28. *Wallace (ID) Coeur d'Alene Miner*, July 16, 1892.
29. Norman B. Willey to Benjamin Harrison, Boise City, June 25, 1892. Idaho Historical Society Collections.
30. Magnuson, p. 224.
31. F. Ross Peterson, *Idaho*. (W.W. Norton & Co.: New York, NY), 1976.
32. *Wardner (ID) Coeur d'Alene Barbarian*, July 23, 1892.
33. Ibid.
34. Magnuson, p. 239.
35. Ibid.
36. *Wallace (ID) Coeur d'Alene Miner*, July 30, 1892.
37. "News from Wardner," *Wallace (ID) Coeur d'Alene American*, Sept. 10, 1892.
38. "News from Wardner," *Wallace (ID) Coeur d'Alene American*, Sept. 17, 1892.
39. 'Happenings at Wardner," *Wallace (ID) Coeur d'Alene American*, Sept. 24, 1892.
40. *Wallace (ID) Coeur d'Alene Miner*, Oct. 1, 1892.
41. Ibid., Oct. 15, 1892.
42. *Osburn (ID) Coeur d'Alene Statesman*, Oct. 19, 1892.
43. *Wallace (ID) Coeur d'Alene American*, Oct. 29, 1892.
44. "The City of Wardner," *Wallace, (ID) Coeur d'Alene American*, Nov. 5, 1892.
45. *Wallace (ID) Coeur d'Alene American*, Nov. 19, 1892.
46. *Wallace (ID) Coeur d'Alene Miner*, Nov. 19, 1892.

47. *Wallace (ID) Coeur d'Alene American*, Dec. 3, 1892.
48. "Events at Home and Abroad," *Wardner (ID) Coeur d'Alene Barbarian*, Dec. 10, 1892.
49. *Wallace (ID) Coeur d'Alene Miner*, Dec. 10, 1892.
50. "Wardner Jottings," *Wallace (ID) Coeur d'Alene American*, Dec. 24, 1892.
51. "The Weather," *Wallace (ID) Coeur d'Alene American*, Dec. 24, 1892.
52. *Wallace(ID) Democrat*, Dec. 29. 1892.
53. *Wallace (ID) Coeur d'Alene Miner*, Dec. 31, 1892.
54. *Denver Rocky Mountain News*, Dec. 25, 1892, Christmas section.

Chapter 22

1. *Wallace (ID) Democrat*, Jan. 5, 1893.
2. *Wallace (ID) Coeur d'Alene Miner*, Jan. 7, 1893.
3. *Wardner (ID) Coeur d'Alene Barbarian*, Jan. 18, 1893.
4. *Wallace (ID) Coeur d'Alene Miner*, Feb. 4, 1893.
5. "A Generous Response," *Wallace (ID) Coeur d'Alene American*, Feb. 25, 1893.
6. "High Rolling," *Wallace (ID) Coeur d'Alene American*, Feb. 25, 1893.
7. Register of Actions and Fee Book, District Ct. J.S. Langrishe vs. George B. McAulay and V.M. Clement June 6, 1893.
8. *Wallace (ID) Coeur d'Alene Miner*, Feb. 25, 1893.
9. "From Wardner," *Wallace (ID) Coeur d'Alene Miner*, March 4, 1893.
10. "Wardner, Idaho April 6, 1893," *Wallace (ID) Coeur d'Alene Miner*, April 8, 1893.
11. "Wardner Items," *Wallace (ID) Democrat*, April 13, 1893.
12. "Theatre—Saturday Night," *Wardner (ID) Coeur d'Alene Barbarian*, June 24, 1893.
13. "Wardner Junction," *Wallace (ID) Coeur d'Alene Miner*, July 8, 1893.
14. *Wallace (ID) Coeur d'Alene Miner*, April 22, 1893.
15. "Our Wardner Letter." *Wallace (ID) Coeur d'Alene Miner*, May 6, 1893.
16. *Wallace (ID) Coeur d'Alene Miner*, May 20, 1893.
17. Register of Actions and Fee Book, District Court. J.S. Langrishe vs. George B. McAulay and V.M. Clement, complaint registered June 6, 1893.
18. *Wallace, (ID) Coeur d'Alene Miner*, Nov. 25, 1893.
19. "Wallace, March 8, 1894." *Wardner (ID) News*, March 10, 1894. Note Langrishe had changed the name of the newspaper to the *News*.
20. *Boise Idaho Statesman*, April 25, 1894.
21. *Wallace (ID) Idaho State Tribune*, Oct. 29, 1894.
22. Ibid., Nov. 22, 1894.
23. Ibid., *Wallace (ID) Idaho State Tribune*, Nov. 8, 1894.
24. Ibid., Nov. 15, 1894.
25. Ibid., Dec. 6, 1894.
26. *Wardner (ID) News*, Dec. 8, 1894.
27. Ibid., *Wardner (ID) News*, March 2, 1895.
28. *Wallace (ID) Coeur d'Alene Miner*, March 9, 1895.
29. Ibid., June 1, 1895.
30. Ibid., June 22, 1895.
31. Ibid., Sept. 24, 1892.
32. Ibid., July 13, 1895.
33. "John Dillon," *Wardner (ID) News*, July 27, 1895.
34. *New York Dramatic Mirror*, Aug. 17, 1895.
35. "The Grand Ball," *Wardner* (ID) *News*, Sept. 14, 1895.
36. "From Wardner," *Wallace (ID) Coeur d'Alene Miner*, Nov. 16, 1895.
37. *Wallace (ID) Coeur d'Alene Miner*, Dec. 7, 1895.
38. *Wardner (ID) News*, Nov. 23, 1895.
39. *Wallace (ID) Coeur d'Alene Miner*, Nov. 23, 1895.
40. "A Good Man Called Home," *Wallace (ID) Coeur d'Alene Miner*, Dec. 7, 1895.
41. Daniel Sylvester Tuttle. *Reminiscences of a Missionary Bishop (*New York: Thomas Whittaker, 1906). pp. 414, 415.
42. Ethelbert Talbot, *My People of the Plains* (New York: Harper Brothers, 1906), pp. 96–97.
43. "The Funeral," *Wallace (ID) Coeur d'Alene Miner*, Dec. 7, 1895.
44. Kellogg Cemetery Records in Idaho State Historical library say his tombstone reads "b. 24 Sept., 1860." The stone has been severely weathered.
45. *Wallace (ID) Coeur d'Alene Miner*, Dec. 7, 1895.
46. No documentary confirmation of his having acted in London has been discovered by these authors. His mother's maiden surname was Boulger.
47. *Madison Wisconsin State Journal*, Dec. 12, 1895.
48. *Marysville (MT) Mountaineer*, Dec., 19, 1895.
49. "The Curtain Falls," *Leadville (CO) Herald-Democrat*, Dec. 14, 1895.

Epilogue

1. "Dates Ahead" and "Montana," *New York Dramatic Mirror,* Dec. 7, 1895.
2. "Routes Ahead," *New York Dramatic Mirror,* Dec. 14, 1895.
3. *Wallace Idaho State Tribune,* Dec. 13, 1895.
4. *Golden (CO) Transcript,* Dec. 25, 1895.
5. "Miscellaneous News," *Wardner (ID) News,* Dec. 14, 1895.
6. "Petition for Justice of the Peace," *Wardner (ID) News,* Dec. 14, 1895.
7. *Wardner (ID) News,* Dec. 14, 1895.
8. "Notice to Subscribers," *Wardner (ID) News,* Dec. 14, 1895.
9. *Wardner (ID) News,* Feb. 16, 1895.
10. *New York Dramatic Mirror,* May 2, 1896.
11. "New Scenery for Pythian Hall," *Wardner (ID) News,* Dec. 14, 1895.
12. "Miscellaneous News," *Wardner (ID) News,* Dec. 14, 1895.
13. *Wardner (ID) News,* Feb. 1, 1896.
14. Ibid., Feb. 8, 1895.
15. Ibid., July 11, 1896.
16. Ibid., July 25, 1896.
17. Ibid., Dec. 19. 1896, Supplement.
18. Note in Shoshone County Commissioners' register, special term, Jan. 8, 1897.
19. Letter, Jeannette Langrishe to "Dear Brother," May 20, 1898, Edwin H. Atwood & Family papers, Minnesota Historical Society.
20. "Mr. Bailey of Idaho," *St. Cloud (MN) Daily Journal-Press,* Aug. 14, 1900.
21. Letter, Jeannette Langrishe to "My Dear Brother" May 5, 1899. Edwin H. Atwood & family, box 5 Minnesota Historical Society.
22. Shoshone county Recorder's books, grantor index, 1/2/1901–11/30/1904 (cq), recorded Nov. 17, 1902.
23. U.S. Census 1900, Idaho, Shoshone county, Wardner, p. 670.
24. "Wardner, Idaho, August 23—, *Spokane Spokesman-Review,* Aug. 27, 1900.

Bibliography

Books

Alter, Cecil. *Early Utah Journalism*. Salt Lake City : Utah State Historical Society, 1938.

Athearn, Robert G. *The Coloradans*. Albuquerque: University of New Mexico Press, 1976.

Bancroft, Caroline. *Gulch of Gold*. Boulder, CO : Johnson Publishing, 1958.

Barney, Libeus. *Letters of the Pike's Peak Gold Rush*. Reprinted from the *Bennington (VT) Banner*, 1859–1860. San Jose, CA : The Talisman Press, 1959.

Bennett, Estelline. *Old Deadwood Days*. Reprint, Lincoln, NE : University of Nebraska Press, 1982.

Burrell, James. *History of Gilpin County, History of Colorado: Clear Creek and Boulder Valleys*. Chicago: O.L. Baskin Co., 1880.

Coutant, Dr. C. G. *History of Wyoming and the Far West*. New York: Argonaut Press, for University Microfilms, Ann Arbor, MI.

Dramatic Compositions Copyrighted in the U.S., 1870 to 1916. Washington: Government Printing Office, 1918.

Furman, Evelyn E. Livingston. *The Tabor Opera House, a Captivating History*. Privately printed, 1972.

Greever, William S. *Bonanza West: The Story of the Western Mining Rushes, 1848–1900*. Moscow, ID: University of Idaho Press, 1993.

Griswold, Don and Jean. *Colorado's Century of Cities*. Denver : Smith-Brooks, 1958.

Hafen, LeRoy. *Fort Laramie and the Pageant of the West, 1834–1890*. Glendale: Arthur M. Clark Co., 1938.

Hartnoll, Phyllis. ed. *Oxford Companion to the Theatre*, 2nd ed. London: Oxford University Press, 1962.

Idaho. *Journal of the Senate of the State of Idaho. First Session Convened on the 8th Day of December, A.D. 1890 and Adjourned on the Fourteenth Day of March, A.D. 1891 at Boise City*, 1891.

An Illustrated History of North Idaho: Embracing Nez Perce, Idaho, Latah, Kootenai and Shoshone Counties, State of Idaho. [Place of publication not identified]: Western Historical Pub. Co, 1903.

Kline, Samuel J. *Recollections and Comments*. Los Angeles: publisher not identified, 1924.

Kroll, Oscar. *The Clarinet*. Trans. by Hilda Morris. New York: Taplinger, 1968.

Leman, Thomas Rede. *The Road to the Stage*. New Ed., London: J. Onwhyn, 1835.

Magnuson, Richard G. *Coeur d'Alene Diary*. Portland, OR.: Metropolitan Press, 1968.

Matlaw, Myron. ed. *The Black Crook and Other Nineteenth Century American Plays*. New York: E.P. Dutton & Co., 1967.

McCutcheon, Marc. *Everyday Life in the 1800s*. Cincinnati: Writer's Digest Books, 1993.

Mencken, H.L. *The American Language*. 4th ed. New York: Alfred A. Knopf, 1962.

Miller, John. *History of Erie County, Pennsylvania*. Chicago: Lewis Publishing Co., 1909.

Moody, Richard. ed. *Dramas from the American Theatre, 1762–1909*. Boston : Houghton-Mifflin Co., 1969.

Morris, Lloyd. *Curtain Time, the Story of American Theater*. New York: Random House, 1953.

Morris, Maurice O'Connor. *Rambles in the Rocky Mountains: with a visit to the Gold Fields of Colorado*. London: Smith, Elder & Co., 1864.

Odell, George C.D. *Annals of the New York Stage*, 15 vols. NY: AMS Press, 1970.

Parker, Watson. *Deadwood, the Golden Years.* Lincoln, NE: University of Nebraska Press, 1981.

Parkman, Francis. *The Oregon Trail.* Garden City, NY: Doubleday & Co., 1948.

Paul, Rodman Wilson. *Mining Frontiers of the Far West, 1849–1880.* Reprint, Albuquerque: University of New Mexico Press, 1974.

Perkin, Robert L. *The First Hundred Years.* Garden City, NY: Doubleday Publishing, 1959.

_____. "Sand Creek," in *A Colorado Reader.* ed. by Carl Ubbelohde. Boulder, CO: Pruett Press, 1962.

Peterson, F. Ross. *Idaho.* New York: W.W. Norton & Co., 1976.

Richardson, Albert D. *Beyond the Mississippi: From the Great River to the Great Ocean.* Hartford, CT: American Publishing Co., 1867.

Sachs, Curt. *History of Musical Instruments.* New York: W.W. Norton & Co., 1940.

Schoberlin, Melvin. *From Candles to Footlights.* Denver: Old West Publishing, 1941.

Settle, Raymond W., and Mary Lund. *Saddles and Spurs, the Pony Express Saga.* Lincoln, NE: University of Nebraska Press, 1955.

Stoll, William T. *Silver Strike: The True Story of Silver Mining in the Coeur d'Alenes.* Moscow, Idaho: University of Idaho Press, 1991.

Talbot, Ethelbert. *My People of the Plains.* New York: Harper Brothers, 1906.

Tallent, Annie D. *The Black Hills or Last Hunting Grounds of the Dakotahs.* Sioux Falls, SD: Brevet Press, 1974.

Taylor, Bayard. *Colorado: A Summer Trip.* New York: G.P. Putnam & Son, 1867.

Tuttle, Daniel Sylvester. *Reminiscences of a Missionary Bishop.* New York: Thomas Whittaker, 1906.

Wells, Charles B. *Memoirs of a Mummer.* Privately printed, 1924. Portions (copies) given to author by Wells's grand-niece, Mrs. Hamlin.

Wolle, Muriel Sibell. *Stampede to Timberline.* Boulder, CO: self-published, 1957.

The World Almanac and Book of Facts, 2005. New York, N.Y.: World Almanac Books, 2005.

Dissertations

Elliott, Craig Clifford. *Annals of the Legitimate Theatre in Victoria, Canada, from the Beginning to 1900.* Unpublished Ph.D. diss., University of Washington, 1969.

Hume, Charles V. *The Sacramento Theater, 1849–1885.* Ann Arbor, MI.: University Microfilms.

Perrigo, Lynn. *A Social History of Central City, Colorado, 1859–1900.* Unpublished Ph.D. diss., University of Colorado, 1936.

Periodical Articles

Bauer, Barbara Perry. "The Main Line Comes to Boise." *Idaho Yesterdays,* v. 44, No. 1 Spring, 2000.

Bowen. Elbert R. "Amusements and Entertainments in Early Missouri." *Missouri Historical Review,* v. 47 (1953).

Davis, Ronald L. "They Played for Gold: Theatre on the Mining Frontier." *Southwest Review,* Spring,1966.

Krone, Charles A. "Recollections of an Old Actor." *Missouri Historical Society* v. II, III, IV (1908–1911).

Krueger, Lillian. "Social Life in Wisconsin, Pre-Territorial through the Mid-Sixties." *Wisconsin Magazine of History,* v. 26, 1938.

Lauterbach, Margaret. "A Plentitude of Senators." *Idaho Yesterdays,* v.1, No. 3 Fall, 1977.

MacMullen, Jerry. "The Orizaba and Johnson Heights." *Journal of San Diego History,* vol. 5, No. 3, July, 1959.

Pollak, Nancy S. "Traveling Nineteenth-Century Ohio." *Ohio Historical* Society Echoes, v. 20, No. 1.

Smalley's *Northwest Magazine,* Oct., 1887.

Tuttle, Daniel S. "Early History of the Episcopal Church." *Contributions to the Historical Society of Montana,* v. 5 (1894).

Youngerman, Henry C. "Theatre Buildings in Madison, Wisconsin." *Wisconsin Magazine of History,* v.30, No. 3.

Zern, Frank W. "Early Day Show Houses and Actors." *The Trail,* vol. III, No. 5, Oct., 1910.

"Private Theatricals—Moore—Miss O'Neil—Chief Justice Bushe." *Dublin University Magazine,* v. XXXV, No. CCX, June, 1850.

Newspapers

Many newspapers cited below were published in Territories, prior to statehood. For clarity, the state name is used.

Bibliography

California

Anaheim Gazette
Bakersfield Kern County Californian
Chico Weekly Butte Record
Eureka Daily Times-Telephone
Fresno Evening Expositor
Galt Weekly Gazette
Grass Valley Union
Marysville Appeal
Nevada City Daily Transcript
Oakland Times
Oroville Weekly Mercury
Red Bluff Tehama County Democrat
Red Bluff Weekly Sentinel
Riverside Press and Horticulturist
Sacramento Daily Record Union
Sacramento Daily Union
Salinas Weekly Index
San Diego Union
San Francisco Daily Alta California
San Francisco Music and Drama
San Luis Obispo Daily Republic
Santa Barbara Independent
Santa Maria Times
Stockton Mail
Ventura Free Press
Visalia Weekly Visalia Delta

Colorado

Black Hawk Daily Mining Journal
Boulder County News
Boulder News and Courier
Breckenridge Daily Journal
Cañon County Fremont County Record
Central City Central City Register
Central City Daily Miners' Register
Central City Daily Register
Central City Register-Call
Central City Tri-Weekly Miners' Register
Colorado Springs Gazette
Denver Commonwealth
Denver Commonwealth and Republican
Denver Post
Denver Republican
Denver Republican and Rocky Mountain Herald
Denver Daily Rocky Mountain News
Denver Times
Denver Tribune
Denver Weekly Rocky Mountain News
Georgetown Colorado Miner
Golden Transcript
Leadville Daily Democrat
Leadville Herald Democrat
Leadville Weekly Herald
Pueblo Chieftain
Tarryall Weekly Miners' Record

Connecticut

Danbury Evening News
Hartford Daily Courant

Idaho

Boise Idaho Statesman
Kellogg Evening News
Kellogg Shoshone Tribune
Murray Coeur d'Alene Sun
Osburn Coeur d'Alene Statesman
Wallace Coeur d'Alene American
Wallace Coeur d'Alene Miner
Wallace Democrat
Wallace Free Press
Wallace Idaho State Tribune
Wallace Press
Wardner Coeur d'Alene Barbarian
Wardner News

Illinois

Aurora Beacon
Chicago Evening Journal
Chicago News Letter
Chicago Times
Chicago Tribune
Freeport Journal
Galena Daily Courier
Galena Daily Gazette
Galena Daily Jeffersonian
Peoria Daily National Democrat
Rock Island Argus
Rock Island Daily Union
Waukegan Gazette

Indiana

Terre Haute Gazette

Iowa

Davenport Daily Democrat
Davenport Daily Gazette
Guttenberg Clayton County Journal
McGregor North Iowa Times

Kansas

Atchison Weekly Champion
Leavenworth Daily Times
Lecompton National Democrat
Manhattan Express

Massachusetts
Boston Evening Transcript
Springfield Republican

Michigan
Detroit Daily Post
Grand Rapids Enquirer
Jackson American Citizen

Minnesota
Mantorville Express
Minneapolis Tribune
St. Paul Daily Minnesotian
St. Paul Daily Pioneer
St. Paul Minnesota Pioneer
St. Paul Pioneer and Democrat and Daily Minnesotian
Stillwater Messenger
Winona Daily Republican

Missouri
Kansas City Western Journal of Commerce
St. Joseph Weekly Free Democrat

Montana
Deer Lodge New North-West
Fort Benton River Press
Helena Herald
Helena Rocky Mountain Gazette
Marysville Mountaineer
Missoula County Times
Virginia City Montana Post

Nebraska
Nebraska City News
Wood River Center Huntsman's Echo

New York
Buffalo Daily Republic
Buffalo Morning Express
Corning Journal
Fredonia Censor
Ithaca Journal and Advertiser
New York Clipper
New York Dramatic Mirror
New York Dramatic News
New York Herald
New York Mirror
New York City Spirit of the Times
Onondaga Standard
Oswego Daily Commercial Times
Rochester Daily Advertiser
Rochester Daily American
Syracuse Daily Star
Syracuse Standard
Troy Daily Times
Utica Daily Gazette

Ohio
Cincinnati Enquirer
Sandusky Clarion
Toledo Blade

Oregon
Ashland Tidings
Astoria Daily Astorian
Marshfield Coos Bay News
Portland Oregonian
Salem Weekly Statesman

Pennsylvania
Erie Observer
Meadville Crawford Democrat
Pittsburgh Daily Gazette
Pittsburgh Daily Morning Post

Rhode Island
Providence Evening Press

South Dakota
Deadwood Black Hills Daily Times
Deadwood Black Hills Pioneer

Utah
Corinne Daily Utah Reporter
Salt Lake City Daily Tribune
Salt Lake City Deseret Evening News
Salt Lake City Daily Union Vedette
Salt Lake City Herald

Washington
Seattle Post-Intelligencer
Spokane Falls Morning Review
Spokane Spokesman-Review
Vancouver Independent
Walla Walla Union

Wisconsin
Baraboo Republic
Beaver Dam Dodge County Citizen
Beloit Free Press
Beloit Journal
Berlin Courant
Chippewa Falls Democrat
Chippewa Falls Herald

Fond du Lac Fountain City Herald
Fond du Lac Journal
Fond du Lac Union
Fort Winnebago River Times
Green Bay Advocate
Green Bay Daily State Gazette
Horicon Argus
Janesville Democrat Standard
Janesville Free Press
Janesville Gazette
Kenosha Democrat
Kenosha Telegraph
Kenosha Tribune
Kenosha Tribune and Telegraph
La Crosse Independent Republican
La Crosse National Democrat
La Crosse Republican and Leader
Madison Daily Argus
Madison Daily Argus and Democrat
Madison Daily Democrat
Madison Daily Statesman
Madison Daily Wisconsin Argus
Madison Wisconsin Daily Patriot
Madison Wisconsin State Journal
Milwaukee Daily Free Democrat
Milwaukee Daily Milwaukee News
Milwaukee Daily Sentinel
Milwaukee Evening Wisconsin
Milwaukee Sentinel and Gazette
Milwaukee Standard
Mineral Point Tribune
Mineral Point Wisconsin Tribune
Monroe Sentinel
Oshkosh Daily Courier
Oshkosh Weekly Courier
Oshkosh Weekly Northwestern
Oshkosh Weekly Times
Pepin Independent
Portage Badger State
Portage Independent
Prairie du Chien Courier
Prairie du Chien Leader
Racine Advocate
Ripon Home
Sheboygan Journal
Shullsberg Lafayette County Herald
Watertown Chronicle
Watertown Democrat
Waukesha Chronotype
Whitewater Gazette

WYOMING

Cheyenne Leader
Laramie Journal

Miscellaneous American Newspaper

Frontier Index [No fixed location. Published at railheads as the Union Pacific was built.]

Foreign Newspapers

Dublin Freeman's Journal
Guadalajara Juan Panadero
Mexico City Two Republics

Public Documents

1850 U.S. Census, Syracuse, Onondaga County, New York.
1880 U.S. Census, Colorado, Lake county, Leadville, enumeration district #81, p. 12.
1880 U.S. Census, Franklin County, Ohio, 6th ward Columbus.
1900 U.S. Census, Franklin County, Ohio.
Arapahoe Count, Colo., District Court, Second Judicial District. Solomon Hexter v. John S. Languishe (sic), Thomas Clifford and Michael D. Clifford.
Arapahoe County, Colo., real estate transfers, Book H.
Charles G. Mayers v. John S. Langrishe, Dane County Circuit Court, v. 4.
Clear Creek County, District Court: John S. Langrishe, Charles A. Cook and Daniel Doyle v. Robert O. Old, transcript of judgement docket, Book 56.
George W. Fuller v. J.S. Langrishe and William McKay, Shoshone County Court, Idaho Territory, exhibit A for mechanics' lien.
Grantee Index, Shoshone County, Idaho, recorder.
Hazel Kirke claim, filed by John S. Langrishe 25 May, 1885 (filed for record May 29, 1885), Book 1, p. 410, Beaver District., Shoshone County, Idaho.
Idaho Senate, 1891 Journal.
J.S. Langrishe v. George B. McAulay and V.M. Clement, complaint registered June 6, 1893, Register of Actions and Fee Book, District Court.
J.S. Langrishe v. George B. McAulay, No. 993, District Court of First Judicial District, county of Shoshone, state of Idaho.
Langrishe claim, filed by John S. Langrishe, Book 1, p. 484, Coeur d'Alene district, recorded Oct. 3, 1885.

Pension War 1812 Papers, Philadelphia, Pa., 2 March 1871, clerk of Orphans court.
Proceedings of Shoshone County commissioners, Idaho Territory, Murray, Idaho, Nov. 17, 1886.
Shoshone County Commissioners' register, special term, Jan. 8, 1897 note.
Shoshone County Recorder's Books, Grantor Index, 1902.
Vol. 72, Ft. Kearney, N.T. Letters Sent, Jan. 1856-Sept. 1860 National Archives, Tape MC3, side 1.
Wisconsin General Laws, General Acts Passed by the Legislature of Wisconsin. Madison: Calkins & Proudfit, 1856.

Unpublished Materials

Barton, Albert O., papers, notebook #1, Wisconsin Historical Society. Bedford Free Public Library].
Byers,' William, Letter: University of Colorado Manuscript Collection.
Kellogg Cemetery records in Idaho Genealogical library report Langrishe's tombstone reads "b. 24 Sept., 1860."
Letter from Langrishe, Geneva, Ill., to F.F. Mackay, held in Rare Book and Manuscript library (801 Butler Library), Columbia University.
Letter, 7 December, 1979, Doyn Inman, P.G.M., Grand Secretary, Grand Lodge Free and Accepted Masons of Wisconsin, to Dr. Charles Lauterbach.
Letter, Jeannette Langrishe to "Dear Brother," May 20, 1898, Edwin H. Atwood Family papers, Minnesota Historical Society.
Letter, Jeannette Langrishe to "My Dear Brother" May 5th, 1899. Edwin H. Atwood Family papers, Box 5, Minnesota Historical Society.
Letter, Laurette Atwater to Augusta Atwood, April 28. E.H. Atwood Family papers, Box 1, Minnesota Historical Society.
Letter, Laurette Atwater to Augusta Atwood, Aug. 8th (1876), E.H. Atwood Family papers, Box 1, Minnesota Historical Society.
Letter, M.J. Dougherty to Capt. Frank Hall, Apr. 27, 1863, Henry M. Teller papers, University of Colorado Historical Collections (Boulder).

Letter, Norman B. Willey to Benjamin Harrison, Boise City, June 25, 1892. Idaho Historical Society Collections.
Notes by Mrs. E.H. Atwood (Augusta Allen Atwood) in Box 5, A.A. 887, E.H. Atwood papers, Minnesota Historical Society library.
Playbills, owned by authors. Chatham Theatre from Boston Public Library and Black Crook from New York Public Library.
Private e-mail from Dr. Allan S. Jackson, emeritus professor of theatre, SUNY Binghamton.
Sayre, Hal, MSS 1-a VIII, Colorado State Historical Society Library.
Smith, Robert Wayne, "History of Placer and Quartz Mining in Coeur d'Alenes," typescript, University of Idaho Library.
Tappan's, Sam. Notebook, Jan. 1, 1865, at Colorado Historical Society.
Whiteman, Dorothy, *History of the Kellogg-Wardner News.* Typescript, 1935–36, University of Idaho Library.
Wilson, N. Avon, "The Pack Mule Press of the Coeur d'Alenes." Typescript, n.d. University of Idaho Library.

Internet

Philip V. Allingham, contributing ed. *The Victorian Web.* www.victorianweb.org/mt/boucicault/pva233.html
www.chicagohs.org/fire/conflag
www.chipublib.org/004chicago/timeline/reatfire.html

Ephemera

Earl B. Crane, "Wardner in the Glory Days: Lively Account of a Man Who Was a Youngster in This Bunker Hill and Sullivan Boom Town," n.d., unknown newspaper, clipping from Idaho Cities and Towns, Wardner, Pamphlet File, University of Idaho.
Oral communication to author from Boulder valley pioneer Mart Parsons, ca. 1953.
Playbill owned by Chicago Historical Society.
Playbills held by the American Antiquarian Society library, printed for Howard & Fox co. by A.C. Greene.

Index

Numbers in **_bold italics_** refer to pages with photographs.

Allen, Ethan 14
Allen, Helen 21, 22, 35
Allen, John H. 12
Allen, Laurette 15, 16, 18, 20, **_39_**
Allen, Lettie 131, 132, 133, 219
Apollo Hall (theatre) 60, 61, **_62_**, 64, 65–66, 70, 72, 73
Atwater, John Bowman 19, 20, 22, **_40_**, 44, 116, 131, 132, 133, 218
Aulbach, Adam 113, 191, 194, 205, 206, 211

Barras, Charles 126
Bella Union Theatre 143, 144, 145
Bernhardt, Sarah 202–203
The Black Crook 97, 121, 122, **_123_**, 124, 126, 129, 183
Black Hawk 33, **_34_**, **_39_**, **_40_**
Black Hills Pioneer 142, 143
Blanchard, Kitty 114
Boucicault, Dion 5, 47, 80, 81, 131, 169
Bunker Hill and Sullivan mine 191, 192, 195, 203, 207, 210, 213
Byers, William N. 61, 62, 88, 115

Camille 46, 66, 76, 93, 166
Carle, Herr Charles 122, 124
Casey, Pat 76, 82
Chambers, Augusta 144, 145, 147, 150
Chatham Theatre 10, 118
Chicago fire 117
Chicago Stock Company 115
Chivington, Colonel 89–90, 91
Clagett, William H. 142, 195, 200, 201
Cleaves, Frank 183, 187, 203
Coeur d'Alene Barbarian 203, 204, 209, 216
The Colleen Bawn 81, 104
Collins, E.R. 61, 63–64, 111, 141, 145
The Corsican Brothers 28, 29, 32, 64
Couldock, Charles Walter 97, 98, 99, **_112_**, 113, 167, 173
Couldock, Eliza 98, **_112_**, 173
Crook, Gen. George 140
Custer, Gen. George Armstrong 138–139

Daymon and Pythias 29, 44
Deadwood Theatre 140, 141
De Bar, Blanche 118, 121
Denver Theatre 78, **_79_**, 96, 141–142
Dillon, Helen 37, 91
Dillon, John 29, 35, 37, 41, **_42_**, 43, 82, 121, 213–214, **_215_**
dogs 69, 91, 99
Dougherty, Michael J. 64, **_65_**, 68, 69, 70, 72, 82, 92–93
Douglas, Miss Belle 178, 180, 181

Edison's Vitascope 220

Fall of the Alamo 75–76
Field, Eugene 207–208
Fisk, Minnie Maddern 169
Floating Dramatic Temple 49
Folds, John S., Sr. 9, 49, 54, 218
Fort Kearny 57, 58, 59, 84
Fort Laramie 58, 59
Fort Riley 56
Frost, Aaron 222

Gilbert, Belle 151, 159
Gilbert, James 151, 159
Glenn, T.R. 127, 130
Globe Theatre (Chicago) 117, 118, 121
Goldrick, Oliver J. 73, 74, 88, 168–169
Gossin, H. 44, 45, 46
Granger, Maud 165, **_166_**
"Great American Desert" 57
Great Eastern mine 163, 164
Great Western Amphitheatre 37, 41
Greeley, Horace 10, 55
Griffith, Jimmy 99, 108, 115, 121, 125, 128, 133, 141, 144, 150, 173
Gross, William J. 111, 115, 121, 135, 141, 144, 146, 149, 151, 153, 160, 173
Guadalajara Theatre 129

Hamlet 46, 84–85, 98
Hickok, "Wild Bill" 139–140
His Last Legs 49, 61, 119, **_120_**
Howard, Charles 50

255

Howard, T.C. 115, 121, 124, 150, 155, 156, 158, 159, 160, 170, 177, 185, 187
Howson Opera Troupe 108

Indians 59, 63, 85, 88, 89, 91, 98–99, 101, 108, 137
Ireland, Dublin 9, 10, 131, 155

Jessie Brown or *The Siege of Lucknow* 80–81, 165

Langrishe, Sir Hercules 10
Leavitt, M.B. 169, 182
Leslie, Mr. and Mrs. N.S. 95, 98
Lind, Jennie 20
Lingham, Matt 118, 121, 164, 169
Lisle, Rose 164, 167
London Assurance 28, 38, 116, 153
Lord Rooney Comedy Company 213

The Magic Talisman 126, 127, 195
Man in a Maze 169, 170, 173, 174, 175, 178, 179, 180, 186, 197
Martin, Jimmy 99, 101, 113, 121, 141, **142**, 144, 145, 146, 148, 149, 151, 160, 162, 198
Mayers, Charles George 44, 49, 131
McAllister, Phosa **153**, 156
McKibben, John 16, **17**, 18, 19, 20, 21, 24, 32, 41, 53, 54, 55, 61
Methua, J. Guido 103, 109
Miles, R.E.J. 52, 53
Miller, R.J. 1, 25
Montana Theatre (Central City, Colorado) 81–82, 88, 89, 95, 108, 122
Moore, Sir Thomas 10
Morlacci, Mme. 160, **161**

Naval Engagements 39, 70, 153, 161, 178, 210
New People's Theatre 73, 74, 76
Nobles, Milton **106**, 107
Northern Pacific Railroad 177

The Octoron 81, 86
Our American Cousin 81, 88–89

Palmer, A.M. 121, 124
Pauncefort, George 82, **83**, 87, 100, 101
Plato, T.W. 16, 18, 21, 22, 25, 26
Platte Valley Theatre 72, 74, 78
The Poor of New York 46–47, 48, 49, 50
Price, Fannie B. 110, 148
Proscher, Jeanette 128

Rankin, McKee 114
Ravel, M'lle Marietta 70, 113
Richelieu 33, 50, 91, 97, 158

Richmond, Harry **55**, 61, 70, 89, 90, 92, 95, 115, 169, 170, 175, 183, 185, 187, 219–220
Rigl, Betty 123–124
Rigl, Emily 123–124
Roberts, J.B. 50, 52
Roche, Frank 158, 160, 162
Runnells, Master Bonnie 128

Sand Creek massacre 55, 89–90, 196
Scheller, Madame Marie Methua 102–103, **103**, 107, 108
The School for Scandal 33, 116
Self or *The Rich of New York* 47, 136, 137, 178
The Serious Family 24, 32, 55, 56, 104, 105, 119, 121, 135, 146, 153, 155, 173, 174
Sherman, Gen. William T. 171
Shoup, Gov. George L. 196
Stark, James 91, **92**
Stewart, Rosaltha Allen 14, 54, 82, 223

Tabor, Horace A.W. 157, 159
Tabor Grand Opera House (Denver) 170, **171**, **172**
Tabor Opera House (Leadville, Colorado) **154**, **155**, 157, 160, 166
Talbot, Bishop Ethelbert 216, 221
Teatro Principal (Mexico City) 130
That Terrible Telegram 185, 186, 187, 200
The Toodles 49, 119, 157
Tuttle, Bishop Daniel S. 99, **100**, 215–216
Twain, Mark 143

Uncle Tom's Cabin 26, 47–48, 52, 86, 145, 160
Under the Gaslight 102, 107

Waldron, George 95, 101, **102**, 103, 108, 109, 113, 128, 173
Walters, Jean Clara 111
Wardner, Jim 150
Wardner News 191, 192, 193, 194, 195, 202, 203, 211, 219
Watkins, H. 50
Waugh, DeWitt C. 72, 76, 81, 118
Waverly (trained horse) 76–77
Wells, Charles 115, 116, 121, 122, 125
The White Crook 127
Wigwam Theatre 162
Wildwood, Nellie 32, 33, 40
Wood's Museum (Chicago) 115
Wright, J.H. 66–67

Yankee Locke 52
Yorick's skull 99, 117, 143–144

Zanfretta, Monsieur 89

www.ingramcontent.com/pod-product-compliance
Ingram Content Group UK Ltd.
Pitfield, Milton Keynes, MK11 3LW, UK
UKHW041934140426
5217IPUK00014B/465